The Classical Style

The Classical Style

Haydn, Mozart, Beethoven

EXPANDED EDITION

Charles Rosen

W.W. Norton & Company

New York • London

The text of this book is composed in 10/11.5 Times Roman
with the display set in Times Roman
Composition by The Maple-Vail Book Manufacturing Group
Manufacturing by Courier Companies

Library of Congress Cataloging-in-Publication Data
Rosen, Charles, 1927–
    The classical style : Haydn, Mozart, Beethoven / Charles Rosen. —
    Expanded ed.
        p.   cm.
    Includes bibliographical references and index.
    ISBN 0-393-04020-8
    1. Classicism in music.   2. Haydn, Joseph, 1732–1809—Criticism
and interpretation.   3. Mozart, Wolfgang Amadeus, 1756–1791—
Criticism and interpretation.   4. Beethoven, Ludwig van, 1770–1827—
Criticism and interpretation.   5. Music—18th century—History and
criticism.   I. Title.
ML195.R68   1997
780′.9′033—dc20   96-27335
                                                                CIP

                        ISBN 0-393-31712-9 pbk

W. W. Norton & Company, Inc., 500 Fifth Avenue, New York, N.Y. 10110
www.wwnorton.com

W. W. Norton & Company Ltd., Castle House, 75/76 Wells Street, London W1T 3QT

    6 7 8 9 0

For Helen and Elliott Carter

Zangler: Was hat Er denn immer mit dcm dummen Wort 'klassisch'?
Melchior: Ah, das Wort is nit dumm, es wird nur oft dumm angewend't.
Nestroy, *Einen Jux will er sich machen*

[*Zangler: Why do you keep repeating that idiotic word "classic"?*
Melchior: Oh, the word isn't idiotic, it's just often used idiotically.]

Contents

Preface to the First Edition   *xi*

A New Preface   *xiii*

Acknowledgments   *xxvii*

Bibliographical Note   *xxix*

Note on the Music Examples   *xxxi*

I INTRODUCTION

1. THE MUSICAL LANGUAGE OF THE LATE EIGHTEENTH CENTURY   19

   Period style and group style, 20; Tonality, 23; Tonic-dominant polarity, 25;
   Modulation, 26; Equal temperament, 27; Weakening of linear form, 28.

2. THEORIES OF FORM   30

   Nineteenth-century conception of sonata form, 30; Twentieth-century revisions, 32; Schenker, 33; Motivic analysis, 36; Vulgar errors, 40.

3. THE ORIGINS OF THE STYLE   43

   Dramatic character of the classical style, 43; Range of styles 1755–1775,
   44; Public and private music, 45; Mannerist period, 47; Proto-classical
   symmetries and patterns, 49; Determinants of form, 51.

II THE CLASSICAL STYLE

1. THE COHERENCE OF THE MUSICAL LANGUAGE   57

   Periodic phrase, 57; Symmetry and rhythmic transition, 58; Homogeneous
   (Baroque) vs. heterogeneous (classical) rhythmic systems, 60; Dynamics
   and ornamentation, 62; Rhythmic and dynamic transition (Haydn Quartet op. 33 no. 3), 64; Harmonic transition (modulation), 68; Decorative vs.
   dramatic styles, 70; Conventional material, 71; Tonal stability and resolution, 72; Recapitulation and articulation of tension, 74; Reinterpretation
   and secondary tonalities, 78; Subdominants, 79; Contrast of themes, 80;
   Reconciliation of contrasts, symmetrical resolution, 82; Relation of large
   form to phrase, expansion technique (Haydn Piano Trio, H.19, 83);
   Correspondence of note, chord, and modulation, 89; Articulation of
   rhythm, weight of individual beat, 90; Sonata style and eccentric material:
   fantasy form (Mozart, Fantasy K. 475), 91; Audible vs. inaudible form, 93;
   Extra-musical influence, 94; Wit in music, 95.

2. STRUCTURE AND ORNAMENT   99

   Sonata forms generalized, 99; Structure vs. ornament, 100; Ornamentation
   in the late eighteenth century, 101; Radical change in function of decoration,
   107.

III HAYDN FROM 1770 TO THE DEATH OF MOZART

1. STRING QUARTET   111

   Haydn and Carl Philipp Emanuel Bach, 111; Beginning in a false key, 112;
   Innovations of the *Scherzi* quartets, thematic accompaniment, 115; Energy
   latent in musical material, 120; Dissonance as principal source of energy,
   120; Directional power of material, 129; Sequence as source of energy, 134;
   Reinterpretation by transposition, 135; Relation of string quartet to classical
   tonal system, 137; Further development of Haydn's string quartets, 138;
   String quartet and the art of conversation, 141.

Contents

2. SYMPHONY   143

Development of the orchestra and symphonic style, 143; stylistic progress, 146; *Sturm und Drang* style, 147; Symphony no. 46, 147; Weakness of rhythmic organization of early Haydn, 149; Symphony no. 47, 151; Influence of opera, 153; Symphony no. 75, 155; New clarity and sobriety, 157; Symphony no. 81, 157; Wit and symphonic grandeur, 159; *Oxford* Symphony, 159; Haydn and pastoral, 162.

IV SERIOUS OPERA   164

Problematic status of *opera seria*, 166; Conventions of *opera seria* and *buffa*, 167; Eighteenth-century tragedy, 168; High Baroque style, 169; Dramatic and elegiac modes, 170; Gluck, 170; Neo-classical doctrine, 171; Music and the aesthetic of expression, 173; Words and music, 173; Gluck and rhythm, 174; Mozart and *Idomeneo*, 177; Recitative and complex forms, 178; Fusion of *seria* and *buffa*, *Marriage of Figaro*, 181; *Fidelio*, 183.

V MOZART

1. THE CONCERTO   185

Mozart and dramatic form, 185; Tonal stability, 186; Symmetry and the flow of time, 187; Continuo playing in the late eighteenth century, 191; Musical significance of the continuo, 194; Concerto as drama, 196; Opening *ritornello*, 197; Concerto in E flat K.271, 198; Piano exposition as dramatization of orchestral exposition, 205; Symmetry of climax, 207; Secondary development within recapitulation, 211; Slow movement of K.271 as expansion of opening phrase, 211; Mirror symmetry, 212; Concerto finale, 213; *Sinfonia Concertante* K. 364, 214; Thematic relationships, 215; K.412, K.413, K.415, 218; K.449, 219; K.456, modulating second theme, 221; Dramatic range of slow movement, 223; Variation-finales, 225; K. 459 and fugal finales, 226; K. 466, art of rhythmic acceleration, 227; Thematic unity, 233; K. 467 and symphonic style, 235; Slow movement, improvisation, and symmetry, 238; K. 482, orchestral color, 240; K.488, articulation of close of exposition, 241; Slow movement and melodic structure, 243; K.503, technique of repetition, 251; Major and minor, 254; Sense of mass, 256; K. 537, proto-Romantic style and loose melodic structure, 258; Clarinet Concerto, continuity of overlapping phrases, 260; K. 595, resolution of chromatic dissonance, 263.

2. STRING QUINTET   264

Concertante style, 264; K.174, expanded sonority and expanded form, 265; K.515, irregular proportions, 267; Expansion of form, 273; K.516, problem of classical finale, 274; Major ending to a work in the minor, 276; Expressive limits of the style, 277; Place of minuet in the order of movements, 280; Virtuosity and chamber music, 281; K.593, 281; Slow introductions, 282; Harmonic structure and sequences, 283; K. 614, influence of Haydn, 286.

3. COMIC OPERA   288

Music and spoken dialogue, 288; Classical style and action, 289; Ensembles, sextet from *The Marriage of Figaro*, and sonata form, 290; Sextet from *Don Giovanni* and sonata proportions, 296; Tonal relations in opera, 298; Recapitulation and dramatic exigency, 301; Operatic finales, 302; Arias, 306; 'Se vuol ballare' from *The Marriage of Figaro*, 308; Coincidence of musical and dramatic events: graveyard scene from *Don Giovanni*, 309; Comedy of intrigue, 312; Eighteenth-century concept of personality, 313; Comedy of experimental psychology and Marivaux, *Così*

Contents

fan tutte, 314; Virtuosity of tone, 316; *Die Zauberflöte,* Carlo Gozzi and the dramatic fable, 317; Music and moral truth, 319; *Don Giovanni* and the mixed genre, 321; Scandal and politics, 322; Mozart as subversive, 324.

VI HAYDN AFTER THE DEATH OF MOZART

1. THE POPULAR STYLE   329

Haydn and folk music, 329; Fusion of high art and popular style, 332; Integration of popular elements, 333; Surprise return of theme in finales, 337; Minuets and popular style, 340; Orchestration, 342; Introduction as dramatic gesture, 345.

2. PIANO TRIO   351

Reactionary form, 351; Chamber music and pianistic virtuosity, 352; Instruments in Haydn's day, 353; Doubling of bass line by cello, 354; H.14, 355; H.22 and expansion of the phrase, 356; H.28, Haydn's early style transformed, 359; H.26, acceleration of motivic elements within a phrase, 361; H.31, luxuriant variation technique, 362; H.30, Haydn's chromaticism, 363.

3. CHURCH MUSIC   366

Expressive vs. celebrative aesthetic, 366; *Opera buffa* style and religious music, 367; Mozart's parodies of Baroque style, 367; Haydn and religious music, 368; Oratorios and pastoral style, 370; 'Chaos' and sonata form, 370; Beethoven's Mass in C Major, problems of pacing, 373; D Major Mass, 375.

VII BEETHOVEN

1. BEETHOVEN   379

Beethoven and post-classical style, 381; Beethoven and the Romantics, 381; Substitutes for dominant-tonic relationship, 382; harmonic innovations of the Romantics, 383; Beethoven and his contemporaries, 386; G Major Piano Concerto, creation of tension by tonic chord, 387; Return to classical principles, 389; *Eroica,* proportions, codas, and repeats, 392; *Waldstein,* unity of texture and theme, 396; *Appassionata* and unity of work, 399; Romantic experiments in Beethoven C Minor Variations, 400; Program music, 401; *An die ferne Geliebte,* 402; Years 1813–1817, 403; *Hammerklavier,* intimate relation between large form and material, 404; Role of descending thirds in construction of sequence, 407; Sequential structure of development of the *Hammerklavier,* 409; Relation to large key-sequence, 413; Relation to thematic structure, 415; A$\sharp$ vs. A$\natural$, 420; Metronome and tempo, 421; Change in style since op.22, 422; Scherzo, 423; Slow movement, 424; Introduction to finale, 427; Fugue, 429; Place of *Hammerklavier* in Beethoven's work, 434; Transformation of variation form into classical form, 440; Op.111, 441; Beethoven and the weight of musical proportions, 445.

2. BEETHOVEN'S LATER YEARS AND THE CONVENTIONS OF HIS CHILDHOOD   449

Beethoven's originality and the style of the 1770s, 449; The cadential trill in op. 111, 449; The traditional final trill in concerto cadenzas, 450; The suspended afterbeat: Sonata op. 101, 457; Conventional concerto figuration transferred to piano sonata, 458; Two stereotypes of the 1770s: Subdominant in the recapitulation, relative minor in the development, 460; Subdominant transferred to coda, 463; Convention and innovation: Relative minor in Mozart's K. 575 and *Coronation* Concerto, 467; Haydn's

Contents

consistent use of the stereotype, 471; Beethoven's naked display of the convention, 474; Stereotype and inspiration in op. 106, 484; The two conventions in op. 110, 488; Integration and motivic alternation in op. 110, 494; Integration of tempi, 499; *Espressivo* and *rubato,* 499; Radical key relations and dramatic structure, 501; Dramatization of the academic elements of fugue, 502; Unity of tempo and the rhythmic notation of the finale, 506; Beethoven's amiability, 507; Pushing back the limits of contemporary style, 508; Synthesis of 18th-century conventions of the variation set, 509; Late Beethoven, 18th-century sociability, and the language of music, 510.

EPILOGUE   513

Schumann's monument to Beethoven (C Major Fantasy), 451; Return to Baroque, 453; Change in tonal language, 453; Schubert, 454; His relation to classical style, 455; Use of middle-period Beethoven as model, 456; Classical principles in late Schubert, 459; Classical style as archaism, 460.

INDEX OF NAMES AND WORKS   523

Preface to the First Edition

I have not attempted a survey of the music of the classical period, but a description of its language. In music, as in painting and architecture, the principles of 'classical' art were codified (or, if you like, classicized) when the impulse which created it was already dead: I have tried to restore a sense of the freedom and the vitality of the style. I have restricted myself to the three major figures of the time as I hold to the old-fashioned position that it is in terms of their achievements that the musical vernacular can best be defined. It is possible to distinguish between the English language around 1770 and the literary style of, say, Dr. Johnson, but it is more difficult to draw a line between the musical language of the late eighteenth century and the style of Haydn—it is even doubtful whether it would be worth the trouble to try to do so.

There is a belief, which I do not share, that the greatest artists make their effect only when seen against a background of the mediocrity that surrounded them: in other words, the dramatic qualities of Haydn, Mozart, and Beethoven are due to their violation of the patterns to which the public was conditioned by their contemporaries. If this were true, the dramatic surprises in Haydn, for example, should become less effective as we grow familiar with them. But any music-lover has found exactly the contrary. Haydn's jokes are wittier each time they are played. We can, of course, grow so familiar with a work that we can no longer bear to listen to it. Nevertheless, to choose only the most banal examples, the opening movement of the *Eroica* Symphony will always seem immense, the trumpet call of *Leonore No. III* will always be a shock to anyone who listens once again to these works. This is because our expectations do not come from outside the work but are implicit in it: a work of music sets its own terms. How these terms are set, how the context in which the drama is to be played out is created for each work, is the main subject of this book. I am concerned, therefore, not only with the meaning or the significance of the music (always so difficult to put into words) but also with what made it possible to possess and to convey that significance.

In order to give some idea of the scope and variety of the period I have followed the development of different genres for each composer. The concerto, the string quintet, and comic opera were obvious choices for Mozart, as were the symphony and the string quartet for Haydn. A discussion of Haydn's piano trios will convey the idiosyncratic nature of the chamber music with piano of that time. *Opera seria* demanded separate treatment, and Haydn's oratorios and masses provided an occasion to discuss the general question of Church music. The relation of Beethoven to Mozart and Haydn clearly needed to be defined by a more general essay, but the major part of the examples could be drawn easily from the piano sonatas. By such subterfuge I have hoped to represent all the important aspects of the classical style.

There is a glaring inconsistency in the pages that follow: 'classical' has always a small 'c,' while 'Baroque,' 'Romantic,' etc., are proclaimed by their initial capitals. The reason for this is partly aesthetic: I have had to use the word 'classical' very often, and the capital letter—turning it into a proper name as if it denoted something that really existed—was too much to face on every page. Although I believe the concept of a style is necessary for an understanding of the history of music, I should not wish to dignify it with the status of solid fact. In any case, I am willing to accept the inadvertent consequences of this whimsical typography. The word 'classical' with a small 'c' implies a style that is exemplary and normative. Like High Renaissance painting, the music of the classical period still provides a standard by which the rest of our artistic experience is judged.

New York, 1970   Charles Rosen

A New Preface

Twenty-five years after this book first appeared, I feel as if it had been written by someone with whom I am only distantly acquainted and for whose actions I am not responsible. Nevertheless, the kindness of the publisher in suggesting a new edition obliges me to face, if briefly, some of the more interesting criticisms that have been made, and perhaps even to try and clear up some misunderstandings. If I were writing this book today, it would be so different that I had to reject the idea of any substantial revision as impractical. I have, however, added a new chapter on Beethoven in order to define more precisely his relation to the two famous composers that preceded him.

In a very generous review, Alan Tyson complained that I began the discussion of Haydn's quartets essentially with op. 33, instead of opp. 17 and 20, which he felt ought to have been treated in greater depth. I asked Tyson whether my account of what we call the classical style was too restrictive and should be altered to include Haydn's opp. 17 and 20, or whether I was mistaken in thinking that the earlier quartets did not already satisfy all the essentials of the definition I had offered. He replied that he was not sure which one of these alternatives was the right one, but that he had always believed one had to study the earlier works in order to understand those that followed. This principle would entail an infinite regress, of course, but that is only to be expected in the writing of history. (Perhaps of greater moment to a lover of Haydn's music is that opp. 17 and 20 are too beautiful not to be given a more extensive examination.)

However, op. 33 displays the first appearance in Haydn's quartets of the 'obbligato accompaniment' as defined by Guido Adler in his article on Viennese classicism in the *Handbuch der Musikgeschichte* (1924)—that is, a texture in which the accompanying voices, while still subordinate to the main voice, are created from the same motifs that make up the principal themes. This technique is essential to the method of thematic development in Haydn, and also in Mozart, Beethoven, and almost all later Western European music. The expression 'obbligato accompaniment' is not known to *The New Grove* (1980), but at any rate, it was known to Beethoven, who once said that he came into the world with an obbligato accompaniment and knew no other.

The technique of deriving the accompaniment from the motifs of the principal voice was, indeed, elaborated in the symphonies that Haydn wrote just before the quartets op. 33.[1] Haydn's declaration that op. 33 was composed

---

[1] I discussed this development in my *Sonata Forms*, rev. ed., New York, 1988, pp. 177–187.

xiii

according to entirely new principles has been characterized as a sales pitch, but I still believe it should be taken seriously: in these works, he applied his symphonic experiments to quartet literature for the first time, and he also developed here an original sense of rhythm partially inspired by *opera buffa*. In any case, I was not concerned primarily with the origins of the style (although I am eager to grant that a knowledge of the origins is an aid to general comprehension) but with its constitution. I wanted to understand what made it so efficient.

Classical texture, of course, had many sources. In 1984, Eric Weimer criticized my neglect of the role played by *opera seria* and pointed out that many aspects of Haydn's instrumental style were developed in the operas of Jomelli and J. C. Bach during the decade that preceded Haydn's op. 33.[2] What he acknowledges as new in op. 33 is only 'the manner in which Haydn took standard accompanimental fragments—one can even say standard accompanimental rhythmic motives—gave them melodic identity and then carefully and consistently used them in both melody and accompaniment.' I am not aware that I was claiming any more than that, but this single innovation still seems to me the touchstone of classical counterpoint. The revival of counterpoint in late eighteenth-century Germany was pointed out in 1801 by Triest (first name unknown) in a brilliant series of articles, published in the *Allgemeine Musikalische Zeitung,* on the development of German instrumental music: the decline of the contrapuntal style under the powerful influence of opera allowed banal accompaniment figures to dominate instrumental works; many musicians after the middle of the century deplored the practice and launched a concerted effort to gain back the richness of the old-fashioned contrapuntal style. We may observe that the fugues in Haydn's opp. 17 and 20 Quartets attest to this ambition, as do the contemporary quartets of Florian Leopold Gassman; to a certain extent, however, they represent a revival of a past tradition. Only with the symphonies of the 1770s and the quartets of op. 33 was Haydn able to accommodate both the modern hierarchy of melody and accompaniment that gave such clarity to his textures and the complex contrapuntal detail that gave new power to his work.

James Webster would also start the classical style a decade or more before op. 33, insofar as he thinks the term has any serviceable value left. In an admirable study, *Haydn's 'Farewell' Symphony and the Idea of Classical Style,* he accuses me, with the greatest possible courtesy, of a prejudice against the earlier works of Haydn.[3] Since he has written the finest account of the earlier period, he goes some way toward convincing me that he may be right. He has certainly given me a deeper appreciation of the works composed before 1780. I should have done them greater justice, and the few pages

---

[2] Eric Weimer, *Opera Seria and the Evolution of Classical Style 1755–1772,* Ann Arbor, 1984, pp. 46–94.
[3] Cambridge, 1991.

where I discuss some of them already betray a feeling of guilt at not having done better. Webster leaves us with the impression, however, that nothing essential changed in Haydn's music after 1780. It is true, as I have written in this book, that the later music rarely displays the extraordinary passion of the finest works from the 1770s, but it shows a sophisticated control in the way it relates phrase rhythm to large harmonic movement and a suppleness never seen before in Haydn's compositional technique.[4] The *London* Symphonies, for example, are perhaps not more powerful than the finest works of the 1770s, but they are certainly more efficient. If Haydn had written nothing after the *Farewell* Symphony he would still be accounted a great composer, but the history of music would have been very different.

The argument about where to start a classical period is inseparable from the reproach, fully justified in certain respects, that I have erred in leaving out all the minor figures. There are two views of history, partly but not completely incompatible. For some scholars, history is what is remembered: they wish to set down only that which has traditionally been thought to be memorable. Others wish to restore the original chaos of an age before the individuals or events of the time were judged worthy of being recalled, and finally to drag from oblivion composers who have been unjustly forgotten, their works unfairly stifled. The first type is a dull fellow who repeats the work of earlier historians with minor variations; we would prefer a more stimulating historian who changes our ideas. The second type, however, cannot represent the full plenitude of all the actions of the past and must invent a personal system of selection, which is likely to be even more arbitrary and obfuscating than the traditional one.

A traditional interpretation or evaluation has, at the very least, this to be said for it. it is a fact of history as solid as any other. We can exaggerate the chaos of the contemporary moment: by the late 1780s there was never any doubt about the supremacy of Haydn and Mozart. The rival claims even of figures as famous as Paisiello and Piccinni were rarely taken very seriously except by a few journalists. The conception of dozens and even hundreds of composers all clamoring equally for attention, all to be sorted out eventually by posterity, is completely fictitious. In the 1780s the emperor Joseph I offered to show Dittersdorf a little essay he had written comparing Haydn and Mozart; he did not write a similar comparison of Wagenseil and Monn. By 1805 Beethoven was respected throughout Europe as the leading composer of instrumental music even by those who disliked much of his work and thought that music had taken a deplorable turn for the worse since the death of Mo-

---

[4] Webster believes that I reproach the early Haydn style of 'a-periodicity.' Since I discuss at length the nature of Haydn's periodic phrasing in the early works, I think he is mistaken. In the later works, Haydn's handling of the period endows the music with great energy; in the 1770s, it is less supple and he needs material of an energetic character to achieve anything like the same drive.

zart.[5] To observe, as some have done, that Haydn, Mozart, and Beethoven were not called classical until well into the nineteenth century is little more than nit-picking. They were considered a coherent group at least as early as 1805, and they, and no others, defined Viennese classical style. Insofar as this style influenced the subsequent history of music, it was through their works alone. Webster has done music-lovers a great service by pleading the cause of Haydn's early works, and I have tried to do something useful by claiming the Haydn trios as unacknowledged masterpieces. Nevertheless, it was the late symphonies and quartets of Haydn that represented the prestige of the classical style during the last decades of his life and for almost two centuries afterward. Reading those articles of 1801 by Triest, we find that connoisseurs at the time agreed not only in dismissing Haydn's operas and liturgical music but in judging the piano music less important than the work of Clementi or even the young Beethoven (if only he would moderate his eccentricity).

Robbins Landon has genially reproached me for the chapter on Haydn's church music: 'The ghosts of our Victorian ancestors are still with us, even in Charles Rosen,' he writes.[6] But the disappointment with Haydn's church music is not an evaluation from the time of Queen Victoria; it is the judgement of Haydn's own contemporaries, of E. T. A. Hoffmann, of Triest, of Ludwig Tieck—and of Haydn himself, who claimed that his liturgical compositions were not as good as those of his brother Michael, a sadly mediocre composer. Of course, there are magnificent pages and sections of Joseph's masses that are splendid, and the last two masses are satisfyingly superb throughout. It is, however, unhistorical to pretend that the setting of religious texts did not present very radical stylistic problems in the last quarter of the eighteenth century, and ideological problems as well. With this approach, we will never appreciate the achievement of Haydn's *Harmoniemesse* or of Beethoven's *Missa Solemnis*. It was exceedingly hard to find a modern form for these settings, and Robbins Landon gives the show away when he describes Haydn's masses 'as brilliantly typical of the *settecento* Baroque in south German or Austrian lands': that style was stone dead when Haydn wrote most of his masses. There is nothing wrong with writing in a worn-out manner except when your contemporaries and you yourself are ill-at-ease with the project. I have—too expeditiously, I admit—tried to indicate what stood in the way of creating a modern liturgical style from 1780 to 1820: the successes came through heroically against the odds.

For similar considerations, the chapter on serious opera could have been made stronger only by trying to discuss the ideological as well as the stylistic reasons for the decline of the genre—the Italian genre, that is, because the

---

[5] See my *The Frontiers of Meaning*, New York, 1994, Chapter 2.
[6] *Haydn: Chronicle and Works, Vol. IV, The Years of 'The Creation,' 1796–1800*, Bloomington, 1980, p. 165.

innovations of French serious opera enjoyed great success (for example, Beethoven's *Fidelio* owes very little to Italian *opera seria,* but a lot to French operatic forms that Beethoven inflected with his study of Mozart, *Così fan tutte* above all). *Opera seria* had lost most of its former importance by the final decades of the eighteenth century. When the young Mozart heard the work of the last really interesting composer of the genre, Niccolò Jomelli, he thought it was good but old-fashioned. After *Idomeneo,* Mozart made no serious attempts to get commissions of that kind: when *La Clemenza di Tito* came his way, it had to be done in a hurry, and he made almost no use of the wealth of invention that we find in the other operas. Serious Italian opera was transformed by Rossini, but that story does not belong in this book—or, indeed, in any book that I would be capable of writing.

I ought perhaps to apologize for language that is misleading, as it has allowed Joseph Kerman to write that

> Rosen likes to give the impression that the Classical style depends perfectly on the perfect integration of melody, harmony, rhythm, and texture, something the minor composers of the time could scarcely achieve. . . . Yet I do not think that we can seriously doubt that in writing his serenade [K. 388] Mozart relied, in Ratner's words, on familiar and universally accepted formulas for its organization and handling of details.' . . . When thirty years later Beethoven began to depart radically from accepted norms he did indeed lose his audience.[7]

I do not, indeed, seriously doubt Mozart's reliance on stereotypes, and have even added several pages on Beethoven in this edition to show that he too relied on them more than one sometimes thinks. I do, however, believe that the use and effectiveness of formulas has been misconstrued by some critics (although not by Kerman).

A basic principle of late eighteenth-century aesthetics is that poetry overcomes the arbitrary nature of language by making the language seem natural—that is, reinvented at the moment to fit what was to be expressed. A similar process is at work in the handling of stereotypes when it is well done: the trick is to make the stereotype sound as if it were invented. In other words, the formula seems as if it were called into being for the occasion. Not even Mozart can pull off this trick every time, but he does it often enough. It takes an exceptional coordination of phrase, harmonic rhythm, thematic content, and structural line to succeed. Mozart's excellence consists not only, or even primarily, in violating the expectations set up by the standard formulas of his time but also in the way he made the stereotypes appear graceful and determined by the piece at hand.

---

[7] Joseph Kerman, *Write All These Down,* Berkeley, 1994, p. 69.

To give a simple example: the return of the tonic together with the main theme is a standard formula of all the various types of sonata form. It can be perfunctory. But a composer can also make it sound as if the tonic was approaching and the first theme about to be played again. There are, of course, stereotyped ways of doing this, but composers could invent more urgent ways of bringing it about: see the first movement of Mozart's G minor Symphony for the most famous example, and I should imagine that even a listener who knew nothing about symphonic form would sense the approach of the full theme played again at its original pitch several bars before the beginning of the recapitulation. In any case, the force of this transitional passage has little to do with conformity or deviation from an accepted norm.

It is clear, however, that my language must be at fault, as Mark Evan Bonds, in an interesting and excellent book on rhetorical structure, similarly accuses me of disregarding stereotype.[8] The example he gives to show the invalidity of my approach is unfortunately chosen, however, as it rather proves the opposite. He cites the first movement of Beethoven's Quartet in F major op. 59 no. 1 where the development section begins by repeating the first bars of the movement, giving the listener the mistaken impression that the exposition is to be repeated, which would fulfill the stereotype. Which listener? Obviously one who hears it for the first time. After that any listener will know that the exposition does not, in fact, return. Will the piece therefore be less effective at future performances?

This is the trouble with analysis in terms of deviation from a norm: it no distinction between expectations that are set powerfully from within the piece each time it is played and those that operate externally. Not that the latter lack importance: they give a work its character, its identity. The odd opening of the development section sets op. 59 no. 1 apart from the other works of its time—although one should add that, just a year or two earlier, Beethoven had written two sonatas, op. 31 nos. 1 and 3, in which the development section begins with the opening measures at the tonic but the exposition is, indeed, repeated. Beethoven directed the repeat in both these cases, and he evidently gave the question about repeats some thought throughout his life. But we also know that performers of the time with weak moral principles did not observe all written repeats. Might these sonatas have been played sometimes without the repeat and would that have created an artistic effect comparable to op. 59 no. 1? In any case, in the way it acts on an informed listener, the deviation from the norm represented by the development of op. 59 no. 1 is negligible compared with the suspended trill in the slow movement of op. 111 or the modulation to D major in the sextet from *Don Giovanni* (see pp. 446 and 297), moments that have a physical power at each rehearing.

Deviation from a standard form can count for a lot or for nothing at all,

---

[8] Mark Evan Bonds, *Wordless Rhetoric: Musical Form and the Metaphor of the Oration*, Cambridge, 1991, pp. 15–16.

depending on the way it has been set up. A recapitulation that begins in the subdominant is very rare at the end of the eighteenth century, but it sounds fairly normal whenever it is tried. That is because it exploits an important aspect of the tonal system as it was understood at the time. It is also very rare for a piece to start in major and turn out to be in the relative minor, but this also works very convincingly (p. 115).[9] Opening in C minor as a way of going to F major, however, still sounds eccentric and queer, if dramatic (p. 112). The slow movement of Mozart's *Musical Joke,* which begins similarly in the wrong key, sounds silly, graceful, incompetent, and charming. Following a norm or violating one has no value in itself. Only if the significance of the norm is understood and exploited does it make sense, and the classical way to convey an understanding of the norm is to make the music imply its existence and necessity. The stereotypes are not either used passively or rejected only to produce a surprise: they demand rejustification. In the best instances, that is what they received.

For this reason the relation of a new work to previous forms is so problematic. To what extent does an innovative work depend on our expectations of standard forms, and to what extent are these expectations merely a nuisance to be cleared away before the new form can be understood for what it is? No one has been more insistent than H. C. Robbins Landon on the need for placing Haydn and Mozart in the context of the composers that preceded them. Yet, when he reaches Mozart's Concerto in E flat major, K. 271, he writes:

> Mozart's concerto, like Haydn's Symphonies Nos. 42, 45, or 47, quietly bursts the form which was bequeathed to him by his precursors: for K. 271 is indeed far removed from the form and content of the pre-classical concerto.[10]

Is the study of the pre-classical concerto, therefore, relevant to our understanding of K. 271? Not irrelevant, clearly, but not as relevant as scholars like to claim. Walter Benjamin remarked about the study of genre that exceptional works either create a genre or destroy it, and the most exceptional do both.[11]

Several minor points in the text could do with revision. On the question of added ornamentation in the Mozart piano concertos, I believe, as Mozart's

---

[9] See the brilliant comments on Haydn's handling of the opening of op. 33 no. 1 and the recapitulation in Webster, *Haydn's 'Farewell' Symphony,* pp. 127–130.

[10] H. C. Robbins Landon, 'The Concerto' in *The Mozart Companion,* edited by Landon and Donald Mitchell, London, 1956, p. 249.

[11] Walter Benjamin, Gesammelte Schriften, Vol. I, 1, 'Ursprung des deutschen Traverspiels,' Introduction, p. 225, Frankfurt, 1972.

sister Nannerl did, that the slow movements not written out by Mozart for the benefit of other performers urgently need filling out in places—the return of the main theme in the slow movement of K. 488, for example. The long leaps from one register to another, however, should not be touched: they are imitations of the vocal leaps in opera that Mozart wrote for his most talented sopranos. The models for ornamentation offered from the period are often idiotic, in particular the one reproduced in the *Neue Mozart-Ausgabe* in the critical notes to K. 488. The only models that should be used are those given by the composer himself.

What I have called slow-movement sonata form might better be called 'cavatina' form. It is the standard form of the outer sections of a da capo aria: an exposition and a recapitulation, neither repeated, and without an intervening development. In the eighteenth century, an aria without a middle section followed by a da capo return was called a 'cavatina.' It was the preferred form of Frederick the Great of Prussia, who seems to have been bored by the da capo form (as many others were at that time), and composers like Graun wrote operas for him in which the arias consisted almost entirely of cavatinas. Its frequent use by Mozart and others for slow movements shows the relation of contemporary instrumental works to operatic forms. Calling it 'sonatina' form is absurd. I do not know any sonatina movements in this form, and it is not a shortened version of 'sonata-allegro' but an independent form, related stylistically to other sonata forms. It is also basic for the overture, and most of the overtures of Mozart, Rossini, and Berlioz employ it.

On the question of playing continuo during a Mozart concerto, I can only reaffirm my belief that it is perfectly fine as long as it is inaudible. In any case, I have recently heard performances on replicas of ancient instruments and can affirm confidently that the continuo part cannot be heard when the orchestra is playing *forte* even when the pianist is thumping away with vigor. The evidence of Mozart's single autograph written-out continuo (K. 246) is that the soloist only fills out the harmony when the orchestra is playing *forte:* when the orchestra plays softly, the soloist either does not play or only doubles the bass line (see p. 193). The idea that this part was written out for a performance without winds may be strengthened by the score of the *Coronation* Concerto in D major K. 537, also intended for an alternate execution with strings alone, according to Mozart's own catalogue. The only place in the work where the winds have a solo part essential to the performance is in the last movement (mm. 137–138, 141–142 and the parallel measures starting at 288), and here the pianist plays only an Alberti bass with the left hand, leaving the right hand free to interpolate the brief wind parts—just as the continuo in K. 246 doubles the melody only at the one point where the winds are not doubled by the strings.

It should be clear enough that Mozart, in his concertos, intended a dramatic contrast between solo and orchestra on the model of the operatic aria, and that this was an important element of his transformation of the genre.

A New Preface

Christoph Wolff pointed out to me that the manuscript of K. 271, discovered after his edition of this work for the *Neue Mozart-Ausgabe* had gone to press, shows that Mozart specifically wrote rests in the left hand of the piano at an important moment of contrast between piano and orchestra to prevent the soloist from playing even a *tasto solo* here.

I am not the only one to complain of the intrusion of continuo-playing where it is not wanted. Robbins Landon quotes a review of a Haydn symphony played in London before the composer's arrival there:

> *Haydn's* Symphonies, which were introduced for the first time at Vauxhall on Tuesday evening, must cease to have their wonted effect, unless Mr Barthelemon will simplify his manner of playing them, and the performer on the organ will confine his finger to those powerful *fortés*, which only require such assistance.[12]

The use of figured bass continued for several decades after it became aesthetically unnecessary, largely because it was practical for giving cues to conductor as well as soloist. When its indications were removed from piano concertos by nineteenth-century editors, however, a few important mistakes were made, and some of the solo part was removed. The most disastrous such omissions are in Beethoven's Concerto no. 4 in G major, where notes in the bass that must be sustained by the pianist with the pedal were removed. There are two such places in the finale, and in the first movement at the opening of the recapitulation the piano should enter on the first beat with a powerful octave in the bass (it would be even better if the pianist continued to play during the two bars of *forte* that precede it, as the music implies a real continuity between tutti and solo at this point).

In a recent assault on the concept of tonal unity in Mozart's operas, led by Carolyn Abbate, Roger Parker, and James Webster, I am named along with Joseph Kerman as one of those principally responsible for propagating this wicked orthodoxy,[13] so perhaps I should add a few words on the subject to supplement what I wrote in this book many years ago. It is true that a lot of nonsense has been produced on this question as on any other. The basic influence in this matter was not, as these writers seem to think, the work of

---

[12] H. C. Robbins Landon, *Haydn: Chronicle and Works, Vol. II, Haydn at Esterhhaza, 1766–1790*, Bloomington, 1978, p. 596.

[13] Carolyn Abbate and Roger Parker, 'Dismembering Mozart,' *Cambridge Opera Journal*, vol. 2, no. 2 (1990): 187–195; and James Webster, 'Mozart's Operas and the Myth of Musical Unity,' *Cambridge Opera Journal*, vol. 2, no. 2 (1990): 197–218. Webster laments (p. 200) that Kerman's *Opera as Drama* was reissued unaltered which 'only emphasizes its dated qualities.' Perhaps there was no need, after all, to bring it up to date as 'today's critical climate' that Webster finds so crucial will be yesterday's very soon.

the Wagnerian theorist Alfred Lorenz but that of Hermann Abert, the greatest of Mozart scholars. Far from being subservient to Wagnerian influence, Abert was principally a student of eighteenth-century opera—Jomelli and Gluck above all—and he was dead before Lorenz published his extravagant improvisations on Mozartean themes. The neglect of Abert even today puts most of Anglo-American Mozart studies at a disadvantage: he has been superseded as to the details of Mozart's biography, but he almost never put a foot wrong on musical questions. His basic account of tonal relationships in the operas appears not so much in his famous Mozart biography as in his introduction to the Eulenberg score of *Le Nozze di Figaro*. There we find an elaborate and systematic examination of the opera's tonal structure and its relation to the dramatic action. A measure of Abert's magnificent good sense is his remark that at the opening of the fourth act (with the arias of Barbarina, Marcellina, and Basilio) there is an absence of effective tonal structure, because the libretto does not provide any action that Mozart could realize in music. The significance of the tonal relationships in the opera depends obviously on the progress of the action in the libretto. Those of us like Kerman who have remarked on the various analogies of Mozart's operatic procedures with sonata technique do not believe that an opera is tightly organized like a symphonic movement, or even that the various numbers are as strictly related to each other as the different movements of a symphony; to argue against these absurdities is to beat not only a dead horse but one that never had any life in it. Nevertheless, the different forces that shape the structure of the purely instrumental works are also at play in the operatic genre, and we can affirm that in eighteenth-century operas only with Mozart did these forces function with effective power. His stylistic principles are the same in both instrumental music and opera, although the exigencies of genre are different.

The notion that Mozart's operas are heavily indebted to sonata style is not a recent perversion of modern analysts. It was already observed by Ernest Newman and George Bernard Shaw, who were far from thinking it was a Good Thing: as Wagnerians they deplored it (although Shaw remarked sensibly that the realization of sonata forms did very little harm in Mozart's operas most of the time).

What is odd today is the air of resentment that seeps into the discussion. The great example to try on the dog has always been the Act II finale of *Figaro,* the longest section in the opera uninterrupted by recitative. It is generally admired for its exciting progress from duet and trio to septet, while the dramatic situation becomes more and more embroiled; the tonal structure starts with an orthodox contrast of tonic and dominant, continues with a dramatic break to a mediant, and leads by a logical series of dominants back to the original tonic. Abbate and Parker claim that the admiration for Mozart's finales was conditioned by the influence of Wagner, although *Figaro's* librettist, Lorenzo da Ponte, explicitly wrote that the structure of a finale was the most important part of an opera, allowing composer, librettist, and singers to demonstrate their full powers.[14] (It is true that Mozart insisted, in a famous letter to his father about *Idomeneo,* that ensembles required a different kind of singing from arias: in the latter the *spianato* or lyric style was proper, while the former had to be rendered *parlando.*) Abbate and Parker term the second-act finale of *Figaro* 'the harmonic juggernaut,'[15] a metaphor they find so apt that they repeat it only a few paragraphs later. A juggernaut is a monstrous chariot under whose wheels the devotees of a divine charioteer were crushed and immolated. It is unclear why Abbate and Parker feel themselves crushed by the monstrous progressions of Mozart's finale. Nor is it reasonable to complain, as they and Webster do, that analysts choose mainly the ensemble pieces to demonstrate Mozart's tonal logic, without mentioning that Mozart himself was known to be proud above all of his ensembles. More than anyone else, Mozart displaced the center of gravity in opera from aria to ensemble, and while I can see that amateurs of Baroque vocal style are unhappy about the change, that is no reason to object to a critic's natural concentration on the ensembles. Many of the most important roles in his operas are characterized principally through the ensemble pieces, the best examples being Don Giovanni and Don Alfonso. It is a pity that more attention has not been paid to the arias, but Mozart's most striking— if not most subtle—innovation in operatic technique is reserved for the ensembles and they, perhaps more than any other aspect, distinguish his work from other contemporary operas.

I suspect that some of the resentment comes from the questions (vexed questions is the proper cliché) of how and how much these tonal relationships are intended to be heard and how important they are. It is clear enough that we can enjoy, and therefore pretty well understand, one of Mozart's operas without consciously being aware of whatever tonal construction there is. Nevertheless, Mozart's decision, starting with *Die Entführung aus dem Serail,* that each opera must begin and end in the same key is unlikely not to have affected the opera's interior construction.

A brief consideration of the last-act finale of *Figaro* may shed some light. The brevity of the final D major section has provoked a lot of comment, and Webster defends its stability against Parker and Abbate's attack by pointing out that it is prepared by a strong dominant passage. He then adds, parenthetically—as if to defend himself from succumbing to the old orthodoxy—'Of course, this resolution has nothing to do with sonata form.' On the contrary, of course it does, unless you take as narrow and literal a view

---

[14] 'In questo [il finale] principalmente deve brillare il genio del maestro di cappella, la forza de' cantanti, il più grande effetto del dramma.' (In the finale must shine the genius of the composer, the power of the singers, the greatest effect of the drama.) *Memorie,* Milan, 1960, p. 96.
[15] Page 194.

of sonata form as Webster does. The end of this last-act finale is preceded by a long section in the subdominant G major. The traditional place of the subdominant in a sonata is just after the beginning of a recapitulation; Haydn very often introduced it just before the recapitulation and Beethoven frequently displaced it into the coda. One may even begin a recapitulation with it. In any case, the importance of the subdominant in this part of the form was understood by almost all contemporary composers of instrumental music. Further, we must recall that this is the end of the opera. The final movement of a sonata or symphony traditionally grants a larger place to the subdominant than any other movement allows. Not only do most rondos have a central section in the subdominant, but even a finale in first-movement form (like the one in Mozart's F major Piano Sonata K. 332) may have an independent subdominant theme in the middle of the development. The subdominant emphasis of the fourth-act finale of *Figaro* is unmistakable. Abert called attention to its symmetry:

D–G–E flat–B flat–G–D

The key structure of the finale as a whole is directly related to the action: the most striking change is to E flat major, the moment when Figaro believes that the Count is making love to Susanna. Mozart's stroke of genius is to make this a moment of magical poetry, almost a celebration of love—and da Ponte gave him an elevated text with a classical reference, as Figaro mournfully compares himself to Vulcan betrayed by Venus. Harmonically E flat is the most remote tonality of the finale and the texture is the most exquisite. It was wonderfully original of Mozart to make this climax of dramatic and harmonic tension an expressive Larghetto between the more quickly moving G major that precedes it and the Allegro molto that follows. It is a breathtaking moment of stasis, in which the horns play the double role of establishing a pastoral atmosphere and of alluding to the traditional antlers of the cuckold. Placing harmonic tension in the center of the work, however, is an integral part of the sonata aesthetic. A passage of calm stasis in a development section was also used with great effect by Mozart in the Concerto in B flat major K. 595, and by Beethoven in the Quartet in B flat major op. 130 (both passages are also associated with a remote tonality).

Even the penultimate G major section of the finale is regulated by sonata principles. After the harmonic and thematic development that accompanies the Count's threat of punishment and the simulated remorse of Susanna and Figaro, the harmony resolves back to the tonic as the Countess enters and adds her plea, and the following *pianissimo* agitation moves it in the flat direction (here the tonic minor), equally traditional at this point in sonata form. One could say that Mozart accommodates his instrumental ideals to the demands of the drama, but it would be preferable to note how these ideals help him to realize the libretto.

The role of E flat major as the point of greatest tension naturally recalls the central second-act finale, which begins and ends in E flat. The principal key of Mozart's central finale is always harmonically distant from the key in which the entire opera begins and ends. In two other important cases, the last finale recalls the key of the central finale at a moment of great tension. In *Così fan tutte*, the D major of the central finale returns in the middle of the last finale (which is centered on C major) when the men pretend to return from the war without their Albanian disguises and precipitate the crisis. In *Zauberflöte*, the E flat that frames the second finale has its dramatic climax in C major, the key of the first finale, for the trial by fire and water. (A polarity between C major and E flat major, however, is established from the beginning of the opera and finds its realization in the last finale.)

To what extent did Mozart expect us to hear these relationships? We do not know, of course, but it is not hard to train oneself to recognize them if one has perfect pitch, as many musicians do and Mozart certainly did. (These relationships were more important to Mozart's contemporaries than to us.) It is true that the D major of *Figaro* is not as firmly fixed as the D minor of *Don Giovanni,* although Bartolo's aria (No. 5) brings back the brilliance of the overture clearly, and the opening sequence of D major, G major, B flat major, F major, and D major is tonally satisfying to those who want their dissonant tonalities in the center and a resolution at the end; the A major duet that follows prolongs the D major area.

What requires notice, however, is the role of E flat major within *Figaro* as a whole. It first appears in Cherubino's description of adolescent erotic disquiet, and the arrival of the key is startling after the A major of the previous duet. It plays an important role in the B flat trio when Cherubino is caught hiding under a dress. It turns up next for the Countess's first aria, an invocation to love. It dominates the second-act finale and its extraordinary imbroglio. In the last act it reappears as the key of Figaro's cuckoldry aria, and Mozart clearly needs that key for the pun on horns (which are traditionally associated with an E flat tonality). Its role in the last finale is given a deeper perspective by the way it has appeared throughout the work. I do not wish to add to the nonsense of key significance and present E flat major as a symbol of eroticism. Nevertheless, it plays a role throughout the work that expresses emotional anguish or disquiet, and this strengthens the idea that Mozart thought of D major as somehow basic to the whole work in a dissonant polar relation to E flat. I do not know if he wanted his public to hear this, but it can be affirmed that some portion of his listeners will be at least subconsciously affected by these relations.

The question of hearing becomes acute because this structure ignores what happens in the recitatives. Mozart's refusal to allow the recitative to play an important part in the tonal structure, however, is central to his sense of the way key relations work in an opera. The basic principle is that any number not interrupted by a recitative or by spoken dialogue must begin and end in the same key. Clearly recitative for Mozart was almost a kind of non-music, like speech. This is directly reflected by da Ponte, who defines a finale in his memoirs as the number in which one *sings* ('canta') without pause. This means that to grasp the key relations in an opera we must disregard the sometimes interesting modulations in the recitatives (which, like the arias, have never been sufficiently studied, except perhaps by Abert). It is also evident that the original versions of the operas before Mozart revised them reflect his tonal conceptions best.[16] In the original production of *Don Giovanni* in Prague, the tritone leap from Don Ottavio's B flat major aria in Act II to the E major of the cemetery scene makes a grand dramatic point. This was certainly spoiled in the Vienna version.

We must also agree with Abert that certain sequences in Mozart's operas are more tightly organized than others. The opening of *Così fan tutte* has a wonderful closed form—C major overture, G major, E major, C major—almost too close for comfort to a sonata aesthetic of tonic–dominant–distant key–tonic resolution. Other sections of the opera are more loosely constructed, but it is perverse to avoid the conclusion that Mozart attempted at the beginning of each opera to establish the initial key as a principal one. It also seems to me absurd to deny that Mozart took advantage of the libretto when it enabled him to plan sequences based on the tonal principles that were so important in his other works. It is equally absurd to force the operas into an esoteric dogmatic scheme that reveals its weakness as soon as we try to apply it. In any case, the tonal framework that Mozart elaborated with considerable suppleness in his operas has intellectual satisfactions and an aesthetic beauty on its own. Even if not all the aspects of his schemes are easy for the ear to grasp, we can learn to perceive enough of it in performance without too much difficulty, and with at least the small increase of genuine musical pleasure that comes with understanding.

New York, 1997

---

[16] The revisions of the Prague version of *Don Giovanni* for Vienna generally attempt to salvage part of the tonal relationship. From 'Or sai chi l'honore' to the champagne aria there is a mediant leap from D to B flat. Interpolating 'Dalla sua pace' in G preserves the basic mediant from the D major area into B flat. Why did Mozart not place the new tenor aria at the point in the second act where he eliminated 'Il mio tesoro'? Surely because he wanted a brilliant virtuoso piece at this point, and he placed here the new 'Mi tradi' that he was forced to write for the Viennese Elvira as a substitute for the tenor brilliance.

Acknowledgments

It would be impossible to acknowledge the contribution of ideas that have come from so many conversations with friends, each one in turn bringing forward a new example to illustrate the other's observation. Many of the ideas in this book are the common currency of musical thought, derived from the experience of all musicians who have played and listened to the music involved. In most instances I could no longer distinguish, even if I wanted to, which ideas are my own and which I have read, or learned from my teachers, or simply heard in discussion.

Much easier to acknowledge is the invaluable help I received in writing this book. I am deeply indebted to—indeed, still marvelling at—the patience and kindness of Sir William Glock, who read the entire manuscript and made hundreds of suggestions which strengthened both the style and the ideas. Henri Zerner of Brown University helped at every stage, and made considerable improvements and corrections; without his excisions, as well, the book would have been slightly longer and much more dubious. I am also grateful to Kenneth Levy, of Princeton University, who read the first half of the manuscript and improved several points. (No one but myself, of course, is to blame for the faults that remain.) I should like to thank Charles Mackerras, David Hamilton, Marvin Tartak, Sidney Charles of the University of California at Davis, and Lewis Lockwood of Princeton University, who gave me material I did not have or did not know, and Mischa Donat, who prepared the index.

My gratitude goes to Donald Mitchell of Faber Music, for his encouragement when only two chapters of this book had been written, and for his invaluable help afterward; to Piers Hembry, who did the reduction of the musical examples; and to Paul Courtenay, who so beautifully copied them.

I owe more than I can express to the continued encouragement and editing of Aaron Asher, both while he was at Viking and after he left, and to the intelligence and tact of Elisabeth Sifton, who helped with the final revisions and made the last stages of producing the book so much more agreeable than any author has a right to expect.

—*From the Preface to the First Edition (1970)*

I am grateful to David Hamilton and Claire Brook of W.W. Norton & Company for making it possible to correct some of the mistakes I had made in

Acknowledgments

the first edition of this book. It has been as great a pleasure for me to correct these errors as it was for my friends to discover them. I am indebted to many people for their help, but I must mention first a detailed and generous letter from Paul Badura-Skoda, which discussed with great kindness a number of points in my book and which has enabled me to make a number of corrections. I have also received communications from John Rothgeb, Alan Tyson, and a student at the University of Toronto who remains anonymous here only because I never learned his name. The way in which I have made use of these different observations is, of course, entirely my own responsibility.

In reading Arnold Schoenberg's essay on Brahms recently, I realized that the analysis given there of two themes from Beethoven's Symphony No. 5 is almost exactly the one I have given. I do not remember reading Schoenberg's essay before, but it is very likely that I did so a number of years ago. I cite this one example among many of unconscious plagiarism only to point out that a great deal of this book is necessarily common property. On a subject so central to our musical experience, whatever value a book might have must lie principally in its setting forth—in however new a light—those aspects of the music that have already been perceived and at least partially understood.

—From the Preface to the Norton Library Edition (1972)

In preparing the new material for this edition I should like to acknowledge the generous help given by Lewis Lockwood, Scott Burnham, Kristina Muxfeldt, and David Gable.

New York, 1997

Bibliographical Note

There is no satisfactory book on the late eighteenth and early nineteenth centuries, but Manfred Bukofzer's *Music in the Baroque Era* (1947) is, with all its limitations, a magnificent work, and I realize how much I owe to many of its general concepts for an understanding of the earlier period.

Hermann Abert's *W. A. Mozart* (1923) has not yet been equalled for its discussion of Mozart's style. The greatest of Tovey's numerous articles on Mozart is his essay on the C major Concerto K. 503. Heinrich Schenker's analysis of the G minor Symphony is perhaps the most stimulating of his discussions of the classical style. Wye Jamison Allanbrook's *Rhythmic Gesture in Mozart* provided new insights, and Ivan Nagel's *Autonomie und Gnade* gave an interesting new interpretation of the operas of Mozart.

On Haydn, we are all grateful for the work of Jens Peter Larsen and of H. C. Robbins Landon, particularly the latter's edition of all the symphonies. Emily Anderson's translation of the Mozart and the Beethoven correspondences, Robbins Landon's edition of Haydn's letters and diaries, and O. E. Deutsch's documentary biographies of Mozart and Schubert have made much of the material available in English. Robbins Landon's five-volume life of Haydn is now indispensable. The best treatment of Haydn before 1780 is James Webster's *Haydn's 'Farewell' Symphony and the Idea of Classical Style*.

Too much has been written on Beethoven to be able to avoid repeating what others have written, but I have tried to acknowledge whatever publication made available information that I did not have or inspired anything relevant to my argument. Priority of publication does not mean very much for a subject so often discussed: for example, Kinderman in *Beethoven Forum,* vol. I (Lincoln and London, 1992, p. 123) mentions the relation of the parallel fourths of the fugue theme to the trio of the scherzo of op. 110 and refers to an essay by Alfred Brendel of 1990, but I discussed this in my sleeve notes to a recording in the 1960s. There must be many pianists who have observed this in the 170 years since the work was written. Uncritical bibliographical references are not interesting, and I have only tried to indicate disagreement when it seemed important.

Thayer's *Life of Beethoven* remains fundamental to all study of this composer; the best edition is that of Elliot Forbes (1964), cited hereafter simply as Thayer. Tovey's unfinished *Beethoven* is underestimated today. Maynard Solomon's biography is now the authoritative one, as is Joseph Kerman's volume on the Beethoven quartets. The best account of Beethoven reception is Scott Burnham's *Beethoven Hero*. Robert Winter and Douglas Johnson have put scholars in their debt with their studies of Beethoven sketches. Among the most interesting recent stylistic studies of Beethoven are those of Robert Hatten, William Kinderman, and Lewis Lockwood. The latter's studies of op. 69 and the *Eroica* are fundamental.

Note on the Music Examples

I am grateful to the generosity of the publishers in agreeing that almost everything of importance discussed would be illustrated, sometimes at great length. We have hoped to make it possible to read the book without regret for the absence of scores. I have not tried specifically to quote my favorite passages, but many of them have slipped in nevertheless. I have, however, tried to balance the familiar with the less known.

In reducing the orchestral and chamber scores by grouping several instruments on one stave, the object has been to combine ease of reading with the possibility of seeing all details of the full score. It should be possible to reconstruct the original score in almost all cases: those examples where not everything has been indicated are marked by an asterisk (*). The examples of orchestral or quartet writing on two staves are, therefore, in no sense transcriptions for piano but transliterations of the originals—although of course I welcome the idea of reading these examples at the piano, which is what I have often done with them myself, faking what my hands cannot reach.

I have used the best texts I could find without normalizing, although I have sometimes found it reasonable not to repeat dynamic markings when successive instruments entered at the same dynamic level. One abbreviation, the plus sign (+), needs a word of explanation: it has been used to indicate doubling (at the unison, unless otherwise indicated). That is, 'Fl.' means the flute takes over the line at the point indicated; '+Fl.' means that the previously indicated instrument continues to play and is now doubled by the flute. Ease of reading took precedence over uniformity, and I hope that the inconsistencies will puzzle no one and give no offense.

Part I

INTRODUCTION

1

The Musical Language of the
Late Eighteenth Century

When Beethoven left Bonn in 1792, he had with him an album in which his patron, Count Waldstein, had written: 'You are going to Vienna in fulfillment of your long frustrated wishes . . . You will receive the spirit of Mozart from the hands of Haydn.' It was, indeed, with Mozart that Beethoven wished to study; he had traveled to Vienna some years earlier and, it seems, impressed Mozart with his playing. But Mozart had recently died, and the twenty-one-year-old Beethoven turned to Haydn, who had already encouraged him during a visit to Bonn.

It would appear as if our modern conception of the great triumvirate had been planned in advance by history. The idea was, in fact, already sanctioned by Beethoven's contemporaries. Years after the death of Haydn, but long before that of Beethoven, when music-lovers complained of the frivolity of Viennese musical life, they compared the infrequent performances of Haydn, Mozart, and Beethoven with the popularity of the new and more modern Italian opera. Even those who believed that music had stopped with Mozart thought of Beethoven not as a revolutionary but as an eccentric betrayer of a great tradition. The more perceptive placed him quite simply on a level with Haydn and Mozart. As early as 1812, in the writings of the finest contemporary music critic, E. T. A. Hoffmann (who loved Mozart so much that he changed one of his names from Friedrich to Amadeus), these were the three great figures, and there was no other to set by their side except Gluck, who stood out for the seriousness and the integrity of his conception of opera. 'Haydn, Mozart, and Beethoven,' Hoffmann wrote in 1814, 'developed a new art, whose origins first appear in the middle of the eighteenth century. Thoughtlessness and lack of understanding husbanded the acquired treasure badly, and, in the end, counterfeiters tried to give the impression of the real thing with their tinsel, but this was not the fault of these masters in whom the spirit was so nobly manifest.'

This new art is, partly by convention, called the classical style. It was not E. T. A. Hoffmann's name for it: Haydn and Mozart were, for him, the first 'romantic' composers. Whatever the name, the originality of this new style and its integrity were felt very early.

Nevertheless, the concept of a style does not correspond to an historical fact but answers a need: it creates a mode of understanding. That this need was felt almost at once belongs not to the history of music but to the history of musical taste and appreciation. The concept of a style can only have a purely pragmatic definition, and it can at times be so fluid and imprecise as to be useless. Confusion of levels is the greatest danger. For example, to compare High Renaissance painting, envisaged as the work of a small group of artists in Rome and Florence and an even smaller group of Venetians, with Baroque painting, conceived as international and as stretching over more than a century and a half, could only lead to methodological chaos, however fruitful the individual observations it may suggest. The scope of the context is not arbitrary, and it is essential to distinguish between the style of a small group (French Impressionism, Ockeghem and his disciples, the Lake Poets) and the more 'anonymous' style of an era (nineteenth-century French painting, late fifteenth-century Flemish music, English Romantic poetry).

This distinction, however, is harder to make in fact than in theory: the style of what is sometimes called the High Baroque in music (from 1700 to 1750) is international, and has no group that corresponds in importance and cohesion to the three classical Viennese composers (none of whom was from Vienna). Yet the High Baroque provided a coherent and systematic musical language which could be used by the three classical figures and against which they could measure their own language. Mozart could produce a good, if not perfect, facsimile of High Baroque style when it was needed, and the combination of his own manner with that of a High Baroque composer (as in his reinstrumentation of *Messiah*) is an example of a clash not so much between two musical personalities as between two isolatable and definable systems of expression. It should be remarked, however, that the High Baroque style for Mozart and for Beethoven meant Handel and Bach above all,[1] and that both Handel and Bach effected a synthesis, a very different and personal one in each case, of the disparate national styles—German, French, and Italian—of their time. The opposing character of the personal styles of Bach and Handel gives them a complementary relation which paradoxically allows them to be considered as a unity.

The reason why the style of a group and the style of an age may sometimes be legitimately confused is that a group-style often appears to realize the imperfectly formed aspirations of the age. A style may be described figuratively as a way of exploiting and focusing a language, which then becomes a dialect or language in its own right, and it is this focus which makes possible what might be called the personal style or manner of the artist, as Mozart worked against the background of the general style of his age, yet with a more specific relation to Haydn and to Johann Christian Bach. But analogies with language break down because a style is finally itself treated

---

[1] In spite of Mozart's acquaintance with later composers who tried to continue the contrapuntal tradition, a remarkable development comes over his work from the moment he begins to know the music of Johann Sebastian Bach.

as a work of art, and judged as an individual work is judged and by much the same standards: coherence, power, and richness of allusion. In current changes of fashion and revivals of interest in one past style after another— Pre-Raphaelite painting, Baroque music—each successive style is almost a solid object, a piece of period furniture to be possessed and enjoyed. Yet such treatment of a period style as itself an *objet d'art* suggests one possible elucidation of the style of a group. More convincingly than the 'anonymous' style of an age, the style of a group represents a synthesis like a work of art, a reconciliation of the conflicting forces of the period into one harmony. It is almost as much an expression itself as a system of expression.

'Expression' is a word that tends to corrupt thought. Applied to art, it is only a necessary metaphor. Accepted as legal tender, it often gives aid and comfort to those who are more interested in the artist's personality than in his work. Nonetheless, the concept of expression, even in its most naïve form, is essential to an understanding of late eighteenth-century art. In any period, of course, the formal qualities of the smallest detail of a work of music cannot be divorced from its affective and sentimental, as well as its intellectual, significance within the work and, consequently, more generally within the stylistic language, and I shall be concerned throughout with the meaning of the elements that make up the classical synthesis. But it is a gross and common error to define a style by specifically expressive characteristics, isolating the 'elegant' painting of the sixteenth century as Mannerist, calling the classical style Apollonian, the Romantic enthusiastic or morbid. Just in so far as a style is a way of using a language, musical, pictorial, or literary, is it capable of the widest range of expression, and a work by Mozart may be as morbid, as elegant, or as turbulent in its own terms as one by Chopin or Wagner. It is true that the means of expression have an influence on what is expressed, and it is the ease or the tension with which the language is used—the grace of expression—that counts so heavily in art. Yet at the point that grace begins to take on such importance, a style ceases to be strictly a system of expression or of communication.

The history of an artistic 'language,' therefore, cannot be understood in the same way as the history of a language used for everyday communication. In the history of English, for example, one man's speech is as good as another's. It is the picture as a whole that counts, and not the interest, grace, or profundity of the individual example. In the history of literary style or of music, on the other hand, evaluation becomes a necessary preliminary: even if Haydn and Mozart improbably differed in all essentials from their contemporaries, their work and their conception of expression would have to remain the center of the history. This stands the history of a language on its head: it is now the mass of speakers that are judged by their relation to the single one, and the individual statement that provides the norm and takes precedence over general usage.

What makes the history of music, or of any art, particularly troublesome is that what is most exceptional, not what is most usual, has often the greatest claim on our interest. Even within the work of one artist, it is not his usual procedure that characterizes his personal 'style,' but his greatest and most individual success. This, however, seems to deny even the possibility of the history of art: there are only individual works, each self-sufficient, each setting its own standards. It is a contradiction essential to a work of art that it resists paraphrase and translation, and yet that it can only exist within a language, which implies the possibility of paraphrase and translation as a necessary condition.

The idea of the style of a group is a compromise that avoids this impossible fragmentation without falling into the difficulties of the 'anonymous' period style, which fails to distinguish between painting and wall paper or between music and commercial background noises for dinner. The style of a group, so conceived, is therefore not necessarily what is called a 'school'—a tightly knit sect of artists and their disciples—although it may sometimes be that in fact. It is a fiction, an attempt to create order, a construction that enables us to interpret the change in the musical language without being totally bewildered by the mass of minor composers, many of them very fine, who understood only imperfectly the direction in which they were going, holding on to habits of the past which no longer made complete sense in the new context, experimenting with ideas they had not quite the power to render coherent.

The relation of the classical style to the 'anonymous' style or musical vernacular of the late eighteenth century is that it represents not only a synthesis of the artistic possibilities of the age, but also a purification of the irrelevant residue of past traditions. It is only in the works of Haydn, Mozart, and Beethoven that all the contemporary elements of musical style—rhythmic, harmonic, and melodic—work coherently together, or that the ideals of the period are realized on a level of any complexity. The music of the elder Stamitz, for example, combines a primitive classical phrasing with the most old-fashioned Baroque sequential harmony, so that one element rarely reinforces the other, but instead diffuses its effect. Later in the century, the works of Dittersdorf, the operas above all, have melodic charm and a certain jolly good humor, but anything more than the simplest tonic-dominant relationship is beyond them. Even in respect to historical importance and influence, but above all as regards the significance of the musical development of the eighteenth century, the work of Haydn and Mozart cannot be understood against the background of their contemporaries: it is rather the lesser man who must be seen in the framework of the principles inherent in Haydn's and Mozart's music—or, at times, as standing outside these principles in an interesting or original way. Clementi, for example, stands somewhat apart, both in his fusion of Italian and French tradition and in his development of the virtuoso passagework so essential to the post-classical style of Hummel and Weber. It is significant that this kind of passagework, which was to be given artistic importance by Liszt and Chopin, was emphatically rejected by Beethoven in most of his piano music; in his remarks on fingering and the position of the hand, he opposes the style of playing most suited to it. Although he recommended Clementi's music for the use of piano students, he disliked a piano technique of the 'pearly' manner, and criticized even Mozart's playing as too choppy.

What unites Haydn, Mozart, and Beethoven is not personal contact or even mutual influence and interaction (although there was much of both), but their common understanding of the musical language which they did so much to formulate and to change. These three composers of completely different character and often directly opposed ideals of expression arrived at analagous solutions in most of their work. The unity of style is therefore indeed a fiction, but one which the composers themselves helped to create. A considerable change is evident in the music of both Haydn and Mozart at about 1775, the date of Mozart's E flat Piano Concerto K. 271, perhaps the first large work in which Mozart's mature style is in complete command throughout; around this time Haydn became more fully acquainted with the Italian comic opera tradition to which the classical style owed so much. The date is not arbitrary; one five or ten years earlier could have been chosen for different reasons, but the discontinuities here seem to me of greater importance than the continuities. It is only from this point on that the new sense of rhythm which displaces that of the High Baroque becomes completely consistent. It is also evident that I take seriously Haydn's claim that the *Scherzi* or *Russian* Quartets, op. 33, of 1781, were written according to entirely new principles.

The musical language which made the classical style possible is that of tonality, which was not a massive, immobile system but a living, gradually changing language from its beginning. It had reached a new and important turning point just before the style of Haydn and Mozart took shape.

There are so many conflicting accounts of tonality that it will be useful to restate its premises, axiomatically rather than historically for brevity's sake. Tonality is a hierarchical arrangement of the triads based on the natural harmonics or overtones of a note. The most powerful of these harmonics are the octave, the twelfth, the fifteenth, and the seventeenth; the octave and the fifteenth may be omitted as being the same note at higher pitches (I shall evade a discussion of the reasons, psychological or conventional, for this); the twelfth and the seventeenth transposed nearer to the original note or tonic produce the fifth and the third, or the dominant and the mediant.

In this triad of tonic, mediant, and dominant, the dominant is the more powerful harmonic and naturally the second most powerful tone. The tonic, however, may be considered as itself the dominant of the fifth below it, called the subdominant. By building successive triads in both ascending and descending directions, we arrive at a structure which is symmetrical, and yet unbalanced:

Introduction

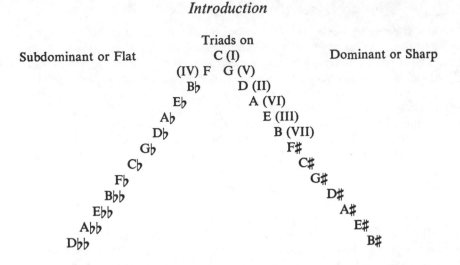

Triads on

Subdominant or Flat   C (I)   Dominant or Sharp

(IV) F   G (V)

B♭   D (II)

E♭   A (VI)

A♭   E (III)

D♭   B (VII)

G♭   F♯

C♭   C♯

F♭   G♯

B♭♭   D♯

E♭♭   A♯

A♭♭   E♯

D♭♭   B♯

The structure is unbalanced, because harmonics all rise from a note, and the dominant or sharp direction, based on the successive second overtones of the previous note, outweighs the subdominant direction, which descends. The subdominant weakens the tonic by turning it into a dominant (that is, by using the tonic note not as the root of the central triad, but as an overtone). This imbalance is essential to an understanding of almost all tonal music, and from it is derived the possibility of tension and resolution on which the art of music depended for centuries. The imbalance can be perceived immediately in the formation of the diatonic major scale (the notes marked with roman numerals above) which uses the root of only one triad in the subdominant direction, but of the first five triads on the sharp or dominant side.

The two directions in just or natural intonation do not lead back to the beginning: following the natural harmonics of the tones, D♭♭ is not the same note as B♯, and neither coincides with C. None of the triads produced on the dominant side is consequently the same as those of the subdominant, but some of them are very close. Almost from the inception of tonality, and even from the very beginning of musical theory itself with the Greeks, musicians and theorists have tried to identify the triads that are significantly close, producing a system which is not only symmetrical but circular, called the circle of fifths:

C (I)

(IV) F = E♯   G (V) = A♭♭

B♭ = A♯   D (II) = E♭♭

E♭ = D♯   A (VI) = B♭♭

A♭ = G♯   E (III) = F♭

D♭ = C♯   B (VII) = C♭

(G♭ = F♯)

24

This entails enforcing an equal distance between the twelve notes arranged in stepwise or scale progression (which produces the chromatic scale), and it distorts their relation to the natural overtones: the system is called equal temperament. Modulating around the circle of fifths in either direction will now bring one back to the original starting point. There were considerable attempts to establish the system of equal temperament in the sixteenth century, where it is essential to much of the chromatic music written then, but it did not become the theoretical basis for music until the eighteenth (and some tuners of keyboard instruments used compromises between equal temperament and just or natural intonation until the nineteenth century).

Equal temperament absolves us from considering at length whether or not tonality is a 'natural' or a 'conventional' language. It is quite evidently based on the physical properties of a tone, and it equally evidently deforms and even 'denatures' these properties in the interests of creating a regular language of more complex and richer expressive capacities. The ear or mind had already learned to make a semi-identification of major and minor thirds, although if the lower third of a triad is major and the upper third minor, this makes for a much closer approximation of the natural overtones; a major chord is therefore more stable than a minor one, which is also—like the relative weakness of the subdominant direction—an essential fact in comprehending the expressive significance of tonal music.

This definition of the universe of late eighteenth-century tonality by means of the circle of fifths may seem more cumbersome than one based on the major and minor scales, but it has the advantage of revealing the asymetrical relation of dominant to subdominant, and, above all, of emphasizing that the center of a tonal work is not a single note, but a triad. The circle of fifths was also the contemporary method of mapping out the chromatic scale, as we can see from Beethoven's early improvisation for organ and, at a later date, from Chopin's *Preludes*. The scales by themselves would imply a system which is not tonal but 'modal': one in which the center is a note, each work is restricted to the notes of its mode, and the final cadences are conceived as melodic, rather than harmonic, formulas. Nevertheless, the scales retain their importance, since the resolution of dissonance at the time was always by stepwise progression—from which arises an ever-present tension within tonality between scale and triad, or between step-wise and harmonic motion. The scales also help to make the essential distinction between the major and minor modes.

The minor mode is essentially unstable, which is why pieces in the minor tend to have endings in the major. It is also a form of the subdominant (and a glance at the diagram opposite will show that notes of the C minor scale which differ from the C major scale all come from the flat or subdominant side). For this reason, the minor mode is often used as a chromatic device, a way of adding color to the major; it does not clearly define a movement to another tonality, but is an unstable and more

25

expressive form of the same key. In a heavily chromatic passage, indeed, it is often impossible to say if the mode is major or minor (see page 256).

The basis of all Western musical form starting with Gregorian chant is the cadence, which implies that the forms are 'closed,' set within a frame and isolated. (Not until the nineteenth century is the final cadence attacked, although the improvisatory introduction attempts to open up the front end as early as the sixteenth century.)

The greatest change in eighteenth-century tonality, partly influenced by the establishment of equal temperament, is a new emphatic polarity between tonic and dominant, previously much weaker. Cadences had still been formed in the seventeenth century with either dominant or subdominant triads, but as the significant advantages of emphasizing the built-in imbalance of the system (the strength of the sharp over the flat direction) began to be realized, the subdominant or plagal cadence was dropped. The dominant cadence became the only one, and was reinforced by the increased importance of the dominant-seventh chord: if the notes of the diatonic scale alone are used in forming triads, then there can be no true fifth or stable triad on VII, which has only a diminished fifth or tritone. VII is the next tone or leading-tone to the tonic, and putting V under its triad produces the dominant seventh (V⁷), at once a dominant chord and the most unstable dissonance demanding immediate resolution into the tonic chord. The pre-eminence of the dominant seventh was reinforced as the medieval distaste for using diminished fifths disappeared from music with the less inhibited use of all dissonances, now integrated and resolved within a more complex arrangement.

The polarity of tonic and dominant was affirmed by modulation, which is the transformation of the dominant (or another triad) temporarily into a second tonic.[1] Modulation in the eighteenth century must be conceived as essentially a dissonance raised to a higher plane, that of the total structure. A passage in a tonal work that is outside the tonic is dissonant in relation to the whole piece, and demands resolution if the form is to be completely closed and the integrity of the cadence respected. It is not until the eighteenth century, with the full establishment of equal temperament, that the possibilities of modulation could be completely articulated, and the consequences of this articulation were only realized in the latter half of the century.

The chromatic modulations of the sixteenth century, for example, do not distinguish clearly between the flat and the sharp directions: the chromaticism

---

[1] In the minor mode, this polarity changed radically from 1700 to 1830. In the early part of the century, the secondary key to C minor, for example, could be either the dominant minor (G minor), or the relative major (E flat major). But the dominant minor triad can never have the force of a major chord, and this weak relation almost totally disappeared by the end of the eighteenth century. The relative major now reigned alone as a substitute for the dominant in the minor mode. This situation, too, could not remain fixed for long. By the time of Schumann and Chopin, the minor mode and its relative major are often identified, considered as the same key, so that no polarity is any longer possible (as in the Chopin Scherzo in B flat minor/D flat major or the Fantasy in F minor/A flat major). The instability of the function of the minor triad is clearly a force for historical change.

is therefore much more what its name implies—a coloring. Even in the early eighteenth century, modulation is more often a drifting movement than the genuine if temporary establishment of a new tonic: in this passage from the *Art of Fugue*, there is a kaleidoscopic shift through several keys with no firm hold on the way:

(Triple Fugue à 4)

But in Mozart and Haydn, the full implications of the hierarchical arrangement of triads are drawn: the various tonalities possible can be contrasted articulately and even dramatically with the central one so that the range of significance is considerably expanded.

The hierarchy is more complex than the place of each triad on the circle of fifths, and depends on many factors, not all of which need be brought into play by the composer at the same time. The tonality on II, for example, although apparently close to I, is actually one of the most remote, or most contradictory in its relation to the tonic, simply because the tonic I creates a dominant seventh chord out of the major triad on II (supertonic) by adding its fundamental note, or root, to it. As a brief summary of the classical use: the keys of III and VI (mediant and submediant) are sharp keys close to the dominant and imply an increase in tension (or dissonance on the level of structure) and to some extent they can substitute for a dominant; the flat mediant and submediant are largely subdominant keys, and are used like the subdominant to weaken the tonic, and lower tension; the other tonalities must be more precisely defined by the context of the music, although the tonalities at a distance of the tritone (diminished fifth) and the minor seventh are most remote or, in other words, most dissonant in their large-scale effects.[1]

All of Haydn, Mozart, and Beethoven is written with the system of equal temperament in mind, even music for string quartet. When Beethoven, in the following passage from the Quartet, op. 130:

writes Db for the first violin and C♯ for the second, he obviously does not intend a different pitch. It is true that Beethoven distinguishes the direction

---

[1] The important pathetic role of the flat supertonic (or Neapolitan) will be discussed later on p. 88.

a note is going in a modulation; in the opening measures of the same movement:

the ambiguity of B flat minor–D flat major is reflected in the B♭♭–A♮. I once heard a quartet play this passage in just intonation with horrible effect. This is not to say that string players play, or should play, in strict equal temperament: pitch is always subtly altered, but for expressive reasons which have little to do with just intonation. Most violinists find it in practice more natural to adjust the pitch in the least 'natural' way. In actual physical terms, here B♭♭ is higher than A♮, but since the A♮ is part of an uncompleted B flat minor cadence, it sounds more expressive and more logical when it is very slightly sharpened, and a leading-tone is more often sharpened than flattened. The theory that string players should play in just intonation seems to be a late nineteenth-century one, mainly due to Brahms's friend Joachim; and Bernard Shaw claimed savagely that Joachim did not play in just intonation, but quite simply out of tune. Such are the dangers of theory applied to performance.

Beethoven did say that he could distinguish between music in D flat and C sharp, but his remark applies even to music played on the piano, and has nothing at all to do with intonation or temperament. What Beethoven was talking about was the 'character' of the different tonalities, a subject that is more relevant to the psychology of the composer than to actual musical language. Donald Francis Tovey ascribed the idea that keys have definite characteristics to their relation to C major, unconsciously treated as basic since that is the first one every musician learns as a child. F major is, therefore, by 'nature' a tonality with a subdominant quality or a release of tension relative to C major, and most pastorals are, indeed, written in F. The traditional use of certain instruments in certain keys, horns in E flat, for example, also influenced the connotations of the tonalities. The dominant character of C sharp and the subdominant character of D flat are bound to have affected any composer's sensibility. Within a classical work, the character of a subordinate tonality (that is, not the main key of a piece) is dependent on the manner of arriving at it—either from the subdominant or the dominant direction—but this does not interfere with the absolute supremacy in theory of equal temperament; in practice the modifications of equal temperament, by vibrato or actual distortion, are expressive and not structural.

The second half of the eighteenth century represents an important stage in the centuries-long process of the destruction of the linear aspect of music. The linearity of music is not only horizontal, as it is most often conceived, with only the independent and continuous voices of a contrapuntal texture recognized as lines. There is a vertical aspect as well. The figured bass of the Baroque from 1600 to beyond 1750, in which the music is structured by a series of chords, is a conception of the flow of music in terms of a series of vertical lines; in fact, the notation yields this vertical linearity easily to the eye. (Even in solo music without any actual continuo instrument there is rarely any doubt, in spite of the independent movement of the voices, where one chord ends and the next begins.) These vertical 'lines' were carried by a strong horizontal bass line throughout the entire Baroque period, and both aspects were heavily attacked by the new style of the later eighteenth century.

The significance of this change appears in the pervasive influence of the many accompaniment figures already developed earlier in the century. The best known of these is the Alberti bass:

This accompaniment blurs the independence both of the three contrapuntal voices which it theoretically contains and of the chordal or homophonic harmony which it supposedly illustrates. It breaks down the isolation of the voices by integrating them into one line, and of the chords by integrating them into a continuous movement. Linear form is essentially the isolation of the elements of music, and the history of music, until our day, may be seen as a gradual breakdown of all the various isolating forces of the art—contrapuntal independence of voices, homophonic progression, closed and framed forms, and diatonic clarity.

The attack upon the tendency to isolate comes paradoxically from within by means of the isolating forces themselves—just as, in painting, Impressionism went beyond Delacroix in its attempt to avoid isolating the larger forms, and yet its method was a doctrinaire isolation and equalization of each brush stroke. In music, the classical style attacked the horizontal independence of the voices and the vertical independence of the harmony by isolating the phrase and articulating the structure. Late eighteenth-century phrasing is emphatically periodic, and comes in clearly defined groups of three, four, or five measures, generally four. Imposing this new periodic system upon the musical flow and blurring the inner progression of that flow by the new accompaniment figures meant that the linear sense of the classical style was transferred to a higher level, and had to be perceived as the continuity of the whole work, and not as the linear continuity of the individual elements.

The vehicle of the new style was a texture called the sonata.

2

Theories of Form

Sonata form could not be defined until it was dead. Czerny claimed with pride around 1840 that he was the first to describe it, but by then it was already part of history. The original meaning of 'sonata' was 'played' as opposed to 'sung,' and it only gradually acquired a more specific, but always flexible, sense. The definitions generally given are far too limited even for the latter part of the eighteenth century, and apply only to the romantic sonata. In any case, the 'sonata' is not a definite form like a minuet, a da capo aria, or a French overture: it is, like the fugue, a way of writing, a feeling for proportion, direction, and texture rather than a pattern.

It is often difficult to distinguish the defining characteristics from the acquired characteristics of a form, partly because as time goes on the latter tend to become the former. That is, we must distinguish between what an eighteenth-century composer would have called a sonata (how far he would have stretched the term and at what point he would have said, 'This is not a sonata, but a fantasia') and the way sonatas were generally written (the patterns they gradually fell into and which were later unhappily considered as rules). The line between the two is often blurred, and it is doubtful if even the composers of the period would have been able to draw it with any certainty. It was not only that the meaning changed, but that the word was intended to cover a large range and even to foresee the possibility of change.

Since Czerny, the sonata has been most often defined as a melodic structure. The account (misleading in a number of ways) generally goes somewhat as follows: the exposition starts with a theme or group of themes in the tonic, followed by a modulation to the dominant and a second group of themes; after a repetition of the exposition comes the development, in which the themes are fragmented and combined in various keys ending with a return to the tonic and a recapitulation of the exposition, this time with the second group of themes in the tonic, and an optional coda. In this presentation of the traditional account, I have avoided the academic analysis of the exposition as first theme, bridge passage, second theme, and concluding theme, all this even more unsatisfactory than the above. Nor have I mentioned the 'rule' that one new theme is 'allowed' in the development. The fact is that while the placing, number, and character of the themes, at least from Scarlatti to Beethoven, have an importance which ought not to be underestimated, they are in no sense the determining factors of the form.

The destruction of the nineteenth-century account of 'sonata form' is a game too easy and too often played. The description's insufficiency is manifest when we consider that Haydn often used only one theme for his sonatas and, in particular, generally marked the modulation to the dominant by repeating the opening measures in their new place even when he used several themes; that Mozart preferred to mark the change to the dominant by an entirely new theme (although he followed Haydn's practice on occasion); and that Beethoven often favored a compromise in which the new theme marking the change is clearly a variant of the opening theme of the work. The presence of a new theme at this point, far from being indispensable as is often thought, is not even remotely a decisive element of the form.

Nor did the presence of a second theme seem even desirable to Haydn's contemporaries. When the great Symphonies 92–94 were first played in Paris, for which city they were written, the critic of the *Mercure de France* wrote admiringly that while less gifted composers needed many themes to sustain a movement, Haydn needed only one. A good tune was always welcome, and it was often used to reinforce and clarify the outlines of a sonata, but a sonata was not built with a succession of themes as its structure.

Although the nineteenth-century description of sonata form is grandly deceptive, it is important to try and understand how and why such a formulation became possible. Inevitably the first generation of Romantics, which thought of structure essentially in melodic terms, tried to arrive at a thematic scheme for the sonata. What is interesting is their apparent success. 'Sonata form' as conceived after 1840 may not work for a great many classical sonatas, but it fits an even larger number. It does so in spite of elevating the purely melodic aspect of music to a position it never held in the eighteenth century, and it satisfies only in so far as there is no tension between this aspect and other determinants of the form. When it fits, it is as misleading, perhaps even more so, than when it does not, but it cannot be easily dismissed. We are allowed one new theme in the development, and it often appears; the 'bridge passages' are most often where they are supposed to be, and sometimes they even sound connective rather than expository; the development not infrequently starts according to rule with the main theme in the dominant.

The trouble with this account of sonata form—unhappily still taught today in most schools and music appreciation courses—is not its inaccuracy but its being couched in the form of a recipe (and for a dish that could no longer be prepared). It admits that a large number of sonatas have heretical characteristics, but ascribes that to licence on the part of the composers, and implies that sonatas ought to be written in the 'orthodox' manner. In fact, except for those of Chopin, most nineteenth-century sonatas *were* written according to the orthodox recipe, and mostly for the worse. The recipe was not only inflexible; it also did not take account of the fact that by 1840 the proper ingredients were no longer being produced. Nineteenth-century tonality had become too fluid for the system of strictly defined modulations, bridge passages, and the like set up by the theorists (indeed, eighteenth-

31

century harmony was itself already too subtle and complex, but it fitted the Procrustean bed later prepared for it more easily). A description of the sonata in fundamentally melodic terms was as unsuited to the eighteenth century's more dramatic structures as the long-breathed melodies of the nineteenth century were inapt for the late eighteenth-century forms. The sonata was as archaic in 1840 as the Baroque fugue in Haydn's day: unfortunately the prestige of Beethoven and, to some extent, of Mozart was so great as to prevent a free adaptation of the form to entirely different purposes comparable to the classical composers' adaptation of the fugue. There was no Baroque composer who weighed upon Haydn as Beethoven did upon Schumann.

The most dangerous aspect of the traditional theory of 'sonata form' is the normative one. Basically the account is most comfortable with the works that Beethoven wrote when he was closely following Mozart's lead. The assumption that divergences from the pattern are irregularities is made as often as the inference that earlier eighteenth-century versions of the form represent an inferior stage from which a higher type evolved.

This is implied, too, but in a more specious way, in a good deal of twentieth-century musical thought. Now the attitude is statistical rather than hortative: the pattern for 'sonata form' is no longer an idealized one but is based on the common practice of eighteenth-century composers. 'Sonata form' is taken to mean the form generally used by a majority of composers at a given time. This is a more attractive procedure, taking better notice of the historical development of the 'sonata,' and it is more scientific in terms of description and classification. The primacy of the tonal over the thematic structure is accepted, along with the importance of periodic phrasing in eighteenth-century form. The defect of this treatment is that it is too democratic. Composers are not equal in the sight of posterity or even in the eyes of their own contemporaries. (We reach here the delicate problem of the relation between the 'anonymous' classical vernacular and the style of Haydn, Mozart, and Beethoven.) The style of any age is determined not only by what is done but by the prestige and influence of what is done, although the prestige of a composer among the public and among his fellow musicians may differ considerably. The importance of a work of music is at least partly contingent upon its success—its immediate attraction for the contemporary public and, in the end, its coherence and depth. But to understand the success of a work, either in the long or the short run, we are not given much help by a theory of style constructed with an eye toward the most conventional and standard procedures. We need to know what may seem impossible to know if music is treated as a conventional language: not what was done, but what artistic purpose these standard procedures were expected, generally in vain, to serve. In keyboard works of Carl Philipp Emanuel Bach, for example, published as late as the 1780s, all kinds of 'sonata' patterns exist, with and without complete development sections, with partial and complete recapitulations, etc.

What should be crucial is the relation of these various forms to the harmonic and thematic material: if they could co-exist, why did the composer choose one in preference to another?

An account of the sonata in purely tonal terms does not falsify the way a classical sonata moves, but it obscures the significance of the form, which must ultimately be considered inseparable from the form itself. There is no question that every sonata-exposition goes from the tonic to the dominant (or to a substitute for the dominant, relative major or mediant and sub-mediant being the only possible ones), but I cannot believe that a contemporary audience listened for the change to the dominant and experienced a pleasant feeling of satisfaction when it came. The movement to the dominant was part of musical grammar, not an element of form. Almost all music in the eighteenth century went to the dominant: before 1750 it was not something to be emphasized; afterward, it was something that the composer could take advantage of. This means that every eighteenth-century listener expected the movement to the dominant in the sense that he would have been puzzled if he did not get it; it was a necessary condition of intelligibility.

The isolation of the harmonic structure, while an advance over a basically thematic definition of 'sonata form,' is therefore generally unsatisfactory; rhythm is given short shrift, and themes are absurdly seen as subsidiary—decorations added to emphasize, or even to hide, a more basic structure. Above all, we are given no hint of the relation of the structure to the material: the terms of the description are either so rigid that the material is only there to fill a pre-existing mold, or so loose that the form is left entirely but vaguely dependent on the material—as if a composer wrote without the example of previous works, his own as well as those of others, to act upon his inspiration, as if an audience expected an ordering of chaos with each new work, as if, in fact, their expectations on hearing a new symphony were not to some extent rhythmic, melodic, and even emotional.

Two more sophisticated rivals in the description of form must be mentioned briefly here. They may be called respectively linear and motivic. Analysis of a work in linear terms is due chiefly to Heinrich Schenker. The complexity of his theory is only partly responsible for the fact that knowledge of his ideas is confined to a small group of professional musicians and historians: some of the blame must be given to a literary style that is often offensive and an arrogance that is easy to confound with fatuity. Music which did not fit his theory was beyond his range, and Brahms is the last composer for whom he had a good word to say. Schenker's theories, as he formulated them, work only for tonal music, and they fit Bach, Handel, Chopin, and Brahms better than the three great classical figures. But there is no question of the relevance and the importance of his ideas (divested of the mystique which has surrounded them) for the period with which we are dealing.

Composers undeniably can think in linear terms in a larger sense than the detailed working-out of polyphony. Nothing is more typical of a fine work than the feeling that the music has moved toward one note which represents and clarifies a point of definition, and the working-out of which has been conceived (and is heard) in larger terms than its most localized and immediate preparation and resolution. (The greater the composer, the larger the terms of his control over the significance of his ideas, even when the range of his conception is deliberately narrowed: that is why Chopin must be considered in the company of the greatest in spite of the limitations of genre and medium that he imposed upon himself.) Both the preparation and the consequent movement are linear before 1900, as linear resolution is the only acceptable form in tonal music, and the search for other resolutions in the twentieth century has had a tangible and yet (so far) only partial success.

In other words, the notes of a tonal composition have a significance beyond the immediate context in which they are found, a significance that can be understood only within the total scheme of the whole work; beyond their meaning in the 'foreground,' there is a 'background' meaning, based principally on the tonic triad, which is the harmonic center of any tonal work. In Schenker's theory, the structure of every tonal work is a linear descent toward the tonic note, and the piece as a whole is the flesh that is put on this skeleton. One might rephrase this by saying that underlying every piece, and mirrored on all levels of its facture, is a simple cadential formula. On historical grounds alone (although Schenker's ideas are fundamentally anti-historical), this conception is justifiable: the cadence is the basic structural element in all Western music from the twelfth century until the first quarter of the twentieth —it is the determining element in all styles; from the cadence grow the conceptions of the modes, tonality, the periodic phrase, and the sequence (which is largely the repetition of cadential patterns). All of this, of course, seems obvious when we reflect that Western music has capitalized more than any other on the passage of time and has rarely tried, like the music of other cultures, to overcome or to disregard this sense of direction toward the final cadence, just as the sense of the frame governs Western painting of the same period.

The psychological accuracy of many of Schenker's observations is unchallengeable: a number of his analyses go further than any others toward explaining the sense of a unity that transcends the apparently sectional exterior form which we find in so many works. It is also true that our sensitivity as listeners to many of these long-range effects is often greater than we consciously realize, and that this sensitivity grows with successive hearings of a work. A small but striking example of this long-range linear sense, overriding the immediate voice-leading and demanding a clear feeling for the separation of different registers, is this passage from the slow movement of Beethoven's *Hammerklavier* Sonata:

where the rising scale progression is broken, or, rather, transposed downward in the middle, leaving a note (G) hanging in the air, unresolved and unconnected. Yet two measures later the melody curves upward with a movement of exquisite grace, resolving the note to an F♯ and, in so doing, connects and resolves audibly, even at first hearing, a part of its own past. This technique—or, better, this sense of line and register, only slightly magnified and transposed to the level of the whole structure—gives us the linear skeleton moving toward the cadence that can be heard in so many works.

An adequate consideration of what we may call linear analysis cannot be undertaken here. Most discussion of it is violently partisan. There are two questions which have never been answered, or even satisfactorily raised. The first is whether, even at its most audible, the linear skeleton that Schenker abstracts and prints in large notes in his diagrams is in all cases the main principle of unity: in other words, the relation of 'background' to 'foreground' does not always seem happily defined. There are other structural principles of unity besides the long-range horizontal one, and in certain works they are not only more striking but even more fundamental. 'Where are my favorite passages?' Schoenberg is said to have exclaimed on seeing Schenker's diagram of the *Eroica*; 'Ah, there they are, in those tiny notes.' Proponents of linear analysis would never claim that the basic line is directly heard in the foreground of our consciousness, but it is disquieting when an analysis, no matter how cogent, minimizes the most salient features of a work. This is a failure of critical decorum.

Introduction

The most signal result of Schenker's frequent disregard of the audible facts is his cavalier treatment of certain aspects of rhythm. It makes no difference to one of his analyses if a piece is fast or slow; nor is there an adequate differentiation in his diagrams between the forms of first and last movements, so widely contrasted in their rhythmic organizations. This omission is not easy to repair, unless one holds that the harmonic and linear structures remain unaffected by the rhythmic development, and it should be emphasized that harmony and rhythm in the late eighteenth century are everywhere interdependent. The rhythmic terminology available to us, which is either primitive or rebarbative, does not encourage analysis, and it is difficult with the present vocabulary even to distinguish pulse from tempo, and rate of harmonic change from the actual duration of notes; but a refusal to face these questions leads to a viewpoint so partial as to be radically false even when useful or stimulating.

The second problem concerning linear analysis is whether it is adequate to the whole range of tonal music. It is remarkable that Schenker's methods of analysis do not differ significantly for Bach, Mozart, Chopin, and Reger. They do not work without considerable revision for non-tonal music or, indeed, for composers like the pre-serial Stravinsky, but even within the tonal field alone, the similarity of approach is *prima facie* suspect. Tonality was not for-two centuries a frozen and unchanging institution, nor is it possible to believe that the gulf between Beethoven and Chopin was one only of sensibility, not of method. Schenker naturally does not concern himself with the historical development of styles: all forms—fugue, *Lied*, sonata, rondo—from 1650 to 1900 are merely differently adapted versions of the long-range linear structure, and a composer's choice of the 'apparent' form takes on an arbitrary coloring. Linear analysis has undoubtedly considerable validity for late eighteenth-century music, but the rate of progression from one point of the basic line to another and the proportions of the form, in particular the length of the final tonic section, are completely irrelevant to the theory. Proportions and dramatic movement are, nevertheless, central to late eighteenth-century style, and they cannot be so dismissed without our feeling that an important aspect of the general intention has been evaded.

Is the unity that we sense in a work of art an illusion? only a critical hypothesis? If it has any reality at all, then a description of its form will not merely name the parts but try to tell us why it seems one whole. The attempt to derive a work of music from one short basic motif uses a method of analysis called 'diminution technique' by Schenker, in whose theory it plays a role less overwhelming than in the work of many of his followers. It is based on a considerable amount of nineteenth-century analytic theory, principally that of Hugo Riemann.

The unity of thematic material in Beethoven, however, was already appreciated during his lifetime. As early as 1810, E. T. A. Hoffmann wrote a review of the C minor Symphony in which he remarked:

36

The inner arrangement of the movements, their development, instrumentation, the manner in which they are ordered, all this works toward a single point: but most of all it is the intimate relationship among the themes which creates this unity, which alone is able to keep the listener held in *one* sentiment (*Stimmung*). Often this relationship becomes clear to the listener if he hears it in the combination of two phrases, or discovers a common ground-bass in two different phrases, but a more profound relationship which does not manifest itself in this manner often speaks only from spirit to spirit, and it is this which reigns in the two allegros and the minuet and magnificently proclaims the controlled genius of the master.

Hoffmann adds elsewhere that this unity of motif is already present in the music of Haydn and Mozart. Anyone who has played the works of the Viennese classics has sensed over and over again the weight of these thematic relationships. What distinguishes more recent critics from earlier ones is their insistence on motivic development as the fundamental principle of structure, taking precedence over harmonic, melodic, or any other more 'exterior' forces.

This motivic development is sometimes presented as a mysterious process, something within the power only of the greatest composers. Nothing could be further from the truth. A really incompetent composer may throw together the most disparate material without any regard for its fitting together, but much the same thematic unity that we find in Mozart can be found in a lesser composer like Johann Christian Bach. In addition, obvious manifestations of thematic unity are not only frequent but traditional. The Baroque suite in which each successive dance begins with the same notes is not an uncommon form; examples may be found easily in Handel. The early Romantics revived this technique with greater power along with their interest in cyclic form, and there are many works in which each section is derived from the same motif: Schumann's *Carnaval*[1] and Berlioz's *Symphonie Fantastique* are only the most celebrated examples.

If the use of a central motif seems less evident, less a part of the work's candid intention, between 1750 and 1825 than before and after, this does not mean that it had become less cogent, let alone disappeared. To some extent it only went underground. Quite often, particularly in Beethoven from the beginning of his career on, it becomes explicit; if we do not feel the 'second' theme of the *Appassionata* Sonata as a variant of the opening, we have missed an important part of the discourse. The less explicit examples of thematic unity, however, arouse the greatest controversy, some of it surprisingly acrimonious. Much of the bitterness is based on misunderstanding.

---

[1] *Carnaval* is derived from *two* short motifs, but they are harmonically very similar and are used in a way that brings them even closer to each other.

Musicians become indignant at the idea that there are thematic relationships in a work of Beethoven, for example, which they think they are unable to hear. Tovey, with a lack of sympathy rare for him, denied the importance of thematic relations if the actual mechanism was not directly audible as an effect: that is, if one could not hear one theme being derived from the other step-by-step during the course of the piece. But a composer does not always want his developments, however carefully he may have worked them out, to take the form of a logical demonstration; he wants his intentions made audible, not his calculations. A newly introduced theme may not be intended to sound logically derived from what precedes it, yet one may reasonably feel that it grows naturally out of the music, fitting in an intimate and characteristic way with the rest of the work. The final melody of the slow movement of Beethoven's *Tempest* Sonata, op. 31 no. 2, is just such a new theme:

and Tovey has claimed that it is vain to try to derive it from anything else in the movement. Yet its harmony is clearly allied to measures 81–89, as is the most poignant part of its melodic curve:

as well as to the diminished chords that are such an insistent feature of the whole movement. Tovey is right to draw attention to the character of this

38

melody as something new, but he leaves as unanalyzable our feeling that it fits in so well with all that comes before. Yet our sense of its organic relation to the rest is not inexplicable. If a composer wishes two themes to sound as if they belong together, it is natural to base both of them on similar musical relationships: to maintain that the effect of these relationships is of little importance unless we can identify them while listening, or give them a name, is like saying that we cannot be either moved or persuaded by an orator unless we are able to identify the rhetorical devices of synecdoche, chiasm, syzygy, and apostrophe with which he works upon our feelings.

Not only the themes but also many of the accompanying details, and even, indeed, the large structure are often derived from a central idea. The coherence of a work of art is, after all, not a modern ideal anachronistic in the late eighteenth century, but the oldest commonplace of aesthetics, handed down from Aristotle through Aquinas. Motivic relationship has been one of the principal means of integration in Western music since the fifteenth century. Direct contrapuntal imitation is its most common form, but motivic development or diminution technique takes on even greater importance in the classical period, although by then it already has a long history behind it. A short motif may not only generate the melody to some extent, but also determine its coloring and the course of what will follow. An example of this kind of expression, on a scale small enough to quote, is the opening of the finale of Beethoven's Sonata in B flat major op. 22:

Here the four-note motif  in the first two measures is echoed in the
bass twice from measures 3 to 6 with the rhythm changed and the accent
displaced. A short repeated motif, particularly a rising chromatic one, always
gains in intensity, and this generates the accelerated echoes of the melody's
graceful swell: becomes transposed to the dominant with and
then to the dominant of the dominant in the seventh measure, and
each of these transpositions has been suggested and prepared in measures 2
and 4. We hear this not as thematic echo, but as harmonic correspondence:
a less intellectual effect, but one more directly affecting our sensibilities. In
this way, the motif calls up the harmonic movement to C (or the dominant
of the dominant) towards which note the first part of the phrase rises, as
well as all the chromatic echoes. When the A♮ is introduced in the twelfth
measure to harmonize with the B♮, all twelve notes of the chromatic scale
have entered as a specific response to the motif: it is for this reason that the
final chromatic scale in measures 16 and 17 appears not simply decorative
but convincingly logical, almost thematic. The short motif has been used to increase the speed and heighten the color; it is, in fact, the prime agent of tension
and transformation, changing its meaning at each successive appearance.

It is easy to neglect this changing significance. To point out the recurrence
of one short motif, and even to remark on its role in the development of the
work, while ignoring its dynamic qualities—its use for musical action—is
to forget that music takes place in time. In too much writing on music, a
work appears like a large system of inter-relationships in which the order,
the intensity, and, above all, the direction of the relations are of secondary,
and even negligible, consideration. Too often, the music could be played
backward without affecting the analysis in any significant way. This is to
treat music as a spatial art. Yet the movement from past to future is more
significant in music than the movement from left to right in a picture.[1] That
is why so many analyses of motivic structure are difficult to relate, not only
to what is heard, but also to the *act* of listening; there is a difference between
what one *can* hear, and how one listens. In this respect Schenker is far superior,

---

[1] Not that the movement from left to right is without significance in painting, as Wölfflin
has shown in a famous essay. But the direction of a picture can be reversed (as in an en-
graving) and still leave many of the significant formal values unchanged.

for his theory rests firmly on the direction of time—the movement towards the tonic, the tendency of resolution to go downward. There must be a coherent interaction between the individual motif and the direction of the piece—the intensity and the proportions of its gradual unfolding.

Above all we must avoid the ludicrous suggestion of a secret art, the idea that composers (only the great ones, naturally) wrote their music by an esoteric process like motivic development, but arranged it into easily understandable forms like sonatas and rondos so that the dim-witted public could grasp it without too much difficulty. This notion, advanced by Schenker and lesser critics like Réti, of an exterior and basically trivial form imposed for the sake of clarity upon a more fundamental process, will not bear even passing scrutiny: it does not correspond to the psychology of any composer—surely not of Haydn, who had not a trace of the conspirator in his nature and whose compositional technique is never *sub rosa*, or of Beethoven, whose disregard for the listening comfort of his public is sufficiently evident in many works; nor, above all, does it bear any relation to even the most perceptive musician's experience of listening to music. It is not true that themes, modulations, and changes of texture are superficial phenomena, less fundamental than diminution technique. This absurdity can be avoided only if a truly intimate relation—not just a marriage of convenience—can be shown between the motivic development and the larger elements of form.

The priorities of hearing must be respected. When relations between themes exist (and they are indeed crucial in the classical period), we ought to know whether they are clarified by the connecting material—that is, if they are part of the discursive logic of the music—or if they are only part of the texture, in which case they are not necessarily less important, but their effect is more an indirect appeal to the sensibility through the total sound of the piece as well as a unifying device. Most important of all, when there is a relation between the details of a work and the larger structure, how is this relation made audible? When there is a correspondence between the detail and the structure, merely to uncover it in the score is insufficient: we must be able to claim that it has always been heard, without being put into words perhaps, but with an effect upon our experience of the musical work.

The cause of our disquiet is above all the rigid linear dogmatism of so much contemporary theory: the insistence that the generating or central idea of composition be conceived only in linear terms, mostly, indeed, as a pure arrangement of pitches without regard to rhythm, intensity, and texture. Much of the malaise in relating this view of the form to the actual music as played arises because our hearing is not exclusively linear—nor is it desirable that it should be. The conception of form as generated by a linear series is no doubt congenial to an age which has seen the development of dodecaphonic music, but it is less natural to the eighteenth century, particularly the second half. (And though a great deal of Baroque music is composed by the elaboration of a short motif, this linear concept is not even very satisfactory for the

41

early eighteenth century.) There is no question that a central idea, a musical idea, often binds together and unifies a late eighteenth-century work, but this cannot be so simply reduced to linear form—either as the working-out of a short linear series or as Schenker's long basic line; both views are too partial to be satisfactory. Nor can 'sonata form' be described simply but ungracefully as only a superficial frame for far weightier processes; both logic and the historical development of the eighteenth century will urge us to a conception that accounts for the profound contemporary feeling for proportions and dramatic movement satisfied by the style.

3

The Origins of the Style

The creation of a classical style was not so much the achievement of an ideal as the reconciliation of conflicting ideals—the striking of an optimum balance between them. Dramatic expression, limited to the rendering of a sentiment or of a significant theatrical moment of crisis—in other words, to a dance movement full of individual character—had already found musical form in the High Baroque. But the later eighteenth century made further demands: the mere rendering of sentiment was not dramatic enough; Orestes must be shown going mad *without his being aware of it*, Fiordiligi must desire to yield while trying to resist, Cherubino fall in love without knowing what it is that he feels, and, some years later, Florestan's despair give way and merge with his delirium and his apparently hopeless vision of Leonora. Dramatic sentiment was replaced by dramatic action. Handel was already capable, in the famous quartet from *Jephtha*, of representing four different emotions: the daughter's courage, the father's tragic sternness, the mother's despair, and the lover's defiance. But the lovers in the second-act finale of *Die Entführung aus dem Serail* move from joy through suspicion and outrage to final reconciliation: nothing shows better than the succession of these four emotions the relation of the sonata style to operatic action in the classical period, and it is tempting to assign to the sequence of emotions the relation of first group, second group, development, and recapitulation.

This requirement of action applies equally well to non-operatic music: a minuet with a character of its own will no longer suffice. No two of J. S. Bach's minuets are alike in character, while there are a number of Haydn's that resemble each other almost to the point of confusion. Yet every one of Bach's has a seamless, almost uniform flow, which in Haydn becomes a series of articulated events—at times even surprising and shockingly dramatic events. The first significant examples of this new dramatic style are to be found not in Italian works for the stage but in the harpsichord sonatas of Domenico Scarlatti, written in Spain during the second quarter of the eighteenth century. Although there is little sign in his works of the classical technique of transition from one kind of rhythm to another, there is already an attempt to make a real dramatic clash in the changes of key, and a sense of periodic phrasing, still small-scale. Above all, the changes of texture in his sonatas are the dramatic events, clearly set off and outlined, that were to become central to the style of the generations that came after him. It was, in fact, under the weight of this dramatic articulation that the High Baroque aesthetic collapsed.

Introduction

What took its place at first was nothing coherent: that is why, although every period is one of transition, the years 1755–1775 may be given this title with particular relevance. Briefly and, indeed, over-simply, during these years a composer had to choose between dramatic surprise and formal perfection, between expressivity and elegance: he could rarely have both at once. Not until Haydn and Mozart, separately and together, created a style in which a dramatic effect seemed at once surprising and logically motivated, in which the expressive and the elegant could join hands, did the classical style come into being.

Before this synthesis, the children of Bach had divided up the principal stylistic possibilities of Europe among themselves: Rococo (or *style galant*), *Empfindsamkeit*, and late Baroque. Johann Christian's music was formal, sensitive, charming, undramatic, and a little empty; Carl Philipp Emanuel's was violent, expressive, brilliant, continuously surprising, and often incoherent; Wilhelm Friedemann continued the Baroque tradition in a very personal, indeed eccentric, fashion. Most of their contemporaries were indebted to them in one way or another. There were, however, many other complex influences in music at that time: a weakened form of the High Baroque style still held sway in most religious music, the serious operatic traditions of Italy and France still had vitality, and the Neapolitan and Viennese symphonic styles were full of experiment, as was the relatively new form of *opera buffa*.

The invention of the orchestral *crescendo* by the orchestra at Mannheim is often credited with a seminal importance, but if ever a development was inevitable, it was this. The dynamic transition is a logical and even necessary corollary to a style that starts with articulated phrasing and develops methods of rhythmic transition from one kind of texture to another. The gradual fitting of Venetian swell shutters to harpsichords is only another and less fruitful aspect of the same stylistic movement. The *crescendo* would have been invented even if Mannheim had never existed, and the music of the Mannheim symphonists is less interesting and less influential than the Italian *buffa* overture.

The greatest contribution of the early Viennese symphonists was their recognition of the need for continuity, quite literally the overlapping of phrases, in holding the attention of audiences. The chamber works of the middle of the century are full of holes, moments where the tension ceases to exist, where the music stops and picks up again with no inner necessity: even in the earlier works of Haydn and Mozart we can see this occurring with sad frequency. The Viennese symphonists had no way of overcoming this defect beyond an occasional injection of the Baroque fugal style and its consequent impression of continuous movement (imitative effects are, for example, used to cover the joins between phrases); but at least they recognized the existence of a problem (or created a problem, which has its own historical merit) that was to be solved quite differently.

The early Viennese symphonists represent the first appearance of a pattern that was to become a regular part of the development of Haydn and Mozart, the return to Baroque complexity to recapture some of the richness lost with the original simplification and destruction that attend any revolution. The articulated Italian manner was essentially thinner than the learned Baroque technique, and each advance entailed a loss that had later to be made good.

The distinction between orchestral style and chamber style, or music for the general public and music for amateurs to play privately, was never absolutely clear-cut, but it is still important for an understanding of the music of the 1750s and '60s. Except in the use of dynamic contrast, the distinction was less clear earlier in the century: at least two of the Brandenburg concertos are intended for one instrument to a part—the sixth, for example, is almost certainly a sextet—while others require a small chamber orchestra with a contrast between solo and ripieno, but the musical style of both kinds is very similar. Toward the middle of the century, however, the symphonies and overtures written for public performance, and the sonatas, duos, and trios written for amateurs are noticeably different in style. The chamber music is more relaxed, diffuse, and simple, in both outline and detail; the finale is often a minuet, the opening movement a set of variations. Public works began to be more formal. The string quartet, for connoisseurs, bridged the gap between the two styles, more formal than music predominantly for keyboard with or without string accompaniment, less richly worked out (until Haydn) than the symphony. This distinction prevails with Haydn even through the last works: long after the quartet, sonata, and piano trio had benefited from symphonic style, the symphonies were more tightly organized, less free, with more massive finales, and with opening movements rarely in the moderate tempi we often find in the chamber works. It remains true, however, that Haydn brought all the weight of his symphonic experience to bear on his chamber music, as Mozart assimilated operatic and concerto style in his sonatas and quartets. The blending of the genres in their music from 1780 on is striking: the finale of Haydn's C major Sonata (H. 48) is a symphonic rondo, and the finale of Mozart's Sonata in B flat major K. 333 is a concerto movement complete with cadenza. The influence went the other way as well: the last movement of Mozart's F major Concerto K. 459 is a symphonic finale in the fugal style that Haydn had done so much to develop, and the slow movements of many of the later Haydn symphonies have the improvised intimacy of much of his chamber music. (Whichever version came first, symphony or piano trio, the slow movement of Symphony no. 102 is closer to traditional keyboard style than to orchestral—which is not to say that it sounds better in the version with piano.)

This development is, of course, related to the history of public concerts in the eighteenth century, as well as to the rise of the amateur musician. Since most public performances in the early part of the century were almost entirely religious or operatic in character, any strong contrast between orchestral and chamber styles would have been unlikely: the real contrasts of the High Baroque are between religious and secular music—although a good deal of music hovers between the two (even if it is understood that panegyric cantatas for royal and ducal houses must be classed as religious music); between vocal and instrumental styles—although here again only the extremes are clear and the dividing-line impossible to draw; between strictly contrapuntal textures and the more popular styles based on the dance and the concerto—although the fugal gigue is by no means uncommon, and Handel wrote fugues on melodies in English hornpipe style; and finally between French and Italian styles, the one decorative and based principally on the old dance forms, and the latter more progressive, dramatic, and relying on the new concerted textures. In the great German masters Bach and Handel, the contrasts are of little importance, the styles fused. They pick and choose where they please; it is perhaps one of their advantages over Rameau and Domenico Scarlatti.

As public orchestral performances grew in frequency, and as at the same time music became more and more a social grace, the difference between public and private music became more distinct. Is the amateur nature of most keyboard music of the latter half of the eighteenth century due to the fact that the pianoforte became the particular province of the female musician? Most of Haydn's piano sonatas and piano trios, many of Mozart's concertos and Beethoven's sonatas were especially written for ladies. One of Mozart's publishers objected to the technical difficulty of his piano quartets, and it should be emphasized that violin-and-piano sonatas and piano trios, quartets, and even quintets were considered basically piano music until well into the nineteenth century, and as such were expected to be simple enough in style and technical difficulty to appeal to amateurs. That Beethoven with his usual ruthlessness made no distinction between amateur and professional, and that Haydn late in life found an English widow equal to the technical demands of his imagination at the keyboard should not blind us to the fact that these are the exceptions. Even the late B flat Sonata K. 570 of Mozart represents a deliberate attempt to accommodate the pianist with a limited technical (and even musical) equipment; and we misunderstand the Haydn sonatas written before 1780 if we interpret them as examples of a still undeveloped style— it was the pianists who were not yet developed, as the far richer and more complex symphonies Haydn wrote during the same period demonstrate.

A newly forged style is a formidable weapon in the conquest of new territory. The temptation to make keyboard and chamber music symphonic (and even operatic) must have been strong: few composers can resist applying the ideas worked out in one genre to another. No doubt the greater frequency of public, or at least semi-public, performance of chamber works helped, and the continuous mechanical changes (improvements?) of the piano were a challenge as well as an answer to changes in style. But that the impetus of the style itself was a major factor in the increasing seriousness of chamber works is without question. The last area to be completely taken over by the classical style was religious music, where the Baroque retained its dominance even in Mozart and Haydn. Here, too, the last defenses fell with the two Beethoven masses—ironically, at the last minute, just as a new interest in the Baroque was beginning to reach the public as well as the professional musician. But a style of such power of integration did not exist before the work of Mozart and Haydn in the late 1770s. Before then the scene was more chaotic with many seemingly equal rival forces; for this reason the period from the death of Handel to Haydn's *Scherzi* (or *Russian*) Quartets, op. 33, is difficult to describe. This is, of course, all hindsight: to a musician of the 1780s there were as many rivals as before, and their claims as difficult to assess. Nevertheless, to appreciate the music of the 1760s, we need all our historical sympathy, we have constantly to keep in mind the difficulties, inward as well as outward, that the composers had to face. On the other hand, from 1780 onward we have only to sit back and watch two friends and their disciple sweep almost every kind of music, from the bagatelle to the mass, into their orbit, mastering the forms of the sonata, concerto, opera, symphony, quartet, serenade, folk-song arrangement with a style so powerful that it can apply almost equally well to any genre. We do not have to call upon any historical sympathy to appreciate the work of Mozart and Beethoven, and the late works of Haydn: they are still in the blood of most musicians today.

It is the lack of any integrated style, equally valid in all fields, between 1755 and 1775 that makes it tempting to call this period 'mannerist.' The word has been so abused that I advance it only with hesitation. In order to surmount the problem of style that faced them, the composers of that time were reduced to cultivating a highly individual manner. The neoclassicism of Gluck, with its wilful refusal of so much traditional technique, the arbitrarily impassioned and dramatic modulations and the syncopated rhythms of Carl Philipp Emanuel Bach, the violence of many of the Haydn symphonies of the 1760s— much of this is the 'manner' that tries to fill the vacuum left by the absence of an integrated style. But so is the sophisticatedly smooth and flat courtly style of Johann Christian, the 'London' Bach; the effect is often chic rather than expressive, and the elegance is chiefly one of surface, as we are always conscious of what is being deliberately renounced for the sake of this grace— what is omitted disturbs the listener as it never does with Mozart even at his most *faux-naïf*. The conscious rejection of his father's style seems to haunt the music of Johann Christian Bach. It is paradoxical that a period which owed so much to Christian and Emanuel Bach, which was so dependent on their craftsmanship and their innovations, could not produce a major style of its own until it had reabsorbed (partly transformed and partly misunderstood) the work of Handel and Sebastian Bach. Nevertheless, this kind of disorganized environment may be stimulating to minor composers: the violin sonatas that Boccherini wrote in the 1760s experiment in much the way Haydn did at that time, and if Boccherini has less crude force and more elegance, this was a disadvantage only when seen in the light of later developments. At any rate, these early sonatas are more estimable than the bland, and even anodyne, music that he was to turn out with such facility in the more ordered classical atmosphere of the latter part of the century.

I have called the period between the death of Handel and the first mature works of Mozart 'mannerist,' with the hope of avoiding both a tone of moral indignation and the fashionable connotation of the term. To strike a strong moral attitude toward an entire historical period inevitably leads to ludicrous misunderstanding—pardonable, perhaps, only when we are dealing with contemporary phenomena: when we have, so to speak, a stake in the next choice that will be made, when our attitude is a hope or an anxiety, and not self-indulgence masking as principle.

But while every age may demand equal consideration it cannot claim equal eminence. From the death of Handel to 1775 no composer had sufficient command over all the elements of music for his personal style to bear the weight of a large series of works, a genuine *oeuvre*. We disapprove nowadays of the idea of progress in the arts, but the deficiency of technique of even the finest talents of the period is a hard fact. It is for this reason that the experiments of the time, rich and interesting as they are, lack direction: the successes are all partial. Even in Haydn's finest works of the 1760s, the rhythmic insecurity is too often impossible to overlook. The relations between regular and irregular phrase-lengths are still unconvincing, and the typical Haydn use of dramatic silence is effective, but illogical within a larger context. The same can be said of Carl Philipp Emanuel Bach's most striking passages: they exist in and for themselves, with little relation to any conception of the whole work. The personal style, or 'manner,' of composers then was defined almost in a void, or, better, against a chaotic background of Baroque workmanship and tradition and half-understood classic and *galant* aspirations. Neither the imperturbable facility of the Romantic and Baroque composer nor the controlled dynamic transformation of the three great classical composers was as yet within reach. For experimentation to succeed, except by accident, one must be able to foresee the result and the import even if only half-consciously.

Perhaps the most glaring weakness of this period is the lack of co-ordination between phrase rhythm, accent, and harmonic rhythm. This is partly due to a contradiction between classical and Baroque impulsion. The motor force of the new style is the periodic phrase, that of the Baroque is the harmonic sequence. When the strongly articulated periodic phrase is combined with a sequence, particularly a descending one as most sequences then were,[1] the result is not an increase of energy, but a loss. The articulation of the phrase, and the powerful new accentuation demanded a corresponding or analogous movement from the harmony: an accented change that comes close

---

[1] Tovey has stressed the originality of the rising bass in Beethoven.

to modulation. Both the accent and contour, which derive energy from their clarity, are weakened by the continuity inherent in the sequence, above all the cherished circle of fifths, which in the middle of a classical work can give the impression of treading water. It is unhappily used by Philipp Emanuel Bach in many expository passages for an illusion of motion. In the great classical works, however, it is mostly used precisely for this quality of *suspended* motion: in a number of Beethoven developments (as in the first movement of the *Waldstein* Sonata), when a point of extreme tension is reached, a sequence, often of considerable length, holds the music poised, immovable, in spite of a violence of dynamic accent. Mozart's most breathtaking uses of the sequence are at the ends of his developments: we sense that the tonic is about to reappear, and with the conviction that Mozart's sense of proportion conveys, we often know in just how many measures, and yet we are led to it by a sequence richly worked out with a felicity of detail that makes us half forget the inevitability of the larger action, or sense it in our pulse while we are dazzled by what appears to be ornament and is really a heightening of the dramatic form.

In this intermediate and confused period between the High Baroque and the development of a mature classical style, certain general conceptions of structure and proportion outline themselves with increasing clarity. The tonal pattern of most pre-classical sonatas is little more than the dance-form of the High Baroque. The first part goes from the tonic to the dominant, the second part from the dominant to the tonic. The return to the tonic in the pre-classical styles is, however, rarely marked by a significant cadence—the strong cadence on the tonic is reserved for the very end. The second part contains a certain amount of what must be called development, and a great deal of recapitulation in the tonic, but the lack of a clear separating tonic chord blurs the distinction between the development and the recapitulation, a distinction that was to be made by the later eighteenth century. In the High Baroque, too strong a tonic cadence long before the end had its dangers: given the fluid, continuous, and self-generating rhythm of Baroque music the only way to stop a piece was a forceful tonic cadence. This was an effect which could be used only with caution before the final page. In order to make a long section after a tonic cadence possible, the classical period had to develop a new and powerful system of rhythm and phrasing.

The composer of a sonata (or of anything else) was concerned with reconciling the demands of expression and proportion. Symmetry withheld and then finally granted is one of the basic satisfactions of eighteenth-century art. By the first third of the century, dramatic expression was beginning to reveal itself not only in detail (the melodic line, its ornaments, the individual harmonic effects) and in texture, harmonic as well as rhythmic, but also in the large structure of the work. A syntactic art of dramatic movement was becoming possible, leaving behind it the more static art of dramatic situation and sentiment.[1] Several of the old Baroque symmetries had to be relinquished: the *ABA* form of the da capo aria, in particular, was too static for the newly developing style, although it was never completely forgotten and had its influence on what was to come. The symmetries of the classical period had to be used for the resolution of dramatic tension, and there were many possibilities. None of them was prescribed or proscribed, although choice was not an arbitrary matter. The most obvious symmetry was originally the most common: the second part repeats the material of the first part, but instead of going from tonic to dominant it goes from dominant to tonic. Thus we have a double symmetry of $A \to B$: $A \to B$ melodically and $A \to B$: $B \to A$ tonally. This does not mean that there is no development; there is plenty of development in Domenico Scarlatti and even in J. S. Bach and Rameau, but it is woven seamlessly into the recapitulation.

Development, in the classical and pre-classical styles, is basically nothing more than intensification. The earliest classical way of developing a theme, and one that was never lost, was to play it with more dramatic harmonies or in a remote key. At times, the more dramatic harmonies all by themselves even without the melodies would serve as development, and we find 'development sections' in many sonatas which make no direct allusion to the themes of the 'expositions.' The most common Baroque means of intensification, the extension of a theme and the avoidance of cadence, never disappeared, and its effect was only enhanced by the classical expectation of periodic cadence. Indeed, the avoidance of periodicity (the breakdown of symmetrical organization) is the fundamental classical means of rhythmic 'development,' and the fragmentation of the melodic material together with the use of contrapuntal imitation is only the thematic aspect of 'development,' corresponding to the rhythmic and harmonic aspects and uniting with them. The move from tonic to dominant in the 'exposition' is already in the direction of greater intensity, and the 'development' in the second part of the sonata form only serves to increase this long-range effect, to make the work dramatic in detail as well as in tonal structure, before it is resolved at the end.

There is a general tendency among historians to judge a pre-classical symphony or sonata as 'progressive' to the extent that it has a separate and lengthy development section. This is to ignore how much of the so-called 'recapitulation' is often given over to development, to an intensification of feeling and direction by the use of all the possible techniques—fragmentation, contrapuntal imitation, the use of remote harmonies or tonalities, the extension of melodies, avoidance of cadence. It also obscures the fact that exposition, development, and recapitulation are not watertight compartments. The addition of one or more new themes in the second half of a sonata means that the 'development section' has taken up the role of exposition. When the

---

[1] How far we find ourselves from the meaning of the terms 'classical' and 'Baroque' in the visual arts!

second half starts, as it so often does, with a complete replaying of the first subject in the dominant, then the 'development' has the role of a thematic recapitulation, just as the recapitulation (and even the exposition) often 'develop.'

Historically, in fact, this frequent appearance in the late eighteenth century of the opening melody at the beginning of the development is a heritage from the pre-classical form of the first years of the century. As the style developed, a purely symmetrical second half became less and less desirable; there always had been a tendency to heighten the feeling and the harmony after the appearance of the first melody played in the dominant at the opening of the second half. This tendency was to increase, and ultimately to create a radical change in the feeling for proportion. The greater dramatic tension that became common soon after the beginning of the second part of a 'sonata allegro' disrupted the simple melodic *AB/AB* symmetry of the Baroque dance-form, and required a more decisive resolution. An emphatic and marked return to the tonic at a point *no more than three-quarters of the way through a movement* is basic in late eighteenth-century style. Its placing is almost always an *event*, and it is never glossed over as the earlier eighteenth century tended to do. It is this dramatization of the return to the tonic that provokes the discussion whether the sonata is binary or ternary, a debate which treats musical proportions as if they were spatial rather than temporal.

Tovey has justly remarked that Mozart's piano concertos are not really in 'sonata form,' but in a variant of 'aria form'; nevertheless, the fact that he needed to make the point is instructive. The concerto at the time of Mozart is an aria that has been affected (or contaminated) by 'sonata form' to the point of resembling it closely. For a while, most major forms began to resemble sonatas: the rondo became a sonata rondo with a full-fledged development and recapitulation. The slow movement absorbed all of 'sonata form,' at first with rudimentary, and then with complete, developments. Minuets and scherzos also took on lengthy developments after their first double bar, and then even marked their opening halves, now become expositions, with a clear section in the dominant, which would be repeated in the tonic at the end. Finally the trios of the scherzos, always simpler and less developed, gradually took on some of the more complex characteristics of the sonata, so that now there was a sonata framed by another sonata. Even the magnificent finales of Mozart's operas, it has been pointed out, have the symmetrical tonal structure of a sonata.

We need a view of eighteenth-century musical style that allows us to distinguish what is abnormal only in a statistical sense from what was genuinely astonishing. For example, the development section of Mozart's Sonata in C major K. 330 makes no overt thematic allusion to the exposition, and this happens relatively rarely in works written during the last quarter of the century, although more often before. But it does not sound at all here as if this were an unusual procedure, either radical or reactionary: it sounds, as do many works of Mozart at this period, normally and normatively beautiful, unpretentious and finely ordered. It would be a mistake to find anything extraordinary in this movement except its balance and the wonderfully expressive detail: its large structure cannot have been intended to surprise. The opening of Beethoven's *Moonlight* Sonata, however, satisfies a definition of 'sonata form' on most counts, but it does not sound like what we expect of a sonata, and even Beethoven called it *quasi una fantasia*. The first movement was obviously intended to sound extraordinary. The principles of 'sonata form' for Haydn, Mozart, and Beethoven did not necessarily include a *thematic* development-section, nor did they require contrasting subjects, a complete recapitulation of the exposition or even a recapitulation that begins in the tonic. These are the patterns most commonly used, the easiest and most effective ways of meeting the demands the public made of the composer or, rather, that he made upon himself. But these patterns were not the form, and they only became so when the creative impulse and the style that generated the form had almost completely died away.

I should not like to set up a mysterious, unverifiable metaphysical entity, a Form, independent of the individual works, and revealed rather than invented by the composer. But a concept of style based mainly on the statistical frequency of certain patterns will never help us to understand irregularities of form or to appreciate the fact that most of these 'irregularities' were not thought to be irregular at all. Nor will it account for historical change—it can only register it. We must comprehend the imaginative significance of these patterns to understand why a recapitulation beginning in the dominant as in Domenico Scarlatti and Johann Christian Bach, gradually became unacceptable, while one that began in the subdominant (at a later point of the work) as in Mozart and Schubert became a reasonable possibility. Three examples may clarify the nature of the problem: the recapitulation of the first movement of Mozart's D major Sonata K. 311 begins with the 'second subjects,' returns to the opening theme only at the end and sounds witty, surprising, and satisfying when the opening finally reappears; the recapitulation of Beethoven's F major Sonata, op. 10 no. 2, which begins in the submediant, sounds witty and thoroughly unsatisfactory, and Beethoven promptly tells us that it was all a joke by going right back to the tonic; the recapitulation of Mozart's C major Sonata K. 545, which begins in the subdominant, sounds neither witty nor surprising but conventionally satisfactory, although it was as rare a form as any of the others at the time it was written.

The idea of a Form striving to define itself, to become flesh in all these different ways, is attractive, but even as a metaphor it sets a trap. It leads one to assume that there was such a thing as 'sonata form' in the late eighteenth century, and that the composers knew what it was, whereas nothing we know about the situation would lead us to suppose anything of the kind. The feeling for any form, even the minuet, was much more fluid. But 'complete liberty' describes the situation no better than 'occasional licence.' In a long-range way, it is no doubt true, or at least fruitful as an hypothesis, that art can do anything it wants; societies and artists call forth the styles they need to express what they wish—or, better, to fulfil the aesthetic needs they themselves have created. It is also true, particularly since the Renaissance, that artists are not so confined by their era as has sometimes been imagined. Not only have some styles offered extraordinary range and freedom, but even the possibility of pastiche exists: Michelangelo and Houdon produced fake antiques and Mozart wrote a suite in the style of Handel. An artist is in many ways free to decide what will influence him: Masaccio turned back a hundred years to Giotto as did Manet to Velásquez, and Beethoven's use of Gregorian chant in the D major Mass and the Quartet op. 132 is a measure of what the classical style could absorb. Nevertheless, for a composer, music is basically what was written last year, or last month (generally by himself, once he has developed his manner). His own work is not determined by it in any rigid sense, but it is what he must work with or against. The 'anonymous style' of an age, the buildings whose architects are without distinction, the books that have only a period interest, the painting that is only decorative—all this comes about by accretion, and it takes a generation to make a really noticeable change. An 'anonymous style' has little tenacity, but a tremendous inertia. If 'style' is used to mean an integrated form of expression—which only the finest artists can muster—there is still a limitation on development: the sustaining of a style in this sense is as heroic an act as its invention and an artist rarely creates his own possibilities, he only perceives them in the work he has just done.

An understanding of the sense of continuity and the proportions of classical style would enable us largely to dispense with a further discussion of 'sonata form.' For the late eighteenth century, a sonata was any *organized* series of movements, and the proportions of the music changed according to whether it was the opening movement, a middle movement, or a finale. Old forms, like the fugue and the theme and variations, were still used, thoroughly transformed; some forms, like the concerto, the overture, the aria, and the rondo, contain vestiges of older forms buried within them; and there are dances, mostly minuets, Ländler, and polonaises. Everything else is sonata: that is to say, plain music. In this case, we cannot be content with the description of a form: we need to know first how the sense of music in general differed from that of the previous age; above all, we need to grasp this in specifically musical terms. The possibilities of art are infinite but not unlimited. Even a stylistic revolution is controlled by the nature of the language in which it is to take place, and which it will transform.

Part II
THE CLASSICAL STYLE

Des Menschen Wesen und Wirken ist Ton, ist Sprache. Musik ist gleich-falls Sprache, *allegmeine;* die *erste* des Menschen. Die vorhandenen Spra-chen sind Individualisirungen des Musik; nicht individualisirte Musik, sondern, die zur Musik sich verhalten, wie die einzelnen Organe zum organisch Ganzen.

Johann Wilhelm Ritter, *Fragmente aus dem Nachlasse eines jungen Physikers,* 1810

[*The essence and the activity of man is tone, is language. Music is also language,* general *language, the* original *one of man. The extant languages are individualizations of music—not individualized music, but related to music like the separate organs to the organic whole.*]

1

The Coherence of the Musical Language

The classical style appears inevitable only after the event. Looking back today we can see its creation as a natural one, not an outgrowth of the preceding style (in relation to which it seems more like a leap, or a revolutionary break), but a step in the progressive realization of the musical language as it had existed and developed since the fifteenth century. At the time, nothing would have seemed less logical; the period from 1750 to 1775 was penetrated by eccentricity, hit-or-miss experimentation, resulting in works which are still difficult to accept today because of their oddities. Yet each experiment that succeeded, each stylistic development that became an integral part of music for the next half-century or more was characterized by its aptness for a dramatic style based on tonality.

It is a useful hypothesis to think of one element of a new style as a germinal force, appearing in an older style at a moment of crisis, and gradually transforming all the other elements over the years, into an aesthetic harmony until the new style becomes an integral whole, as the rib-vault is said to have been the creative, or precipitating element in the formation of the Gothic style. In this way the historical development of a style seems to follow a perfectly logical pattern. In practice, things are rarely so simple. Most of the characteristic features of the classical style did not appear one by one in an orderly fashion, but sporadically, sometimes together and sometimes apart, and with a progress despairingly irregular to those who prefer a hard-edged result. The final product does, however, have a logical coherence, as even the irregularities of a language, once investigated, become consistent. So the procedure of isolating the elements and considering how one leads to the other, implying the other elements and completing them, is unhistorical but helpful.

The clearest of these elements in the formation of the early classical style (or proto-classical, if we reserve the term classical for Haydn, Mozart, and Beethoven) is the short, periodic, articulated phrase. When it first appears, it is a disruptive element in the Baroque style, which relied generally on an encompassing and sweeping continuity. The paradigm is, of course, the four-measure phrase, but historically this is not the model, but only, at the end, the most common. Two-measure phrases are almost a trademark with Domenico Scarlatti, becoming four-measure phrases when they are, in turn, grouped by twos. Haydn's Quartet op. 20 no. 4 starts with seven completely independent six-measure phrases, and this is only one example among thousands. Three- and five-measure phrases appear frequently from the very beginning, and 'real' seven-measure phrases become possible in the latter part of the century ('real' as opposed to eight-measure phrases where the last measure disappears by overlapping with the beginning of a new phrase). Not until about 1820 did the four-measure phrase gain its stranglehold on rhythmic structure. Before then, its supremacy was purely practical—it was neither too short nor too long, and it was easily divisible into balanced and symmetrical halves as three- and five-measure phrases were not. But there is no magic in the number four, and what is important is the periodic breaking of continuity.

Naturally, the periodicity makes this possible by providing a continuity of its own. The periodic phrase is related to the dance, with its need for a phrase pattern that corresponds to the steps and to groupings. In Italian instrumental music of the early eighteenth century, this phrase grouping is reinforced by the harmonic sequence, and it is amusing to see the most basic device of High Baroque rhythm contribute to the effectiveness of an element that was eventually to lead to the fall of the Baroque system. Not that the sequence was ever abandoned; it has remained an important part of music until our own day. In the classical style, however, it loses its primacy as a force for movement (some of which it regained during the nineteenth century). A Baroque fugue is kept moving largely by sequence: a classical sonata has other means of locomotion as well. In a classical work, in fact, a sequence is often a means of decreasing tension: after a series of surprising modulations, it is a way of calling a halt, and is often used for this purpose, placed over a pedal point, particularly toward the end of a development section. All large-scale movement has ceased, and the sequence is only a kind of pulsation. In this way the basic impulsive element of the Baroque is employed but down-graded in the classical system.

Articulated, periodic phrasing brought about two fundamental alterations in the nature of eighteenth-century music: one was a heightened, indeed overwhelming, sensitivity to symmetry, and the second was a rhythmic texture of great variety, with the different rhythms not contrasted or super-imposed, but passing logically and easily into each other. The dominance of symmetry came from the periodic nature of the classical phrase: a period imposes a larger, slower pulse upon the rhythm, and just as two similar measures are almost always necessary for us to understand the rhythm of the music and to identify the downbeat, so now a comparable symmetry of phrase structure was necessary to hear and to feel the larger pulse. The preference for articulation also increased the aesthetic need for symmetry. When the main consideration was rhythmical flow, as in the High Baroque, the balancing of one half of a phrase by another was not of predominant concern; it was more important for the end of each phrase to lead imper-ceptibly and urgently to the next. As each phrase assumed a more independent existence, the question of balance asserted itself with greater clarity. One example, the opening measures of perhaps the first unequivocal masterpiece in a classical style purified of all mannerist traces, Mozart's Concerto for Piano and Orchestra K. 271, will show how this balance was achieved, and also illuminate the variety and integration of rhythmic textures:

Measures 1–3 and 4–6 are the extreme form of balance, absolute identity. Yet it would be a mistake to think that the identical halves are identical in meaning. The repetition has greater urgency (a third would be exasperating), and gives the phrase greater definition, a clearer existence as an element of

the work we are about to hear. This is an astonishing and delightful opening, surprising not only for its use of the soloist at the very outset, but also for the wit with which he enters, as he replies to the orchestral fanfare. For this wit, the exquisite balance of the phrase is essential: the orchestra falls an octave and rises a fifth, the piano then rises an octave and falls a fifth within an equal length of time. We are not by any means intended to hear this as an inversion, as would be the case with a theme inverted in a fugue. That is the last thing the style requires, and the most ruinous of effect. The symmetry is concealed, delicate, and full of charm.

The concealment and, above all, the charm depend on the rhythmic variety: in effect the orchestra is in *alla breve*, with two long beats to the bar, while the piano is in a clear four (¢ and C). The stately is opposed to the impertinent, and balanced perfectly by it. The High Baroque is capable of such contrast, but rarely aimed at this kind of balance. The extent of the classical achievement is not, however, seen in the first half-dozen measures but in the ones that follow, where a convincing fusion of the two kinds of pulse is heard. The phrasing in measure 8 is a synthesis; it beautifully combines the pulse of *alla breve* and common time, while the melody in the first violins in measures 7–11 combines the opening motives of both the piano and the orchestra. It is this that makes the transition from measures 6 to 7 masterly: the urgency of the repeated phrase justifies the increased movement in eighth notes of the accompaniment in measure 7, while the first violins, who play the repeated B♭'s of the first measure half as fast, keep the change from being obtrusive and draw the two phrases together. With this seventh measure, the animation begins to increase, but the transition is imperceptible, a natural growth of what comes before. This kind of rhythmic transition is the touchstone of the classical style; never before in the history of music had it been possible to move from one kind of pulse to another so naturally and with such grace.

The High Baroque preferred music with a homogeneous rhythmic texture, using different kinds of rhythmic movement only under certain conditions. Contrast of rhythm could occur in two ways: by the superimposition of one rhythm over another, in which case the dominant rhythm of the piece inevitably becomes the faster one; and by the placing of large blocks of one kind of rhythm next to another (as in the plague of flies from *Israel in Egypt*), in which case the two or even three sorts of rhythm are superimposed before the end, generally at the climax, thus being reduced to the first case. In both cases, the rhythms remain essentially distinct; no transition is envisaged or attempted. A sudden and violent change in the rhythmic texture is sometimes attempted by Bach and other composers for dramatic reasons, as in the organ chorale-prelude *O Lamm Gottes* and in the last movement of the Fourth Brandenburg Concerto. Here the effect is one of wilful rhythmic eccentricity, always giving a moment of shock to the listener, deeply emotional in the one piece, dramatic but amiable in the other. But even these works are exceptions:[1] the most common Baroque form is one of simple and unified rhythmic texture. When a rhythm has been established, it is generally continued relentlessly until the end, or at least until the pause before the final cadence (at which point a change of rhythm is possible without giving the impression that something very out-of-the-way is happening). A fugue theme, for example, may open with long notes and finish with ones of smaller value (rarely the other way round), and it is the faster notes that become the basic texture of the whole: the longer notes of the theme are invariably accompanied by the faster rhythm in the other voices. Once the piece is under way an impression of *perpetuum mobile* is not uncommon.

The *perpetuum mobile* is occasionally found in classical works, and it is interesting to compare the difference in treatment. The chief rhythmic interest of the classical *perpetuum mobile* is focused on the irregular aspects: that is, the rhythmic variety is as great as in any other classical work. In the finale of Haydn's *Lark* Quartet op. 64 no. 5, the phrases are clearly articulated and never overlap, in spite of the continuous movement; the strong off-beat accents of the middle section in the minor provide still greater assurance of variety. The syncopated accents of the finale of Beethoven's F major Sonata op. 54 are even more surprising: they occur alternately on the second and third sixteenth notes of groups of four as follows:

This provides two contradictory forces that challenge the weight of the downbeat. The *sforzando* on the tonic in the bass reinforces the second sixteenth note, which is the weakest in the measure, making the accent most destructive to a sense of unvaried flow. For a classical composer the *perpetuum mobile* is only an added challenge to his desire to break up the rhythmic texture, and the tension adds dramatic force. It is, however, typically a device for finales, where the greater rhythmic stability of a continuous

---

[1] The one real exception that I know in the High Baroque, where a form of rhythmic transition, as opposed to contrast, is attempted, is the 'Confiteor' of the *B minor Mass*. In this profound work, the means used are, however, almost anti-classical, and a gradual change of tempo is meant, not a fusion of different pulses.

movement can serve as an alternative to a squarely articulated melody. The *perpetuum mobile* of the last movement of the *Appassionata*, a piece more stable than the first movement, has its dynamic share of rhythmic violence, and finally breaks down just before the return to the tonic in an access of passion followed by a moment of complete exhaustion. Indeed, the rhythmic violence of this movement often makes us forget its ceaseless flow. The Baroque *perpetuum mobile*, on the other hand, is not a dramatic form, or one that generates any particular tension. It is the normal procedure, and there are so many examples that citation is unnecessary—any work in which the thematic material moves evenly (almost any Allemande, for example) will do.

Baroque dynamics provide a perfect analogy with Baroque rhythm, perhaps because dynamic inflection is as much a part of rhythm as it is of melodic expression. Just as the rhythmic motion may be constant throughout the work, or different rhythms may be either superimposed horizontally or juxtaposed vertically without mediation, in the same way a Baroque work may be played at a fairly constant level of sound, or two levels may be superimposed or juxtaposed without any use (at least structurally) of *crescendo* and *diminuendo*.[1] A great deal has been written about 'terraced dynamics,' but the typical performance, except when a solo or several soloists were to be contrasted with a larger group, was probably at a constant level: 'terraced dynamics' were not a necessity but a luxury of Baroque music. Most harpsichords were built with only one keyboard, so that two levels of sound were impossible at the same time, and sometimes even the quick juxtaposition of two levels was made more than difficult by the inconvenient placing of the stops at the side of the instrument. Changes in registration on the organ during the middle of a piece generally required the presence of an assistant with a plan of operations: only an important virtuoso work would have been performed in this way, and then only when practicable. It should be remembered, too, that the use of two keyboards does not imply two dynamic levels, but rather two kinds of sonority. In reality, this contrast of sonority is more fundamental to High Baroque music than the contrast of dynamic levels, which is only a special form of it. The division between tutti and soli in the concerto grosso is less an opposition of loud and soft than of two different qualities of sound, which clarify the structure as the two keyboards clarify the voice-leading in those of the *Goldberg* Variations where the voices cross each other. Equally matched levels are, however, normal in the Baroque, though we are sometimes prevented from realizing it by nineteenth-century habits that have led us to demand greater dynamic variety from music. Often we badly distort the music even when we do not exceed what was possible on an early eighteenth-century instrument. Much of Domenico Scarlatti's

---

[1] *Crescendo* and *diminuendo* as ornamental and expressive nuances were, of course, important to the Baroque period, particularly in vocal music.

music, for example, is made up of short passages played twice or even three times in a row; to play these repetitions as loud-soft echoes is to betray the music, for much of the effect should come from its insistence. The belief that everything that appears twice should be differentiated is an unconscious and sometimes noxious principle in the mind of almost every performer today. The High Baroque looked for variety mainly through ornamentation and not through dynamic contrast, 'terraced' or not.

Even here circumspection is necessary. Some music (a great deal of Handel's) needs heavy ornamentation even the first time round; other music (most of Scarlatti's and almost all of Bach's) needs very little or absolutely none. Scarlatti had worked out an early form of the more articulated classical style, and an indiscriminate application of ornament would cause his phrases to overlap. And it was already a contemporary complaint against Bach that he wrote everything out and left no space for the performer to add his ornaments; the answer, quite rightly made at the time, was that this is one of the great beauties of his music. It is sometimes held that the repeats of all the *Goldberg* Variations should be decorated. This is what comes of reading eighteenth-century theorists (or about them) and paying no attention to the music. A few of the variations could indeed be ornamented, but most of them resist any attempt beyond the addition of a mordent or two, and this would only make the performance sound fussy. The problem is that performance has become largely a public affair since the eighteenth century: and with the formality has come a need for variety of effect and dramatization. The purpose of ornamentation (except in opera) was not to capture and retain the attention of a large audience: one ornamented to please oneself and one's patron and friends. The *Well-Tempered Keyboard* and the *Art of Fugue*, for example, were indeed intended to be performed, but only in private, as many fugues at a time as one wanted, on any keyboard instrument that was handy. It is obvious from suites and partitas that the early eighteenth century could bear longer stretches of the same tonality than any succeeding period, along with lengthier works in the same rhythm and at the same dynamic level.[1] The chamber music of the High Baroque was certainly played with subtle dynamic inflections, and required, what is most difficult to recapture, a *rubato* proper to the style and a decorative system for emphasizing these inflections, for its expression, in fact. But it was not an art that relied heavily upon large dynamic contrasts, or in any way at all upon transition between dynamic levels. What dynamic contrasts there were can be found mainly in the public genres: opera, oratorio, and concerto. This distinction between genres developed greater importance in the middle of the eighteenth century, becoming blurred only at the end. The symphony, for example, demanded a greater overlapping of phrases—i.e., less articulation and more directional movement—than the solo sonata, but by the time the late eighteenth-century

---

[1] Even if these suites were treated to some extent as anthologies, a work like the Handel Chaconne, which *was* played in its entirety, makes a modern ear impatient.

theorists had pointed this out, Haydn and Mozart were already writing their solo works in a more symphonic style.

The articulated phrase required its individual elements to be discrete and set off from each other in order that its shape and symmetry might be clearly audible, and this in turn brought about a greater variety of rhythmic texture and a much larger range of dynamic accent. In the opening phrase of the Mozart Concerto K. 271, cited above (p. 59), the Baroque contrast between a section of music for orchestra and a new section for solo has been concentrated into a single phrase. When the most emphatic extremes are forced into one detail, then a style must be found that can mediate between them: a work made up of such contrasts so dramatically juxtaposed at close range with no possibility of long-range transition between them would either be very short or intolerable. It is this style of transition or mediation that the later eighteenth century created. The development of the *crescendo* in orchestral music, particularly at Mannheim, is well known, but also the possibility of mediating between different kinds of rhythms now appeared for the first time. One of the most common practices of the classical period was to introduce a faster rhythm first into the accompaniment and only some measures later into the main voices, thus smoothing over the join until no break is felt. Beethoven's Fourth Piano Concerto opens with a feeling of two slow beats to a measure:

and by the end of the exposition we hear eight quick beats per measure:

where the *sforzandi* on the weak eighth notes double the pulse from the previous four. As the movement proceeds, the transition from two to eight is imperceptible.

Rhythmic transition in the late eighteenth century is achieved with discrete, well-defined elements, generally related to one another by each in turn being twice as fast, or half as fast, as the preceding, so that all the rates of speed tend to come from the series 2, 4, 8, 16, etc. But the movement from one rhythm to another is felt as a transition and not as a contrast. This sense of unbroken continuity is achieved not only by starting the faster rhythm in a subsidiary or accompanying voice so that its entrance is less noticeable, or by subtle nuances of phrasing, as in the above example from Mozart, but also by the placing of accents and by harmonic means as well. Mozart and Haydn were the first composers to understand the new demands on harmonic movement made by the periodic phrase, and it is in their works that a convincing relation is first heard. Much of their success hangs on a comprehension of dissonance and harmonic tension: it is often an exceptionally dissonant chord that introduces a new and faster rhythm,[1] and both composers made full use of the added animation that is so natural at the end of a musical paragraph in its drive toward a cadence and resolution. Both also succeeded after 1775 in handling the introduction of triplets into duple time convincingly—always a difficult matter in a style so heavily concerned with symmetry and with the clear independence of the individual elements.

With the classical style, a means of transition can even become a thematic element. In Haydn's Quartet in C major op. 33 no. 3 of 1781, the *crescendo* is perhaps the most important element of the main theme:

Here is the classical style during its first years of perfection; not only is there symmetry from phrase to phrase, but even within the phrase itself. The *crescendo* of the first three measures (to which the grace notes and turn in the violin are a contribution) is balanced by the descent of the first violin in measures 4 to 6, itself counterbalanced by the rising figure of the cello, so

---

[1] See the new triplet rhythm introduced at the end of the example from Mozart's D major Quintet K. 593 on p. 283.

that the general effect is still one of ascending. More important, the opening measures are not only a *crescendo* but also a gradual acceleration little by little from the uninflected pulsation of the opening measure to the sixteenth-note rhythm of measures 4 to 6. The first four bars represent an increase of pulse (0, 1, 2, and 4 in each successive measure) within the same tempo. The *sforzando* on the second beat that accompanies the entrance of the cello strengthens the sense of four beats in that bar, and also foreshadows the emphatic halt of the first violin on the second beat in the next bar. Even the transition back to the feeling of zero beats per measure is beautifully handled. Bar 4 has a *sforzando* on the second beat, bar 5 has only the accent that comes from the sustained notes, and bar 6 withholds all accent from the second beat and follows it with a surprising silence; all this prepares the return to the uninflected pulsation of the opening. The silence is as much a part of the theme as the *crescendo*; it is even developed afterwards, first by being filled up with the violin's decorated notes from bar 3 played twice as fast:

and later by being doubled in length:

These examples introduce another kind of transition, thematic transition, which is sometimes used for development. In this movement, a closing theme of the exposition quoted on the following page is derived from the same violin motif of bars 2 and 3, played at double tempo, and its connection with the opening is made through measures 31–32 quoted above and the surrounding section. In this way, each theme appears to grow from the preceding one, gaining an independent identity and still keeping its relationship to the whole. This delightful five-measure theme (or four-measure theme with an echo in the middle) demonstrates a kind of thematic relationship in which the logical steps are successively spelled out in the music itself:

It should be noted here that the quartet's opening six-measure phrase (quoted p. 65) can be looked at either as a four-measure phrase with a one-bar introduction and an echo at the end, or (since a new figure is introduced at the climax at the opening of bar 4) as two three-measure phrases. Both interpretations, of course, are right; or, rather, we hear the rhythmic tension between these two patterns as part of the phrase. The harmony of this opening phrase is more subtle than it appears at first: nothing but tonic with a little dominant thrown in at the end to define the key, it sounds grandly simple, but tension is introduced by withholding the root position of the tonic, so necessary to this style, until the end of the *crescendo* and then by bringing it in on an off-beat. The spaciousness is tempered with wit: no chamber music before this had ever achieved such a combination.

The capacity of the classical style to go imperceptibly from one dynamic level to another, from one kind of rhythm to another, was limited only in the direction of how slowly it could be done: how fast was unimportant, since, at a very fast rate of change, a transition disappears and becomes a contrast. A slow transition, however, was always more difficult, and the immensely long and very gradual changes that Wagner was to perfect were impossible within a classical scheme. The stability of the tonal sense and the need for balance were there as a barrier; not until nineteenth-century tonality became less stable could the pace at which things happened (as opposed to the tempo) be slowed down. The third act of *Parsifal* is, in a formal sense, an enormous modulation from B major back to the A flat major of the Prelude to the first act, and Wagner can make it last so long because he is able to take so much time defining his first key: the third act prelude is in a vague region floating between B flat minor and B major, and this lack of tonal definition allows Wagner's rhythm to proceed in a series of waves and the tension to be increased at a very slow pace. The dynamic level can then be raised at a similarly slow rate, and the range can be greatly enlarged.

For Haydn, Mozart, and Beethoven, no such technique was available or even conceivable, although Beethoven extends the power of the style and slows the rate of change almost miraculously in such places as the slow *crescendo* and *accelerando* ('poi a poi di nuovo vivente') in the finale of the A flat Sonata, op. 110, from the inversion of the fugue to the end. Here all the discrete thematic units of the classical style are used so that they appear to blend with each other, and to achieve this continuum Beethoven uses an abnormal harmonic movement, modulating from the key of the leading tone to the tonic (G minor–major to A flat). The distance of the relationship, although classically lucid, blurs the force of the tonic and allows for a great expanse of time so that its eventual return and re-establishment may carry the full weight demanded by the triumph of the last pages. Beethoven's method, with the relationships sharply defined, has nothing to do with the Romantic procedure of withholding the tonic. In general, for an event to happen in slow motion we must wait for the middle of the nineteenth century: the classical style is capable of very slow tempi, but the music is always event-ful, and a single continuous movement longer than twenty minutes is beyond its reach.

There is, however, a sense in which the classical style moves more slowly than is sometimes thought. The modulation to the dominant is not always an affair of a few measures; sometimes it starts with the opening phrase, and the whole first page of a movement may be a series of successively stronger approaches and withdrawals. In Haydn's E flat major Quartet op. 20 no. 1, bars 7–10 are already in the dominant and there is a return to the dominant in bars 14 and 15; the tonic reappears after each of these places, and the final move to the dominant is not made until bars 21–24. All this must, of course, be changed in the recapitulation, which is completely re-written. We can speak here of a long dominant preparation, but it is more accurate to describe it as a general drift to the dominant made articulate at a given moment. The extent of the drift is often obscured by the terminology of 'sonata form,' which concentrates on the moment of articulation: what are called 'bridge passages' between tonic and dominant are common enough in classical expositions (how could they not be?), but there are innumerable cases where the movement to the dominant begins right at the opening, with the establishment of the tonic. This is often found in Haydn and is even more frequent with Beethoven. The drift away from the tonic starts at the opening of the *Eroica* Symphony, and the *Waldstein* Sonata establishes the tonic only after the movement away from it has apparently started. The Sonata in A major op. 101 marks the extreme development of this technique as Beethoven here starts directly with the movement to the dominant. The tonic is established by implication with an extraordinarily poetic effect of beginning in the middle, and only a firmness that is taken for granted without being emphasized could make possible the emotion that is built on it.

Sometimes the change of key is startling and abrupt, and the new tonality is introduced without modulation. When this happens, something in the opening section has made it possible. The first of Haydn's op. 33 Quartets, in B minor, restates the main theme in D, the relative major (the 'normal' secondary key for a movement in the minor after 1770), after a fermata and without any modulation at all:[1] this is possible because the main theme was originally announced, at the very opening of the work, in what appeared to

---

[1] Quoted on page 116.

be the relative major, the B minor becoming clear only in the third bar. The movement to the new key is therefore accomplished simply by reharmonizing the melody in the way already implied by the first two measures. The preparation of the new key is not explicit, but implicit in the material itself.

We can see from this example both how free classical form was, and how closely it was tied to tonal relationships. At this point Haydn is drawing the logical conclusion of his opening. He is bound less by the practices of his contemporaries than by a sensitivity to harmonic implication; the suggestion of D major placed at a point as critical as the opening measure makes Haydn realize that he can dispense with a modulation. The same sensitivity will lead Mozart, after *La Finta Giardiniera*, to write each opera in a definite tonality, beginning and ending with it, and organizing the sequence of numbers around it.

An articulate movement to the dominant (or its substitute) is all that is required harmonically of a sonata exposition: how it is done is completely free, or, rather, bound only by the nature and material of each individual work. There is a movement toward the dominant in most Baroque music, too, even in the early Baroque, but it is rarely made either articulate—that is, decisive—or dramatic. What the late eighteenth century did was to intensify this movement toward the dominant and give it a stronger feeling of direction.

A clear hierarchy of tonal strength was demanded by the classical style. Tovey and others have commented on the difference between being *on* a tonality and being *in* it. In reality, a subtle series of degrees is set up by the classical composers: stronger than being *in* a key, is its establishment as a secondary key, a weaker pole of force reacting against the tonic. Still stronger, of course, is the tonic itself. This hierarchy (a continuous one, with each stage blending into the next) explains how Mozart's G minor Symphony K. 550, for example, can have a development section which goes through a kaleidoscopic succession of keys, without ever reaching the stability achieved by the relative major at the end of the exposition. As an example of even greater resourcefulness, the first tutti of Beethoven's Fourth Piano Concerto also goes through a series of tonalities but without once really leaving the tonic. It is a mistake to speak of classical modulation without specifying an order of magnitude; unfortunately, we lack a concise technical language. A Baroque *composition* moves to another tonality in much the same way that a late eighteenth-century *phrase* goes normally from tonic to dominant or back. In the classical style, modulation is given a power commensurate with its role.

In short, the larger harmonic structure was transformed in order to make it fit the proportions as well as the nature of the classical phrase. It had, indeed, already been remarked in the eighteenth century that a sonata exposition was an expanded dance-phrase. This expansion was accomplished not merely in the Baroque fashion of extending and repeating the motion of individual motifs, but by dramatization as well.

69

The Baroque and classical styles are sometimes contrasted as decorative and dramatic respectively. This leads to misunderstanding only if taken to refer to expressive character rather than to the technical procedures of the two styles. A Baroque work is undramatic in that its tension remains fairly constant until the final cadence, and only rarely rises above the level set at the beginning. Nothing can be more dramatic in character than the opening chorus in E minor of Bach's *St. Matthew Passion*, yet it achieves its dramatic effect by transcending the variation (chorale prelude), a decorative form, and the concerto grosso form (which, like the Baroque rondo, works by alternation and generally does not build to a specific area of climax). This chorus moves like a sonata from the minor to the relative major, but the cadence on G major actually lowers the dramatic energy, which is recaptured only with the entrance of the third chorus singing the chorale. Through its throbbing rhythm, anguished harmonies, and the cumulative effect of its three choruses, the music acts as a dramatic image, not as a scenario. On the other hand, in a classical sonata in a minor key the apparent relaxation of the relative major is always compensated for by Haydn, Mozart, and Beethoven, who make certain that the tension is raised, not lowered, at this point. The second subject of Beethoven's *Appassionata* is both more lyrical and more nervous than the opening; it moves faster and the bass steadily mounts. There were, of course, no rules about second subjects in the late eighteenth century, nor were second subjects even necessary, but when they occur in Haydn, Mozart, and Beethoven, they are usually more intense than the first subject. The dramatic character of the sonata calls for contrast, and when the main theme is vigorous, some of the succeeding themes generally take on a softer character. But then their harmonic movement tends to be faster (as in Beethoven's opps. 53, 57), more agitated (Mozart K. 310, Beethoven op. 31 no. 2) or more chromatic and passionate (Beethoven op. 109). Haydn prefers themes of equal intensity and relies on harmonic movement for the necessary dramatic effect. It is true that in Schumann and Chopin, the second themes are generally more relaxed in every way than the first, but by that time the sonata was an archaic form, fundamentally unsuited to contemporary style, with the initial tonic section so unstable emotionally that a decrease in tension was inevitable.

The stability and clarity of the opening and closing pages of a classical sonata are essential to its form, and they make the increased tension of the middle sections possible. The difference between the Baroque movement toward the dominant and the classical modulation is not only one of degree: the classical style dramatizes this movement—in other words, it becomes an event as well as a directional force. The simplest way to mark this event, to articulate it, in fact, is by a pause on the dominant of the dominant before continuing, and sophisticated versions of this device can be found even in the latest works of Beethoven.

This event can be further articulated in two ways: it can be emphasized by the introduction of a new theme (the practice of Mozart and the majority of his contemporaries), or by the repetition of the opening theme, preferably in such a way that its new significance at the dominant is clear (the device preferred by Haydn). Beethoven and Haydn often combine both methods, first restating the main theme with changes and new details that show how it is reinterpreted by being transposed from the tonic, and then adding a new theme. The presence or absence of a new melody is of less moment than the extent to which the new key is dramatized, and how continuity is achieved to offset the articulated structure.

This moment of dramatization and where it occurs make an essential contrast with the Baroque style. Modulation already exists in all dance-forms of the early eighteenth century; but in High Baroque style a pause to mark the arrival at the dominant is hardly ever placed in the middle of the first half but at the end of it; the music is a gradual flow to the dominant with a resolution at the end of the section. Early in a sonata, however, there must be a moment, more or less dramatic, of awareness of the new tonality: it may be a pause, a strong cadence, an explosion, a new theme, or anything else that the composer wishes. This moment of dramatization is more fundamental than any compositional device.

For this reason, the classical style needed more forcible means of emphasizing new keys than the Baroque, and it used for this purpose a quantity of 'filling' almost unparalleled until then in the history of music except in pieces of an improvisatory character. By 'filling' I mean purely conventional material, superficially unrelated to the content of the piece, and apparently (and in some cases, actually) transferable bodily from one work to another. Every musical style, naturally, relies on conventional material, principally at cadences, which almost always follow traditional formulas. The classical style, however, further magnified and elongated the cadence in order to strengthen the modulation. A Baroque composer worked mostly with vertical filling (the figured bass), and the classical composer with horizontal: long phrases of conventional passagework. Aside from accompaniment figures and cadential ornaments, the two basic forms of conventional material are scales and arpeggios, and they fill classical works to a degree that would only have been possible for a Baroque composer in a toccata, or in a form that tried to sound improvised rather than composed. The means employed by an early eighteenth-century composer to give the impression of freedom were needed by Mozart to organize the form; he used whole phrases of scales and arpeggios the way Handel used sequences—to tie sections of the work together. But in the finest Baroque work the sequence is generally clothed and covered by thematic material, while even in the greatest works of Haydn and Mozart the 'filling' is displayed nakedly, and appears to have been prefabricated in large pieces.

Another reason for the use of large conventional phrases and their deployment in block-form was the increase of instrumental virtuosity, although it is moot whether the instrumentalist inspired the composer or vice versa: probably both. In any case, the following passage from one of Mozart's finest works, the Sonata for Piano K. 333, is absolutely conventional:

It could be transferred to any work in common time which needs an F major cadence. The passage has a certain amount of brilliance and is obviously derived from concerto style. It also provides a climax by sounding the first high F in the piece, the top note of Mozart's piano. But that is not its only *raison d'être*; it is placed where it is because Mozart needs four bars of emphatic cadence. In fact, less conventional, more thematic material will not do; thematic interest would distract from the essential—which is exactly what it appears to be: four bars of cadence. We have reached a style in which proportion has become a major interest. Starting with conventional passages, such as the one in K. 333, we shall end with the unbelievably long final cadence of Beethoven's Fifth Symphony, where fifty-four measures of pure C major are needed to ground the extreme tension of that immense work. But already in Mozart, the length of this conventional material is sometimes astounding.

It should be remarked that this passage in Mozart is not arbitrary but grows logically out of the phrase that precedes it. The block use of conventional material often goes, however, much further in this style. The opening movement of Mozart's C major Symphony K. 338 has no melody at all in the first forty measures. There is nothing but completely conventional march-like flourishes and a harmonic pattern that eventually moves to the dominant, and only at this point are we finally given a melody. Yet it is one of Mozart's most brilliantly laid-out pages, serving not only to define tonality as a Baroque opening would do, but also to set up an area of great stability: much of the power of this opening comes from its avoidance of any thematic expressivity. (This is also why a good part of this first page is reserved for the end and not the beginning of the recapitulation: the classical style demands a resolution midway through the second half of a movement but a resolution of such magnitude would make the remainder of the recapitulation an anticlimax.)

It is the classical sense for large areas of stability, impossible before and lost since, that establishes what might seem to be the one fixed rule of sonata recapitulation: material originally exposed in the dominant must be represented in the tonic fairly completely, even if rewritten and reordered, and only material exposed in the tonic may be omitted. This is, of course, not a rule at all but a sensitivity to tonal relationships. (It is amusing to recall that

Chopin was censured by contemporary academic critics—and called un-orthodox even by some in the twentieth century—for omitting the recapitulation of much of the first subject in his sonatas, a well-worn eighteenth-century device.) Material presented outside the tonic must have created, in the eighteenth century, a feeling of instability which demanded to be resolved. When the tonic was reaffirmed in the second half of the piece, the material already presented in the tonic could be, and often was, drastically cut, but the rest of the exposition cried out for resolution in the tonic. Today, our harmonic sensibilities have become coarsened by the tonal instability of music after the death of Beethoven, and the strength of this feeling is perhaps difficult to recapture.

It is worth examining this in some detail, at least briefly. First for an exception to prove a rule. There is one Haydn quartet, op. 64 no. 3 in B flat, in which one of the second subjects appears nowhere in the recapitulation. It is a strange quartet with an eccentric and comic opening. The first melody in the dominant, F major, is also the first regular-sounding melody in the quartet (mm. 33–42). A four-measure phrase, it is played first in the major and immediately repeated in the minor, and it clearly functions in the exposition to reaffirm the dominant. (It is not the only theme so used: the opening theme is replayed in the new tonality, and yet another new theme is then introduced, also in F major.) The repeated four-measure phrase does not, as I said, reappear in the recapitulation, but it does, however, reappear *in its full form* in the development section, *and on the tonic*. This time the phrase is played twice in the minor. In this way the theme is satisfactorily recapitulated, as one half of it was already in minor to begin with; in addition, the tonic major is avoided in the development. All the various classical demands for balance and tonal resolution have thus been reconciled.

A use of the tonic minor after the recapitulation has been reached in-variably means a reduction in stability, and this explains Haydn's reluctance to employ it.[1] In another quartet, op. 50 no. 6 in D major, four measures of the exposition (26–29) are in the dominant minor, and again they are not in the recapitulation; again, however, they appear in the *tonic* minor in the development section. In this way, Haydn manages to avert a difficult situation: the tonic minor may be used towards the end of a recapitulation in major only if its effect is successfully countered. In the first movement of the *Waldstein* Sonata, for example, Beethoven has a phrase in the exposition that is played twice in the minor; it is played twice in the recapitulation, but the second time in the major (mm. 235–243).

The danger of using the tonic major in the development is obvious, as it weakens the dramatic effect of its return. Unless it occurs briefly in passing, it, too, needs to be offset, generally by following it with the tonic minor. The

---

[1] In Symphony no. 85 (*La Reine*), a section of the exposition in the dominant minor is also avoided in the recapitulation, and there are other examples.

most important use of it in a development is naturally the false reprise, or false recapitulation. But this dramatic effect of incongruity cannot be used with impunity if it lasts beyond a few measures; when it does, Haydn makes it do an important part of the work of the main reprise. In the Quartet, op. 77 no. 1 in G major the opening subject is repeated in the exposition at the dominant with the theme in the cello; this is the way it appears in the tonic in the false reprise, and accordingly it does not have to be recapitulated in this form later. In this same movement there is a further example of the absence of a theme in the 'second group' from the recapitulation: again it is played in the tonic (major) in the development, but only at the end of the development, as it is used to re-establish the tonic and reintroduce the main theme.

These are the rare cases in the Haydn quartets of material exposed in the dominant and missing from the recapitulation, and at each point we have seen that some form of tonic recapitulation has been provided. This is not a rule of form but a rule of the classical aesthetic—a part of the age's, or of Haydn's, musical sensibility. The amount of material exposed in the *tonic* and omitted from the recapitulation could be as much or as little as the composer wished. In one earlier form of the sonata, of course, current around 1750, the recapitulation normally began with the second subject (did Chopin use this form because Warsaw, provincial by comparison with Vienna and Paris, preserved the older version?), and Haydn, Mozart, and Beethoven generally shortened the tonic material in the recapitulation, or omitted part of it and intensified what remained.

Remarkably, the quartets of Haydn mentioned in the past few pages are almost the only ones in which the recapitulations[1] are noticeably shorter than the developments. In most of the others (and there are more than eighty in all), the two sections are approximately equal in length, or else the recapitulations are longer, sometimes very much so. In the examples just given, we have seen that the development has taken over, even tonally, part of the role of the recapitulation. That is, we are dealing here not only with the rare exceptions of thematic material remaining unresolved after the return to the tonic, but also with the infrequent cases where the final area of stability is somewhat shorter than the area of dramatic tension called development with which the second part of a sonata begins. This firm area of final stability is an essential part of the classical style, as vital to it as the dramatic tension that precedes it; its proportions are vital, too, and they are demanded by the articulated nature of the form and required for the balance and symmetry central to the expression.

The emotional force of the classical style is clearly bound up with this contrast between dramatic tension and stability. In this respect, a fundamental

---

[1] I use 'recapitulation' here to mean everything that follows the final reintroduction of the tonic, including what is generally called a coda, if there is one.

change took place towards the middle of the century. In most Baroque music, a relatively low level of tension is created and sustained, with certain fluctuations, only to be resolved at the end of the piece: the music works cumulatively—it is rare that one moment is notably more dramatic than another. The middle section of a da capo aria, however, unlike the center of a sonata movement, is almost always less brilliant and intense, if more expressive, than the outside sections: it is often in a more relaxed key (the relative minor, for example) and scored for a reduced orchestra, sometimes for continuo alone. This lessening of tension and weight towards the center is characteristic of the High Baroque sectional work: Bach's Chaconne for unaccompanied violin, for example, or the great A minor Fugue for organ, where the central section omits the pedal—when the pedal re-enters in the tonic to accompany the return of the main subject, the effect of the recapitulation is not the classical one of resolution, but of a fresh injection of energy. The climax of a Baroque work is to be found in the increase of motion towards the final cadence: a stretto is one of its typical manifestations.

The climax of a classical work is closer to its center, and that is why the proportions of the final area of stability are so important. Temporal proportions are not like spatial ones: we cannot refer back and forth at a performance, and we must rely on memory, emotional and sensuous as well as intellectual, for comparison. The sense of balance in music is not arithmetical; a set of factors larger and more complex than a mere count of measures come into play. As we have seen, if a phrase is played twice, the effect is not like that of the repetition of an architectural motif on a façade; each playing has a different weight. In addition, the resolution of harmonic tension, and the symmetry of material (and of phrase) were not the only questions affecting classical proportions: the variety of large-scale rhythmic elements within a dramatic pattern demanded the resolution of rhythmic tension, a resolution that had to be combined with the need for keeping the piece moving until the end. With all of these forces interacting, the proportions of each classical work are individual, torn in every case between drama and symmetry. One requirement remains fixed: a long, firm, and unequivocally resolved section in the tonic at the end, dramatic if need be, but clearly reducing all the harmonic tensions of the work.

Common technical terms are often exasperating in their inappropriateness to particular cases, and none more so than 'recapitulation.' If we use it to mean a simple repeat of the exposition with the secondary material put into the tonic, then the whole idea must be thrown out as unclassical: this type of recapitulation is the exception rather than the rule in the mature works of Haydn, Mozart, and Beethoven. There is always a reinterpretation of the exposition after the return to the tonic. Even Mozart, who uses polythematic expositions with long melodies, and who can therefore afford a more literal repeat, often reinterprets considerably. An added short development section following the reappearance of the first theme is a common feature in his works, and by no means is it always used as a replacement for the exposition's modulation to the dominant. Haydn, who tends to the monothematic and whose motifs are shorter, needs even greater reinterpretation: the whole exposition has generally been conceived as a dramatic move to the dominant so that a literal repetition at the tonic would be nonsensical. It is understandable that Tovey, irritated by the academic use of 'recapitulation,' should write that 'the very idea utterly breaks down' in late Haydn, and that he 'used fully developed codas instead of recapitulations.' This is only to substitute one injudicious term for another in the hope of correcting an abuse: if 'coda' is to have any meaning for audible experience, then it is not possible to use the word for everything that comes in Haydn after the return to the tonic. Although Haydn's music is too dramatic in conception for an exact repeat transposed to the tonic, he never neglected the function of 'recapitulation' as 'resolution.' By this I mean not merely a firm re-establishment and concluding reassertion of the tonic—a 'coda' could indeed do that, as in Chopin's G minor Ballade—but a 'resolution' of material, that is, of the 'exposition' as well as of the 'development.' There is a moment in the exposition when the dominant appears established as a secondary pole, and everything that occurs after that moment invariably has its counterpart in a Haydn 'recapitulation,' rewritten, reinterpreted, rearranged in another order, perhaps. Haydn had understood that there are more complex forms of symmetry than naïve repetition. 'Recapitulation' may be a poor term, but we still need it to describe the resolution of the exposition, of which a literal repeat at the tonic is only a limiting form.

This insistence on stability at the beginning and, above all, at the end of each work allowed the classical style to create and integrate forms with a dramatic violence that the preceding Baroque style never attempted and that the Romantic style that followed preferred to leave unresolved, the musical tensions unreconciled. For this reason, a classical composer did not always need themes of any particular harmonic or melodic energy for a dramatic work: the drama is in the structure. A Baroque composition reveals its dramatic character in its first measure by the nature and shape of its melody, but nothing except the pianissimo of the opening two measures of the *Appassionata* would allow us to suspect the storm to be unleashed, and even the dissonance in the third measure adds only another hint. In particular, the most placid Baroque melody becomes more urgent as it proceeds; even when it rises and falls as in the first fugue of the *Well-Tempered Keyboard*:

the effect of its fall is annulled by the second voice's appearing to grow from the first and to continue its rise. Classical melodies for the most part are rounded off, resolved as they end—and the fact that they end at all sets them apart so clearly from many themes of the Baroque. The Baroque melody (like Baroque structure) is extensible, almost indefinitely so; none of the three great classical composers could have written a melody anywhere near as long as the one in the slow movement of Bach's *Italian Concerto*; such a melody seems to end only when compelled to, when a tonic cadence is at last unavoidable, while the climax is left largely undefined, the tension diffused rather than concentrated—this diffusion making it possible to sustain the melody at such length. Both the energy and the tension of a classical theme (often uniting a variety of rhythmic elements) are much more clearly concentrated, and this climax logically demanded a symmetrical resolution of the melody.[1] Historically, symmetry preceded drama. It was the symmetrical organization of the Rococo style[2] from the early eighteenth century on that made the dramatic concentration of the later classical style a reality. The balance and the stability provided a framework for the drama.

The classical recapitulation does not differ from the exposition for the sake of variety; the changes made are rarely ornamental, except in slow movements and in some rondos. Even variation form begins to be conceived dramatically. This is not to say that ornamentation did not exist, or that it was not occasionally added by performers (a subject best considered in relation to concertos and the operas, where a long virtuoso tradition was still influential). But the music itself implies that at no time in history had musicians less objection to hearing the same thing twice the same way. Beethoven, for example, insisted upon the repeat of the exposition of the *Eroica* Symphony (still often omitted in performance today) in spite of the abnormal length of the movement. The Baroque tradition of improvised ornamentation was certainly moribund, if not actually dead, except in opera; even there it is sometimes difficult to say whether the composers wanted the ornaments that the singers were certain to add, or whether they merely tolerated them because they were forced to. (About the appoggiaturas in recitatives, there is no question; the composers expected them, but recitatives are a special case, and have little to do with the other forms of the late eighteenth century.)

Haydn's symphonies before 1790 generally have recapitulations that follow the expositions more closely than do those of the quartets, although much of the tonic section or 'first group' is likely to be cut, and a good deal of development added. The melodies themselves reappear with less change than in the quartets, but this is not because Haydn was less concerned with variety and interest in his more public compositions, which would be astonishing. It is because the symphonies, written for larger audiences, are composed with

---

[1] The concentration of tension without clear resolution could be achieved only at the cost of weakening the firm tonal foundations of the style. It took many years for this to happen (with Schumann and Liszt), and much else in music had to change as well, the large rhythmic conceptions in particular.

[2] The Rococo in the other arts (painting and architectural decoration) tends to the asymmetrical, and no comparison is intended.

broader strokes, while the expositions of the quartets imply a degree of complex harmonic tension that cannot simply be transferred to the tonic at the end of the movement. The themes of the symphonies, less fluid than those of the quartets, neither need nor support so much alteration, and it is the structures of the symphonic recapitulations which tend to differ from the expositions, and in ways that are dramatic and rarely ornamental. Even these dramatic changes are generally implied by the preceding development. It is the nature of these changes that allowed Tovey to claim that, given a page of an unknown work by Haydn, Mozart, or Beethoven, one could tell whether it was from the beginning, middle, or end of a movement, something which could not be done with a page of Bach or Handel.

The classical style is a style of reinterpretation. One of its glories is its ability to give an entirely new significance to a phrase by placing it in another context. This can be done without rewriting, without reharmonizing, and without transposition: the simplest, wittiest, and most superficial form of this is an opening phrase which becomes a closing phrase as (one example from so many) in Haydn's Quartet op. 33 no. 5:

A more refined case of reinterpretation is a phrase in Mozart's Piano Sonata K. 283:

which in the exposition is a modulation to the dominant, and in the recapitulation is a return to the tonic. In the exposition it is preceded by

where the strong tonic cadence makes what follows sound like a movement away from the tonic. The second time, in the recapitulation, it is preceded by

where the indecisive feminine cadence and the strong subdominant coloring now imply a return to the tonic. With this feeling for tonal coloring, we have arrived at one of the most important distinctions between the style of the three great classical masters and the preceding generations.

Mozart is the first composer consistently to use the subdominant with a full sense of its relaxation of long-range harmonic tension; he generally introduces it as a regular feature of the recapitulation immediately after the re-entry of the tonic. Haydn's practice was similar, but less consistent, and Mozart's sensitivity to large tonal areas remained unequalled until Beethoven.[1] Johann Christian Bach and the other composers Mozart followed show none of his feeling for the balanced relations between the main and subordinate tonalities in a work, and have generally nothing more than a sense of the tonic-dominant effect. C. P. E. Bach's horizon is wider harmonically, but his practice is incoherent: he is more interested in local effects— he delights in harmonic shock, as did Haydn; but Haydn knew how to weld his effects together, and his most disparate harmonies are not only reconciled but even explained by what follows as well as implied by what precedes. (The first composer with a fine ear for the more complex relationships is probably Scarlatti; the logic of his movement from one tonal area to another is generally impeccable, but the style remains unclassical in that the areas follow one by one and neither blend nor interact.)

The classical sensitivity to the secondary tonalities and their relation to the

---

[1] Beethoven often uses the subdominant at the opening of the development section (*Waldstein* Sonata, Quartet op. 18 no. 1); the dimensions of his developments are considerably larger than those of Mozart or Haydn, and he needs the momentary retreat before starting to build the climax.

tonic can produce moments of astonishing poetry. The opening theme of the *Eroica* Symphony is essentially a horn-call, but the horn is never allowed to play it solo until the recapitulation is under way: at this point the orchestra modulates from the tonic (E flat) to the supertonic (F) and the horn enters *dolce* with the theme, followed by the flute playing it in D flat major. Much of the sweetness and delicacy, and the air of stillness, come from the new keys as well as from the orchestration: D flat major, the key of the flat leading-tone, is heard as a remote and exotic subdominant, and Beethoven, in an extension of Mozart's practice, is using it exactly where Mozart always uses the subdominant. Most remarkable is that the F major is also heard as a subdominant: it not only leads to D flat major but is introduced itself by a D♭, the unexplained dissonance in the main theme already played at the opening of the movement. Beethoven's practice here is different in range from Mozart's, but not different in kind, and Mozart was capable of effects of the same complexity. The emotional power is dependent on our hearing these phrases a few moments after the tonic has been re-established following the unprecedentedly long development section; as substitutes for the sub-dominant, the supertonic and the flatted leading-tone have a feeling of tran-quillity, while as remote keys coming at such a crucial moment they bring a tension to the heart of the stillness.

This complex, almost contradictory, emotion is another achievement of the style: it is not the kind of emotion that had changed since the early eighteenth century—Bach's sentiments were surely as complex as Beethoven's—but the expressive language. The affective character of a Baroque composition is much less complex; the emotion is sometimes deeply poignant, and it can attain an expansiveness that the classical style reaches with much greater difficulty, but it is generally more direct, and always more unified. The emotional complexity of the classical language is what makes the operas of Mozart possible. Even irony was possible in music now, as E. T. A. Hoffmann remarked of *Così fan tutte*. This complexity depends in large part on the classical harmonic relationships. The proto-classical composers—Rococo, mannerist, or early classical—increased the tension between tonic and domi-nant, and, for most of them, large-scale harmonic effects began and ended with that. It was Haydn and Mozart who took this tension, understood its implications throughout the entire area of harmony, the circle of fifths, and created a new language of the emotions.

The new emotional complexity entailed the use of contrasting themes and of themes in which a contrast was already built-in. The use of contrasting themes, however, has often been overemphasized: in a style essentially dramatic, and in which the different sections of a work are marked clearly enough for their proportions to be audible, it is only natural for melodies of differing character to occur. But the contrast of themes is not an end in itself, nor is the contrast of different sections of the movement. A fusion of dramatic effect with a profound sense of symmetry and proportion demands an evident sense of the degree of tension and stability in each part of the work and a clear articulation of these parts, but this can be, and sometimes is, achieved without any contrast of character, either in the various themes or in the different sections of a movement. The first movement of Haydn's *Military* Symphony has two themes of much the same character, both jolly, and both fairly square in rhythm (the second has only a more popular style, and rounds off the form). Nor do the tonic and dominant sections of the exposition of this movement differ much in character, as the dominant section begins with the first theme played exactly as it was at the beginning (enabling Haydn, in the recapitulation, to omit the entire section in the tonic). The sections are articulated by orchestration and not by contrasting themes, as each begins with woodwinds alone, then continues with strings alone (or, in the dominant section, antiphonal strings and winds), and finally allows the full orchestra with timpani to be heard—a pattern that has a remarkable clarity. (In the recapitulation the pattern is reordered both for dramatic surprise and increased stability, as the opening woodwind section is followed immediately by the theme in the full orchestra, and only then by the antiphonal strings and winds.) Contrasting themes are, of course, an aid in articulating a structure; but it is the clarity of outline that is essential, and not the contrast. As for the dramatic effect of contrasting themes, the power of the same theme played in different ways is as great, if not greater, and it is through the transformation of themes and not their contrast that the classical composer affects us most.

It is for this reason that we can dismiss as merely quaint the observation that in sonatas the first subject tends to be masculine and the second subject feminine. The very terminology of first and second subjects is already distressing enough, although it has become so ingrained that it is now difficult to excise it altogether; calling them 'first' and 'second groups,' however, does not help much in identifying themes, when the same melody may appear in both groups. (I should prefer to speak of tonic and dominant areas in an exposition, always remembering that the composer has often created a no-man's land between the two.) In any case, the masculine–feminine distinction amounts to nothing more than the fact that the very opening of a sonata is most often more direct and more forthright than the later material—reasonably and naturally so, as the opening must define the tonality and the tempo, and create the energy to move to the dominant. This can be done with a non-'masculine' sounding theme: there are numerous examples from all three classical composers, especially Mozart. It has even been said that Mozart's F major Piano Sonata K. 332 starts with what would be a second subject in another composer's hands: I should like to see a sonata with a second subject that so firmly and irrevocably, although gracefully, defines a tonality. In Beethoven's op. 31 no. 1, both subjects seem to me equally masculine; op. 31 no. 2 has hermaphrodite subjects; and as for op. 31 no. 3, the first subject is decidedly the more feminine. So much for the sex of themes.

Contrasting themes are, however, an inevitable, if not an invariable, part of the classical style. Perhaps even more significant are the themes of internal contrast, both rhythmic and dynamic. Before 1750, such contrast is almost always external—between voices, between different phrases, between separate orchestral choirs—and rarely internal, rarely within a melodic line. In classical melodies, however, internal contrast is not only frequent, but essential to the style, which relies so heavily upon dynamic inflection.

The need to reconcile dynamic contrast is as important and as typical as the contrast itself. This reconciliation, or mediation, takes many forms. One of the simpler ways to resolve a contrast of loud and soft is to follow it with a phrase that goes gradually from one to the other. In the opening phrases of the minuet from Mozart's Sonata K. 331:

the *crescendo* in measures 7 and 8 bridges the gap between the *forte* and the *piano* of the first four bars. It also prepares the more expansive and dissonantly expressive form of the downward scale motif; the *crescendo* is as much an element of continuity as of mediation. This reconciling of dynamic opposites is at the heart of the classical style, and is analogous to the mediation between two kinds of rhythm cited from Mozart's K. 271 on page 59. An entirely different way of resolving a dynamic contrast is shown in the *Jupiter* Symphony; the opening phrase

is played twenty measures later with a counterpoint

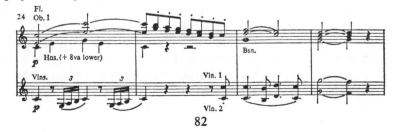

that binds the two halves together; even though both parts of the phrase are now played *piano*, their appearance in this form so soon after the opening is to turn opposition into unity.

This synthesis is, in small, the basic classical form. I do not want to turn Haydn, Mozart, and Beethoven into Hegelians, but the simplest way to summarize classical form is as the symmetrical resolution of opposing forces. If this seems so broad as to be a definition of artistic form in general, that is because the classical style has largely become the standard by which we judge the rest of music—hence its name. It is, indeed, clearly a style that is normative in aspiration as well as achievement. In the High Baroque, on the other hand, there is resolution indeed, but rarely symmetrical, and the opposing forces, rhythmic, dynamic, or tonal, are not very sharply defined. In the music of the generation of 1830, the symmetry is less marked or even evaded (except in academic forms, like the Romantic sonata), and a refusal of complete resolution is often part of the poetic effect. Not only, however, does the description fit the large classical form, but, as we have seen, the classical phrase as well: in no other style of music do the parts and the whole mirror each other with such clarity.

It is interesting to be able to document a composer's consciousness of this relation of large-scale form to phrase. Around 1793, Haydn wrote a Piano Trio in G minor for Prince Anton Esterházy which begins with a set of double variations. The second theme, in G major, is derived from the last phrase of the first theme, a procedure that Haydn often employs in sectional movements (particularly minuets with trios) to tie them together, and which Brahms copied faithfully. The second variation of this second theme is a complete sonata movement, and it is amusing to see how Haydn expands a 20-measure theme into a larger work[1].

---

[1] I omit the violin and cello parts where they merely double the piano.

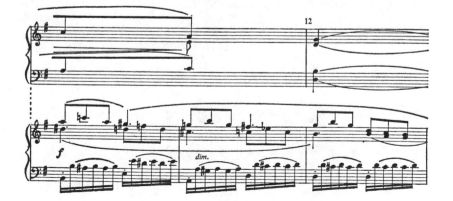

Last eight measures repeated with violin figuration
in piano and then four measures of Coda

From this witty expansion it can be seen that sonata form is an immense melody, an expanded classical phrase, articulated, with its harmonic climax three-quarters of the way through and a symmetrical resolution that rounds it off in careful balance with the opening.[1] Haydn not only elongates and repeats elements of the phrase, he also amusingly magnifies four little thirty-second notes in measure 6 into eight full measures of virtuoso passagework to become a full new closing theme. The *sforzando* in measure 18 of the melody, the loudest chord of the unexpanded form, becomes a pedal point over the dominant in the sonata, replacing the alternative movement of the bass of the exposition; the accented A♯ in measure 6 of the theme becomes a little two-measure sequence.

The points of his theme that Haydn expands most significantly are the central modulation and the end. This corresponds to the historical development of the sonata, and explains the gradual increase of importance during the century of the 'development section' and the 'coda.' An expansion of the end of a phrase is the articulated form of an older technique, and the foundation of the cadenza; it is essentially the High Baroque method of expansion, which works by extending and developing the last few notes of the phrase. But the expansion of the *center* of the phrase is peculiar to the classical style, and is the key to its sense of proportion.

Most revealing of all in this central expansion is the elaboration of the initial subdominant harmony at the beginning of measure 11 of the theme into a full-scale modulation to the subdominant in the sonata. Haydn does this simply by sitting on the fundamental note of the chord for two measures. No more delightful audible and visible proof could be offered that a modula-

---

[1] In about the same year that Haydn wrote this trio, the most impenetrable, although most acute, of contemporary theorists, H. C. Koch, published a method for expanding an 8-measure bourrée-phrase into a sonata exposition (see L. Ratner, 'Eighteenth-Century Theories of Musical Period Structure,' *Musical Quarterly*, October, 1956). His methods are more pedestrian than Haydn's and less up to date. There is no reason to think that Koch knew Haydn's trio, or that Haydn had read Koch's book.

tion is only the expansion of a chord, its transference to a higher level of the structure.

On this new level, the modulation naturally requires more elaborate resolution than a chord, and the succeeding measures of the little sonata form lead by way of a series of sequences back to the tonic area with a half-cadence on the dominant. The status of a subordinate tonality within any classical work is exactly the relation of its chord to the tonic triad.

No composer was a greater master of the expansion of the center of a phrase than Mozart, and in this lies part of the secret of his breadth in dramatic writing. The string quintets offer perhaps the most impressive examples of this central expansion:

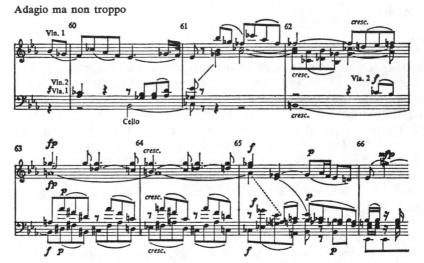

The first measure offers a simple cadence, and the next five measures repeat it but expand the center into one of Mozart's most passionate and intense ideas. The intensity depends in part on the original cadence's presence as model: not only a resolution but a symmetry is implied, withheld, and then granted.

This passage from the slow movement of the G minor Quintet shows that the Neapolitan harmony (a minor second above the tonic) draws its pathos from being conceived as an expressive appoggiatura, again on the more powerful level of large structure. The B♮ of the cello in measure 62 appears in the place of an expected B♭, and it demands resolution (like the first violin's F♭): the anguish and the intensity come not only from withholding the resolution of the minor second, but from raising the cello astonishingly through B♯, C♯, and D♮ to E♭ before letting it sink back into the cadence. The relations of note to chord to modulation are preserved at separate and articulated levels throughout the classical style. It is not until the nineteenth century that these levels are confounded, and one arrives with Wagner at the possibility of phrases which are tonally dissonant, but at the level of the chord and not only of the larger form.

This relation of modulation, chord, and note appears with great simplicity on the first page of Beethoven's *Appassionata* Sonata (the tonalities are again a minor second apart, and the work makes the most striking use of the Neapolitan throughout):

The alternation of the keys of D flat major and C major is followed by the laconic motto of the single notes D♭-C in the left hand in measure 10, in which the appoggiatura which is the basis of the harmonic effect is presented thematically, its significance isolated and detached. The relation of individual note to modulation is further exemplified by the duration. The alternation of D flat major and C major takes almost four bars, the rhythmic motto based on the alternation of notes only two beats. The weight of harmonic significance is reflected in the length of the rhythmic units, and it would not be fanciful to consider the whole passage as an expression of the motto stated at its end.

This correspondence among the elements is, of course, characteristic of every style at its maturity: the extensible Baroque form is intimately related to the Baroque melody, which seems to generate itself, spin itself out to exhaustion; the rigid eight-measure phrase pattern of a good deal of Romantic music corresponds to the frequently obsessive use of one rhythm within the phrase. What is unique in the classical style is the clarity of the audible and symmetrical pattern given to the phrase and reflected in the structure as a whole. The audibility of the pattern depends on the way in which the motifs which make up the classical phrase are isolated and set in relief. The little four-note motto at the end of the example from the *Appassionata* Sonata is typical, and the thematic treatment of the four opening drum beats of Beethoven's Violin Concerto is perhaps the most spectacular instance of such high relief. It is fundamental to the compositional technique of Haydn and Mozart as well. The clarity of definition in their works requires just this separate and isolatable nature of the different parts of the phrase. What we call 'thematic development' today is generally the detaching of these separable parts and their arrangement into new groupings. This detachability, indeed, makes possible the high degree of characterization and contrast within the phrase itself.

The clarity of the phrase is not only reflected in the total structure but at the lowest level of detail as well. The most striking rhythmic consequence is the

89

characterization and inflection of the individual beat. In the first half of the eighteenth century the beats are much more nearly equal in weight; the first, or downbeat, is somewhat heavier, and the last, or upbeat, is given importance by a slight lift; but the inequalities are never underscored. In a classical work, each beat in a measure has a distinctive weight of its own: in 4/4 time the upbeat has now a much greater weight than the second beat. It is understood that this new differentiation is not used relentlessly throughout a work of Haydn or Mozart but is present as a latent force, to be called upon as needed. A comparison of a minuet by Bach with one by Haydn will show what had happened in half a century:

In the Bach the beats are almost exactly equal in weight: even the downbeat is given only slightly greater importance by the melodic pattern. But the sequence of strong, weak, and moderately strong is evident in every measure of the Haydn. The examples are tendentiously chosen to prove a point, of course, but they are not atypical. No minuet of Bach attains the strong characterization of the beat so clear in Haydn, while no minuet of Haydn reduces the beats to something so close to undifferentiated pulsation.

The life and energy of classical rhythm depends on this distinctive character—the possible isolation, in fact—of each beat. The hierarchy of weight resulting from this individualization is given dynamic form in these dramatic and witty measures from the slow movement of Haydn's Quartet in E flat op. 33 no. 2:

The Coherence of the Musical Language

The succession in measures 22 and 24 of *f*, *pp*, *p* is the classical gradation, and the brilliance of Haydn's dynamic conception comes from the fact that each successive stage is an echo of a beat and not a beat itself, so that the weight of the beat is felt in the silence and reflected in the sound.

The articulated movement between detail and total structure made possible that intimate relation between the material and the large-scale proportions of the 'sonata' style. For this reason, along with the ideal shape of the sonata, we must abandon any idea of second subjects, bridge passages, closing themes, and so on as determinants of the form. Not that they do not exist; they mostly do. But it is not abnormal or eccentric when Haydn dispenses with a bridge passage between the tonic and dominant in op. 33 no. 1; it would be eccentric only if the material demanded one.[1] The symmetry of sonata form which the nineteenth century tried to codify was in the eighteenth a free response to symmetrically ordered material, and the symmetry could take many forms, some of them surprisingly complex. That some form of symmetrical resolution was felt as essential to the sonata (and to almost everything else) is unquestionable: in the rare cases where the material implied either a markedly asymmetrical resolution, or a form (like that of the *Moonlight* Sonata) that is relatively unarticulated, the result was a Fantasy. But the structure of a Fantasy was no less strict than that of a sonata, equally bound by sensibility and not by formalities.

The kind of material impossible for the ordered resolution of the sonata may be seen in the opening of Mozart's C minor Fantasy K. 475:

It is wrong to think only of the opening theme as the material of a work, and this Fantasy is created out of a much larger conception, but even in these

---

[1] See discussion of this point on page 116.

few bars we can see the direction the music is taking. The phrases are as symmetrical as one could wish, but the abrupt, poignant changes of harmony destroy all the stability of the tonic, creating instead a mysteriously expressive atmosphere. With the stability of the tonic disappears any possibility of clear harmonic tension and thus any chance of clear resolution. We do indeed reach the dominant (G major) a dozen measures later

but it has become a remote foreign key. This music offers, within the classical style, no way of continuing without the introduction of new material, new tonalities, and new tempi. Even in this work, the final pages have a firm symmetry, with the tonic re-established dramatically and all the opening material repeated, but it is not possible to speak of symmetrical resolution of the first section. When the tension between tonic and dominant has been so weakened with no substitute offered, resolution loses its meaning. What the 'recapitulation' resolves is not the harmonic tensions of the opening, but the tensions set up by all the different tonalities in the course of the piece (which has six clearly distinct sections). The resolution is less like that of a sonata (except in its use of the same material) than of the final section of an operatic finale— although in no opera does Mozart ever weaken the tonic as he does at the opening of this work. This is not to say that the Fantasy is in any way unsuccessful; it is a magnificent piece, but for once we have a work that is truly abnormal by classical standards.

The unusual form of this work is explained by its purpose: it is not a separate piece but an introduction to a sonata and, brilliantly and tightly constructed as it is, it is intended to have something of the quality of an improvisation.[1] In K. 475, to give the effect of improvisation, the opening tonal

---

[1] The other C minor Fantasy by Mozart, K. 396, is quite different; it is not a Fantasy at all, but a slow sonata movement, unfinished, for piano with violin obbligato, although the idea of the obbligato was perhaps only introduced in the course of composition.

firmness so characteristic of the period is deliberately weakened, and only gradually returns as the piece continues, finishing with a massive establishment of the tonic just before the final section. The form has a very subtle balance:

    I Tonic: C minor with the tonic weakened by immediate modulation, going finally to B minor

    II Dominant of the dominant: D major (since G major has been weakened, its dominant is used in its place)

    III Continuous modulation

    IV Subdominant of the subdominant: B flat major (used as subdominant in place of F major, by analogy with section II)

    V Continuous modulation, affirmation of C minor

    VI Tonic: C minor throughout

The symmetry is clear, as is the relation of the form to the use of tonic, dominant, and subdominant in the sonata. The music has the sound of improvisation and all the advantages of organized form: only in this way could it give such an impression of unity while sounding so rhapsodic.

This relation of the individual detail to the large form even in apparently improvisational works, and the way the form is shaped freely in response to the smallest parts, give us the first style in musical history where the organization is completely audible and where the form is never externally imposed. In the Baroque period, the form of the chorale prelude is decidedly imposed from without; it is not just that the counterpoint that accompanies the *cantus firmus* is generally inspired by the first phrase of the chorale, but that even in some of the greatest works of Bach we have, not a total conception, but a successive modification to respond to the changing phrases of the chorale. This is a way of writing that suits the additive nature of Baroque style: a building that has been conceived little by little, modified as it proceeds, may give an impression of unity in the end, but it is a different kind of unity from one designed as a whole and as a single form, although the former may be no less beautiful. The order of the canons in Bach's *Goldberg* Variations is not an audible one; that is, the idea of arranging them as canon on the unison, on the second, third, fourth, and so on, is mathematical rather than musical: this order, too, has its own beauty and gives pleasure, but not a specifically musical pleasure. Much has been written about Bach's musical symbolism, perhaps too much, but there is no doubt that a number of details in his work—the startling rhythmic and harmonic change in the chorale-prelude *O Lamm Gottes*, for example—demand a knowledge of their symbolism, and cannot be understood strictly musically. This is never true of Mozart, except in the operas, and even there musical considerations predominate: Figaro's chromatic moan about his twisted ankle is both a final cadence in C for one section and a modulation to F for a new beginning; the chromaticism has a musical function completely independent of the words. But the distinction between *legato* and *staccato* in 'Et in unum Deum' from Bach's *B minor Mass* is there to illustrate the difference in identity of the Father and the Son: it sounds charming in itself but it has no further musical consequence in the piece. Even the Baroque fugue, the freest and most organic of the forms of that period, sometimes has a structure that is not determined in a fully audible fashion: the form of a *ricercar* fugue, for example, is not dependent on the sound of its theme but on its capacity for stretti. Each stretto can, of course, be heard, but it is only latent when the theme is first played; the *possibility* of stretto is a fact, but not an audible one. It has been pointed out that the opening theme of the slow movement of Beethoven's F minor Quartet op. 95 can be combined with the fugato that forms the middle section of the movement, but that Beethoven does not take advantage of this. A Baroque composer writing a fugue would probably have been unable to resist the temptation.

The structure of a classical composition is related to the way its themes *sound*, not to what might be done with them. This principle of audibility even extends to the cancrizans, or backward version of a melody: in the finale of the *Jupiter* Symphony, the cancrizans may not be immediately clear as such, but at first hearing it sounds evidently derived from the main theme; and the fugue theme of the *Hammerklavier* Sonata finale has a shape so individual that one is always aware, when a performance reaches the cancrizans, which part of the melody is being played backwards—perhaps with the minuet of Haydn's Symphony no. 47[1] the only cancrizans of which this is so. In the late eighteenth century all extramusical considerations, mathematical or symbolic, have become completely subordinate, and the whole effect, sensuous, intellectual, and passionate, arises from the music alone.

This is not to say that extramusical considerations play no role in the classical style, but they do not play a determining role. Even politics can enter into music. When Don Giovanni welcomes his masked guests with 'Viva la libertà,' the context does not specifically imply political liberty (or the opera would certainly have been banned at once). Coming after 'È aperto a tutti quanti' ('anyone is welcome'), the words have a meaning much closer to 'freedom from convention' than to 'political freedom.' However, this is to reckon without the music. Starting with a surprising C major (the last chord was E flat major), Mozart brings out the full orchestra with trumpets and drums *maestoso* in an exhilarating passage full of martial rhythm. In 1787, during the ferment that followed the American Revolution and preceded the French, an audience could hardly have failed to read a subversive meaning into a passage that may look fairly innocuous in the libretto, particularly

---

[1] Quoted on p. 152.

after hearing 'Viva la libertà' repeated a dozen times with full force by all the soloists, accompanied by fanfares from the orchestra. Even here, however, there is a purely musical reason for this passage. It is the central moment of the first act finale, and Mozart's finales are conceived as complete movements in spite of their separate numbers, and begin and end in the same tonality, in this case C major. Just a few minutes before the entrance of the masked guests, there is a change of scene, and the C major needs a massive restatement to hold the finale together.[1] The section can be interpreted in purely musical terms (which again is not to deny the importance of the extramusical significance).

This musical independence illuminates the originality of classical comedy. Even humor becomes possible in music without outside help; the music of the classical style could be genuinely funny, not merely jolly or good-natured. Truly musical jokes could be written. There are jokes in music previously, but they are based on non-musical allusions: the Quodlibet of the *Goldberg* Variations is only amusing if one knows the words of the combined folksongs; some of the popular atmosphere comes through, but without the words the effect is only one of grandiose good humor. The contrasts of dynamics and register in the 13th of the *Diabelli* Variations of Beethoven, however, are grotesquely funny by themselves with no outside reference:

---

[1] The finale then proceeds, in Mozart's usual fashion, to an intensification (for the attempted rape of Zerlina) by the dominant G major and a series of modulations, which is resolved by the subdominant and a final tonic section, a pattern harmonically close to sonata form.

as is the following passage at the end of Haydn's Quartet op. 33 no. 3; the tempo is *Presto*:

It was, indeed, for passages like this that Haydn was attacked as a 'buffoon' by his contemporaries.

The buffoonery of Haydn, Beethoven, and Mozart is only an exaggeration of an essential quality of the classical style. This style was, in its origins, basically a comic one. I do not mean that sentiments of the deepest and most tragic emotion could not be expressed by it, but the pacing of classical rhythm is the pacing of comic opera, its phrasing is the phrasing of dance music, and its large structures are these phrases dramatized. This relation between the classical and comic styles was remarked by Carl Philipp Emanuel Bach, who at the end of his life deplored the loss of the contrapuntal Baroque style, and added: 'I believe, with many intelligent men, that the present love for the comic accounts for this more than does anything else.'

If the taste for the comic in music grew in the second half of the eighteenth century, this was at least in part because the development of style had at last made a genuinely autonomous musical wit possible. The incongruous seen as exactly right, the out-of-place suddenly turning out to be just where it ought to be—this is an essential part of wit. The classical style, with its emphasis on reinterpretation, made a wealth of double meaning a part of every composition. Finally, the highest form of wit, the musical pun, came into being. In the finale of the D major Trio H. 7 by Haydn, the E♭ as a dominant of A flat major is turned as a joke into the D♯ which is the third of B major:[1]

---

[1] I do not wish to suggest that any distinction between D♯ and E♭ was made by the late eighteenth-century composers. The joke would still be there if the note remained E♭ and the key changed to C flat.

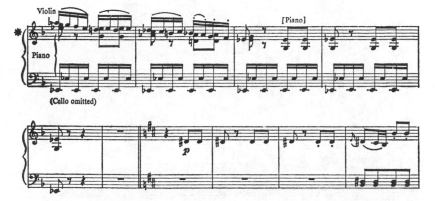

The sharp distinction between tonalities in the classical style gives this passage its wit, along with the pause and the insistent repetition. Clarity of articulation is essential to this kind of comedy. The contrast between the melodic and accompanying parts in classical style (replacing the Baroque autonomy of the individual parts and the use of figured bass) allows us the delicious moment in Haydn's *Clock* Symphony when the accompaniment is transposed into the upper register:

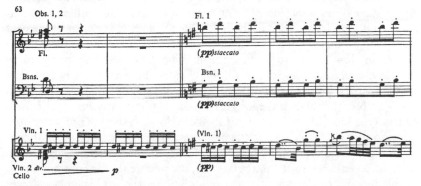

where the double meaning is made even more evident by giving the figure to the solo flute and bassoon.

The comic becomes not only the characteristic mood of a work but often, particularly with Haydn, an essential technique. In the delightful B flat major Quartet op. 33 no. 4, the modulation to the dominant is a joke:

If wit can take the form of a surprising change of nonsense into sense, a classical modulation gives a splendid formula: all we need, as here, is one moment when we are not sure what the meaning of a note is. Haydn sets up his joke by having the three little notes at the end of the phrase in bars 8–9 and 10–11 played in unison with no harmonies, and *piano*. Then the cadence, symmetrically repeated, seems to finish a section at the middle of bar 12—but the three notes occur inexplicably once more, still *piano*, still unharmonized, and played by the cello alone in its low register. It is not until the next chord that we understand why the little motif was left without harmonies: because the low D was to become the dominant of G minor, and thus to start the modulation to the dominant. Playing the three notes softly each time sets them apart, hides their true significance, and so contributes to the joke; indispensable, of course, is the irregularity of the phrase rhythm, particularly the last repetition of the little motif in the cello, and the tone of witty conversation that characterizes the thematic material. For a quick shift of context or a witty reinterpretation of a note, a dramatic and forceful modulation is also indispensable. In the Baroque style, the preference for continuity over articulation and the lack of clear-cut modulation leave wit little place except as a general tone or atmosphere in some very few works; the Romantic modulation, on the other hand, at times so heavily chromatic that the two keys blend into each other, and often much slower and more gradual, nullifies the effect of wit altogether, and we return, with Schumann, to something resembling the Baroque good humor and air of jollity. The civilized gaiety of the classical period, perhaps already somewhat coarsened, makes its last appearances in the Allegretto of Beethoven's Eighth Symphony, and in some of the movements of the last quartets. After that, wit was swamped by sentiment.

2

Structure and Ornament

The feeling for a closed, symmetrical structure, the central position of the most extreme tension, and the insistence upon an extended and complete resolution, together with a newly articulated and systematized tonality, produced a variety of forms, all with a right to be called 'sonata.' To distinguish them does not imply that they existed as norms or even as molds. They were only the result of musical forces and not to be identified with these forces themselves. For this reason, they should not be described too closely in the abstract, much less defined, or one would miss seeing how each of them could blend into the other, and how much freedom remained latent in these forms throughout the latter half of the eighteenth century.

1) FIRST-MOVEMENT[1] SONATA FORM falls into two sections, either of which may be repeated[2]: some symmetry between the two is essential but it is not very strictly defined. The movement begins by establishing a strict tempo and a tonic as frames of reference. The first section, or *exposition*, has two *events*, a movement or modulation to the dominant, and a final cadence on the dominant. Each of these events is characterized by an increase in rhythmic animation. Because of the harmonic tension, the music in the dominant (or second group) generally moves harmonically faster than that in the tonic. These events are articulated by as many melodies as the composer sees fit to use. The second section also has two events, a return to the tonic, and a final cadence. Some form of symmetrical resolution (called *recapitulation*) of the harmonic tension is necessary: an important musical idea played anywhere except at the tonic is unresolved until it is so played. The return to the tonic is generally (but not always) clarified by playing the opening measures again, as they are most closely identified with the tonic. If the return to the tonic is long delayed to heighten its dramatic effect (by modulating to other keys or by sequential progressions at the dominant), then the work has an extensive *development section*. The breaking of periodic rhythm and the fragmentation of the melody serve to reinforce the harmonic movement of this development. The harmonic proportions are preserved by placing the return to the tonic or beginning of the recapitulation no later than three-quarters of the way through the movement. The most dramatic point is generally just before (or, more rarely, just after) the return.

---

[1] This form may, of course, be used for second movements or finales, but it is most commonly associated with the more complex first movement.
[2] The second half was scarcely ever repeated alone, although the finale of the *Appassionata* is an exception, and similar forms may be found in the Mozart operas.

2) If the return to the tonic is not delayed at all, so that there is a symmetrical resolution but no 'development,' then the form may be called SLOW-MOVEMENT SONATA FORM.

3) MINUET SONATA FORM is in two parts, but always in three phrases: phrases two and three belong together. The two parts are always repeated. The three-phrase shape may be expanded, but the proportions and the essential outline are always in evidence. The first phrase may end on the tonic or on the dominant. (Tovey sees a profound difference between these two possibilities, but Haydn, Mozart, and even Beethoven use both, and the two forms often produce minuets of exactly the same shape, size, and dramatic effect. The second form is naturally easier to expand, and became more frequent; it merges with first-movement form.) The second phrase often plays the double role of a development section and of a second group of an exposition, and the third phrase resolves or recapitulates. The minuet is generally part of a larger ternary *ABA* form, with a trio usually more relaxed in character.

4) FINALE SONATA FORM is more loosely organized and is conceived as resolving the tensions of the entire work. This looseness gives rise to a greater range of patterns than in any other movement. If a first-movement form returns to the opening theme in the tonic before the development section, then it is called a sonata-rondo. There is often a new theme at the subdominant towards the center of the movement, sometimes placed in the 'development section,' sometimes as a substitute for it. This new subdominant theme may be found in finales which are not rondos, like the last movement of Mozart's A major String Quartet. Both the return to the tonic before the development and the theme in the subdominant are reductions of tension and a loosening of formal structure. What is essential in this movement is a relative squareness and clarity of rhythm and phrasing.

These forms are arranged here in a progressively relaxed order, and the order itself parallels the interior pattern of tension and resolution within the individual forms. From this we can see that they are less to be viewed as pre-existent shapes to be followed than as the habitual working-out of unifying principles. The main principle is one of recapitulation through the resolution of previous tensions, harmonic and rhythmic, and the return of the thematic material is always in an aspect significantly different from its first appearance in the exposition.

There is a radical distinction between all these forms and the ternary form of the Baroque in any one of its guises—da capo aria, dance-form with trio— or its extensions—the early rondo, and the concerto grosso form. In all these variants of *ABA*, the initial *A* returns unaltered at the end—unaltered on paper, that is, as in practice the return was often considerably decorated by the performers.

The idea of the recapitulation as a dramatic reinterpretation of the exposition attacks the practice of decoration at its root: the structure itself now does the work of the improvised ornaments. The ornamentation of the repeat of the exposition becomes an actual embarrassment: it implies either that the material heard in a dramatically different form in the recapitulation will be less ornamented and inevitably less elaborate than the repeat of the exposition, or that the recapitulation must also be ornamented, which can only obscure and minimize the structural changes with their radically different expressive significance. This is why the three great classical composers added almost nothing to the art of ornamentation, whatever their interest in it may have been. Only with Rossini, Chopin, Paganini, Liszt, and Bellini did a skill and originality in decoration comparable to that of Bach and Couperin reappear at last. The practice of improvised ornamentation, however, did not die, although it was largely superfluous in the classical style. Performance always lags behind composition in its adaptation to new conditions. By the last quarter of the century, the most famous of the guides to performance, Türk's book on keyboard-playing, advises against any ornamentation in a piece 'where the reigning character is sad, serious, nobly simple, solemnly and exaltedly grand, proud, and the like.' This seems to leave only the merely pretty to be ornamented. Hardly a slow movement of Mozart's would not fall into one of the categories where ornament is to be shunned. We must wait for the Italian opera of the early nineteenth century for ornamentation to gain new vitality and to be more than a dead weight from an earlier style.

Nevertheless, several problems remain. They arise not from the music itself but from the complex relation of contemporary performance to a changing style. For example, there is no doubt that ornamentation can, and even should, be added to some passages in Mozart's concertos and arias. But how much, and where? Our guides are most unreliable. The ornamented versions published by well-meaning admirers of Mozart some years after his death are mostly vile. Hummel's versions are, of course, better than most—he was a pupil of Mozart as well as a fine musician—but they are impossibly rich. To use them would be to forget how musical taste can change in twenty-five years. Hummel belongs, in his musical outlook, to the age of Rossini, not to the age of Haydn and Mozart; the development of Beethoven who carried on the classical tradition against the current of his time must have been incomprehensible to him. Indeed, the whole tendency of the classical style is against the heavy ornamentation of the Baroque and mannerist styles, and it considerably purifies the lighter ornamentation of the Rococo. The music of Haydn after 1775 cannot be ornamented, and as for Beethoven, we know what he thought of musicians who added anything to his music from his explosion when Czerny did so, and his subsequent apology: 'You must pardon . . . a composer who would have preferred to hear his work exactly as he wrote it, no matter how beautifully you played in general.'

The principal document in favor of heavy ornamentation in Mozart's concertos is by no means as straightforward as is sometimes thought. In answer to a letter from his sister complaining of the bareness of a certain passage in the slow movement of the D major Concerto K. 451, Mozart sent her an ornamented variant. This is generally taken to imply that the custom of the time was to ornament all such passages whenever they occur. Nevertheless, the exchange of letters cuts both ways: it may also be interpreted as meaning that one never added ornamentation without asking the composer first, even if one were a close relative as well as an accomplished musician. The most cogent evidence we have for Mozart's attitude to improvised ornament unfortunately describes only the position he took on the matter when he was seven years old. In 1780, when he was twenty-five, his father wrote to him about a certain 'Herr Esser, whom we met in Mainz eighteen years ago, and whose playing you criticized by telling him that he played well, but that he added too many notes and that he ought to play music as it was written.' There is, moreover, no reason to think that Mozart changed his mind about this in later years.

Mozart stands apart from Haydn and Beethoven, however, because of his closeness to the operatic style, and the tradition of ornamentation in opera was very powerful. It is known that arias in Mozart's operas were sung with added ornaments during his lifetime. How much of this did he plan for, how much did he merely tolerate, and how much did he deplore? We do not know. The existence of two versions of some concert arias, unornamented and ornamented, both by Mozart himself, proves the relevance of ornamentation to Mozart's vocal style. But it may also indicate that if an aria was to be ornamented, Mozart preferred to write out the ornaments himself. It does not prove the unornamented version to have been inacceptable.

That Mozart was not averse to ornamentation, we know, too, from several other authentic variants. The slow movement of the Piano Sonata in F K. 332, and the eleventh variation of the finale of the Sonata in D K. 284 were both published in 1784 (by different publishers) with extra ornaments certainly added by Mozart himself. It is significant that both these pieces are marked Adagio. Mozart's Allegros can absorb ornamentation no better than Haydn's; the style had transformed them to a point where the technique of improvised ornament was irrelevant. It was still possible in a slow movement, however (although by no means as essential as in a work of the 1740s), while at certain points of a decorative form like a set of variations, it was indispensable. When, as in the A major Sonata for Piano K. 331, Mozart has not written out the repeats of the penultimate variation (traditionally an Adagio in a set of variations, and so marked here), one should add ornaments during performance, using the analogous place in K. 284 as a model; even here, discretion is necessary, as the melody of this variation is more complex than the one in K. 284, and less well adapted to a generous addition of ornaments.

It should be noted that the original manuscript of K. 284 already contains rich ornamentation and that the principal additions to the published version are directions for dynamics and phrasing. The following measures give a good idea of the additions:

from all of which we may safely conclude that dynamic contrast was beginning to replace decoration, and that Mozart added ornaments to those of his compositions which were already in an ornamental style. The operatic manner of the concerto, however, demanded a more decorative style from the soloist than from the orchestra. In the variation sets in the concertos, the heavier decoration for the piano has already been written out by the composer: this is even true of movements like the variation finale of the C minor Concerto K. 491, where the left hand was sketchily indicated and filled in later, while the decorated form of the melody for the soloist was written out from the very first.

Slow movements present a touchier problem than variation sets; tradition is less of a guide here, as Mozart was changing tradition more radically in this instance. It is even difficult to use the added ornaments of the slow movement of K. 332 as a model for later works: the original form of its melody is already full of decoration, and in the last years of his life Mozart was developing and refining melodic lines of deliberate simplicity. It is possible to add ornaments to 'Dove sono' in *Figaro* (although questionable whether there is any musical gain in doing so), but the music for the three boys in *Die Zauberflöte* cannot be ornamented at all without becoming nonsense. Nor can the duet between Pamina and Papageno, 'Bei Männern,' be decorated: Mozart has himself added the most sparing decoration for the second verse, making the melodic line more expressive in the most economical way; any further addition would only mean a loss. The music of Haydn and Mozart killed Rococo decoration, and how dead it was in Vienna can be seen in the music of Hummel, where it appears swollen and unsupported by the structure, insubstantial as a ghost. As for Beethoven's music, decoration is unthinkable[1]: in all the vagaries of operatic production has anyone anywhere ever tried to decorate the canon in *Fidelio*?

Our knowledge of contemporary performance from descriptions, memoirs, and treatises can help here, but we must beware of letting it lead us blindly. I have never read a didactic book on contemporary performance which could be trusted very far: most so-called piano methods will appear wrong or irrelevant to any pianist. We all know how misleading almost all descriptions of performances are: the few that are relatively accurate will be almost

---

[1] Except, of course, for the necessary vocal appoggiaturas in recitatives and in a few cadences like the end of 'Abscheulicher, wo eilst du hin?'

indistinguishable in twenty years from the others. There is no reason to think that writing about music was any better in the eighteenth century than it is today. Almost any rule about eighteenth-century performance-practice will find its contemporary contradiction somewhere or other. Above all, when we remember how fast musical fashions change, we must beware of applying the ideas of 1750 to 1775 or to 1800.

At once the best and the worst evidence for improvised ornamentation are the written-out versions contemporary with the composer, or prepared shortly after his death. The best evidence, because they were actually performed; the worst, because they are, in most cases, abominably crude, and even when they are not, there is no reason to think the composer would have approved. Most performance is already bad enough without our being hamstrung by the habits of inferior eighteenth-century musicians and the aesthetic of the worst eighteenth-century taste. I sometimes wonder about the response, a century from now, to tapes or recordings of the music of today in which the tempi are misjudged, the ensemble is sloppy, and the rhythms have come out all wrong. Will this be taken as the true style of our time? Will the fact that a 5/8 section of one of the best-known works of a famous composer was generally omitted by an equally famous conductor because he had trouble beating it be understood in a hundred years as evidence of the composer's approval (his protest was, of course, private and unavailing)? Is there any reason to think that performance has deteriorated since the eighteenth century? One needs merely to remember how Mozart was forced to spoil *Don Giovanni* for the Vienna production or recall the première of Beethoven's Violin Concerto, at which the soloist fiddled a sonata of his own composition for one-stringed violin held upside down between Beethoven's first and second movements.

This leaves us, for the most part, basically with the musical text, but this in turn does not imply that literal treatment is desirable. Nothing disconcerts a composer more than an exact but lifeless performance of the notes. In the end, it is painful to think what little good erudition alone can do us. From Mozart's own description of *rubato*, for example, it is certain that he sometimes played with his hands rhythmically apart like Paderewski and Harold Bauer, but in the where, the how often, and the how far apart lies all the difference between music and nonsense. How tricky the problem is may be seen if we recall that Chopin is reported (correctly?) to have played with great freedom, taught his students with a metronome, and made a public scene when he heard Liszt play one of his mazurkas with too much liberty.

On the whole, if anything is to be added to a work of Mozart, we should consider in each case whether or not the manuscript is completely written-out and for whom. The E flat Concerto K. 271, written for Mlle. Jeunehomme, for example, is obviously complete down to the last notes of the cadenzas; the C minor K. 491, written for the composer himself, was hastily set down.

Cadenzas must *almost* always be provided at fermatas, and if other ornamentation is added at all, it should mostly be in the slow movements.

One rule often given today as in the eighteenth century is always to preserve the original shape of the melody. This admirable rule, however, brings the besetting problem of added ornamentation into clearer focus. In spite of contemporary theory, it is not a rule that anyone at the time would have subscribed to in practice. Not even Mozart. Throughout the eighteenth century, the preservation of the original melody's outline was a relatively minor consideration when ornaments were to be added. Much more important were the interest, grace, and expressive quality of the additions: if the original idea was buried or transformed, so much the worse for it. The ornamentation that Handel, Bach, and even Mozart wrote out often changed the original shape considerably. A few examples should suffice; here is a phrase of Handel, in its original, simple form and then as ornamented by the composer:

here is the first measure of the adagio variation of the Sonata K. 284, and Mozart's own writing-out of the repeat:

and here, finally, are the first and last appearances of the slow movement's melody in the Sonata in C minor K. 457:

Handel buries his melody; Mozart reshapes his for expressive effect.

When we listen to Mozart, are we interested in the music or in an authentic eighteenth-century performance? The two interests coincide only up to a certain point. The Caravaggios of San Luigi dei Francesi cannot be seen easily in the place where they are hung and for which they were painted; taken down and placed on exhibition recently they became really visible for the first time in centuries. The original ambiance is not always the most helpful one for seeing a work of art. Similarly, eighteenth-century practice, no matter how authentic, is of no use to us when it distracts from, and even renders inaudible, those qualities of Mozart's music that were most revolutionary and most personal; and it becomes intolerable when we are offered the worst traditions of the past as a model, as we often are.

Ornament must be related to style, and it is necessary to decorate only when the musical sense requires it. For this, each composer and each work must be reconsidered individually. A very brief cadenza must be inserted at fermatas like this one in the slow movement of the Concerto in C minor K. 491:

because the melodic outline makes no sense in the context of Mozart's style without a bridge. The appoggiaturas must be added to recitatives in operas because a cadence like the following:

is (or should seem to be) ugly when we consider the nature of Mozart's melody and harmony (or that of any other eighteenth-century composer) outside the recitative, and also because we know that recitatives were written in a kind of shorthand conventionally filled out by the singer—melodic originality had no place in a *secco* recitative. Handel's solo melodies should be ornamented because they make more sense and sound better that way—

they are structures built for decoration, unlike his choruses—but if we find the original outlines beautiful, we should allow them to be audible through the decoration. The early sonatas of Haydn cry out for ornament, particularly when they are played on a harpsichord: it would be folly to add a note to the last ones, even in the repeats. A performance is not an archaeological dig. Paradoxically, in so far as the purpose of a performance of a Mozart concerto is reconstruction of eighteenth-century practice rather than pleasure or dramatic effect, just so far does it differ from an actual performance by Mozart.

There is, furthermore, little reason to provide what we imagine to be completely 'authentic' ornamentation on instruments which are radically 'inauthentic.' The sound of the modern piano, the modern bows of string instruments, the increased power of the woodwinds—all this changes the significance of ornamentation, which largely provided the possibility of expressive and dynamic emphasis. In the modern context it makes for a fussy effect. An entire string section attacking a trill in a Handel oratorio with an explosive vigor unimaginable on eighteenth-century instruments does not add to our better understanding of the music. Ornamentation in an opera or a concerto against the heavier sound and, above all, the more intense sonority of the modern orchestra has nothing like the significance it had in the late eighteenth century. The reproduction of eighteenth-century sonorities with modern instruments is, however, a disastrous solution. Music is as much idea and gesture as sonority. If a fortissimo on an eighteenth-century instrument produces mezzo piano by our standards, it is the violence and the drama that are important and not the actual volume of sound.

In all the arts, the taste for ornamentation changed radically in the last quarter of the eighteenth century. To take only one example, the infinitely repeating designs for fabrics used in the upholstery of chairs and sofas were gradually replaced by centralized compositions. For mural decoration the simple folds of hanging draperies were preferred to more elaborate systems. These tendencies are obviously reflected within the musical style of the period, with its centrally placed point of tension and its clarity of form.

Most important of all, the function of decoration became the exact contrary of what it had been. In Rococo interiors, the decoration was used to hide the structure, to cover over the joints, to enforce a supreme continuity. Neoclassical decoration, however, always much more sparing, was used to emphasize structure, to articulate it, and to sharpen the spectator's sense of it. The analogous change in the function of musical ornaments does not need a mystical correspondence of the arts to explain it. The solid body of aesthetic doctrine which condemned ornament as immoral dominated the second half of the century, and there were few pockets of resistance. To equate the practice of Mozart (and Haydn after 1780) with that of J. S. Bach or even C. P. E. Bach is to ignore one of the most sweeping revolutions of taste in history.

The musical ornamentation of the first half of the eighteenth century was an essential element in the achievement of continuity: the decoration not only covered the underlying musical structure but kept it always flowing. The High Baroque in music had a horror of the void, and the *agréments* fill what empty space there was.

The decoration of the classical style, on the other hand, articulates structure. The chief ornament retained from the Baroque is, significantly, the final cadential trill. Other ornaments are used more rarely, and they are almost always fully written out—necessarily so, as they have become *thematic*.[1] This development was carried by Beethoven as far as it could go. In his later music, the trill lost its decorative status: it is no longer an ornament but either an essential motif—as in the *Archduke* Trio or the fugal finale of the *Hammerklavier*—or a suspension of rhythm, a way of turning a long sustained note into an indistinct vibration which creates an intense and inward stillness. In the last works of Beethoven the notion of ornament often completely disappears, drowned in the substance of the work.

---

[1] See the purely thematic use of an *acciacatura* in Haydn's Quartet op. 33 no. 3 in C major, quoted on pp. 65–67.

Part III

HAYDN FROM 1770 TO THE DEATH OF MOZART

———

Wer den Witz erfunden haben mag? Jede zur Besinnung gebrachte Eigen-
schaft-Handlungsweise unser Geistes ist im eigentlichsten Sinne eine neu-
entdeckte Welt.

Novalis, Blütenstaub, 1797

[*Who may have invented wit? Every attribute/procedure of our mind that
is made conscious is in the strictest sense a newly-discovered world.*]

1

String Quartet

The musical scene in Europe during the third quarter of the eighteenth century, with its many conflicting national traditions, makes a cluttered impression today. In Italy, indeed, there was barely even a national style but rather several municipal ones, each with its own claims. The greater unity of the end of the century is not an illusion, or an historical scheme imposed by our own evaluation. Although some of the independent national styles— French grand opera, for instance—continued to exist and to develop in a direction not much affected by Viennese classicism, the supremacy of the Viennese style, or rather of Haydn and Mozart, is not just a modern judgment, but an historical fact, internationally acknowledged by 1790. As for Beethoven, in spite of difficulties in winning acceptance for his larger works, by 1815 even most of those musicians who did not like his music would have admitted that he was the greatest living composer: some of the admiration he won may have been unwilling, but it was uncontested (except of course, by the lunatic fringe that is the normal burden of the taste and criticism of any age).

It would be romantic to think of Haydn as arriving like Malherbe to bring order and logic into a 'mannerist' chaos and irrationality. To begin with, Haydn was as interested as anyone else in the disruptive and shocking effects of the music of the 1760s: he retained a taste for such effects to the end of his life, remaining a master of the surprise modulation, the dramatic silence, the asymmetrical phrase; and he added to this an aptitude for the facetious that no other composer enjoyed. The proportions of his works became 'classical,' the harmonic vision more logical, but he never abandoned his earlier 'manner': his latest works, in fact, are at times even more shocking than the earlier ones. His eccentricity lost none of its power, but it was integrated into a conception of musical form larger and more coherent than any other composer of the 1760s had imagined.

The qualities of Haydn's music that we often find most astonishing today are oddly his least personal: daring juxtaposition of remote keys, abrupt use of silence, irregular phrasing—all this was a legacy from the music of the 1750s and 1760s. Every one of these traits can be paralleled, often more startlingly if less coherently, in the work of other composers, Carl Philipp Emanuel Bach in particular. In Haydn's last Piano Sonata in E flat major, the slow movement is in E major, and the surprise of the distant new tonality is much admired; Tovey has pointed out that C. P. E. Bach in his D major

111

Symphony also wrote a slow movement in the flat supertonic, but, for once more timid than Haydn, conciliatingly placed a modulating coda after the first movement by way of explanation. But a B minor Sonata by C. P. E. Bach, published in 1779, has a slow movement in G minor, an even more startling relationship than the Neapolitan tonic-supertonic, and this time there is no transition to mitigate the effect, although the end of the movement modulates back to B minor. (The strange sound of the G minor second movement is enhanced by Bach's use of F sharp minor, and not D major, as the secondary key, or 'dominant,' of the first movement.)

Next to Carl Philipp Emanuel Bach, Haydn appears like a cautious, sober composer: his irregularities of phrase and modulation are almost tame compared to those of the elder man. What is unprecedented, however, is the synthesis that Haydn gradually developed, in the late 1760s and the early 70s, out of dramatic irregularity and large-scale symmetry. Until then, the symmetry of his forms had been exterior, and sometimes even perfunctory: the dramatic effects either broke the structures, or depended upon a very loose organization for their existence. Haydn developed a style in which the most dramatic effects were essential to the form—that is, justified the form and were justified (prepared and resolved) by it. Haydn's classicism tempered his ferocity, but in no way curbed or tamed his irregularities. It was the tradition of eccentricity that protected him against the insipidity of the 'Rococo' or 'galant' mode. Mozart, of a generation younger than Haydn's, was raised in the latter style at a time when the late Baroque manner of C. P. E. Bach was itself already somewhat out of fashion. He therefore had to develop his own taste for dramatic discontinuity and asymmetry, mostly from within himself but partly inspired by his contact with the music of Johann Sebastian Bach.

The greatness of Haydn's synthesis may perhaps be estimated if we compare the way he and C. P. E. Bach treated an effect deliberately outrageous to an eighteenth-century ear: beginning a piece in the wrong key. It would be fairest to take works written close to each other in time. Of the sonatas published in 1779 by C. P. E. Bach, no. 5 in F major begins:

in which the strange C minor opening and the sequence it initiates continue to disturb the tonal stability as far as their echoes in the sixth and seventh measures. The last movement of Haydn's Symphony no. 62 in D major, written around the same time, opens in a fashion at once more troubling and more stable:

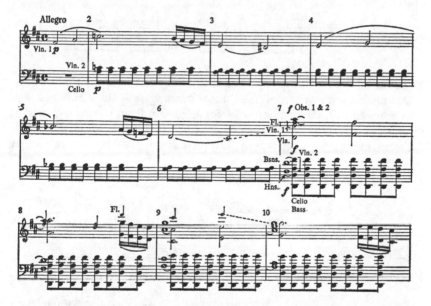

more troubling because the first two measures mysteriously define no definite tonality at all—the 'wrong' key, E minor, is implied clearly only in measure 3, while C. P. E. Bach defines his false key at once; more stable because Haydn's sequence moves simply and logically into the D major tonic, so that the real tonality is a consequence of the false opening, and is established merely by continuing the sequence thematically. Haydn's opening is, of course, additionally stable in that it begins a finale, and we have the D major still in our ears from the previous movements (all, unusually, in the tonic): this means that the surprise is greater in C. P. E. Bach when the real tonality appears, but it also enhances the mystery of Haydn's opening. C. P. E. Bach certainly comprehends the larger harmonic consequences of his ideas (as we have seen, his 'false' opening continues to color the movement after the tonic is established), but Haydn's scheme is on a wider scale to begin with. It is also capable of greater elaboration, as at the recapitulation:

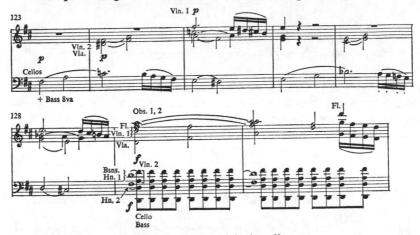

where the added contrapuntal voices enrich the effect.

One further comparison of 'false' tonal openings will show Haydn's logic even more clearly, the two examples coming again from the same period as those previously quoted. The 1779 Sonata no. 3 in B minor of C. P. E. Bach, the one with the slow movement in the remote key of G minor, has an opening which implies D major for two measures:

The end of the first measure, with its G♯, suggests that something is wrong, and B minor soon arrives. The following modulation to F sharp minor also has several surprises, the most conspicuous being the sudden turn to G major, emphasized by the *forte* and the startlingly heavy chord. Thus the 'false' opening is once again not without its consequences, and perhaps it even makes the G minor slow movement more plausible, just as Haydn prepares the E major movement of the E flat major Sonata by an emphasis in the first movement on the remote key to come. C. P. E. Bach's most subtle touch here is that the opening, while apparently in D major, hides the B minor triad of the real tonic in its first three notes. By Haydn's standards, or even by J. S. Bach's, this work is not completely coherent; yet it is a pity not to accept the standards that it lays down for itself. Even so, resistance is almost inevitable, because the style implied by these standards is a little thin even at its most dramatic, and small-scale even when it achieves an effect of brilliance. C. P. E. Bach's grandeur lacks breadth just as his passion lacked wit.

Two years after this sonata was published, Haydn wrote the Quartets op. 33, of which the first also pretends to begin in D major and quickly turns to B minor.[1] But the logic is more rigorous, the dramatic force far more compelling:

---

[1] Tovey thought that Haydn got the idea of the quartet from the Bach sonata, but this seems unlikely: the works are too different in procedure, and the idea of a false beginning was not uncommon.

115

A♮, the one note in D major to clash with B minor, appears innocently in the melody in the second measure, but the accompaniment, which had already introduced the A♮, now contradicts with an A♯ two beats later. Then Haydn seizes on this as a pivot to establish B minor, the expressive detail and the fundamental harmonic structure becoming identical here: in measures 3, 4, 7, and 8 he plays the A♯ and the A♮ together again and again, along with a *crescendo* and the rising line in the first violin. Although we are now fully in B minor, resolution is withheld until the eleventh measure, with the appearance of a new but related theme. The effect is at once broader and more concise than in C. P. E. Bach, more logical and yet no less strange: the only way in which Haydn's new 'classicism' could be said to temper oddity, to rein in eccentricity, was by avoiding the root position of the D major chord in the first two measures. The change to B minor seems, therefore, not a modulation, as in Bach, but a reinterpretation, a new clarity. In return, he can dispense with a modulation when he goes to the relative major as a dominant; he merely reharmonizes the opening with a D major chord, in root position for the first time:

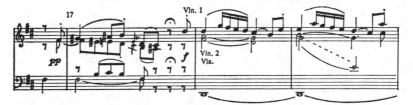

sweeping away all unnecessary transitions.

This opening page just cited is a manifesto. Haydn's claim that the Quartets op. 33 were written 'in an entirely new and special style' has sometimes been discounted as mere sales talk, but his last series of Quartets, op. 20, written almost ten years before, had circulated widely and was well known: he must therefore have thought that his claim had some chance of seeming plausible. In point of fact, this page represents a revolution in style. The relation between principal voice and accompanying voices is transformed before our eyes. In measure 3, the melody is given to the cello and the other instruments take up the little accompanying figure. In measure 4, this accompanying figure has become the principal voice—it now carries the melody. No one can say just at what point in measures 3 and 4 the violin must be judged the principal melodic voice, and where the cello shifts to a subordinate position, as the passage is not divisible. All that one knows is that the violin starts measure 3 as accompaniment and ends measure 4 as melody.

This is the true invention of classical counterpoint. It does not in any way represent a revival of Baroque technique, where the ideal (never, of course, the reality) was equality and independence of the voices. (J. S. Bach's admirers boasted that he could print keyboard works like the six-voice ricercar from the *Musical Offering* in full score.) Classical counterpoint generally abandons even the pretense of equality. The opening page of this quartet, for example, affirms the distinction between melody and accompaniment. But it then transforms one into the other.

No doubt there are precedents for any revolution, and it would not be surprising if one turned up for this. But I do not yet know an earlier instance of an accompaniment figure changing imperceptibly and without a break into the principal melodic voice.[1] If one should be found, the Quartets op. 33 would remain the first application of this principle—i.e., the accompaniment conceived at once as thematic and as subordinate—on any scale and with any consistency. In this way the texture of the string quartet is incomparably enriched without disturbing the late eighteenth-century hierarchical scheme of melody and accompaniment. It meant, of course, that the thematic elements in Haydn often became very short since they were to be used as accompanying figures. In compensation the new-found power was considerable, as can be seen in this B minor Quartet from what happens to measures 5 and 6 when they reappear in the recapitulation:

---

[1] In Haydn's Quartet op. 20 no. 2 in C major, an accompanying cello figure in measures 16 and 17 becomes melodic in measure 19, but only on being transferred to the violin. There are, of course, many previous examples, generally witty, of accompanying figures

where the little two-note accompaniment now has the force of an explosion. This is one example of Haydn's placing the true climax of the work not just before, but just after the beginning of the recapitulation.

There are other changes of equal importance in the style of op. 33. Transitional figures and phrases are almost completely eliminated. Earlier, in op. 20, to get from one phrase to another, Haydn had had to write:

where the cello figure in measure 4 has a purely transitional function, and is never needed except in this place. Ten years later, Haydn is more economical. The end of each phrase implies what is coming, generates it. New themes (or new versions of old ones) enter without transition: they do not need to be introduced, they are already implicit. This is partly because the phrasing has become more systematic. For those who love the passionate irregularity of the phrasing in earlier Haydn, no doubt this means a loss. There is, however, a gain: the more intimate relation between the larger structure and the small detail that starts with op. 33 makes the slightest irregularity more telling —its consequences are more considerable, and less localized. The most insignificant elements achieve a sudden power, as with the expressive meaning given to the distinction between the staccato and legato in the twelfth measure of the opening of op. 33 no. 1 quoted above. Some of this new power comes

---

used melodically, but then they make no pretense at any point of being accompaniments; and many Baroque accompaniments are thematically derived but lack classical subordination.

from the thematic relationships, but most important and original is the sense of pace that comes from the greater concision and regularity of the phrase.

Where did this new feeling for pace come from, and what had Haydn been doing for a decade since his last set of quartets? The nickname of the Quartets op. 33, *Gli Scherzi*, hints at Haydn's source of new strength. Between 1772, when the *Sun* Quartets op. 20 were published, and 1781, most of Haydn's output consisted of comic operas written for the court at Esterházy. Even a considerable part of his symphonic works then consisted of arrangements from his comic operas.[1] The Quartets op. 33 are called *Gli Scherzi* because they replace the traditional minuet with a scherzo; the change is largely one of name, Haydn's minuets having frequently had a jocose enough character in the past, but the new title is significant. The quarters are informed through-out by the pacing of comic opera. They are informed, too, by the comic spirit, but that is nothing new for Haydn. The Quartets op. 20 have moments of pure fun that equal anything Haydn was to compose later. The *Scherzi* Quartets are, indeed; generally comic in style, but this has, I think, been exaggerated. The fugal finale is absent here, but Haydn for the moment feels no need to buttress the originality of his thought with the complexities of an older style. Many of the movements are as serious as any in the previous set of quartets. (Tovey finds only wit in the false tonal opening of op. 33 no. 1, and feels that it is a device that Brahms elevated into the pathetic with the Clarinet Quintet; on the contrary, it seems to me that if the procedure in Haydn is wit, the intent is deadly earnest, the effect as pathetic as in Brahms, and more powerful if less nostalgic.) But the *Scherzi* Quartets have the rhythmic technique that comes from the experience of writing comic opera: a rapid action demanded a regularity of phrasing in order to be intelligible, and the music needed a tight continuity articulated logically to keep time with what happened on the stage. What Haydn had learned in ten years, what these new quartets show, is, above all, dramatic clarity. Expressive intensity had previously caused Haydn's rhythm to clot, and rich, intricate phrases had been followed all too often by a disappointingly loose cadence. With the *Scherzi* Quartets, he was able to construct a framework in which the intensity and the significance of the material could expand and contract freely and still be supported by the basic movement. They are, above all, lucid.

Haydn was not a successful writer of opera, comic or serious; his musical thought was too small-scale—or, if one prefers a gentler word, too concentrated. But he learned from comic opera, not freedom of form—he had never needed to be taught that—but freedom in the service of dramatic significance. When the words in a libretto denied his musical ideas their implied development and balance, he invented new ways to restore both. In his operas, too, we can see the strengthening of his sense of the dynamic force of his material.

---

[1] Starting in 1776, the number of operatic productions at Esterházy considerably increased.

119

This sense that the movement, the development, and the dramatic course of a work all can be found latent in the material, that the material can be made to release its charged force so that the music no longer unfolds, as in the Baroque, but is literally impelled from within—this sense was Haydn's greatest contribution to the history of music. We may love him for many other things, but this new conception of musical art changed all that followed it. It was for this reason that Haydn did not tame his eccentricity or his coarse humor, but used them, no longer self-indulgently, but with respect for the integrity of each individual work. He understood the possibilities of conflict in musical material within the tonal system, and the way it could be used to generate energy and to create drama. This accounts for the extraordinary variety of his forms: his methods changed with the material.

By 'material,' I mean largely the relationships implied at the opening of each piece; Haydn had not yet arrived at Beethoven's conception of a musical idea unfolding gradually, let alone at Mozart's larger vision of tonal mass which in some ways surpassed even Beethoven's. Haydn's fundamental ideas are terse, and stated almost at once, and they give an immediate impression of latent energy that Mozart rarely looked for. They express an immediate conflict, and the full play and resolution of the conflict is the work: it is Haydn's view of 'sonata form.' The freedom of this form is no longer just the exercise of a whimsical imagination in a loosely organized scheme, as in some of the great works of the 1760s, but the free play of an imaginative logic.

The two principal sources of musical energy are dissonance and sequence— the first because it demands resolution, the second because it implies continuation. The classical style immeasurably increased the power of dissonance, raising it from an unresolved interval to an unresolved chord and then to an unresolved key. The 'false' tonal opening of Haydn's B minor Quartet op. 33 no. 1 is a dissonant *tonality*, for example, and the movement resolves it in two ways, first by treating it as the dominant or secondary key (temporarily making a tonic of it, which is a half-resolution), and then by expanding this in the 'development' and resolving everything in a recapitulation which—except for two measures at the opening—insists dramatically on the tonic. One important aspect of Haydn's genius lay in his sense of the energy latent in his material (or, to put it another way, in his invention of material that gave him the requisite energy): so, in the B minor Quartet, he at once plays over and over (six times in measures 3 to 8) the painful dissonance of A♮–A♯ (quoted above, page 115).

Haydn's invention cannot be given full justice without going into most of what he wrote, but some idea can be given of the variety and logic with which he treated the sonata style. The first movement of the Quartet in B flat major op. 50 no. 1 is built from almost nothing at all: a repeated note in the cello and a six-note figure in the violin. Everything in the exposition is restricted to these two small elements:

String Quartet

There are two measures of one note softly repeated by the cello (motif *a*), a tonic pedal. This is a charming joke: op. 50 no. 1 is the first of the quartets written for the King of Prussia, who was a cellist. Accordingly the set opens with the cello all by itself, playing a motif hardly taxing to the royal virtuosity—a solo on one note. The six-note figure, which I call (*b*), is used in sequence in measures 3–8, with its rhythm and accent delightfully transformed halfway up. The sequence, rising by thirds, is then balanced by a vigorous descent, which starts with (*b*) in measure 9 and continues in a scale, stopping on the way to emphasize the E♭–D which are the outer shape of (*b*) in its first appearance, harmonized, at the *sforzando* climax in measure 10, on G minor, a harmony that prepares the later movement away from the tonic. (The F♯ in measure 9 is the first chromatic alteration in the movement and it will be emphasized and finally used in measure 28 to begin the modulation to the dominant.) In measures 12–27, (*b*) is used with expressively altered harmonies to form a cadence, the final cadential figure four times repeated (measures 20, 24, 25, 26), while the pedal (*a*) is gradually transferred upward with amusing effect: it is a pun, as an ostinato that is typically bass in character is raised to the alto and then to the soprano voice.

The gradual increase in harmonic intensity can be seen by comparing measures 3–4, 9–10, 14–16, and 28. At measure 28, the F♯ that has appeared so prominently is made more striking by being presented as the bass of an augmented triad. Its new form starts a downward sequence, ending on a C major triad (the supertonic, or dominant of the dominant). The motif (*b*) has still the same shape at measure 35, but develops a unified triplet rhythm as at measure 7: the sequences now all move downward and the rhythm has naturally become more animated. In measures 33–40 (and 45–46 and 51–53), (*a*) is no longer a tonic, but a dominant pedal (at the dominant), which gives it, of course, greater energy. The first cadence at measures 47–50 again recalls measures 9–10, and is an augmentation of (*b*). New forms are found for (*b*) (measures 50–54), its shape twisted but still audibly derived from its original statement, until a second cadence at measures 55–56. At 56, (*a*) becomes a tonic pedal again (at the dominant), and still another form is found for (*b*); the final F major cadence at measures 59–60 is a more decisive version of the B flat cadence at measures 11 and 12.

One could say that in this exposition Haydn treats the six-note figure (*b*) as a row, except that his procedure has absolutely nothing to do with serial technique. The way its shape is twisted, while remaining always recognizable, shows us that Haydn may be said to work topologically—his central idea remaining invariant even when its shape is deformed—while a serialist works geometrically. More to the point, however, is that (*b*) alone is not the source of the piece, but rather the tension between (*b*) and the calm one-note ostinato (*a*). The fixed, unmoving sound of that one repeated note allows (*b*) to be set up against it as a series of sequences, from which all the rhythmic animation of the work comes. In fact, the ostinato (*a*) by itself largely explains much of the shape of the piece—in particular, why Haydn does not, as he generally does, leave the tonic as soon as he can, but stays without moving from it for a considerable space, even closing strongly on the tonic in measure 27. Neither (*a*) nor (*b*) alone, however, is sufficient, but from the opposition between them and from their shape Haydn derives his larger structure. There are no tunes, few rhythmic surprises, fewer dramatic harmonies. Yet it is fascinating and witty music, in which Haydn, intent on dazzling us with his technique, makes splendid bricks with hardly any straw at all.

Haydn reserves all his harmonic surprises for the development, which begins by reinterpreting the outer shape of (*b*) (E♭–D):

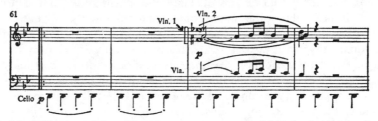

and this falling second unifies the movement, marking (as it did in the exposition) the points of structural importance.[1] The recapitulation enters without warning in the middle of a phrase:

so that the precise moment of the return to the tonic is almost unnoticed. The recapitulation rephrases the exposition, moving to the stabilizing subdominant, but with greater rhythmic animation and an exhilarating brilliance. One final stroke is reserved for the very end of the movement where, along with the final appearance of the falling second (E♭–D), the rhythm of (*a*) is quietly tripled:

---

[1] It insistently appears to shape each climax of the recapitulation (mm. 114–115, 121, 133–138, 145) as well as at the beginning and end of this section. The development section from measures 87 to 102 is a large-scale movement from E♭ to D.

If we ask why the two notes E♭–D play such a large role, we must look back to their first appearance at the beginning where the E♭ enters softly and magically after the mysterious one-note ostinato in the cello: it is the melodic note of the first chord, a sweetly dissonant harmony and an unforgettable opening. The E♭ is also present in every dissonant chord for the first fifteen measures. The entrance, marked *dolce*, and the repetition of the pattern make this not a hidden relationship—a recondite compositional element—but an immediate audible experience, far easier to hear than to see on a page. The most important musical relationships in Haydn are never theoretical, but those which immediately strike the unprejudiced ear as significant, as the extraordinary hushed chord at the opening of this quartet does. 'Unprejudiced ear' is perhaps a misleading expression; we not only need to recapture an innocence of nineteenth- and twentieth-century developments, but we also need the prejudices of the eighteenth century. The opening ostinato pedal, the strange, soft chord, and the little six-note figure—the significance of these in the language of eighteenth-century tonality give Haydn all he needs: his imaginative understanding of the dynamic impulse they contain shapes the form the material itself seems to create.

This movement, with its obsessive use of one six-note figure, may seem atypical (although there are many such pieces in Haydn, whose material could be even more laconic). When the material is more complex, however, Haydn's procedure remains the same; an entirely different shape results, of course, as the relation to the material is central to his method. The tensions implied at the opening determine the course of the work. The exposition of the D major Quartet op. 50 no. 6 only appears so different a way of writing a sonata from op. 50 no. 1 because the musical material is so radically different:

125

String Quartet

Here, wit is omnipotent. The opening phrase is a final cadence. No tonic is defined by the first measure; we start on an unexplained, unharmonized, and therefore ambiguous E. If a dissonance is a note that requires resolution, then the E, standing by itself, is dissonant although we are only aware of its dissonance after it has disappeared; surprise will, however, keep it ringing in our ears long enough to realize that we have been fooled. The line then descends to the E below, and we resolve it with the cadence II–V–I. The *diminuendo* is the wittiest stroke of all and the tonic chord, when it arrives, does so unassumingly. The good humor of this opening is boundless.

In the most straightforward terms, we have been given an E in place of a D (or at least in place of an A or an F♯: almost all the pieces written at that time start with a note of the tonic triad, and the few exceptions at least do not puzzle us for a full measure with a mysteriously unexplained note). With the imaginative logic that he had both invented and tempered with experience, Haydn proceeds to exploit this contradiction between the D we ought to have had and the E that we were given instead. From measures 5 to 15, he continually sounds the E dissonantly against a D, more and more insistently. Meanwhile, the rhythm of the opening measure ♩. ♫♫, which we may call (*a*), appears in varied guises throughout. The tonic cadence at measure 16 closes the first period.

This dissonant E is, of course, the dominant of the dominant: its very nature implies the traditional first modulation almost by definition. Accordingly in measure 18, E is established as the climax of a stretto using (*a*); and then in measure 23, after decorated forms of (*a*), it is established as the bass. It is interesting to note the octave transpositions, and to see at how many levels the E is made prominent. The note now has such force that it no longer demands resolution, but can itself be used to resolve. To bring out this force, an F♮ is set up against it with a *sforzando* repeated four times under (*a*) in measures 26–29, an F♮ that also serves to prepare the splendid surprise cadence on an F major chord *subito piano* at measure 38. This F is now prolonged for six measures (measures 39–44) with all the orchestral power Haydn's string quartet can manage, using the opening phrase (*a*): measures 38 to 47 are essentially an inner expansion—a withholding of the cadence at measure 37. A new theme, square and decisive, is finally introduced in measure 48 to round off the form. To appreciate the full mastery of this exposition, we must play it with the repeat. When the opening phrase returns it has an entirely different sense: it is now a modulation from the dominant back to the tonic.

The difference between the expositions of these two quartets does not imply freedom or variety in the usual sense, but comes from a new conception of the demands of the material, the central idea. A long and completely separate tonic section in the B flat Quartet above arises from the opening tonic pedal, while the uninterrupted flow of the D major Quartet's exposition is in answer to the tension at the beginning which immediately directs the music towards the dominant of the dominant. It should be noted that, because of this impulsion, there is no cadence on the dominant until almost the end of the exposition: again, this is not a whimsical evasion of normal practice, but a sensitivity to musical forces. That is why the F major section (measures 38–45) is both so astonishing and so logical. (It is, naturally, not really in F major; these ten measures act on the E as an appoggiatura raised to a higher power.) In both these works, as in almost all of Haydn from 1780 on, the most eccentric musical ideas (and both works are astonishing) are purged of mannerism by an understanding and a display of their full musical significance. There are no plums or (to mix a metaphor) purple passages in this style, as there are in the great works of the 1760s.

To speak of any of Haydn's structures without reference to their material is nonsense. Any discussion of second themes, bridge passages, concluding themes, range of modulation, relations between themes—all this is empty if it does not refer back to the particular piece, to its character, its typical sound, its motifs. Haydn was the most playful of composers, but his frivolity and his whimsicality never consisted of empty structural variants. After 1770 or so, his recapitulations are only 'irregular' when the expositions demanded an irregular resolution, his modulations surprising when the logic of their surprise was already implicit in what preceded them.

Briefly, Haydn is interested in the directional power of his material, or, what is much the same thing, its dramatic possibilities. He found ways of making us hear the dynamic force implicit in a musical idea. The primary directional element is generally a dissonance which, strengthened and properly reinforced, leads to a modulation. Before Haydn, the modulation of any sonata exposition was imposed almost always from without: the structure and the material were not strangers to each other, and the material could, indeed, demand a certain kind of structure (a movement away from the tonic) but without itself providing the full impulse necessary for its form. With all of Haydn's works of the 1780s, as well as some of those before, it becomes more difficult to disentangle the central musical ideas from the total structures in which they work themselves out. Secondary directional forces implicit in the material were its capacity to form sequences (a way of fixing interest and enforcing continuity already part of High Baroque technique, which created its material with that possibility in view) and its aptness for reinterpretation—development, fragmentation, and, above all, for creating new significance when transposed. This aptness was certainly recognized and appreciated before Haydn, but with nothing like his acuteness and his largeness of vision.

As to the primary element, dissonance, Haydn developed a remarkable sensitivity to its most delicate implications, an imaginative ear that caught each expressive accent. In the Quartet in B flat major op. 55 no. 3, the most dramatic effects follow from a clash between E♭ and E♮ in the opening measures; the emphasis given to this opposition is swift and controlled:

The E♭ is made prominent as early as its first appearance in the second measure by the hint of a tritone with the preceding A, and this sets into relief the surprise of an E♮ (m. 4)—which is at once contradicted, *forte* (m. 5),

130

and then the bass (m. 6) plays both E♭ and E♮, resolving one into the other. (The other chromatic alterations—B♮ and then A♭—are called up harmonically by the E♮ and help to sustain its significance.) The impulsive power of this relation is first realized in measure 20, where the two notes together (in the viola) start the modulation to the dominant, a passage immediately reiterated (m. 22). The most sensitive detail is the playing of the main theme at its original position, but reharmonized with an E♮ in the bass (m. 27), so that the opening melody is now itself the bridge passage to its own appearance in the cello at the dominant (m. 31).

There is no end to the subtleties of Haydn's ear at this time; the second theme depends on the same opposition of E♭ to E♮:

but it is now the E♭ which is the dissonant note, an inversion of harmonic function that complements the inversion of rhythm, emphasized by *sforzandi* which substitutes (♩ ♩) for (♩ ♩). In the recapitulation, where the second theme is transposed to the tonic, Haydn now inverts the theme:

in order not to relinquish the E♭–E♮ relation (which would otherwise have become A♭–A♮ here). The delicacy of Haydn's procedure and the large range of effects it reached is unprecedented: no composer before him had depended so exquisitely on the facts of hearing to form his larger structures.

Haydn's close interest in the *immediate* audible effect may best be seen in his understanding of the implications of his openings. The first striking dissonance we hear is generally used later as the means of launching the first large harmonic movement. The F major Quartet op. 50 no. 5 begins:

and the witty C♯ in measure 5 makes its effect at once. It is both charming and logical when, twenty measures later, the same note is superimposed on the first measure to begin the modulation to the dominant:

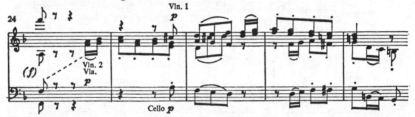

This is not a prepared modulation, in the academic sense, but a comprehension of the drama that could be played out in tonality.

It is not only that Haydn's 'irregularities' of form must be seen in the light of his interest in working out the possibilities of his material; in addition, his infractions of the academic rules of harmony must be interpreted as a desire for dramatic emphasis. At the opening of the beautiful E flat major Quartet op. 64 no. 6, there are surprisingly exposed parallel unisons between independent voices in measures 9 and 10:

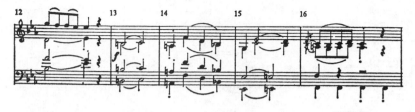

The little two-note motif, the rising second in the second violin, which is thus called to our attention, appears throughout the opening measures (m. 1: 1st violin; m. 2: viola; m. 4: cello, etc.), but it is not just passively the principal element in the melody: it is about to take on an active role, to become the agent of movement in measure 13. The parallel unisons are a hint, an apparently decorative way of bringing it to the listener's attention. This dynamic change, perhaps the most essential creation of the classical style, affects the rhythm significantly: the difference in phrasing of the same figure in measures 2 and 14 is the result of a new significance; the later form moves towards a new tonality as the earlier affirms the tonic. This conception of phrasing is original, transforming a decorative and an expressive element into a dramatic one.

More daring are the parallel fifths in measures 147–149 of the recapitulation of the opening movement of the C major Quartet op. 64 no. 1:

133

but here the more brutal emphasis in measures 147 and 149 is not a fore-warning of changed significance, but the height of an accumulation of force, as this phrase, in its various forms, has been the agent of much harmonic movement.[1] Most important, however, is that it is a way of resolving the surprising change of harmony in measure 133, a dominant-seventh chord on A♭ which has remained suspended so long that its resolution demands this painful intensity. The whole passage from measures 133 to 147 is an expansion of this chord, one of the most remarkable in Haydn, and an example of the physical excitement this kind of expansion can generate. The dramatic intensity is curiously appropriate, as Haydn works out at this place a climax that rivals the end of the development section in power. A secondary climax of such importance in the recapitulation was only occasionally used by Haydn and Mozart, but it was to become almost second nature to Beethoven after the *Waldstein* Sonata.

What I have called the secondary directional forces—sequence and re-interpretation by transposition—are most important only when the material does not provide a dissonance sufficiently dynamic for Haydn's purpose. The opening of the finale of the quartet just cited, op. 64 no. 1, obviously implies the formation of sequences based on its sharply defined rhythm:

---

[1] It is used dramatically at most of its appearances before, particularly throughout the development section, and the expansion of this passage is prepared by what has preceded. It is the climax of the movement.

but nothing in these first two measures prepares us for the spectacular crescendo of sequences that makes up its development:

This *tour de force* transforms Baroque sequential technique beyond all recognition, even if it would be difficult to conceive without the rediscovery of Handel and Sebastian Bach in the early 1780s. The gradual reconquest of contrapuntal mastery was necessary, but the energy of this passage is a classical one, arising from the brilliant articulation of phrase which makes the opening of the sequential phrases on weak beats so forceful, the one-and-a-half measure phrases in the violin at measures 49–52 so striking.

Reinterpretation by transposition as a directional force also exists in the Baroque, but the greatly enhanced force and clarity of modulation in the late eighteenth century give it a new power. Its most common form (in Haydn as in earlier composers) is the replaying of the main theme at the dominant, where a new place and a new meaning give thematic shape to the harmonic

135

form. There are, however, subtler uses, the most interesting, perhaps, being to reinterpret the material by transposing the harmony while leaving the melody at the same place. At the beginning of the F sharp minor Quartet op. 50 no. 4, the melodic line of measures 5 to 8 is played three times, changing only instrument and register, but at the end we have reached A major:

The same melodic shape has a new harmonic meaning; only the last note has to be altered at the end. Haydn was particularly given to this kind of wit in movements in a minor key, treating the minor mode as a whole as an unresolved dissonance. Transposition within the sonata implies, in general, a dissonance on a higher plane, or, better, a tension with the original or potential tonic form of the transposed phrase.

Most of the examples I have given come from opening movements because these are almost always the most dynamically conceived of the four, and such dynamism was Haydn's most original achievement. The first movement and the finale were evidently the difficult ones for him to write: in his old age, he only had the strength to finish the middle movements of his last quartet. But his new conception of musical energy makes itself felt throughout the quartets, transforming even the relaxed middle sections of those slow movements that are in ternary form into a kind of development, and much the same thing happens in many of the trios of the minuets. The finales are as daring as the opening movements, looser in structure, yet more concise in their use of fundamentally less concentrated ideas.

String Quartet

By the early 1770s, in the dozen quartets of op. 17 and op. 20, Haydn had affirmed the seriousness and richness of the string quartet. With the application, in the *Scherzi* Quartets op. 33, of thematic transformation to the entire texture including the accompaniment, so that a linear vitality now present in every instrumental part does not entail a return to the Baroque ideal of largely unbroken and always unarticulated linear continuity, Haydn established the string quartet as the supreme form of chamber music.

For most people, the string quartet is almost synonymous with chamber music, yet its prestige comes entirely from its pre-eminence in the classical period, from 1770 to the death of Schubert. Outside these limits, it is not the normal form of expression, nor even an entirely natural one. In the first half of the eighteenth century, the use of continuo for all concerted music makes at least one of the four instruments redundant: the trio sonata (three instruments and a harpsichord) was then a more efficient combination. After Schubert, music generally seeks to avoid the kind of linear definition implied by the string quartet, and it becomes an archaic and an academic form—a proof of mastery, and a nostalgic recall of the great classicists. Fine works were still written in this form, of course, but they all bear the mark either of strain or of the composer's increasingly special adaptation of his style to the medium (or the medium to his style, as with Bartók's imaginative use of percussive string effects).

Nevertheless, the leading role of the string quartet is not the accidental result of a handful of masterpieces: it is directly related to the nature of tonality, particularly to its development throughout the eighteenth century. A hundred years earlier, music had not yet shaken off the last traces of its dependence on the interval: in spite of the central importance of the chord—the triad in particular—dissonance was still conceived in intervallic terms, and the resolution of dissonance, consequently, even in late seventeenth-century music, very often satisfies the aesthetic of two-part counterpoint and ignores the tonal implications. By the eighteenth century, dissonance is always dissonance to a triad, stated or implied, although music theory naturally lagged far behind practice. Rameau's heroic and awkward attempt at reformulating harmonic theory must be seen against this background of changing practice and of the new but absolute harmonic supremacy of the triad. It is rare in later eighteenth-century music that the full triadic form of every chord except brief passing ones is not explicitly played, either by three voices or by the outline of one voice's motion (just as, in the first half of the century, when a note was missing from a triad, it was supplied by the continuo). The few exceptions are always for special effect, as in Haydn's Trio in B flat major H. 20 where the piano plays a melody for left hand alone (and the dissonances are *without exception* resolved in terms of the previously implied triad), or where a single note is used in such a way that it could imply one of several triads—an ambiguity which is always dramatic when it is not merely incompetent.

The string quartet—four-voice polyphony in its clearest non-vocal state—

is the natural consequence of a musical language in which expression is entirely based on dissonance to a triad. When there are fewer than four voices, one of the non-dissonant voices simply must play two notes of the triad, either by a double stop or by moving quickly from one note to the other: the richness of the sonority of Mozart's Divertimento for string trio, which mainly uses the latter method and is sparing of double stops, is a *tour de force* almost miraculous in its ease and variety. (The resolution of certain dissonances will, of course, itself create a triad and therefore demand no more than three-part writing, but some of the basic dissonances of late eighteenth-century harmony, like the dominant seventh, require four voices.) More than four voices gave rise to questions of doubling and spacing, and the woodwind quartet created problems of the blending of tone-color (and, in the eighteenth century, of intonation as well). Therefore only the string quartet and the keyboard instrument allowed the composer to speak the language of classical tonality with ease and freedom, and the keyboard had the disadvantage (and the advantage!) of less striking linear clarity than the string quartet.

After the Quartets op. 33 of 1781, Haydn waited for almost five years before returning to the form, except for the masterly single Quartet op. 42, simple to the point of austerity. From 1786 until his first trip to England in 1791, he produced no less than eighteen works in this form. All these quartets follow the six that Mozart dedicated to him, and many historians find an influence of Mozart in the works of this period. That there was an influence is easy to believe, but isolating it is not without its risks: the beautiful A flat Piano Sonata H. 46 was once dated about twenty years too late because of a supposed influence of Mozart in the slow movement. It is perhaps more practical to assume that by 1785 Mozart and Haydn were working on parallel lines that occasionally converged. Tender and graceful 'second themes,' in particular, generally ascribed to Mozart's ascendancy, are found often enough in earlier works by Haydn for their slightly greater frequency after 1782 to be attributed to the increasing complexity of Haydn's technique, which now enabled him to encompass very different moods within one movement without sacrificing any of the nervous muscularity of his style. Nevertheless, Haydn was certainly strongly affected by Mozart's harmonic range and ease of phrasing.

Written for the King of Prussia, the six quartets op. 50 of 1786 are grander than those of op. 33. The solo cello passages placed as a tactful homage to the royal amateur call forth complementary solo displays from the other instruments, the long solo for second violin at the opening of the slow movement of op. 50 no. 2 being perhaps the most remarkable. The F sharp minor Quartet op. 50 no. 4 contains Haydn's greatest fugal finale, in which the element of academic display present in almost all classical fugues loses itself completely in pathos. In this work, too, Haydn's sense of the unity of a whole quartet has grown immensely; the F sharp major minuet seems only to be an interlude in the major: its key is unstable, continually drawn back to the minor of the first movement. The third quartet of the set, in E flat major, starts with a logically refined, subtle version of the famous joke in the last movement of op. 33 no. 2, which pretends to be finished before the end; in op. 50 no. 3 the recapitulation begins in the middle of the opening theme and continues for considerable length until the cadence on the tonic, one which just lacks that last degree of firmness which would make it absolutely conclusive. Then after a silence of two measures the beginning of the opening theme appears at last, and starts a short but brilliant coda. In all these quartets, the independent solo writing entails an emphatic and complex contrapuntal display, even in the slow movements, which consequently attain a lyrical breadth and a tranquil gravity rare in Haydn until now. The opus as a whole represents a solidification and an expansion of the light-hearted revolutionary procedures of op. 33.

The greater contrapuntal richness of op. 50 may also have a more significant purpose. With the change in style of op. 33 came a considerable simplification: the music was leaner than the great quartets of ten years previously. It is not so much that every advance involves a loss, but rather that Haydn was forced to simplify his textures in order to deal with a new and more complex system of phrasing (the co-ordination of asymmetry within a larger periodic movement) and a new conception of thematic relationships. The partial return to the rich and more 'learned' technique of the High Baroque is an attempt to compensate for this consequent thinness. A simplification to try out a new technique and then a swing back to an elaborate, and sometimes even old-fashioned, counterpoint, was a strategy common to both Mozart and Haydn at various stages of their careers. (The pattern had, in fact, already appeared in Haydn's life before the 1780s. The Quartets op. 17 are sparer and, in most ways, less extravagant than those of op. 9: that was the price of their more advanced technique, and to recapture a former richness, Haydn turned to strict counterpoint in the great Quartets op. 20 of 1772.) For both Haydn and Mozart, as well as for Beethoven, there was an attempt to reconquer the past once the present had been won.

The six quartets, op. 54 and 55, published two years later in 1789, are more experimental: the slow movements, in particular, take on a character even more dramatic than Haydn had ventured before. The swifter pacing of the Allegretto slow movement of op. 54 no. 1 may derive as much from the slow movement of Mozart's F major Concerto K. 459 of 1784 (also an Allegretto) as from previous essays of Haydn in a flowing 6/8 time (op. 33 no. 1, for example). Not only the continuity and the apparently artless and melancholy simplicity, but the chromatically sensuous harmonic movement are more often found in Mozart than in Haydn. The second movement of op. 54 no. 2 is far stranger, with a rhapsodic solo violin part in a written-out rubato that delays melodic notes so as to produce painful cross-harmonic effects. The rubato of the classical period (as we can see from those passages where

Mozart, Haydn, and Beethoven wrote it out) was used to create the most affecting dissonances: unlike the romantic *rubato* (and the one most in use today), it was not just a delaying of the melody, but a forced overlapping of the harmony as well. I should imagine that as a kind of suspension it was originally related to the appoggiatura, the most expressive of ornaments and almost always a dissonant note. (The dramatic middle section of the slow movement of op. 54 no. 3 also shows a brief use of the same *rubato* in a strangely violent passage, and this movement has a nervous rhythmic power characteristic of Haydn, but unusually and even astonishingly effective here.) Even more curious is the presence, in op. 54 no. 2, of a second slow movement, as the finale is an extended Adagio, with a Presto middle section which is actually a concealed variation, a rare example of an enigmatic form in this period. The ear is oddly satisfied, but the mind can only grasp the relation with difficulty in performance. The harmonies in the trio of the minuet that just precedes sound equally enigmatic and equally right as they derive from the strange harmonic effects arising in the solo violin's *rubato* in the first slow movement.

The second movement of op. 55 no. 1 is monothematic and in 'slow-movement sonata form' (i.e., without a central development section), but the customary secondary development after the recapitulation is so impressive that Tovey has held up the piece as a rare example of rondo form in a slow tempo. The last movement is almost a sketch for the great finale of the *Clock Symphony*: it starts in rondo style, squarely cheerful, but the first return of the main theme becomes an extended triple fugue. At the end the theme returns amiably, in all its original simplicity, and the triple fugue has served as a development section. Op. 55 no. 2 in F minor starts with its slow movement, a double variation form of great depth: the stormy Allegro in first-movement form takes second place.

The mature power and variety of the six quartets op. 64, which followed a year later, were never surpassed by Haydn. The B minor Quartet no. 2 looks back to op. 33 no. 1 not only in its ambiguous opening in D major, but even in the shape of its thematic material in the first movement. The exquisite Adagio uses a slow four-note scale figure, transposing it to the dominant, inverting it, and ornamenting it: for all its presence everywhere in the melody, the figure is not used as a series, but as a *cantus firmus* on which a florid and expressive decoration is draped. Op. 64 no. 3 in B flat major is one of the great comic masterpieces: the listener who can hear the last movement without laughing aloud knows nothing of Haydn. Both op. 64 no. 4 in G major and no. 5 in D (the *Lark*) have a double recapitulation of the main theme, but for entirely different reasons: the *Lark*, because its principal melody is a violin solo high on the E string, which cannot be developed, only played simply in all its glory—it appears untouched in the development at the subdominant and is then abandoned until the recapitulation; the G major, partly because the main theme appears briefly a second time in the exposition, but mainly because the first recapitulation goes almost at once to the tonic minor, and appears to be a false reprise—it is nothing of the sort, however, as it stays at the tonic to recapitulate essential material of the second group (much of which was in the dominant minor). A false false-reprise is an exceptionally sophisticated irony even for Haydn, and a second beginning of the main theme at the tonic after an emphatic pause restores equanimity. Most original in the *Lark* is the wide spacing of the registers, with a new range and openness of sonority.

I have hesitated to mention perhaps the most striking innovation of Haydn's string-quartet writing: its air of conversation. Subjective impressions are awkward to analyze, but this is too important a characteristic of Haydn's to leave without trying to isolate it. The combination of independence of voice-leading with a retention of the early classical emphasis on hierarchy of melody and accompaniment, the conception of the phrase as an articulated member with a clearly marked cadence or half-cadence at the end which gives it the air of a lucid proposition—all this will only go part of the way to an explanation. The opening of the Quartet in E major op. 54 no. 3 may help us further:

The second violin and viola begin a melody, and are literally interrupted at once by the violin, which takes immediate precedence. In the fourth and fifth measures the two middle voices try once more, and are again interrupted. The sociable comedy of Haydn's art becomes radiant at the end of the eighth measure: the second violin and viola, resigned, give up their phrase and accept the first violin's melody; begin it—and are again comically interrupted. Perhaps the wittiest point is that now (m. 9–10) the first violin retorts this time with the emphatic *end* of his opening phrase (m. 3–4) transposed up a ninth, and telescoping the original periodic movement. All the dramatic asymmetries melt into the regular phrasing, and what seems at one moment to be pure musical pattern appears suddenly as dramatic wit.

This passage is like a model for a dramatic and yet conversational dialogue in a comedy, in which the content of the words has become irrelevant to the wit of the form (although I should not wish to imply that the harmonic significance of this opening does not contribute to its vitality). The isolated character of the classical phrase and the imitation of speech rhythms in all of Haydn's chamber music only enhance the air of conversation. Eighteenth-century prose in England, Germany, and France had become, in comparison with the previous age, much more syntactic, relying more exclusively on balance, proportion, shape, and the order of the words than did the heavier cumulative technique of the Renaissance. The eighteenth century was cultivatedly self-conscious about the art of conversation: among its greatest triumphs are the quartets of Haydn.

2

Symphony

Our time has blurred the line between public and private forms of art, but Haydn's symphonies speak primarily to the listener, not to the players, as the quartets do. This distinction between symphonic and chamber music was, if anything, accentuated during Haydn's lifetime. Many solo passages in the earlier symphonies seem to exist as much for the performers' enjoyment as for the audience's, and in the small musical world at Esterházy, where Haydn worked for so many years, it may have been politic to keep the important musicians happy with frequent opportunities to display their virtuosity. Orchestral music in the 1760s at Esterházy and elsewhere was still in conception a relatively intimate affair, in spite of the existence of several famous orchestras, but in the last quarter of the century composers began to take more and more notice of the possibilities of very large ensembles, and their music reflects this new fact of concert life. In 1768, Haydn was still able to write: 'I prefer a band with three bass instruments—cello, bassoon and double bass—to one with six double basses and three celli, because certain passages stand out better that way.'[1] By the 1780s, Haydn's orchestration had certainly progressed beyond this stage, which represents a taste midway between chamber and orchestral styles. Ten years later, the Viotti orchestra he used in London for his last concerts there was a large one, and by this time the different orchestral colors are less contrasted and opposed than blended to form a new kind of mass sonority. The orchestra that Mozart preferred is surprisingly large, but he is quite clear about what he wanted: 40 violins, 10 violas, 6 celli, 10 double-basses (!) and double wind on each part.[2] Even remembering that all the instruments of the time were a little softer than those of the present day, this is still a force almost twice that which any conductor dares to use now for a Mozart symphony. Of course Mozart did not often get an orchestra of such size, but there is no reason today to perpetuate those conditions of eighteenth-century performance which obtained only when there was not enough money to do the thing properly.

Most interesting is the exceptional weight given, towards the end of the century, to the bass instruments. It is evident that as the Baroque contrapuntal style was superseded, and as the figured bass disappeared, the massive

---

[1] *Collected Correspondence & London Notebooks of Joseph Haydn*, ed. H. C. Robbins Landon, London, 1959, page 9.
[2] Mozart, *Letters*, ed. Emily Anderson, London, 1966, Vol. II, page 724.

sound of the bass became as important as the clarity of line. From the letter cited above, it is also apparent that this development was proceeding too fast for Haydn's taste in the 1760s, and it was more than ten years before his own writing took full account of the new sonority. But today's performances of all the later symphonies of Haydn and of Mozart suffer from an insufficient reinforcement of the bass line as well as from a belief that the small orchestras that were so common in the late eighteenth century represent the sonority that Haydn and Mozart had in mind as ideal, and not merely the one they were forced to accept for lack of anything better. From 1780 on, composers wrote their symphonic works with large, heavy-sounding ensembles in mind; performance by smaller groups was only a makeshift, like the performance of some of the Mozart piano concertos with string quintet in place of full orchestra.

The distinction between public and private music implied a distinction in style of performance, too. The virtuoso conductor did not exist until he was invented during the lifetime of Beethoven. When Beethoven explained to individual members of the orchestra how he wanted certain passages played and demanded slight, expressive variations of tempo, it was an orchestral innovation for the time and noticed as an eccentricity. The solo music of the late eighteenth century allowed, of course, for a good deal of freedom and flexibility in performance, but even a quick comparison of one of Haydn's symphonies with a solo sonata will show that the symphony avoids all those effects which require the individual nuances and refinements of *rubato*, even slight, that the sonata demands throughout. The symphonic music is always more coarsely organized, and more tightly written as well: the relative loose-ness of the solo sonatas of the 1770s, with their clearly marked cadences, which can be given so much individuality by the performer, and their more elaborate detail intended to be interpreted and expressively shaped, gives way in the symphonies to overlapping phrases which enforce continuity and to the broader strokes implied by the heavier sonority. To play a symphony of Mozart or Haydn as if it were a sonata, interpreted and molded in an indivi-dual way by a conductor, is to betray its nature, to obscure rather than to reveal. It is not that music in general should be allowed to speak for itself—an impossible principle and doubly mistaken as regards any work written with a solo interpreter in mind—but rather that it should be performed with-out distorting its character, and the freedom of the virtuoso conductor does not add a new grace to Mozart but only obscures an old one. Above all, the elaborate but firm rhythmic organization of a Mozart symphony requires a steady tempo in order for it to speak to us clearly.

The music of the nineteenth century, on the other hand, demands the services of the virtuoso conductor, and Brahms, Tchaikovsky, and Strauss are unthinkable without him. With Beethoven, however, some prudence is still required. Even the late orchestral works like the Ninth Symphony clearly imply a performance with few of the individual refinements of tone, accent, and tempo of the sonatas and quartets: the music stands alone without these embellishments, which are, in the more intimate works, not embellishments but necessities of style. Here, some variation of tempo as well as other nuances are essential: Beethoven himself, in sending a metronome mark for a song to the publisher, said that the indication was only valid for the opening measures because no metronomic restriction could be put upon sentiment. In late Beethoven, in particular, *espressivo* certainly means a *ritenuto* as can be seen in the markings of the Sonatas, op. 109 (*un poco espressivo* followed by *a tempo*) and 111 (where every *espressivo* is accompanied by *ritenente*). Changes of tempo, however, must always be understood as coming under a large and controlling idea of the rhythm. I have no wish further to impugn the testimony of Beethoven's friend Schindler—who wrote many years after Beethoven and under the influence of a much later aesthetic, and who has been sufficiently attacked for his romantic overinterpretations—but even he is quite firm that when Beethoven said that the pace of the Largo of the D major Sonata op. 10 no. 3 must be changed ten times, the composer himself added, 'but only so as to be heard by the most sensitive ear.' It is evident from this that Beethoven wished a movement, whatever the variations in pace motivated by the expression, to sound throughout *as if it were in one tempo*, and in this he remains firmly within the bounds of the tradition of Mozart and Haydn. The solo music of the period just before Mozart, from 1750 to 1770, however, does not by any means require this kind of rhythmic unity. It is even inappropriate to much of the work of Gluck and Philipp Emanuel Bach, although it should be added that in the latter's work the rhapsodic freedom of the solo music can never be transferred to the orchestral works.

This need, not only for rhythmic strictness but also for a much simpler and even more literal interpretation of late eighteenth-century symphonic music, is more easily grasped when we read Haydn's letter of October 17, 1789, about the advanced and difficult Symphonies 90–92:

> Now I would humbly ask you to tell the Princely *Kapellmeister* there that these 3 symphonies [90–92] because of their many particular effects, should be rehearsed at least once, carefully and with special concentration, before they are performed.[1]

This represents, again, the worst traditions of the eighteenth century, and it would be ridiculous to take it as a standard or guide for the present. But it explains the existence of a special symphonic style in which even the greatest complexity of musical idea was conceived in terms of a straightforward execution, and which can only be marred by the imposition of later standards of orchestral virtuosity. A straightforward execution, of course, is by no means a straightforward affair any longer, and every musician, orchestral or otherwise, when playing the music of the classical period, has irrelevant and ingrained habits of performance derived from later styles.

---

[1] Haydn, *Correspondence*, page 89.

The development of Haydn as a symphonist raises one of the great pseudo-problems of history: the question of progress in the arts. The achievements of 1768 to 1772 are very great ones in a style that Haydn almost at once abandoned. In these years he wrote a series of impressive symphonies in minor keys—dramatic, highly personal, and mannered. The most important, in roughly chronological order, are the G minor no. 39, the *Passione* no. 49, the *Trauer Symphonie* no. 44, the C minor no. 52, and the *Farewell* no. 45. To these symphonies, more significant than all but a few of those in the major mode of the same years, must be joined the great Piano Sonata in C minor of 1770, H. 20.[1] The Quartets opp. 17 and 20, written in 1771 and 1772, are all—in major or minor—on a level that no other composer of Haydn's time could equal or even approach, and in assessing the level he had reached, one must also add the beautiful slow movement of the Piano Sonata in A flat H. 46. None of these works gives a clear indication of the direction that Haydn was to take, and one might imagine the history of music to be very different if only he had explored the paths suggested in some of them. They seem to presage not the sociable and lyrical wit of his later work (and of Mozart's), but a style harshly dramatic and fiercely emotional without a trace of sentimentality. Taken on their own terms the works of the late 60s and early 70s inspire admiration: they are defective only when measured by the standards of Haydn's later works. Why then do we impose these standards? Why do we refuse the same tolerance to the early work of an artist that we grant—indeed, insist upon granting—to an earlier style? No one, for example, would reproach Chaucer with a failure to shape his verse in the dramatic speech rhythms of the Elizabethans, Masaccio with a lack of the atmospheric integration of High Renaissance painting, or Bach with a refusal to seek the rhythmic variety of the classical style.

The analogies are, however, less pertinent than we who love so many of the early works of Haydn would like them to be. A style is a way of exploiting and controlling the resources of a language. J. S. Bach's mastery of the contemporary language of tonality was as complete as could be imagined, but in the twenty years between his death and the *Sturm und Drang* symphonies that Haydn wrote in the early 70s, this language had changed significantly: the syntax was less fluid, the relation between tonic and dominant more highly polarized. Haydn's style of 1770, while it had taken account of the development, was not yet able to embrace its full implications. The higher degree of articulation of phrase and polarity of harmony raised problems for continuity that were difficult to solve: the shapes and rhythms move without

---

[1] The G minor Sonata H. 44 may belong here as well, but I think it is now being dated too early as it used to be dated too late. Its co-ordination of harmony, accent, and regular cadence would place it later than 1770, and perhaps after 1774. Its publication with works of the late 60s does not give so cogent a reason for dating it with them when it is recalled that one of the other sonatas in the group is not by Haydn at all as the publisher claimed. A batch as mixed as that could have been heterogeneous in other ways as well.

transition from the squarely regular to the unsystematic, relying in the latter case almost entirely upon repetition or upon Baroque sequences to justify the sense of motion. This dichotomy can be felt most strongly in pages like the opening of the *Farewell* Symphony, where all the phrases are not only of the same length but of exactly the same shape, and where a later departure from this regularity (mm. 33 on) is almost entirely sequential in nature. The classical ideal of balanced asymmetrical variation within a large period is only dimly foreshadowed.

It should be clear, in fact, that if today we judge the fine symphonies of 1772 by a standard of coherence that the works themselves do not impose (and which were only arrived at by Haydn years after), this standard is met not only by the later work of Haydn but also, within an earlier state of the tonal language, by Bach and Handel. It is not therefore paradoxical that we should refuse the criteria of excellence implicit in the *Sturm und Drang* works, while granting those of the early eighteenth century. There is no 'progress' between Bach and late Haydn, only a change in the musical 'vernacular.' There is, however, a genuine progress in style between early and late Haydn: the younger Haydn is a great master of a style that only imperfectly realizes what the language of his time had to offer, the later is the creator of a style that is an almost perfect instrument for exploiting the resources of that language. (In all this, I am, I hope, begging the question of the extent to which changes in style themselves precipitate changes in the common language.)

It is a delicate point, and an idle one, whether Haydn could have arrived at so richly complex and so controlled a style by continuing in the direction that may have seemed so finely promising in 1770. Hindsight is cruel to un-realized possibilities. Yet it is worth remarking that the greatest success of Haydn's early style, its fierce dramatic power, was inseparable there from a harsh simplicity, a refusal of complex control, and a willingness at times to break almost any rhythmic pattern for the sake of a single effect. It is diffi-cult to see how a richer art could have arisen from this often brutal contrast between a coarse but urgent regularity and a dazzling eccentricity, except by abandoning the very virtues which made the style of the early 1770s so compelling—which is, indeed, what Haydn did. It is, perhaps, a pity that with the attainment of a more disciplined style, some of the fierce energy that was so admirable had gone out of his art. His later style could support such fierceness (as Beethoven was able to show almost at once), but the dis-cipline of comedy which transformed and enriched Haydn's style left an ineradicable impression on his musical personality.

I do not wish to give the impression that his art around 1770 was all emotion, drama, and effect: it had already a formidable intellectual power. A fine example of this musical logic is the Symphony no. 46 in B major, of 1772, with the surprising return of the minuet in the middle of the finale, an anticipation of the return of the scherzo in the last movement of Beethoven's Fifth Symphony. As in Beethoven, it is not the opening of the minuet that returns: Haydn has chosen to begin at exactly the moment that the minuet resembles the main theme of the finale. The opening measures of the last movement are:

and here even the phrasing, emphasized by the omission of the accompanying voice on the third beat, is related to the return of the minuet:

But these measures are themselves, for the ear if not on paper, a backward version of the original opening of the minuet:

(Haydn was concerned with cancrizans or back-to-front effects at that time, and it is interesting to see how it takes a freely audible, rather than theoretically strict, form here.) All these shapes come directly from the third and fourth measures of the first movement:

thus demonstrating the logic of Haydn's imagination. It should be clear, however, that these are striking effects with little power to range beyond their immediate context.

Thematic relationships of this sort, while the easiest to write about and in some ways the easiest to perceive, are actually the least persuasive and the least compelling. They work less directly on the nerves, communicate less physical excitement than harmonic movements and relationships of pulse and rhythm. (Of course, any hard-and-fast separation of these elements of music is nonsense, and even a theoretical division can be abused.) The kind of thematic relationships that Haydn employs to such effect in Symphony no. 46 are, in fact, common enough throughout the early eighteenth century; what is interesting here is that they are used with dramatic point as never before. They have, in short, become events. But these events arrive unsupported by the rhythmic and harmonic conceptions, which allow them to take place but in no way reinforce them. The thematic logic remains isolated.

The weakness of Haydn's early style, in fact, viewed from the heights of his later work, is not in its logical relations, nor in its moments of drama and poetry, but in the passages of necessary prose. Haydn could manage tragedy or farce, and even magnificent strokes of high comedy. His middle style was awkward. It was at times difficult for him to impart urgency or energy to material of a more sober cast. Even in the opening of as fine a symphony as the *Mercury*, no. 43 in E flat major, his struggles are apparent:

The series of weak endings on the tonic is viable only if one does not expect anything from the phrase which will imply an articulate shape and a necessary continuation. The relaxed beauty of this beginning is evident, but a style which will accept it at the price of such a flaccid co-ordination between cadential harmonies and large-scale rhythm can reach a dramatic effect only through the extraordinary. The later Haydn is dramatic without effort, as a matter of course and with the most everyday material. In this passage, we can see Haydn beginning to struggle: not only the opening *forte* chords for each phrase but also the successive elongation of the phrase-length attempt to enforce a sense of growing energy. We must not ask for more success as we listen further, but the faster rhythm of measure 27 is not persuasive because it is not what it would like to be: it is not faster at all, but only an extra excitement in the violins.

This kind of writing is not rare in Haydn around 1770; the opening of the Quartet in D major op. 20 no. 4 almost duplicates the above:

The beginning of the A flat Sonata H. 46 for piano shows the same limping tonic cadences, which enforce nothing beyond themselves:

and the same unprepared animation, convincing only if one does not put too high a price upon one's convictions.

To characterize Haydn's symphonic development after 1772 is not easy, partly because of its continuity. The break in quartet-writing made the difference between the new achievement of op. 33 of 1781 and the earlier op. 20 of 1772 much simpler to grasp; the change in symphonic style appears more tentative because it was more gradual. Many of the symphonies of the 1770s, too, are arrangements of music originally intended for the stage. The composition of operas, mainly comic, was evidently occupying too much of Haydn's time now for him to devote so much concentration to either chamber music or pure symphonic works. But there are still twenty symphonies written between 1773 and 1781, a large, varied, and uneven production. The broad outlines of Haydn's progress are clear enough, starting with the restraint put upon his most characteristically violent inspirations, and the new smoothness of surface. Most significant, however, in the late 70s is the synthesis of continuity and articulation, a beautiful understanding of the ways that accent and cadence could be combined to form an impelling sense of movement without falling back on the unvaried rhythmic textures of the Baroque.

Sometime during the 1780s, Mozart jotted down the opening themes of three of Haydn's symphonies, nos. 47, 62, and 75, undoubtedly with an eye to conducting them at his concerts. Symphony no. 47 in G major is a typical work of 1772, one of Haydn's most brilliant and satisfying. The second parts of the minuet and trio, which are their first parts played backward note for note, are only the least subtle of the surprises in this work. Most agreeable about these cancrizans, however, is Haydn's device for ensuring our awareness of what he has done:

The *forte* accents on the first beat, reappearing on the third, turn an academic exercise into a witty and intellectual effect. Mozart evidently found the melody of the slow movement particularly successful, as he recalled it in the B flat major serenade for winds, K. 361, but thickened its two-part counterpoint. Haydn's melody has, indeed, an almost Mozartean grace:

and the later inverting of these two voices displays a skill in double counterpoint that rivals the minuet's *al rovescio*. As with every composer except Schubert, Haydn's real education took place in public; however, the use of contrapuntal technique was not experiment but the necessary reinforcement of a style too thin as yet to be commensurate with Haydn's ideals. Even in the slow movement, these devices remain somewhat extraneous to the music's inner tensions and to its essential feeling for harmonic conflict. Still more of an alien intrusion upon a blandly formed scheme is the opening of the recapitulation of the first movement, which uses an effect derived from the Neapolitan symphonists: beginning in the minor without any previous warning or preparation.[1] It is a measure of Haydn's art of the period that any

---

[1] The tonic minor can be used in a recapitulation as a substitute for the subdominant, but its startling appearance here in place of the tonic major precludes any such interpretation: the key does not resolve tensions but adds a new one.

attempt to integrate his most dramatic ideas into a coherent scheme would only ruin them. Nevertheless, that Haydn became a significantly greater composer ten years later is no reason for not admiring this splendid symphony as Mozart evidently did.

The influence of operatic style is evident in the second of the symphonies that interested Mozart, no. 62 in D major, recently dated around 1780, but perhaps composed a few years earlier—the manuscript of the first movement, in any case, which existed separately as an overture, is dated 1777. A brilliant, lively piece, this movement was also used as an alternate finale to the *Imperial* Symphony, no. 53, a function for which its operatic style clearly fits it: it is lightweight for a first movement. In other symphonies of this time made up of music originally meant for the theater, Haydn's concern for unity is as minimal as it is here; *Il Distratto*, no. 60, 'that old pancake' as Haydn later called it, is particularly heterogeneous. In no. 62 the air of potpourri is increased by the fact that all the movements are in the same key, as in a Baroque suite; the contrasts of key had by then become almost taken for granted in a symphony. The slow movement, an Allegretto, is a most curious work: the opening measures

and, indeed, most of the piece, are not only derived from the least possible material—two notes and a banal accompaniment *con sordini*—but impudently display it in a way unusual for Haydn. The ostentatiously naïve sound of the accompaniment, in spite of the poetry that is drawn from it, seems to imply some exterior motivation, as if derived from music written for the stage, like so many of Haydn's works at that time. The last movement has been cited above (p. 113) for its ambiguous opening and for the smoothly efficient logic of Haydn's growing technique.

Haydn's operatic experience as both conductor and composer gave him an invaluable lesson in the relation of musical form to action. The eternal problem in opera is not of expressing or reinforcing action and sentiment—

this would leave us with background music for poetry readings or the films—but of finding a musical equivalent for action which will stand alone as music. It is an insoluble problem: Mozart and Wagner came closest of all composers to solving it, and none of their operas would entirely hold up as a work of absolute music without the words or the actions. Moreover, the problem is meant to be insoluble: when the music achieves absolute intelligibility without the drama, it detaches itself, lives on as independently as the Overture to *Leonore* no. 3, and ceases to exist as opera. The attainment of the ideal would kill the species almost by definition, but it remains as the goal, the point of infinity towards which each work tends: a state in which every word, every feeling, every action on the stage has not only its musical parallel, but its musical justification as well. For this, one needs a style in which violent disruptions of texture—harmonic, rhythmic, and purely sonorous—can be integrated and given a purely musical coherence.

Haydn found this style at about the same time as Mozart, and, although he never arrived at Mozart's sense of long-range movement or his handling of harmonic areas on a very large scale, he applied this new coherence magnificently to the field of purely instrumental music. The relation of music to action in opera has its analogue in absolute music as well. In a style as articulated as that of the late eighteenth century, where the music had become a series of clear events and not merely a cumulative flow, a powerful emotion or a dramatic intensity could no longer rely on High Baroque continuity and would have ended—did, indeed, so end in many works —by smashing the frame of the piece and by dissipating its force. Haydn learned from opera a style that could concentrate that force as he had never been able to do in the 1760s, and with it he effected a synthesis between the tuneful Rococo *Gemütlichkeit* of Austria and North German expressive mannerism, both of which he had already mastered, but rarely been able to combine.

Mozart, brought up in the more comfortable style and already the composer of music whose prettiness alone amounted almost to genius, arrived at the same point from the opposite direction. *Opera buffa* was his school, as well. It stimulated and developed his talent for dramatic expression; Haydn's needed no stimulating, but a chance to be organized and to achieve balance. Operatic experience serves to curb and tame as well as to inspire the feeling for drama. In opera a composer has a certain freedom that purely instrumental music does not grant: the public will forgive coarseness of conception and lapses from musical decorum for the sake of drama, and, in general, the logic of the music and of the book can be considered loosely as intertwined strands, only at rare moments becoming completely unified. But the composer must pay for his freedom by the constraint of bending his imagination to a form not originally musical. The cleverest librettists of the century, like Metastasio, prided themselves on supplying books that gave the musician all he needed and left him full play, but all they actually did at their best was to provide words which fitted the operatic forms that had served in the past—the cavatina, the da capo aria—and to construct scenes in which the singers could give vent to the static display of sentiment that was so ingrained in the style of the High Baroque. Until Mozart forced the hand of his librettists,[1] even comic opera, hidebound by habit, cliché, and a limited repertory of forms, was a strait-jacket as confining as a crab canon, and could have been satisfactory only to a composer like Piccinni, whose urge to dramatic gesture was minimal in spite of all his spirited tunefulness. *Opera buffa* could be a discipline as rigorous as the most academic forms, and it was of the highest importance for two crucial and related aspects of the classical style: the integration of dramatic events within symmetrically resolved closed forms, expanding these forms without changing their essential nature; and the development of a rapidily moving and clearly articulated large rhythmic system that unified the smaller phrase articulations, and gave a cumulative force to the animating impulses sufficient to override the inner cadences. With the sense of the event or individual action and the new technique of an almost systematized intensity, the classical style became at last capable of drama even in non-theatrical contexts.

The application of dramatic technique and structure to 'absolute' music was more than an intellectual experiment. It was the natural outcome of an age which saw the development of the symphonic concert as a public event. The symphony was forced to become a dramatic performance, and it accordingly developed not only something like a plot, with a climax and a dénouement, but a unity of tone, character, and action it had only partially reached before. Unity of action was, of course, one of the classical requirements of tragedy, and the symphony as drama gradually abandoned every trace of the looseness of the suite. By 1770 Haydn needed no lessons in dramatic character or expression: what he added to his equipment by 1780 is something of the economy of the stage. His music becomes, not more concise, but less: true dramatic economy is not concision, but clarity of action. His most striking inspirations now unfold with less of the old laconic harshness, and with more reference to their place in a total conception.

This new efficiency is already evident in the third of Haydn's symphonies that Mozart noted, no. 75 in D major, which dates from around 1780 or a little later. It attains grandeur at once in the slow, grave introduction, without the nervous, sinewy brilliance that had generally served Haydn before as a substitute for weight: the musical line is everywhere deeply expressive and unforced. When the introduction turns into a somber minor for more than half its length, and is then followed by a Presto which opens quietly:

---

[1] It is possible that da Ponte understood the dramatic necessities of Mozart's style without prompting; but before his association with da Ponte, Mozart had already bullied several librettists into giving him the dramatically shaped ensembles he so clearly loved.

it is impossible not to think of the overture to *Don Giovanni*, which was to be written only a few years later.

An instructive part of operatic writing is the achievement of symmetrical balance when the words or the action will not admit of a literal repetition of the music: one of the few great strengths of Haydn as an opera composer was his ingenuity at finding splendid formal subterfuges and hidden solutions for problems of this kind, and he transferred to the symphonies of the 1780s some of this new technique. An example of his skill may be found later in the same movement from Symphony no. 75. One part of the 'second group' of the exposition never reappears in the recapitulation:

replacing it is a canonic passage based on the opening theme:

Significantly the two passages, otherwise so unlike, have the same harmonic elements, their shapes emphasizing the same dissonances. They have also the same harmonic function in the larger design, while the later, canonic passage has, in addition, the more typically cadential effect of a *stretto* in a fugue, and its more explicit reference to the opening theme rounds off the form more strikingly. The slow movement, too, must have been exceptionally interesting to Mozart, as the soft hymn-like theme, a type of melody that Haydn appears to have been the first to write, is a model for much of the music that Mozart was later to develop in the *Magic Flute*.

Symphony

Haydn's witty play with the elements of form is now controlled within the structure of the whole work: his effects are far-reaching as well as immediately astonishing. His orchestration, too, now uses color to emphasize and underline form as well as to charm. Solo instruments no longer give the effect of an independent *concertino* (except, of course, in the *Sinfonia Concertante* of the London period), but are integrated within a truly orchestral conception; they play from within the larger body of sound, and rarely in contrast or opposition to it. As a consequence, they play less often alone, but are now given remarkable chances to double each other, as at the opening of the beautiful slow movement of the Symphony no. 88, where the melody is played by the solo oboe and violoncello an octave apart. In the earlier symphonies, the solo passages often stand out as the most exceptional and striking moments, but they are only loosely related to the rest of the piece.

The clarity of definition in Haydn's works of the 1780s together with his new sense of proportion makes possible the greatest play of imagination without disturbing the equilibrium of the whole work. In the first movement of the Symphony no. 89 in F major of 1787, for example, the development and recapitulation delightfully exchange roles. The development section, with all its wide and continuous modulations, contains an almost complete and orderly recapitulation of the melodic outline of the exposition, while the recapitulation fragments the themes and regroups them, resolving everything harmonically at the same time into the tonic of F major. The displacement of function does not disturb the large symmetry of this movement, but only adds to it, as Haydn is now empowered, by the regrouping, to form a mirror symmetry by placing the opening theme's full appearance *after* the second theme, with an enchanting reorchestration for violas and bassoon accompanied by horns, flute, and strings. No work shows better the gap between the academic *post facto* rules of sonata form and the living rules of proportion, balance, and dramatic interest which really governed Haydn's art.

Haydn's new-won classical sobriety was easily mated with his fantasy and his wit. It is now rare when the odd and the eccentric (still as frequent as ever in his work) are not transfigured by poetry. In the little-appreciated Symphony no. 81 of 1783, the opening measures are conceived so as to admit of a subtle and blurred return to the tonic at the recapitulation. The opening is mysterious after the straightforward first chord:

but the recapitulation is far more evasive:

Where is the exact point of return? Somewhere between measures 105 and 110, but it steals in upon us. The pivot upon which this fine and deeply felt ambiguity turns is the mysterious F natural at the opening of the movement above (at measure 3), which inspires the two soft poignant long-held notes at the return (B♭ in measure 96, E♭ at 103). The means of development are the three suspensions at the opening (measures 4–6) which turn into a much longer sequence of suspensions (measures 104–109), ever more expressive as all the winds enter softly one by one. The rapid eighth-note motion is stilled: the tonic does not appear but makes its presence felt gradually, like a light whose distant glow precedes its brilliance. In spite of the blurred contour, the arrival of this recapitulation is a true classical 'event.' The sudden stillness of the rhythm with only the pulsations of the violas and cellos (at measure 94) is a sign that something is about to happen, and the disappearance of this animation (at measure 104) with the tranquil entrances of the winds into the serene harmonic movement tells us that it is happening now. The absence of articulation is not a coquettish reference to traditional ways of beginning a recapitulation, a withholding of the habitual and the expected for the sake of an effect: to refuse to articulate by means of such an extraordinary and moving transition is itself a form of articulation and a decided setting into relief of the moment of resolution.

During the 1780s Haydn wrote more than twenty symphonies, among them the two great sets of six and three symphonies for the Comte d'Ogny (82–87 and 90–92). Haydn's success in Paris was only part of his general European triumph, which had proclaimed him the greatest living composer even before his first trip to England in 1791. There is not a measure, even the most serious, of these great works which is not marked by Haydn's wit; and his wit has now grown so powerful and so efficient that it has become a sort of passion, a force at once omnivorous and creative. True civilized wit, the sudden fusion of heterogeneous ideas with an air paradoxically both ingenuous and amiably shrewd, characterizes everything that Haydn wrote after 1780.

The finest of the symphonies written for Paris is the last, no. 92 in G major, called the *Oxford* because Haydn played it when he received a degree there, having no new one ready in time. The trio of the minuet is high farce: it is impossible for a listener not already in the know to guess where the first beat is at the beginning:

The orchestration is part of the joke, as the winds and strings seem to have different downbeats. Later, by the time the listener has caught on, Haydn shifts the accent, and introduces pauses long enough to throw him off again. This minuet is the greatest of all practical jokes in music. The deeply felt slow movement may be cited for the economy of adding expressive color to a little motif and building a climax:

The chromatic motif in measure 15 reappears in measures 17, 19, and 21, and each time it is less detached, more expansive, and harmonically warmer until the full rich legato at the end. The method is still that of wit, but at the point where it is indistinguishable from fantasy.

The first movement of the *Oxford* is Haydn's most massive expansion of sonata form until then. The material is stripped down to a bare minimum to offer the greatest ease of construction, and every possible event of the recapitulation—the return to the tonic, the move to the subdominant (here the tonic minor is used as a normal substitute), the playing of each of the themes—is a cue for a new development. In one respect, Haydn's technique of expansion in the recapitulation is less sophisticated than Mozart's, as it consists of a periodic return to the first theme, largely unaltered, as a springboard for quasi-sequential developments, while Mozart is able to expand the phrase,

160

or the individual member of the larger form, as he expands the whole. But this distinction cannot be made a reproach to Haydn, as he has deliberately contracted the phrases of the exposition in preparation for the great expansion of the second half of the movement: the recapitulation seems to be made up of separate small bits of the exposition, like a mosaic, but the spirit that put the pieces together had a tough, dynamic conception of the total controlling rhythm that even Mozart could rarely attain outside opera. The following passage from the recapitulation is, indeed, based wholly on one tiny motif, a two-note upward leap:

but this leap—although it is the only *thematic* element that counts here—is not the center of interest, which is now entirely directed to the larger movement, the downward chromatic progression in the bass answered by the swifter and more powerful diatonic rising motion. The sense of detail is still sharp, but everything is commanded by a musical sense that hears far beyond the individual motif. With this work and with Mozart's *Prague*, the classical symphony finally attained the same seriousness and grandeur as the great public genres of the Baroque, oratorio and opera, although without ever aspiring to their enormous dimensions. Haydn equalled but never surpassed the *Oxford* Symphony.

E. T. A. Hoffmann once wrote that listening to Haydn was like taking a walk in the country, a sentiment destined to make anyone smile today. Yet it seizes on an essential aspect of Haydn; the symphonies of Haydn are heroic pastoral, and they are the greatest examples of their kind. I am alluding not only to the deliberately 'rustic' sections of the symphonies—the bagpipe effects, the Ländler rhythms in the trios of the minuets, the imitation of peasant tunes and dances, the melodies based on yodeling. Even more characteristic is the pastoral tone, that combination of sophisticated irony and surface innocence that is so much a part of the pastoral genre. The rustics in pastoral speak words whose profundity is apparently beyond their grasp; the shepherds are not aware that their joys and sorrows are those of all men. It is easy to call the simplicity of the pastoral artificial, but it is this simplicity which is most moving, the country simplicity that speaks with a sharp nostalgia to the urban reader. The symphonies of Haydn have that artful simplicity, and, like the pastoral, their direct reference to rustic nature is accompanied by an art learned almost to the point of pedantry. Haydn's most 'rustic' finales generally contain his greatest display of counterpoint. Nevertheless, the apparent naïveté is at the heart of Haydn's manner. His melodies, like the shepherds of the classical pastoral, seem detached from all that they portend, unaware of how much they signify. Their initial appearance is almost always without the air of mystery and unexplained tension that introduces the themes of Beethoven. The importance of this polished surface for Haydn cannot be exaggerated: his seriousness would be nothing without his air of amiability. His genial tone is the triumph of his new sense of phrase and of the dancing, energetic pulse that unifies so many of his longest works.

Sophisticated simplicity of surface is typical of most seventeenth- and eighteenth-century pastorals, as well as a pretence of opacity, a claim that the surface was everything—with the understanding that if the claim were granted, the whole traditional structure would collapse. This is the irony that underlies the poetry of Marvell, and even the poignance that flows from the landscapes of Claude and Poussin. The pretence that Nature is as we have imagined her to be, and that Phillis and Strephon herd sheep, gives us a form of art more direct than the realistic novel in that its unabashed artificiality openly calls for an act of faith. Pastoral is perhaps the most important literary genre of the eighteenth century: it infected all other forms—the comedies of Marivaux and Goldoni; the philosophical novels of Goldsmith and Johnson; the erotic novels of Prévost, Restif de la Bretonne, and the Marquis de Sade; and the satirical novels and stories of Wieland. Even Voltaire's Candide is basically the shepherd who speaks innocently of truths more universal than he suspects—it is only his world that has turned Nature upside down. In most of these works, the dominant stylistic pattern is a naïveté or simplicity that demands absolutely and without appeal to be taken at face value, even though it is belied by everything else in the work.

The pretension of Haydn's symphonies to a simplicity that appears to come from Nature itself is no mask but the true claim of a style whose command over the whole range of technique is so great that it can ingenuously afford to disdain the outward appearance of high art. Pastoral is generally ironic, with the irony of one who aspires to less than he deserves, hoping he will be granted more. But Haydn's pastoral style is more generous, with all its irony: it is the true heroic pastoral that cheerfully lays claim to the sublime, without yielding any of the innocence and simplicity won by art.

Part IV

SERIOUS OPERA

———

Vous avez écrit votre pièce d'après les principes de la tragédie. Vous ne savez donc pas que le drame en musique est un ouvrage imparfait, soumis à des règles et à des usages qui n'ont pas le sens commun, il est vrai, mais qu'il faut suivre à la lettre.

Carlo Goldoni, *Mémoires,* 1787, Chapter XXVIII

[*You have written your play according to the principles of tragedy. You evidently do not know that musical drama is an imperfect work, controlled by rules and traditions which lack common sense, but which must be followed to the letter.*]

Serious Opera

The problem of eighteenth-century tragedy can only be considered with the limitations of the artistic language in mind—rather, the problem of the failure (or, if you like, the non-existence) of eighteenth-century tragedy. Not only in literature, but in music as well, secular tragedy was the unattainable ideal. *Opera seria* is today a curiosity on the stage; the finest examples have a sort of twilight existence, not as whole works of art, but only by virtue of the fineness of their parts. If we limit, perhaps unwisely, the meaning of 'form' to a way of integrating details within a larger conception, then *opera seria* is not a form at all: it is only a method of construction. The total form was never made to live; the sub-forms are sometimes very much alive indeed—arias from the operas of Cavalli, Alessandro Scarlatti, and Handel, ensembles from Rameau's, almost any page of Mozart's *Idomeneo*. The composer who came closest to real success with the form was Gluck, during the period of experimentation when the classical style had not yet been really fixed and the High Baroque seemed no longer capable of inspiration. At least three of Gluck's operas reached dramatic heights unknown in secular music in the hundred years since Monteverdi (and religious drama in music posed entirely different problems). Yet even here there are pages of such incoherence, harmonically and in particular rhythmically, that Gluck's musical supremacy can be granted only with misgiving.

The failure of Mozart is the most striking. The harmonic and rhythmic coherence that Gluck arrives at only by an effort which leaves the signs of his struggle still perceptible seems to have come to Mozart with an ease granted to no other composer. Yet sometimes in *Idomeneo*, the mastery of large rhythmic movement over a long stretch of time inexplicably seems to have deserted him. The musical action is unconvincing, and yet the inspiration is consistently high. More puzzling still, in an entirely different way, is the case of *La Clemenza di Tito*, Mozart's last opera. Written (in haste, it is true) at a time when Mozart was composing some of his greatest music, it is a work of exquisite grace and rarely redeemed dullness. I have heard it performed, but have never seen it and cannot believe that even the greatest of stagings could save it. *La Clemenza di Tito* has all the finish of Mozart's finest works—Mozart's music is never less than beautiful—but it is difficult to convey how unmemorable it is. Mozart was, indeed, capable of tragedy in his dramatic works, but in comic opera—*opera buffa* and *Singspiel*.

Serious Opera

The inability of even the greatest composer to breathe life into *opera seria* has been blamed on the restricting conventions of the genre. There is, indeed, a certain comic side to a convention that forces the hero, just so that he may be able to return and take a bow, to leave the stage without waiting for an answer immediately after a proposal of marriage couched in the form of an aria. But Mozart himself, in his comic operas, dealt with situations equally destructive of illusion. Constanze, in *Die Entführung aus dem Serail,* when informed by the Pasha of the tortures that await her if she does not yield to his demands, must stand and listen to an introduction at least two minutes long in full concertante style before replying. In present-day performances, the stage director's problems with this aria are almost greater than the singer's, difficult as the coloratura may be with its full-blown written-out cadenza accompanied by solo winds. The director's conscientious realism invariably distracts our attention from the ritornello—how to explain the long wait before the reply? Is Constanze thinking it over? Speechless with rage? Trembling with fear before she can screw up her courage to say that torture will be unavailing? Should she pace? Sit down? Strike one attitude and hold it for the full two minutes? None of this, of course, was a problem during Mozart's time; no such psychological questions were asked. Mozart realized the aria was unconscionably long, and said apologetically that he could not stop, but the problem of holding an audience's interest was not, in the *Singspiel,* more than partially coincident with the question of preserving naturalistic illusion. The soprano waited because a concertante aria of that size and dramatic importance required a long ritornello.

It may be objected that the aria concertante is one of the conventions of *opera seria* rather than of the *Singspiel,* and that the ridiculousness of the situation is a reflection on that already unfortunate genre. But the situation need not seem ridiculous if it is accepted without qualms by the stage director; the aria is dramatically necessary as well as a fine piece of music. The trouble arises partly because directors continue to work in a tradition of naturalistic psychology entirely foreign to eighteenth-century opera, and partly because they cannot conceive of music going on with the curtain up without inventing business to fill what seems to them so much empty time. Today, if Constanze did nothing during the ritornello, this, too, would be felt as an obtrusive effect. What is clear even in a misguided production, however, is the dramatic rightness and force of the aria, and of its place in the opera as a whole, giving the needed weight to the first act, and bringing back the brilliance (and the tonality) of the overture (and therefore of the opera as a whole). There seems to be nothing wrong with the conventions of *opera seria,* provided that they appear within the framework of comic opera.

Even characteristic *buffa* conventions can seem ridiculous enough to any-one who refuses to suspend his disbelief. At the beginning of *Le Nozze di Figaro,* the floor must be measured twice by Figaro only so that his music may be combined with Susanna's. Wagner rejected the convention of repeating everything four or five times mainly because the musical forms which required repetition were obsolete by his time; of course, he gave more philosophical reasons for his decision. But Wagner's own conventions are, in other ways, no less formal and unrealistic: in a Mozart aria, passages are repeated four times mostly at a pace approximating normal speech; in Wagner, everything is sung once but generally four times as slowly. In any case, *opera buffa* has conventions as artificial as those of any other art form: one must accept the idea that it gets dark enough outdoors for a valet to disguise himself as his master by the mere exchange of cloaks; that a young man can go unrecognized by his fiancée if he puts on a false mustache; and that if someone is to get a box on the ear, it is almost always somebody else standing nearby who receives it by mistake. As for the *Singspiel*, its preposterousness is grandiose even when compared to *opera seria*. The failure of eighteenth-century heroic and tragic opera to create enduring works which could still seem artistically relevant to us today cannot be explained by its conventions. Handel and Mozart, at least, succeeded with everything else they put their hands to, and they came near to succeeding with *opera seria*.

A popular explanation of the weakness of *opera seria* is the general failure of tragedy throughout the eighteenth century. The ideal of poetic tragedy was as important in literature as in music, and its failure there was even more disastrous. Individual arias from Handel's operas have lost none of their effect, isolated revivals of *Idomeneo* reveal magnificent sections of great beauty, and Gluck came close to creating a viable style for musical tragedy. Yet the tragedies of Voltaire and Crébillon can only be read today for their historical interest, and Metastasio is intolerable except in the smallest of doses. Even lovers of Addison and Johnson cannot get through more than one act at a time of *Cato* and *Irene*. Undeniably, respect for the high art of tragedy and a failure to produce anything above mediocre examples of it are both characteristic of the period. The evidence for the century's incapacity for tragic art appears to be overwhelming. Why should we expect more from the musicians than from the poets?

The arts often show roughly parallel developments (sometimes by mis-understanding each other), but we cannot assume that success in one is relevant throughout a culture. Elizabethan music has none of the large-scale dramatic qualities to be found in the plays; French painting of the sixteenth century produced nothing to set beside Rabelais; Verdi's operas have no peers in the Italian theater of their day. Even within the confines of one art, two genres may show a striking inequality: eighteenth-century French poetry is a wretched affair compared with the magnificent prose of the time. Yet it is only primitive taxonomy to say that the century of reason and light was a prosaic age. The English eighteenth century, too, we are told, was a prosaic age, but there are Pope, Johnson, and Smart: in France, we must settle for Parny and Jean-Baptiste Rousseau, and it is not much consolation to invoke the spirit of rationalism. It is a mistake to hold the *Zeitgeist* responsible for a crime when one cannot be sure of the *modus operandi*. The eighteenth century may not have been able to produce tragedy, but it was not for lack of aspiration, appreciation nor popular interest. Neither talent nor effort could create an enduring tragic form, while pastoral, a genre equally antique and sclerotic, could be made to live again.

It may be that our understanding is parochially blind to the ideals of another age. The heroic operas of Rameau and Handel, the tragedies of Voltaire and Addison had their admirers, even passionate ones, in their time. It is not, however, the success of eighteenth-century tragedy on its own terms that is being challenged, but its claims to transcend those terms and to break out of its localization in historical time. The exercise of taste is often a definite act of will: Stravinsky was counseled by Rimsky-Korsakov not to listen to Debussy as he might come to like that sort of music. The effort to like *opera seria* has been made. Handel's operas have been brought out of oblivion, and no one can deny that they contain scores of beautiful pages; his invention and imagination were as great in *Giulio Cesare* as in *Israel in Egypt*, but the result is far less satisfactory in the former. Nothing can redeem the weaknesses in every one of Gluck's finest scores, and it is sad to think that a staging of his works is generally an act of archaeological piety. To resuscitate Rameau's operas, even performances with perfume and a Wagnerian orchestra have been tried. As for *Idomeneo*, if it could have been saved for the repertory, it would have happened by now. In this century, opera managers have been delighted to find that *Cosi fan Tutte* and *Die Entführung* could be produced with a success almost equal to that of the already popular *Don Giovanni*, *Figaro*, and *Die Zauberflöte*, and they would be even happier to add a grand tragic opera to the pentalogy. Performances are, indeed, no longer rare. Yet every one, riddled with cuts and rearrangements born of desperation, has the air of a revival.

Neither the High Baroque style of Bach, Handel, and Rameau nor the classical style of Haydn and Mozart was apt for the rendering of secular tragedy, not even of contemporary works like the tragedies of Voltaire. With little possibility of transition, High Baroque rhythm was almost unmanageable for dramatic purposes, and the constant reliance upon falling sequences for harmonic motion only added to the heaviness. Dramatic movement was impossible: two phases of the same action could only be statically represented, with a clear division between them. Even a change of sentiment could not take place gradually: there had to be a definite moment where one sentiment stopped and another suddenly took over. This reduced the heroic opera of the Baroque to a succession of static scenes, with all the rigid nobility of Racine and little of his extraordinary and supple inner movement. The monotony of Baroque opera has been blamed on the massive use of the da capo aria; but the da capo aria is the form best suited to this rhythmic conception, and, in fact, offers the greatest chance of variety and relief in its contrasting middle section. No doubt Handel and Rameau transcended this style and worked miracles with it at moments, but it was not one which lent itself with any ease to dramatic action.

I have spoken above of 'secular' tragedy in order to avoid a quibble about the Passions of Bach and the oratorios of Handel, but the quibble is worth discussing. There can be no question of the dramatic intensity of these works, and it is interesting to see how this is achieved. The dramatic parts of the Bach Passions are concentrated entirely in the recitatives and in some of the choruses; these are set within a framework of personal meditations in the form of arias, and of public meditations in the form of hymns. The whole of the *Passion according to St. Matthew* is framed by two great tableaux: the first, superbly visual, is the road to Golgotha, and the final chorus is the burial of Christ. In this way the static nature of High Baroque style is both accepted and magnificently overcome. Just as Mozart could realize his most heroic and tragic effects only in the setting of *opera buffa*, so Bach arrives at his dramatic effects only in what must be called an elegiac setting. Even the recitatives are not strictly drama but narrative epic, and recitative all by itself is not a musical form that can sustain much interest for any length of time. The dramatic power of Bach's works depends upon the juxtaposition of the recitative with the elegiac arias, the chorales, and the descriptive choruses. High tragedy is achieved only through means that remain largely narrative or pictorial.

Dramatic development being impossible within Baroque style, dramatic juxtaposition must act as a substitute, and this, too, is Handel's solution in the oratorios. In Handel as in Bach, it is the contrast of chorus and solo voice that makes possible the development of a dramatic logic. No oratorio of Handel is organized with the intensity of the two great Bach Passions, with their tight relationship between each part and its neighbors, and the significance of the movement from recitative to commentary in the chorales and the arias. But within the choruses, Handel often shows a dramatic, if not an emotional, force that Bach rarely attempts: where Bach's choruses are generally built from one homogeneous rhythmic texture, Handel can deploy two or more rhythmic blocks, and without making any attempt at transition between them, place them side by side with the most vigorous contrast, and then pile them one on top of another, all of this with a motor energy that has never been surpassed for excitement.[1] This is accomplished with a texture that is considerably thinner than Bach's, and a consequent loss of intensity is compensated by a gain in clarity. Unlike the Bach Passions, the oratorios of Handel are truly public, meant for a concert performance or with simple staging, almost out of place in a church. Handel went bankrupt twice as an operatic impresario and made a good deal of money from his oratorios; the

---

[1] The supremacy of Handel's choruses was recognized throughout the eighteenth century: when Wieland preferred them (and those of Lully) to the arias, he claimed to be expressing a common judgment.

contemporary public may only have reacted with the same kind of enthusiasm to Handel's subjects that an audience today shows for Biblical epics at the movies, but their judgment has endured.

It is therefore not the dramatic or tragic instinct which was lacking in the first half of the eighteenth century, or even the capacity and the genius to achieve it. Missing was a style that could encompass a sustained theatrical effort with the use only of recitative, aria, and solo ensemble; even the latter is rare in Handel's operas and of much greater interest in the oratorios, and the solo ensembles of *Jephtha* and *Susanna* have no parallels of equivalent dramatic force and characterization in the operas. Concentration on the aria, given a style in which interior dramatic development was close to impossible, made Baroque opera a series of display pieces for the singers. There was nothing to set off or enliven the static nature of the individual numbers as convincing as the use of narrative form in the Passions and the oratorios, together with the use of choruses for description and of arias for religious meditation and commentary.

Rameau's avoidance of narrative and elegiac forms—the one so natural for recitative and the other so well adapted to the normal musical structures of the High Baroque—may partly account for his failure to create a large musical work that is completely satisfactory. He makes magnificent use of the chorus, and many of the ensembles are highly developed, but with the unyielding rhythm of the period and a magnetic attraction to the tonic more typical of contemporary French music than of the German school, his scenes tend to separate into marble reliefs, noble, graceful, and oppressively immobile. If heroic tragedy was to be possible in French music, a chorus providing a background and philosophical commentary was necessary, and the possibility of rendering in one musical form a progressively developing conflict rather than a clearly defined opposition would have to be evolved. In other words, French Baroque opera had to become more like Greek drama, if it was not to start all over again on an entirely new basis. This, of course, is exactly what Gluck tried to achieve, with a neoclassic dogmatism and a daring originality typical of the period. If the success was only partial, the effort was heroic.

Gluck is generally described as a composer of genius with astonishingly defective technique. About the genius there is no question at all, and there is little question, if much misunderstanding, of the 'imperfections' that can be found in any of his works. It would be interesting to ask if these 'defects' arose, not from lacunae in Gluck's equipment, but from what he was trying within his historical moment.

The history of music is encumbered by half-exploded theories about the deficiencies of the greatest composers: Beethoven's lack of ease in contrapuntal writing, Chopin's difficulties with large forms, Brahms' awkward orchestrations. These dead horses rise like ghosts, and still require occasional beating. But with Gluck's operas, the faults are, at times, too glaring to be denied or to be turned into virtues by any aesthetic and historical reconsiderations. Nevertheless the faults, to a large extent, derive from the nature of the contemporary style applied to the task that Gluck set for it. To say that the style of the 1760s and 1770s was unequal to the problems of creating a tragic work for the stage may seem only a less specific way of saying that it was Gluck who failed to bend his art to the demands of tragedy. But the first way of putting it has a certain advantage, as it draws our attention to the nature of the style and the demands made upon it by *opera seria* and the renewed interest in Greek tragedy. We may then find some idea of the problems facing Gluck, the purpose of many of his innovations, and the reason for some of his failure. To talk of Gluck's defective technique explains little, and is only an excuse for dismissing that part of the music which we dislike. Not that the criticism is irrelevant or even untrue, and it is in any case sanctioned by tradition. It was Handel who said that Gluck 'knows no more counterpoint than my cook,' and although Tovey has pointed out that Handel's cook, who was also a singer in Handel's opera company, probably knew a good bit of counterpoint, it was surely obstinate of Gluck not to have remedied a defect which would have needed no more than a year's study to bring him up to snuff. It would be more reasonable to assume that Gluck no longer had a need for Handel's counterpoint. When we miss contrapuntal mastery in Gluck, we should recall that he had broken with Handel's style and his kind of mastery, and created something that had not yet arrived at Mozart's ease or at Beethoven's range but which was moving towards them. This kind of historical hindsight is cheap, as Gluck was not in any conscious or unconscious way working towards the same goals as Mozart and Beethoven; but a small dose of teleology may be useful in approaching an historical figure as irritating and as admirable as Gluck.

Motives are generally mixed, and the most variegated of all are the unconscious and unconfessed ones that we of necessity conjecture and read into the past in order to explain historical change. The most evident of Gluck's operatic innovations is his drastic simplification—of action, of form, and of texture. What were the reasons for this reform? The official answer, and Gluck's own, is greater dramatic naturalness. The return to Nature is the reason for almost every dramatic reform, and it is even, of course, true in each case, but it is not always easy to fix what was natural as opposed to artificial, particularly as regards eighteenth-century tragedy: to some extent it meant getting rid of the crippling conventions of the previous generations. The more interesting puzzle, why these conventions just at that time suddenly seemed crippling, is complicated by a further consideration, the rising interest in Greek art and the development of neoclassicism. The Renaissance, largely Roman in the fifteenth and sixteenth centuries (except in France), became predominantly Greek by the eighteenth. This growing enthusiasm for Greek culture, however, was colored by a curious kind of primitivism. The eighteenth-century belief in progress was offset by a nostalgia for a utopian past, which gave an easy outlet to the old belief that the world was continually degenerating, not improving. If the Greeks had achieved an ideal civilization, it was because they were less complicated and sophisticated than the moderns. The eighteenth century tried not so much to imitate the Greeks as to improve on them by attempting a drastic simplicity which had little to do with the Greeks. Writers and architects went back not so much to Greek art as to what they considered the theoretical source of Greek art, to Nature, in short. Greek architecture is not as ostentatiously 'natural' as neoclassic eighteenth-century style could become when it deliberately tried to recall or reconstruct the primitive origin of architectural elements. The derivation of columns from tree trunks so evident to the rationalist mind implied that the use of bases for columns was over-sophisticated, unnatural: the columns in many neoclassic buildings grow straight out of the ground. Neoclassic painting is distinguished not so much by the use of classical subjects—they were common enough since the Renaissance, and even before—but by the moral earnestness with which they were treated; in addition, classical mythology became less important than subjects drawn from history illustrating the civic virtues. Above all, neoclassic painting pretends to none of the emotional complexity of Poussin or Raphael in their treatment of classical subjects: it makes a direct appeal to simple and basic emotions, or such, at least, was the claim.

Neoclassicism is aggressively doctrinaire: it is art with a thesis. This makes the relation of practice to theory a peculiarly sensitive one. Normally, in most styles, the relation is loose and somewhat muddled: artistic theories— that is, those accepted by the artists themselves—may be nothing more than pious sentiments which are justified by tradition or appear to sound well; they may be rationalizations, *post facto* attempts to justify the works already finished by principles which had little to do with their creation (while foreshadowing, perhaps, the direction in which the artist hopes to go); they may, finally, reflect in an oblique or even a direct way the actual practice of the artist. If these different kinds of principles are most often confused (so that artists are either reproached or commended for not practicing what they preach), the excuse for historians—a lame one—is that they are difficult enough to disentangle. In the case of a style like neoclassicism, the problem becomes the more complex as there is a conscious attempt on the part of the artist to make practice follow theory, even when this theory, professed and expounded, collides head on with artistic habits and with less conscious principles which only practice can gradually bring to light. In most neoclassic works, a considerable tension results from this conflict, a desire for theoretical coherence which leads paradoxically at moments to an incoherence within the artistic language, forced into contradiction with itself in order to conform to something exterior. The deliberate cult of the natural leads in neoclassicism to an effort of self-denial and repression which becomes indistinguishable from the 'perverse': it gives the greatest neoclassic works—the operas of

Gluck, the architecture of Ledoux, the paintings of David—an explosive force that is in excess of the works' own pretensions.[1]

What this comes to, in fact, is that the greatness of so much of neoclassicism arises from the incomplete repression of instinct by doctrine (instinct being here nothing more mystical than unformulated doctrine). It has, therefore, the curious result that the theory of neoclassicism is in a special sense built into the works themselves. In Gluck's operas, the examples of classical virtue on which they are based—Alceste, Iphigenia, Orpheus—are not only expressed, but literally illustrated by the chastity of the music itself: the refusal to permit vocal display, the absence of ornament, the endings of arias which leave no possibility for applause, the simplicity of the musical texture with contrapuntal enrichment reduced to the barest essentials. The austerity is not only a form of stoicism, a holding back from pleasure, but one of the main sources of pleasure in itself. There is, of course, no virtue in refusing to yield to what does not tempt; Gluck's reduction in the number of roulades he would write for singers and his attempt to escape the da capo form which would allow them the chance to improvise are no longer artistically impressive. What is far more significant are the moments of strained simplicity, where Gluck is obviously denying himself something he loved. The severity of much of his finest work is analogous to the box-like space and metallic colors of David, and the pure geometrical forms of Ledoux, all of which have a significance as much ethical as aesthetic.

The theory of art as an imitation of Nature is an ancient piety: neoclassicism gave it a new force by a simplistic and even primitivist view of Nature. The doctrine of the imitation of Nature gave rise to such difficulty in music (in painting the application was so self-evident as to retard aesthetics for centuries) that it had to be completely rephrased: music imitated—or, better, represented and expressed—the purest and most natural feelings, and was to be judged by its success or failure at this task. Along with neoclassic doctrine, eighteenth-century psychological ethics implied a considerable reduction of sophistication of feeling; coloratura virtuosity did, surely, express feeling, but of an 'unnatural' and unacceptable kind. In any art so closely involved with its own theory, the influence of political and educational thought was inevitable: Gluck's music is as much affected by the ideas for which Rousseau was the greatest spokesman as by the revived interest in classical virtue. This restressed relationship between music and feeling tied operatic music emphatically to the words almost at the very moment that Mozart was about to achieve its emancipation by making the music not so much an expression of

---

[1] I have used 'neoclassicism' in a narrow sense of a return to the assumed simplicity of Nature through the imitation of the ancients. The body of doctrine in the eighteenth century was coherent, cohesive, and supranational. Gluck claimed that the accent of Nature in music would abolish the absurdity of national styles. The aesthetics of neoclassicism may be summed up in Winckelmann's belief that the thinnest line was the most apt for the portrayal of a beautiful form.

the text (although still partially that) but an equivalent for the dramatic action. Mozart's achievement was revolutionary: for the first time on the operatic stage, the music could follow the dramatic movement while still arriving at a form that could justify itself, at least in its essentials, on purely internal grounds.

Before Mozart (or before the development of the Italian comic opera for which Mozart was to find a definitive form), a musical drama had always been so arranged that the more formally organized music was reserved for the expression of feeling—generally only one sentiment at a time—in an aria or duet, while the action was left to be conveyed in recitative. This meant that except in so far as the music had values of its own unrelated to the drama, it remained essentially an illustration and expression of the words; it could only be combined with the action in the most primitive way and in the least interesting fashion. This primacy of the text reigns from the start, even in Monteverdi, where the difference between aria and recitative, between more and less formally organized structure, is not always clear-cut. This does not at all imply that the music took a servile position, but it does impose a hierarchy in the transmission of meaning: the music interprets the text, and the text interprets the action—the words standing in almost every case between the music and the drama. An aesthetic of music as the expression of feeling was ideal for Baroque opera: it fitted the da capo aria like a glove, with its homogeneous rhythmic texture, its principle of additive extension of a central motif, and its relatively equal distribution of tension throughout—even the contrast provided by the middle section was so static as to raise no contradiction. The difficulty—leaving aside for the moment the rupture between music and the essential scenic movement—is that in so far as music is an expressive art, it is pre-verbal, not post-verbal. Its effects are at the level of the nerves and not of the sentiments. For this reason, in music like the Baroque da capo aria, devoted to the depiction of one sentiment or *Affekt*, the words come to seem like a commentary, generalized and denatured, on the music. The musical line speaks directly to the listener, and the singer adds, as a bonus, the words which can act only as a sort of dampening program notes. Opera cannot exist without an aesthetics of expression, but a complete subservience to it destroys the possibility of drama. It is from this fundamentally static aesthetic that arise all the problems, all the malaise encountered in the production of Baroque opera today, and it is significant that the Mozart comic operas, which partially broke with the aesthetic of expression, have held the stage continuously and successfully since their composition. *Figaro*, *Don Giovanni*, and *Die Zauberflöte* are the first operas that have never had to be revived.

If Gluck appeared to accept an aesthetic of expression and, indeed, to give it a new force by an exquisite and unparalleled concentration on details of declamation, there are signs in his work that its static implications caused him a certain uneasiness. There are a number of experiments of arias in continually changing tempi, the most remarkable being Alceste's 'Non, ce n'est point un sacrifice.' For the most part, these different tempi are treated as

173

separate blocks; in all of Gluck's music there are only a few hints that a rhythmic transition is even attempted. The aria from *Alceste* is one of Gluck's most successful works, and without calling either its greatness or its beauty into question, it must be said that the scheme of so many different tempi is a measure of desperation. Within the frame of one piece, Gluck seems almost always to experience grave difficulties in changing the rhythmic movement. The following measures from the Overture of *Iphigénie en Tauride* have an effect of clashing gears when the change arrives:

and such passages are not infrequent.

Seen from the viewpoint of the classical style, Gluck's rhythmic system contains an important contradiction. The phrasing is classically articulated, while the pulse-beats are only very weakly differentiated in a manner better suited to Baroque continuity. In Paris' aria 'Di te scordarmi,' from *Paride ed Elena*, one phrase appears in two forms:

The second form in the minor takes half a measure less, and surely gains in concentrated force. Comparing the two forms, it is difficult, however, to see whether much distinction has been made between the force of a first and of a third beat: the phrase in the minor begins with a more dramatic accent, but after this the rhythmic impulse is oddly more fluid than the phrasing. In the music of Haydn and Mozart, such shifts in 4/4 time occur frequently, but (at least after 1775) it is always clear exactly what has happened: either there is a phrase of unusually irregular length, so that the downbeat has now shifted temporarily to the third beat (later composers would write a single 2/4 measure and move all the bar-lines), or the downbeat retains its force and we are to hear the phrase-articulation as a syncopated accent against the beat. The choice is not so clear-cut in Gluck, and there are many such ambiguous passages throughout the operas.

Because of this rhythmic looseness, Gluck's greatest achievements resolve into a series of tableaux, some of them magnificently conceived. In one important respect, there is an astonishing advance upon earlier *opera seria:* that is, in the idea of psychological contradiction and tension within the frame of a single movement. The most famous of such moments is Orestes' pathetic belief that he has found peace while his inner turmoil is so evident in the music, but the anguished hesitation of Helen in *Paride ed Elena* is as striking:

the syncopations, the cross-rhythms, and the half-parlando declamation are combined with great originality.

Still more original is Gluck's conception of dynamic accent. It is true that the rhythmic texture retains the almost total homogeneity of the High Baroque, but the dynamics thrust in an entirely new element. Most of the greatest passages in Gluck rely in one way or another upon a rhythmic ostinato, which is given shape by accent and by an irregularity of super-imposed articulation: the conception of the static tableau is being destroyed by pressure from within. The most remarkable and largest construction of this kind is Iphigenia's aria with chorus from *Iphigénie en Tauride*, Act II, scene VI, but it must be quoted at great length before any of its power can be understood. An almost equally moving ostinato is found in the trio of the last act of *Paride ed Elena*:[1]

---

[1] Gluck was sufficiently pleased with this trio to use it in *Orphée* as well.

The free-flowing declamation against the syncopated ostinato, the tension imposed on the texture by the *sforzandi*—all this has no parallel within the classical style. It appears in opera again with the Italian romantic style, above all with the ostinati of Verdi (an example close to the above is Otello's exhausted monologue in Act III). However, the true inheritor of Gluck is, to no one's surprise, Berlioz, for whom the conception of a syncopated ostinato reinforced by accent is central: the 'Lacrimosa' from the *Requiem* could never have come into being without Gluck.

Mozart owes an important artistic debt to Gluck, above all in the dramatic power of his accompanied recitatives. There are even occasional clear references to Gluck's personal style, as in the Chaconne from *Idomeneo*. Nevertheless, it is surprising how many of Gluck's most successful and suggestive innovations seem not even to have existed for Mozart. He owed almost nothing to Gluck's declamation in the arias, or to his conception of accent; he never tried Gluck's experiment of multiple and fluid tempo changes within an aria; and only at the end of his life, in *Zauberflöte,* did he use an operatic chorus with Gluck's majesty (and even then did not aim at Gluck's dramatic force, except in the off-stage pianissimo phrase for chorus at the end of Tamino's scene with the priest). Beethoven owes perhaps even less to Gluck, in spite of his attempt to write a thoroughly 'serious' opera, although Florestan's hallucinatory vision of Leonora at the opening of Act II of *Fidelio* has both Gluck's fluidity of rhythm and phrase and even something of his orchestral sonority in the lone oboe high above the pulsating strings.

Mozart destroyed neoclassicism in opera. This was quite clearly understood by his contemporaries, and it accounts, at least in part, for the opposition to his style. Already in 1787 in his *Italian Journey*, Goethe wrote: 'All our endeavor . . . to confine ourselves to what is simple and limited was lost when Mozart appeared. *Die Entführung aus dem Serail* conquered all, and our own carefully written piece has never been so much as mentioned in theatrical circles.'[1] Goethe's ideals were much the same as Wieland's: the latter (one of the few authors Mozart is known to have admired) wrote in his essay on the German *Singspiel* that 'the greatest possible simplicity of plan is proper and essential to the *Singspiel*. Action cannot be sung.' It was, of course, just this point that Mozart was so triumphantly to prove wrong.[2] It was not, however, in *opera seria* that Mozart succeeded in setting action to music.

With *Idomeneo,* written when he was twenty-five, Mozart is already aware of the problem of dramatic pacing. In one respect, *Idomeneo* is unique among Mozart's operas in its concern for a very special point of dramatic continuity: the integration of the beginning or end of an aria with the recitative that precedes or follows it. The beginning of the first aria shows the subtlety expended on this problem:

The first bar of the *Andante con moto* has a double function: it closes the recitative with a cadence, and formally opens the aria. Yet both these functions are accomplished ambiguously: the cadence is not a true close but a surprise cadence on VI instead of the tonic, and the opening bars do not initiate the rhythm of what is to follow, but accelerate into it by a series of graded steps. The rhythm moves in quarter notes for two bars,

---

[1] Cited by Abert, and by Deutsch, *Mozart*, Black, London, 1965.
[2] Mozart's practice was less opposed to Wieland's other views on *Singspiel*. Wieland had complained of overtures that had nothing to do with the operas and no one, not even Gluck, linked his overtures so intimately with what followed as Mozart. With Wieland's complaint of overlong ritornelli Mozart cannot have been much impressed, and the writer's distaste for overdecorated display arias, unnatural da capos, and perfunctory recitatives would have been shared in the late 1770s by any musician of taste.

eighth-note movement appears at the end of bar 3, and a syncopated sixteenth-note rhythm is only achieved with the true beginning of the aria in bar 5.

This aria, too, ends with a phrase designed to prevent any applause and to move immediately into the recitative:

This is a rare device elsewhere in Mozart; Tamino's aria 'Wie stark ist nicht dein Zauberton' in *Die Zauberflöte* is one of the few exceptions, and it is conceived as a part of the first-act finale. Mozart's arias almost always begin after a firm close to the preceding recitative, and are themselves rounded off at the end. But in *Idomeneo,* Electra's aria 'Tutte nel cor vi sento' (no. 4) begins in the wrong key coming out of the recitative, and moves without pause into the following chorus, which itself does not end but changes into an accompanied recitative, which in turn, without warning becomes a *recitativo secco.* Idomeneo's aria 'Vedrommi intorno' (no. 6) opens, like the first aria, with an orchestral bridge passage, and is also precipitated into the next recitative with no hesitation. Electra's aria 'Idol mio' is interrupted by a march. A similar concern is apparent throughout the opera.[1]

The relation of the more organized form (aria) to the less organized (recitative) was the fundamental problem of opera from its sixteenth-century origins: it embodies in a striking way the tension between music and speech. The terms were posed by Monteverdi's introduction of set-forms into the continuous recitative, and the history of opera may even be viewed as a battle between formally organized musical structure and recitative. The problem was exacerbated by the Italian composers of the first half of the eighteenth century when they abandoned the *arioso,* a form midway between aria and recitative. The musical structures were consequently polarized into extremely formal patterns on one side and the looser rhythms of speech on the other. (Only the accompanied recitative in the occasional introduction to an aria or in the *scena* remained as a

---

1 See nos. 15, 17, 18, 19, and the beginnings of nos. 20, 21, 22, 24, and 29.

transitional form.) There was a corresponding polarization of the dramatic movement: action was reserved for the recitatives, and the highly formal patterns of the arias became fit only for the most static role, the expression of sentiment and the display of virtuosity—the two are often indistinguishable. This polarization was less an individual solution to the difficulty of representing drama in music, than a refusal to seek a solution. With this development, *opera seria* was obliged to renounce all its traditional high-flown claims—even its genuine hope—to be a match for classical tragedy, and we can understand why critical observers then as now could view it only as a degenerate form of dramatic art. Président de Brosses remarked that he enjoyed opera because he could play chess during the recitatives while, on the other hand, the arias distracted him from the boredom of uninterrupted chess-playing.

The paradox is not that so much great music was written in early eighteenth-century *opera seria,* but that the music demands to be understood and accepted not merely in purely musical terms but in dramatic ones as well. Yet these dramatic terms could never be defined coherently enough to produce anything more than a brilliant series of scenes and set-pieces, a succession of dramatic pictures. With the wreck of its aspirations to emulate classical tragedy, *opera seria* gave up even the attempt to find a musical and dramatic equivalent for the great baroque plays. The tragedies of Racine are a mute presence behind many eighteenth-century operas, not only Mozart's *Mitridate,* but their presence is above all a reproach. The stumbling-block was the lack of a musical style that could provide both the long-range sense of continuity that the French and German baroque tragedies demanded and a complexity and richness of formal structure sufficient to allow its purely musical significance to carry dramatic weight.

The attempt to develop this continuity, to unify recitative and more richly organized form, that Mozart essayed in *Idomeneo* was a cul-de-sac. It is only a small-scale, localized answer to the more general problem of the rhythmic conception of a large work. It was, indeed, only for specific, localized effects that Mozart was to return to this method: Guglielmo's aria in *Così fan tutte* which is never finished because the girls leave in indignation and the young men are overcome by laughter; the *arioso* into which Don Alfonso breaks in the same opera when he wants to convey the shocking news that the two young men have been called away for military service; the trio in *Don Giovanni* [1] when the Commendatore lies dying, which trails off with a sinister fall into the hushed recitative. Gluck's move towards a revival of *arioso* technique, his search for a texture intermediate between recitative and formal aria, was not acceptable to Mozart, who

---

[1] This trio is, however, part of a large and perfectly balanced symmetry (see pages 302–303).

relied on the richness of formal patterns for so much of his art. Within the contexts of Gluck's reforms, *Idomeneo* is a deeply reactionary work. It is also a masterpiece, which Mozart was to equal musically but never to surpass. Within his own lifetime, however, it was already to become viable only in concert form, and it has taken a century and a half for its greatness to be appreciated.

The style that Mozart had inherited and developed was only applicable to the tragic stage with difficulty, and the sense of strain is inevitable. The classical style was, indeed, one which dealt clearly with events, and its forms were anything but static, but its pace was too rapid for *opera seria*. Tovey has remarked that Beethoven was not insufficiently dramatic but rather *too* dramatic for the stage: his music compresses into ten minutes the complexity of a three-act opera. Although the principal modulation within late eighteenth-century style is conceived as an event, there is no way that this event can be evaded for any length of time without the delaying action of a considerable amount of chromaticism, and Mozart's language was essentially diatonic, at least in its long-range aspects. He could write a love-duet with as much passion (on his own terms) as Wagner, but the prospect of making it last more than an hour, or, indeed, more than a few minutes would have seemed absurd to him. The slow, dignified pace of a tragic opera broke into small pieces in his hands, as it did in everyone else's at that time: *Idomeneo* remains a beautifully conceived mosaic, and if its limitations are those of the contemporary language, it is not true that every language is equally apt for every form. On the other hand, the pacing of the classical style worked supremely well for the comic theater, with its quick changes of situation and the numerous possibilities of accelerated action.

The dénouements of both *Idomeneo* and *Fidelio* are curiously alike: in both, the heroine steps forward at the last moment to save the hero, and offers to die with him. Leonora, it is true, has a more masculine character than Ilia, and the revolver she holds out is a more vigorous argument on her side. But there is another difference, too: in Mozart, the dramatic scene takes place entirely in accompanied recitative, in Beethoven in a fully worked-out quartet. The almost intolerable excitement of the quartet, 'Er sterbe,' is something entirely new and original on the musical stage, and was made possible by Beethoven's expansion of sonata form: the double climax of Leonora's, 'First kill his wife' and the off-stage trumpet (both symmetrically centered on an electrifying B♭ within a D major sonata form) is an example of extreme harmonic tension both just before and after the beginning of the recapitulation—such as we already find in Haydn and Mozart, but which Beethoven was to carry far beyond its original form. Mozart, however, at the moment of writing *Idomeneo*, was not yet able to manage either modulations of that power and gravity or violent shifts of rhythmic texture within a 'sonata form,' and he was obliged to stay within the framework of recitative to match the dramatic movement of his text. It is the weakest point of the score.

What finally enabled him to break out of the intolerable choice between action and musical complexity was quite simply the rhythm of *opera buffa.* Some purists have been shocked that Leporello is present throughout the most serious scenes of *Don Giovanni.* The objection seems to me misplaced even on purely dramatic grounds; but about the musical utility of Leporello at such moments, there can be no question. He is essential to the rhythm of the action. When Donna Anna tries to hold back the man who has just tried to seduce her (and perhaps succeeded), Leporello sings a patter that could have been taken over by Sir Arthur Sullivan:

LEP.
Stä a ve-der-che il li-ber - ti-no mi fa-rà pre-ci-pi - tar, stä a ve-der-che il li-ber - ti-no mi fa-rà pre-ci-pi - tar,

and in the scene where Don Giovanni braves the Commendatore and descends into hell, Leporello has a similar figure:

LEP.
La ter-za-na d'a-ve-re mi sem-bra   e le mem-bra fer-mar più non sò;   la ter-za-na d'a-ve-re' mi sem-bra,

He provides a rhythmic base upon which the more serious actions can play themselves out. Even were we to allow a sense of dramatic decorum already outmoded by the 1780s to influence our judgment of Leporello's presence at such points, he would still be the price that must be paid for music and drama to meet as equals. Mozart transformed *opera seria* by finding an outlet for many of its conventions and all of its power within the frame of *opera buffa.* He made opera adequate to the demands of drama by refusing the ancient classical dramatic models which had always been implied by the history of *opera seria.* Not only in the *Singspiel* did he ruin the neo classical program; he also destroyed the ideal of a purely serious musical-dramatic genre by successfully grafting the most brilliant achievements of *opera seria* on to the living tradition of *opera buffa.*

The introduction of *seria* characters into comic opera was a standard procedure starting with the Neapolitan *opere buffe* of the early eighteenth century, but no one before Mozart had been able to integrate them successfully into the comic action. At the age of nineteen, with the *Finta Giardiniera*—the first of his stage works to give a real sense of his power —Mozart had already given his comic opera weight and dignity by the more elaborate musical style and the brilliance and richness of the *seria* characters' more formal musical structures. It is an advantage to consider the two genres, *seria* and *buffa,* as independent if only in order to see that it was *opera buffa* that provided the large-scale organization into which the individual elements of *opera seria* could be incorporated. Nevertheless, the eighteenth century, with all of its feeling for the emotional intensity conferred by purity of genre, was not rigidly dogmatic—at least the composers were not, if the critics were—and Mozart's mature operatic achievements are all in great part a fusion of *buffa* and *seria* traditions. The distinction between the two traditions is kept alive in the later operas sometimes to effect a dramatic contrast and sometimes to distinguish the aristocratic characters from the lower orders, but much of the music takes place in a world where the synthesis is complete.

The first masterpiece of this fusion is *The Marriage of Figaro*.[1] Da Ponte claimed that with this work Mozart and he had created an entirely new kind of spectacle. It has, indeed, a moral gravity unprecedented in *opera buffa*. It is also—perhaps as a corollary—immensely long for its time, so long, in fact, that when it was imported to Italy, the first production had to be spaced over two evenings (and even then the last two acts were rewritten by another composer since Mozart's were considered impossibly difficult). To sustain a length and a seriousness never before attempted in *opera buffa*, Mozart had literally to create a new sense of dramatic continuity.

In doing so, he did not revive the small-scale devices of musical integration that he had previously essayed in *Idomeneo*, but accepted—and even emphasized—the integrity and isolation of the individual number. The *secco* recitative is less expressive in *Figaro* than in any one of his previous operas, the symmetry of the set-forms more highly worked out and more complex. The dramatic rhythm of the whole is defined in a truly classical manner: by the relation of the articulated and independent units to each other, by their proportions, and by their symmetrical grouping according to a scheme of increasing tension towards the center of the work. The concept of continuous rhythmic change as a series of carefully graded steps is basic to the classical style, and with *The Marriage of Figaro* it is applied to rhythm on the largest scale. Dramatic continuity is achieved by respecting the independence of the closed set-forms.

Mozart's ability to define character by purely musical means, to write for each of the three sopranos (the Countess, Susanna, and Cherubino) in an individual and characteristic way, provides the variety necessary for his structure. The essential innovation that was the keystone of his success was his extraordinary development and expansion of the ensemble. The quartet in *Idomeneo* was his own favorite number in that opera, but the rest of the work could offer nothing like the richness of the ensemble writing of *The Marriage of Figaro*. The first six numbers of *Figaro* ingeniously

---

[1] In the *Entführung*, Constanze's arias in *seria* style are less well-integrated with the rest of the music, particularly as the first two follow each other with nothing but spoken dialogue to separate them.

combine three duets with three arias of very different character: Figaro's cavatina 'Se vuol ballare', Bartolo's revenge aria, and Cherubino's expression of awakening adolescent sensuality. The dramatic trio that follows, in which Cherubino is discovered hiding in the chair under a dress, is the focus of the development, which moves towards an increased complexity of music and action. The chorus of peasants that comes next and Figaro's martial aria 'Non più andrai' provide a brilliant close. The *tour de force* of this new conception of musical continuity in drama as an increasing complexity of independent units is the famous second act finale, which moves from duet, through trio, quartet, and quintet to septet in a magnificently symmetrical tonal scheme.

This synthesis of accelerating complexity and symmetrical resolution which was at the heart of Mozart's style enabled him to find a musical equivalent for the great stage works which were his dramatic models. *The Marriage of Figaro* in Mozart's version is the dramatic equal, and in many respects the superior, of Beaumarchais' work, and for the first time in the history of opera, the musical version could accept, and even welcome, comparison with the greatest dramatic achievements. *Don Giovanni,* too, loses nothing in stature placed beside the versions of Goldoni and Molière; *Così fan tutte* is one of the most subtle and perfect of psychological comedies in the tradition best represented by Marivaux; and *The Magic Flute* transformed the genre of the Viennese magic-play as well as that of the magic fable created by Carlo Gozzi. If this development was possible only within the tradition and structure of *opera buffa,* it could not have been achieved without Mozart's mastery of all the elements of *opera seria* as well. The solidity of Mozart's achievement is astonishing when one considers the hollow nobility of almost all *opera seria* after Monteverdi, the lightweight flimsiness of eighteenth-century *opera buffa,* and the enforced naïveté of the neo-classical *Singspiel;* without these traditions, however, the later Mozart operas would not have been possible.

Since classical rhythm could not, as we have seen, easily manage long-range non-comic dramatic pacing, Beethoven, in writing *Fidelio*, went to the much more loosely organized traditions of French grand opera, of Cherubini and Méhul, mostly in an attempt to slow the movement to a pace commensurate with his subject's moral dignity. This is even more evident in the original version of the opera, where there is a continuous and heavy repetition of small phrases and parts of phrases: this repetition, much of it cut in the final version, gave both clarity and a kind of loose dignity to French opera, and also diluted its dramatic force. Beethoven's rewriting reflects a decision to return largely to the much tighter *opera buffa* organization, and this is particularly evident in the substitution of the *Fidelio* overture for the earlier ones; in spite of romantic horn calls, its lighter movement is far closer to comic style. Except for the inspired revision of Florestan's air, this return to classical concision accounts for the largest part of the rewriting (although the unfortunate change in the opening melodic line of the final duet in G major of the dungeon scene must have been motivated by singers' difficulties with the original form, which is musically more spontaneous).[1]

The mixture of traditions is most noticeable in the first act, where the opening duet is almost pure *opera buffa*, while the Mozartean models are only too evident behind the exquisite canon 'Mir ist's so wunderbar' (the canon of *Così fan tutte*) and Rocco's aria (which has parallels with many Mozart arias, especially 'Batti, batti, bel Masetto'). The melodramatic scenes that follow are more diffuse in character except for Leonora's aria, heavily influenced again by Mozart, and the prisoners' chorus. Pizzarro's aria, effective as it is, is more musical gesture than substance. The dungeon scene, however, is pure Beethoven, and it is the weight of his symphonic style that makes the digging of the grave and the giving of the crust of bread so moving.

With all its greatness, *Fidelio*, in comparison with the ease of style of Mozart's comic operas, is a triumph of personal will. It is a work which shows its strains. Like a language, a style has unlimited expressive capacities, but ease of expression—which carries more weight in art than in communication, and can even overpower content in importance both for artist and public— is very severely tied to the structure of the style. Even the innovatory nature of a style is bound by its own rules, and only those stylistic changes which fit most comfortably into the already established system are acceptable in the long run. Like most of Beethoven's work, *Fidelio* is not a beginning but the end of a tradition, and in this case it is an almost completely isolated effort within that tradition.

---

[1] Beethoven's difficulties with *Fidelio* have been overemphasized: much of the failure of the first version of the opera can be ascribed to the bad luck of a production in time of war. Nevertheless, Beethoven was not ordinarily willing to rewrite a piece merely because it had failed to find favor with the public, and his successive revisions (in large part a tightening of the rhythmic structure) showed that he acknowledged a problem. If even the final version cannot be accounted completely satisfactory, it stands easily by the side of Mozart's successes.

Part V

MOZART

En musique, le plaisir de la sensation dépend d'une disposition particulière non seulement de l'oreille, mais de tout le systême des nerfs . . . Au reste, la musique a plus besoin de trouver en nous ces favorables dispositions d'organes, que ni la peinture, ni la poésie. Son hieroglyphe est si léger & si fugitif, il est si facile de le perdre ou de le mésinterpréter, que le plus beau morceau de symphonie ne feroit pas un grand effet, si le plaisir infaillible & subit de la sensation pure & simple n'étoit infiniment au-dessus de celui d'une expression souvent équivoque. . . . Comment se fait-il donc que des trois arts imitateurs de la Nature, celui dont l'expression est la plus arbitraire & la moins précise parle le plus fortement a l'âme?

Denis Diderot, *Lettre à Mademoiselle* . . .
Appendix à la *Lettre sur les sourds & muets,* 1751

[*In music, the sensuous pleasure depends upon a particular disposition not just of the ear, but of the entire nervous system . . . Besides, music has a greater need to find in us those favorable organic dispositions than either painting or poetry. Its hieroglyphic is so light and so fleeting, it is so easy to lose it or to misinterpret it, that the most beautiful symphonic work would have little effect if the infallible and immediate pleasure of the sensation pure and simple was not infinitely above that of an often ambiguous expression . . . How is it then that of the three arts that imitate nature, the one in which expression is most arbitrary and least precise is that which speaks to the heart most powerfully?*]

1

The Concerto

Mozart's most signal triumphs took place where Haydn had failed: in the dramatic forms of the opera and the concerto, which pit the individual voice against the sonority of the mass. At first glance, the disparity of achievement may seem inexplicable. The surface of Haydn's music is, if anything, more, not less, dramatic than that of Mozart's. It is the elder composer who is inclined to the *coup de théatre*, the surprise modulation, the sudden farcical deflation of pomposity, the scandalously excessive dynamic accent. It may even be argued that Mozart's melodies are not only more conventional than Haydn's, but in general less 'characteristic,' less immediately descriptive of a specific sentiment or action. Mozart's musical references rarely descend to the particularity of Haydn's tone-painting and sentiment-painting in his two great oratorios. The 'characteristic' moments that we find throughout Haydn's symphonies differ from the tone-painting in the *Seasons* only in their lack of explicit reference, and they are no less marked and individual. The personages of an opera by Mozart live with a physical presence never found in Haydn's operatic work, but their music is neither more dramatic nor more 'expressive.' And while Mozart's psychological penetration may seem to give a satisfying explanation of his success in opera, it cannot account for his equal success in the closely related form of the concerto.

Mozart's early career as an international virtuoso performing concertos and his first-hand acquaintance with opera in all the capitals of Europe are experiences that Haydn missed. Nevertheless, Haydn's knowledge of opera should not be underestimated, and his interest in spectacular instrumental virtuosity in some ways surpassed Mozart's. Haydn was neither indifferent to virtuosity nor unable to handle it, and his relative insecurity with concerto form must have other roots. How evident this is may be seen by comparing the tame display of his last piano concerto, a good but unremarkable work, with the extravagant virtuosity of his piano trios and late sonatas, and the surprisingly complex demands he made upon the solo orchestral players in the symphonies, both early and late. Haydn's interest in virtuosity evidently flowered best in chamber music and in the symphony. The reasons for Mozart's superiority to Haydn in opera and concerto are more specifically musical than wider experience, or a taste for virtuosity and dramatic expression: they must be sought both in his handling of long-range movement and in the direct physical impact of his music.

The unsurpassed stability of Mozart's handling of tonal relations paradoxically contributes to his greatness as a dramatic composer. It enabled him to treat a tonality as a mass, a large area of energy which can encompass and resolve the most contradictory opposing forces. It also allowed him to slow down the purely formal harmonic scheme of his music so that it would not outstrip the action on the stage. The tonal stability provided a frame of reference which allowed a much wider range of dramatic possibilities. The firmness of this frame of reference may be heard even in Mozart's most daring harmonic experiments. If we stop the famous chromatic introduction to the String Quartet in C major K. 465 at any point and play the chord of C major, we find that not only have Mozart's complex and weirdly disquieting progressions established the key from the outset without once actually sounding the tonic chord, but they never leave that key: the chord of C major will appear always as the stable point around which every other chord in these measures revolves. The opening of a work by Mozart is always solidly based, no matter how ambiguous and disturbing its expressive significance, while the most unassuming first measures of a quartet by Haydn are far more unstable, more immediately charged with a dynamic movement away from the tonic.

The balance of harmonic relations needed to achieve this stability is a delicate one, but even the most dissonant material was dealt with by Mozart with an ease which is itself the outward sign of the harmonic equilibrium. The opening of the E flat Quartet K. 428 shows how widely Mozart could range without losing the larger harmonic sense:

The opening measure is an example of Mozart's sublime economy. It sets the tonality by a single octave leap (the most tonal of intervals), framing the three chromatic measures that follow. The two E♭'s are lower and higher than any of the other notes, and by setting these limits they imply the resolution of all dissonance within an E flat context. They define the tonal space:

and the resolutions trace the fundamental tonic triad of E flat major. The melodic line is unaccompanied, but not unharmonized: it is given complete harmonic meaning by the opening octave. We hear all these chromatic alterations so resolved into a completely diatonic significance because of the resonance of that opening measure: the fact of the octave leap is as important as everything that comes after. The 'unharmonized' chromatic progression is not only resolved, and harmonized by the first measure, but itself implies the harmonies that follow:

The fifth measure, which outlines the chord of II against the tonic note, has already been defined by the melodic line. The dramatic effect of full harmony after a unison passage is in no way minimized by the impeccable logic.[1]

This extraordinary power of Mozart's allows him to use a range of subsidiary modulation, of remote tonalities, in his expositions which Haydn generally had to reserve for the development sections. Haydn's more energetic conception of his material implies, too, a recapitulation that is very different from the exposition, as the nervous energy of the exposition must be completely reconceived when it is used at the end of the movement to affirm stability. Mozart's more massive treatment of the tonal areas of the exposition often results in recapitulations that are symmetrically equivalent, in which the musical discourse that resolves is almost a literal transposition of the pattern that established the initial tension. The large-scale symmetry is mirrored in the rich symmetry of the details, so that the music seems to achieve a state of constant balance, untroubled by the expressive violence that nevertheless so frequently characterizes Mozart's work. The symmetry is a condition of grace.

The complexity of the equilibrium in Mozart has sometimes been contrasted with the bland, mechanical symmetry in the music of his contemporaries, notably Johann Christian Bach and Dittersdorf, whose details echo themselves tamely and monotonously. Mozart's avoidance of strict repetition is not primarily for variety's sake: symmetry is not the same thing as literal reproduction, above all not in music, where the cumulative force of repetition is directly opposed to the feeling for balance. Music is, of course, asymmetrical with respect to time, which moves in only one direction, and a style that depends on proportion must seek in some way to redress the inequality. The

---

[1] The symmetry is always expressive. The second violin in measures 5 to 8 resolves its own motif ♪♪♪ by playing it backwards ♪♪♪

'sonata' is itself a form based on a partial compensation of the one-way movement of time, as the pattern of the exposition is not literally repeated at the end but rewritten so as to suggest that the music is drawing to a close. The inner symmetry of a Mozart phrase takes similar account of the direction of time, and its apparent variety is a subtle adjustment of balance, a more perfect symmetry.

The combination of power and delight that Mozart gained by adjusting his sense of symmetry to an irreversible forward movement is difficult to illustrate only because one would like to quote everything. The following eight-measure phrase from the finale of the *Hunt* Quartet must suffice:

The last four measures are a hidden repetition of the first four (as one can see at once by playing the first violin parts of both halves together, and noting the parallel octaves). In addition, there is also a mirror symmetry, as the second part of the phrase descends almost exactly as the first part rises; that is why the second half sounds so much like a resolution of the first half, in spite of their closely parallel structure. Along with these symmetries, however, there is another force at work, revealed most directly in the faster note-values of the second half of the phrase. This sense of forward movement is already apparent in the first half, which not only doubles the tempo of the initial motif as it transposes it upward, but plays it at the faster speed in the bass, so that the motif generates the harmonic movement as well as the melody. Controlled within the framework of symmetries are the elements reflecting the flow of time: the increased animation and the cumulative repetition of the motif reinforce each other. Both the symmetrical control and urgent sense of motion are essential to Mozart's dramatic genius.

This profound understanding of the relation of symmetry to movement in time appears as the sign of Mozart's mature style with *La Finta Giardiniera*, written at the age of nineteen. This new dramatic power can be felt throughout, most strikingly at the opening of the finale of Act I, with Sandrina's sensuous and despairing cry:

The symmetry of this seven-measure phrase is concealed, but it is nevertheless absolute. The last three measures not only balance the first three, with the fourth measure standing as a pivot, but also outline essentially the same melodic shape. In repeating and decorating this shape, however, they give it a new and more agitated rhythm and a harmonic movement of greater tension. The symmetrical balance is caught up in the dramatic movement, but gives it a stability that allows the drama to unfold as if impelled from within.

A sense of drama had become more important to the age in general. We can see this in one detail in the development of the keyboard concerto during the period that preceded Mozart's maturity. From 1750 to 1775 a figured-bass or continuo accompaniment on the keyboard was sometimes still harmonically necessary in all the purely orchestral sections, or ritornelli. Accompaniment by the soloist, however, was already felt as injurious to the dramatic effect of his entrances as a soloist, and to reinforce the contrast between the orchestral and solo passages, the continuo was generally suppressed for a few measures before each solo entrance. The following solo entrance from a concerto by Johann Christian Bach represents the common practice of the time:

Here the *unisono* implies the disappearance of the figured bass so as not to spoil the solo that is about to begin. It is a device obviously derived from a special form of the Baroque aria and concerto in which the entire ritornello is *unisono,* but by the middle of the century it is generally used only at the close of the opening orchestral tutti: this is the norm rather than the exception.

Mozart, however, never bothers to set off his solo entrances in this way. If we were to believe, as some would now have us do, that he continued to use the solo instrument in the tutti, it would imply that the minor composers of the preceding age were more interested than Mozart in the dramatic effect of the solo. This conclusion is plainly not easy to accept. In every way, Mozart made the soloist of his concertos even more like a character from an opera than before, and emphasized the dramatic qualities of the concerto. The derivation of concerto form from the aria was more than an historical fact for Mozart, it was a living influence.

Nevertheless, the evidence for the piano's role as continuo-instrument in Mozart's concertos after 1775 is attractive. It consists of the following: (1) the manuscripts of the concertos clearly show that Mozart has almost always written *col basso* in the piano part (or actually copied out the bass into the piano part) wherever the piano is not playing solo; (2) every one of the editions of the concertos published in the eighteenth century, most of them not during Mozart's lifetime, give a figured bass for the piano during the tutti sections; (3) there is a realization in Mozart's handwriting of a continuo for the Concerto in C major K. 246, of 1776, and some of the manuscripts of the early and lightly scored concertos contain continuo figures written in Leopold Mozart's hand; (4) the Artaria edition of K. 415, one of the few printed before Mozart's death, has a figured bass for the tutti which is not only very richly indicated, but carefully distinguishes sections of mere doubling of the bass from full chordal accompaniment: it has been conjectured[1] that the figured bass, generally added by the publishers, is in this case by Mozart himself, as it is so carefully worked out.

This last piece of evidence may be dismissed almost out-of-hand: the figured bass of the 1785 edition of K. 415 may be richly indicated, but it cannot be by Mozart. It is full of the kind of mistakes that Mozart cannot have made and which cannot be ascribed to printer's errors. The figured bass is the work of a publisher's hack.[2]

We must remember the conditions of public performance during the late eighteenth century. No one played from memory, and a full score at the

---

[1] H. F. Redlich; introduction to Eulenburg edition of the score, 1954.

[2] For example: in measure 51, the F in the bass is figured $^6_5$. Yet at that point the full orchestra *forte* (trumpets, drums, horns, oboes, bassoons, and strings) plays only the notes F, A, and C—if Mozart had wanted the D required by the figured bass, he would not have asked the piano alone to play it against so much opposition. The figuring, of course, makes a perfectly sensible cadence at that place from the point of view of the bass alone, and it is a way of harmonizing that the hack evidently preferred; when the same cadence occurs for full orchestra in measure 156 as the end of quite a different phrase, he again harmonizes a note with 6, while the other instruments play a triad in root position. In similar fashion in measures 56, 57, and 58 he puts a 7 to a chord accompanying a simple triad: the dominant seventh *would* make harmonic sense in this place, except that Mozart did not write it, and if it were played, even on a modern nine-foot concert grand, nobody would hear it—a consoling thought. There are many more mistakes in the figuring of K. 415 as given in the Eulenburg score. In the second movement, bars 15–16 make no sense, and the natural is not indicated in bars 5 and 6; in the third movement the second 6 in bar 21 should be a $^6_4$, the 6 of bar 46 should be $^6_\#$, and there is something wrong in bars 138–139 (where $5\,^6_3$ are written for $7\,^5_3$). How many of these mistakes are due to misprints, and where they come from (Artaria or Eulenburg), I do not propose to find out. If Mozart did not write it, I do not care how they print it.

191

keyboard would have been too cumbersome. Not even the conductor always used a full score at that time; it was common to use only a first violin part. The pianist used the violoncello part for cues, a tradition that dates back to a time when he actually had to play continuo. Even Chopin's concertos were published with a continuo part; this persistence of an old-fashioned notation has, indeed, created some textual problems; there are notes at the beginnings and ends of phrases in concertos by Beethoven and by Chopin about which there remains some uncertainty as to whether they belong to the solo part, and are therefore to be played, or to the continuo part, in which case they are only cues, or an aid to performance. In the concertos of Mozart there is absolutely no place where an extra note is needed to fill in the harmony, or where the texture of the music requires the kind of continuity that the steady use of figured bass can give. Continuo playing in secular music died out in the second half of the eighteenth century, although only gradually, and everything about the music of Haydn and Mozart tells us that it was *musically*, if not practically, dead by 1775. An analogue to the purely notational aspect of the continuo as a mnemonic aid in performance is the score of Mozart's Clarinet Concerto, where, in flat contradiction to all that we know of Mozart's delicacy and tact in doubling the string parts with wind instruments, we would have to believe that whenever the clarinet is not playing solo, it incessantly doubles the first violin part throughout; this doubling is, of course, nothing but a system of cueing.[1]

Eighteenth-century performance was, in general, a less formal affair than it is today, and the attitude to the musical text was decidedly more cavalier. (Haydn's letter about the *Paris* Symphonies, suggesting that at least one rehearsal would be advisable before a performance, gives an idea of what went on.) Did a pianist ever play some part of the continuo, if not all of it? When the pianist conducted from the keyboard, he did play chords to keep the orchestra together, and perhaps even to add a little extra sonority to the louder sections. The tradition among soloists of playing the final chords of a concerto with the orchestra dates back a long way, but whether to the time of Mozart I do not know. A tradition may be as mistaken as an innovation, but it undoubtedly looks better if the pianist does not relax measures before everybody else. Eighteenth-century piano sound was so weak that even if the pianist played some of the continuo, he would have been inaudible most of the time except to members of the orchestra unless he tried to play very loud, and there is no reason, musical or musicological, to suppose that anyone in the late eighteenth century ever tried to play a continuo part other than discreetly. As the size of the orchestra for concertos increased, the

---

[1] In Haydn's *Mass in Time of War*, when the organ is silent (and Haydn writes '*Senza Org.*'), the continuo figures together with the bass line are still put into the organist's part. These figures have no meaning except as cues, either for the organist or—if the work was conducted from a bass part instead of full score—for the conductor.

continuo became not only unnecessary but absurd as well. From the point of view of modern performance, it would be acceptable if the pianist played the figured bass provided that no one could hear him.

There was, however, a way of playing the more lightly scored concertos, and that was at home with a string quintet. Mozart himself apologized for not sending his father the manuscripts of some new concertos, but 'the music would not be of much use to you . . . [they] all have wind-instrument accompaniment and you very rarely have wind-instrument players at home.'[1] The continuo figures in Leopold Mozart's hand could have been used only for performance in private of the concertos which did not need winds, and the keyboard then surely filled out the string sonorities. Mozart, after all, would not have needed the figures—and Leopold could only have used them at home.

The continuo part of K. 246 in Mozart's handwriting adds much more cogent evidence that this was the case. The piano accompanies the orchestra in the outer movements solely during the passages marked *forte,* and (most striking characteristic of all) in the Andante, measures 9–12, it doubles the melody at only one point—significantly at the only place in the entire concerto where the melody is played by the winds alone without help from the strings. This realization, then, must have been for a performance without winds, almost certainly with string quintet alone. This unique piece of evidence in Mozart's own hand has, therefore, no bearing on public performances of the concertos.

The indication of continuo in the Mozart concertos should be considered together with the evidence for piano parts in the later Haydn symphonies. Haydn himself conducted the first performances of the *London* Symphonies from the keyboard; there is even a little eleven-measure piano solo that has come down to us for the end of Symphony no. 98. Yet in all of the half-dozen editions of this symphony published during Haydn's lifetime, the solo is omitted: it is found only in an edition published after his death, and in arrangements for piano quintet and piano trio—and in one of these arrangements it is assigned to the violin. Against the background of the immense amount of solo writing for all other instruments in the Haydn symphonies, eleven optional measures for piano exist only as an example of Haydn's wit. The responsibility for keeping the orchestra together at the first performance was divided between the concert-master, Salomon, and the composer at the keyboard; it must have been delightful at the end of a symphony to hear an instrument suddenly begin to play a solo when, until then, it had had only the musical significance of a prompter at an opera. The charm of this passage is not that the piano was used for symphonic works, but that, except for these eleven measures, it was seen but not heard. (It would be impossible to appreciate the joke at a modern performance, although the sonority of the little piano solo is so enchanting that it is a pity to leave it out.) The keyboard had,

---

[1] Mozart, *Letters,* ed. Emily Anderson, p. 877, letter of May 15, 1784.

by then, long since lost its function of filling in the harmonies,[1] and it was already losing that of keeping an ensemble together.

One might add that Mozart's indication *col basso* in the manuscripts of the concertos is absolutely mechanical: proponents of the theory that the figured bass was meant to be heard as well as seen make a great deal of the fact that Mozart sometimes writes rests into the piano part during the tutti. But these rests have no musical significance whatever: in almost every case they are added only when the cello is not playing. They were an aid to the copyist, not a direction to the performer. The cello part (and nothing else) was printed in the piano part when the piano was silent as automatically and traditionally as it is printed in the organ part of Beethoven's *Missa Solemnis* along with the direction *senza organo*. Why bother printing it, then? Simply because the keyboard performer had had the cello part in front of him for at least 150 years and it helped him to keep his place.[2]

Now, in all this discussion, there has been one important absence, an empty chair for the guest of honor who never turned up. It is a question absent from all the literature on the subject, as far as I know. We have asked whether the continuo was used and whether it was necessary, but never what the musical significance of the continuo is. There should, after all, be a difference between a performance of any work with a keyboard instrument adding harmonies and a performance without one—a *specifically musical* difference. If a continuo was a practical aid to performance, a help with the ensemble, why was it abandoned? The disappearance of its harmonic function is an answer that begs the question. Why did composers cease to use the keyboard instrument to fill in the harmonies when it was so much easier than distributing notes elsewhere over other instruments, and also such an advantage in keeping an orchestra together? Why, for example, would the addition of even a discreet continuo to a Brahms quartet or a Tchaikovsky symphony seem so ludicrous?

A continuo (or any form of figured bass) is a way of outlining and isolating the harmonic rhythm. That is why it can be indicated generally by figures under the bass rather than by writing out the exact notes. The emphasis on

---

[1] Even in the early symphonies of Haydn, the stylistic evidence for continuo-playing is only a thinness of texture typical of Haydn and which continued to delight him to the end of his life, as a glance at the late quartets will show.

[2] It is amusing to note to what extremes those in favor of the continuo function of the soloists are sometimes driven to save their theory. In bars 88–89 of the D minor Concerto K. 466, Mozart wrote four low notes into the left hand (doubling the timpani) along with some chords two octaves above while the right hand plays some rapid passage-work. Obviously since no one hand can stretch three octaves, these bars have elicited some fancy explanation. A second piano to play continuo on the low notes has been suggested, along with the use of a piano with pedal keyboard (which it seems Mozart actually owned at some time). It now appears most probable that Mozart originally wrote the low notes and then changed his mind and added the chords without crossing out the first version. What this passage shows, if anything, is that when Mozart wanted the soloist to fill in the harmony, he wrote down the notes for it.

the change of harmony is the only important thing—the doubling and the spacing of the harmony are secondary considerations. This isolation—this setting in relief of the rate of change of the harmony—is essential to the Baroque style, particularly the so-called High Baroque of the early eighteenth century. This is a style whose motor impulse and energy comes from the harmonic sequence, and which depends upon this to give life and vitality to a relatively undifferentiated texture.

But the energy of late eighteenth-century music is based not on the sequence but on the articulation of periodic phrasing and on modulation (or what we may call large-scale dissonance). The emphasis of the harmonic rhythm is therefore not only unnecessary but positively distracting. The tinkle of a harpsichord or a late eighteenth-century piano is a very pretty sound when it is heard in a Haydn symphony, but its prettiness has no relevance to the music and no significance beyond its agreeable noise-value. The fact that Haydn and Mozart were unable to conceive of a more efficient way of conducting an orchestra puts them along with all the other *performers* of their day, whose idea of performance had not yet caught up with the radical change of style which had occurred since 1770 and for which Haydn and Mozart themselves were so largely responsible. This raises the question—does the composer know how his piece is to sound?

The problem is a delicate one, and it lies at the heart of our conception of music. If music is not a mere notation on paper, then its realization in sound is crucial. We assume generally that the ideal performance is the one the composer imagined as he wrote the piece, and that this imagined ideal performance is the real piece, not the notes on paper or the wrong notes of an actual performance. But this assumption is flimsy and fails to stand up under examination. And none of these—not the imagined or the actual performance or the schematic representation on paper—can be simply equated with a work of music.

Let us put this in the simplest possible terms. When a conductor in 1790 conducted from the keyboard, we know from contemporary testimony that he often stopped playing to wave his hands. There is no way of knowing when he did this, but he did not play throughout. When Haydn imagined the sound of one of his symphonies, he must indeed have expected a certain amount of piano or harpsichord sonority as being likely here or there, but there is no place in the music where he implied this as necessary or even desirable except for the little joke in the Symphony no. 98.

This means that a composer's idea of his work is both precise and slightly fuzzy: this is as it should be. There is nothing more exactly defined than a Haydn symphony, its contours well outlined, its details clear and all audible. Yet when Haydn wrote a note for the clarinet, that does not indicate a specific sound—there are lots of clarinets and clarinettists, and they all sound very different—but a large range of sound within very well-defined limits. The act of composing is the act of fixing those limits within which the performer may

195

move freely. But the performer's freedom is bound—or should be—in another way. The limits set by the composer belong to a system which is in many respects like a language: it has an order, a syntax, and a meaning. The performer brings out that meaning, makes its significance not only clear but almost palpable. And there is no reason to assume that the composer or his contemporaries always knew with any certainty how best to make the listener aware of that significance.

New ways of composing precede new ways of playing and singing, and it often takes as long as ten to twenty years for performers to learn how to change their own styles and to adapt themselves. The use of the continuo in the piano concerto was, by 1775, a vestige of the past that was to be completely abolished by the music itself, and we have every reason to believe that the figured bass was already nothing more than a conventional notation which provided the soloist and the conductor with a substitute for a score during performance, or, at most, a way of keeping an orchestra together which had no longer any musical significance. The occasional indignation about its omission either from performance or edition is historically unwarranted and musically unjustifiable.

In 1767, Rousseau complained that the conductor at the Paris opera made so much noise beating a rolled-up sheet of music paper on the desk to keep the orchestra in time that one's pleasure in the music was spoilt. The audible use of a keyboard instrument during a symphony or the orchestral section of a concerto written after 1775 is no doubt less irritating, but its authenticity and its musical value are the same.

The most important fact about concerto form is that the audience waits for the soloist to enter, and when he stops playing they wait for him to begin again. In so far as the concerto may be said to have a form after 1775, that is the basis of it. This is why the concerto has so strong and so close a relationship to the operatic aria; in fact, an aria like 'Martern aller Arten' from *Die Entführung* is nothing less than a concerto for several solo instruments, the soprano being only the principal soloist of a concertante group. The relationship is perhaps closer at the end of the eighteenth century than at any other time: essentially what the classical period did was to dramatize the concerto, and this in the most literally scenic way—the soloist was seen to be different.

In the Baroque concerto, the soloist or soloists were part of the orchestra, playing with them throughout; the contrast of sound was achieved by having the ripieno, or the non-solo elements of the orchestra, stop playing while the soloists continued. There is scarcely ever any effect of dramatic entrance in the early eighteenth century, except from the full orchestra; even when the famous cadenza in the Fifth Brandenburg Concerto begins, there is a sense of the soloist continuing without a break from the previous texture, as the orchestra has gradually effaced itself by a beautifully timed series of gradations in which Bach for once overcomes the contemporary style's resistance to dynamic transition. (The slight pause with which many harpsichordists mark the opening of the cadenza is an anachronism, an intrusion of our modern theatrical idea of the concerto.) With the classical concerto, things are on a different footing: in every concerto by Mozart from 1776 on, the entrance of the soloist is an event, like the arrival of a new character on the stage, and it is set off, emphasized, and colored by a bewildering variety of devices. It should be noted here that this detachment of the soloist from the ripieno was not an invention of Mozart's but a gradual development during the century, a part of the general evolution of the articulated form and a consequence of the taste for clarity and dramatization; but only Mozart, of all the composers before Beethoven, understood the implications of this dynamic contrast between soloist and orchestra, and its formal and coloristic possibilities. Even Haydn remained tied largely to the conception of the soloist as a detachable part of the orchestra.

The Baroque concerto is a loose alternation of ripieno and solo sections, with a strong tonic cadence avoided except at the end of the first and last orchestral passages, and with the solo sections derived from the tutti, almost always generated by the opening motifs. This account overlooks the sources of energy within the Baroque style, which make the great concertos of Bach and Handel more than a loose succession of contrasts, but these sources, in any case, had long since dried up by Mozart's time. The development of the concerto after 1750 has often been described as a fusion of the new sonata form and the older concerto form, but this way of looking at it, even if not positively misleading, has the disadvantage of leaving it as a puzzle why anybody should have wanted arbitrarily to fuse such opposed conceptions. Why not drop the old form and write a completely modern work, a sonata for soloist and orchestra? It will be easier to look at the subject from a viewpoint at once simpler and less mechanical. Treating the sonata not as a form but as a style—a feeling for a new kind of dramatic expression and proportions —we may see how the functions of a concerto (the contrast of two kinds of sound, the display of virtuosity) are adapted to the new style. There is not much point in listing the variety of Mozart's formal devices in concerto form unless we understand their expressive and dramatic purpose.

To return to the opening orchestral pages, or the first ritornello: once it is accepted that the soloist's role is to be a dramatic one, the ritornello poses a problem, simply (as I said) that the audience is waiting for the soloist to enter. In other words, to a certain extent the opening tutti always conveys an introductory atmosphere: something is about to happen. If it is very short, as in most arias, the problem disappears, but in a work of larger dimensions, this introductory character trivializes the opening, and the material first heard in it tends to lose its importance and its urgency. To turn it completely into an introduction—to give it harmonically the character of a dominant rather than a tonic chord—and to have the soloist expose the principal material alone or only accompanied would be an outrage to the classical sense of decorum, given the comparative weight of the orchestral and solo sonorities (this was possible only more than a century later as a joke, in a work like Dohnanyi's *Variations on a Nursery Theme*, although Beethoven's *Kakadu* Variations adumbrate the effect). To drop the opening ritornello altogether and to have the material presented by soloist and orchestra as almost equal partners (as in the concertos by Schumann, Liszt, Grieg, and Tchaikovsky) is to renounce the classical delight in large-scale effects, to make the contrast between solo and orchestra one of short alternations, losing the breadth of the long sections. On the other hand, to make the opening ritornello overdramatic in an attempt to raise its importance and seize the audience's attention would be to undercut the dramatic effect of the soloist's role and to destroy one of the principal advantages of the concerto form.

At the age of twenty, with what may be considered his first large-scale masterpiece in any form, Mozart solved this problem in a manner as brutal and as simple as breaking the neck of a bottle to open it. At the opening of the Concerto in E flat K. 271 (quoted above, p. 59), the piano participates —as a soloist—in the first six measures, and is then silent for the rest of the orchestral exposition. It was a solution so striking that Mozart never used it again (although it was developed by Beethoven in two famous examples, and by Brahms in an expansion of Beethoven's conception). With one stroke, the opening presentation is made more dramatic and the orchestral exposition is given the weight it might have lacked. For this purpose, the most striking entrance of the soloist—the first one—is thrown away at the second measure, before we have heard enough of the orchestral sonority to deepen the contrast. And this, in turn, creates a problem for the next entrance of the solo instrument, solved with equal daring and brilliance. The piano enters before the orchestral exposition has had time to close, in the middle of what is evidently a long final cadence[1]; coming in with a trill, which serves doubly and ambiguously as a signal of solo virtuosity and as a coloristic accompaniment to the orchestral phrase, the piano continues with a witty insouciance apparently in the middle of a phrase of its own, as if continuing a conversation.

The orchestral exposition of K. 271 remains in the tonic throughout without modulating: it is, in fact, exactly like the orchestral opening of an operatic aria. The dramatic modulation is left to the soloist; in so far as there are two real expositions in a concerto, one is necessarily passive and the other active, and the nineteenth century, which did not understand this, was often forced to do away with the orchestral exposition as tautological. In Mozart's E flat Concerto, however, not only is the harmonic direction different, but also the thematic pattern is not the same in the two expositions. The ritornello fixes the nature of the work, providing the tonal and motivic foundation; the piano's exposition gives the concerto its dramatic movement, dropping some of the thematic material and adding new material for the purpose. Almost

---

[1] See themes (9) and (10) cited below, p. 202.

all this material, various and rich as it is, holds together by a logic that is immediately convincing: much of it is audibly derived from the opening phrase.

The two expositions, different as they are, have a relationship that is by no means arbitrary, and, still leaving aside for the most part all ideas of concerto form and sonata form, it is interesting to see how Mozart molds his material and how he dramatizes it. The motto of the work is its opening measures, a theme (1) from whose two opposing parts much of the rest of the movement follows. The orchestral fanfare I label (*a*), and the concealed symmetry of the piano's witty answer (*b*):

After being repeated, this is immediately followed by a theme (2) which ingeniously combines both the rhythms and the shapes of (*a*) and (*b*) together in a dancing movement:

which brings a faster rhythm in the accompaniment, and a fanfare (3) that clearly resembles (*a*) while the oboes continue the phrasing of (2):

Then a transitional four measures, made up of two completely conventional elements, which I call (3A) and (3B), although it is an idle question to decide whether the phrase belongs more with what precedes or with what follows. I cite it not only for its mastery of transition, but because of its importance in

199

later sections, as Mozart will use it like a pivot to make the listener associate in his mind two sections of different material but similar function:

(3A–B) slows the movement down: the whole phrase functions, of course, as a pedal-point on the dominant, and the music is poised before continuing with a new kind of motion. Then follows a melody of the most ravishing grace (4), apparently new, and so derived from (*b*) that it fits everything that precedes: it is an augmentation of the basic thematic pattern, and has an effect of breadth, of giving greater space to the original terse motif:

A new theme follows immediately (I call (5) a separate theme although it is never presented apart from (4) except in the cadenza: for any other composer, without Mozart's richness of invention, it would have done service as an independent melody); it is derived from (4) through the graceful movement upwards at the opening of each measure:

and the derivation is intended to be heard as part of the music's conversational logic. But it is a rhythmic and an expressive intensification, with one out of two leaps made twice as fast with a *sforzando* on a weak beat: even the accompaniment becomes contrapuntally richer and more chromatic. There is a heightening of the expression and of the pace which accelerates towards the end and breaks immediately into (6):

derived directly from (*a*), echoing the trill heard a few seconds before at the end of (5), and coming to an expressive climax and to a sudden stop. Until this point of the work, every note of the chromatic scale has been played except one, D♭. It is now sounded, syncopated and fortissimo.

This is not only the first fortissimo in the movement, but, in a sense, the only one, as the others are all literal repetitions. The D♭ is also the longest melodic note so far, and the silence that follows its immediate resolution into an F minor chord is the longest silence we have heard until now. A study of the phrase patterns reveals an even more interesting aspect of this climax: all the phrases until this point except one have fallen into a symmetrical and regular rhythm. The opening measures are no exception: they are clearly a four-measure phrase played twice, with the first playing interrupted at the opening of the fourth measure. The slight asymmetry is compensated by the symmetrically literal repetition. Other phrases are not only squarely regular, but have symmetrical echoes: bars 8–9 mirror 10–11, 18–21 exactly repeat 14–17, as 43–44 repeat 41–42. The only interruption of this regularity before the climax we have just reached is in measures 12 and 13, which stand out as an exception in the procession of four-measure groups and which outline an F minor sixth chord:

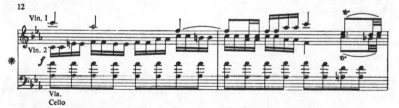

the same chord which resolves the fortissimo diminished seventh under the D♭ in measures 45–46—a resolution which itself needs to be resolved in turn. In this way, the climax at measures 45–46 is prepared; and it, too, is an interruption of the regular four-measure pattern, but a much more violent and dramatic one.

If the climax is beautifully prepared, it is also itself a preparation and a foreshadowing of what is to come. The phrase that follows, indeed, insists on the importance of what has just happened. So far, the large rhythmic pattern has come in two waves, the increase of intensity from (1) to (3), and the even greater one from (4) to (6). At this point the rhythmic motion breaks down completely, and the climax of (6), its last two notes, is turned into a recitative (7) which again outlines an F minor chord:

201

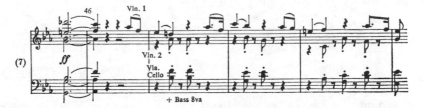

This recitative acts as a fermata (or, in broader terms, as a cadenza), an expressive wait before the closing phrase, a refusal to resolve the tension. Here is a mastery of rhythm that Mozart derived from opera, and that no other composer has ever employed with such ease. A closing phrase, a fanfare (8) based on (*a*), follows:

and there is a splendidly witty effect when it appears that it is not a closing phrase at all; a second cadence (9) follows, which is nothing but (*a*) inverted:

202

interrupted by the piano (10), with its second dramatic entrance.[1] Two closing phrases are by no means a luxury: Mozart needs both of them later in the work.

The role of the piano is to dramatize this pattern with such force as to make its resolution urgent and demanding enough to support the weight of the symmetrical patterns that so delighted Mozart even in his operas. In terms of Mozart's style, dramatization means development (thematic fragmentation and extension) and modulation (large-scale harmonic opposition or dissonance), and we find both kinds in the piano's presentation of the form already outlined by the orchestra. Even the orchestration of the same material is more dramatic and more colorful in the second exposition than in the first. This double exposition has very little to do with the repeat in the exposition of a sonata: the solo exposition is an expansion and a transformation as much rhythmic as harmonic. It is the most crucial misunderstanding of Mozart to think, in this concerto, of his repeating a pattern and adding color, drama, and variety to the individual elements: the entire pattern is what Mozart is dramatizing—the real material is not the individual themes but their succession—and the second exposition is not a repeat but a transformation. Only when the creative impulse had died out of the concerto form, as from the sonata, did the double exposition become like the repeat of the first half of a sonata allegro (as in the concertos of Chopin, for all their poetry). But no one who listens to a Mozart concerto without formal preconceptions has any doubt that the soloist's exposition is not a repeat with variations and an added modulation, but a radically different presentation of ideas heard first in the orchestra, with the significance of the pattern completely altered by new ideas and a new approach.

The transformation starts at the beginning. The opening theme (1) interrupts the piano's new entrance (10) and is played twice as at the opening. But we do not go on with (2) as before; instead, the piano, accompanied by two oboes, begins to develop (*a*) along with a cadential trill (found in so many of the themes, above all in (6) and (10B)):

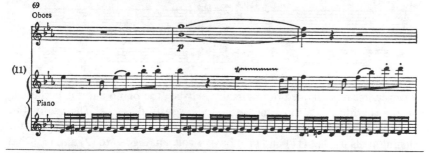

---

[1] Details are wearisome, so I reserve this for a note: the entrance of the piano returns in measure 60 to the F minor sixth chord, and its opening trill and the whole phrase that follows serve once again to resolve the top C of this chord into a B♭.

The accompaniment speeds up its motion and the music modulates immediately to the dominant, B flat major, and reinforces the modulation with a passage of mechanical and conventional brilliance:

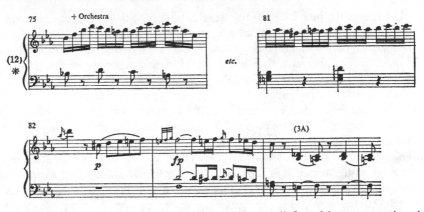

The brilliance is used to set the modulation into relief, and less conventional material would not do: the inexpressive nature of the music here, its banality serves as a contrast to the more complex logic of a development which fragments the opening theme and forces it into another key. The virtuosity stabilizes the new tonality.[1]

To re-establish the pattern, themes (4) and (5) are now played, but first preceded by the transitional passage (3A–B), which appears to grow logically out of the end of (12):

However, it is now divided dramatically between the piano and the orchestra, and the rhythm of its third measure is vigorously different. The use of this transitional phrase (and a part of the logic we unconsciously accept while listening) tells us that (11) and (12) have a role analogous to (2) and (3): that

---

[1] As part of the more expansive art of the second exposition, it should be remarked that measures 78–81 are harmonically a magnified version of measures 12 and 13.

is, (2) and (11) are both developments of (*a*), and (3) and (12) both close a section by adding brilliance and increasing the sense of movement. But the new version of (3A–B) responds to the greater intensity of the piano's exposition by its more dramatic orchestration and rhythm.

The graceful melodies (4) and (5) are also not merely repeated by the piano, but (5) is played twice, the second time by the piano supporting the oboe with an accompaniment that moves twice as fast as before, and the theme is then further lengthened by a deeply expressive phrase (13) that is like a fermata over measure 115, a refusal to accept the inevitable descent:

We hold our breath here, waiting for the phrase to finish, and we are kept suspended by the surprise cadence in the middle (m. 114); the end of the phrase, however (m. 117), leaves us harmonically at exactly the same unresolved point as the opening. This tension is immediately relieved by a final and lengthy burst of virtuosity, played twice (14):

This closes and by measure 135 completely grounds the modulation started in measure 70; once again the conventionality of the material is necessary for the feeling of a stable cadence. This is also the perfect point for an extensive display of pianistic brilliance, which is, after all, the essence of the concerto form.

It is natural (as well as traditional) to re-establish the symmetry by having the orchestra return here and end this exposition with the closing phrases of its own ritornello; (6), (7), and (8) accordingly follow in order and in the

205

dominant. But the recitative of (7) is given to the soloist after the orchestral climax, an operatic gesture so natural and yet so effective that it is hard to know whether to ascribe it to imagination or logic. Mozart's most fantastic strokes are always his most reasonable. The climax at the opening of (7), now transposed to the dominant, is less imposing than on its first appearance, because it has followed a very long display of virtuosity from the soloist which rises several times to the highest note on Mozart's piano. The virtuosity is part of the dramatization. The piano's exposition is, as we have seen, a free adaptation of the orchestral ritornello, which is only a concise introductory statement: both expositions are, however, a development and an expansion of the motto with which the work opens, and both are shaped towards a climax, but a different one in each case. The orchestral climax leading from a high D♭ to a sustained F minor chord[1] is not so much transposed by the piano's exposition as replaced by the greater dramatic power of the modulation to the dominant and by the brilliance of the solo writing. But it is, in the end, the original orchestral climax which will play the more important role in the total form of the movement.

Only two phrases of the orchestral exposition—here labelled (2) and (3)—do not appear in the piano's exposition, and both are played by the piano in the section that follows (which we may call the 'development,' an intensification of the exposition's modulation to the dominant and an increased dramatization of its material); but the two phrases are no longer continuous, being widely separated to frame the 'development.' The piano begins to play (2), now at the dominant, in a way that cuts off the orchestra's cadential phrase before its finality has a chance to make its effect, and blurs the distinction between the exposition and the development; certainly, since we have not heard (2) either in the piano or at the dominant, it would be hard to decide whether this passage does not have as much right to be called 'exposition' as 'development,' and our doubt is strengthened by the new and graceful arc with which the piano rounds off the phrase and which leads directly to the opening fanfare of (1). The motto theme (1) is played, complete with its repeat, and seems as much as ever to be a beginning, and to mark once again an initiation of the pattern twice presented.

This section does, indeed, follow the sequence already described, but with greater intensity. As in the piano's exposition, (1) is followed by (11), which is a development of (1a), and as if to emphasize its parallelism with the exposition, it is again scored as before with the piano accompanied only by the two oboes. But the development is more extensive, and modulates immediately to F minor, the key that played so important a role in the orchestral exposition. It leaves this key to touch briefly and inconclusively on the tonic, and then returns with this dramatic passage, where the orchestral climax cf

---

[1] Sustained by the phrase that follows, which dwells on the notes of the F minor triad even while the harmony changes beneath it.

the ritornello in (6) (with the D♭ resolved as before into a sixth chord of F minor) is here reiterated four times[1]:

This hammering of D♭ is the extreme point of tension, the center of the work.

This moment is a synthesis as well as a culmination, a fusion of the aims of the two expositions. Using the developmental material initiated in the second exposition, and starting from the modulation to the dominant effected there, Mozart arrives at the dissonant climax of the first exposition, now more urgent and more expressive, and with much greater rhythmic energy. The symmetry is not the mechanical symmetry of textbook form, but implies a new dramatic level. It is the understanding of symmetry as a dramatic force that gave Mozart his supremacy in opera and the concerto, an understanding that extended to the most insignificant detail. Even the resolution of the climax just quoted has its parallel: it is resolved by (3) in the orchestra, and repeated, at long last, by the piano. At its first appearance (3) was preceded, exactly as it is here, by an F minor sixth chord, in a passage singled out by its irregular phrase-length. In other words, the conventional little phrase (3)—the most ordinary stock-in-trade of the contemporary composer—is the resolution both of the initial moment of tension and of the central climax of the movement, binding the two together.

---

[1] It has already been played just eleven measures before, so that the repetition is even more striking.

After the playing of the short phrase (3A) and a transitional passage[1] which replaces (3B), the original pattern begins again ('recapitulation') with (1) played, as always, twice—or almost twice. This time, however, the scoring is symmetrical mirror-fashion: the piano, not the orchestra, begins and is answered by the orchestra and then the order is reversed. In the second playing of (1), the piano answers with a difference—it accompanies the melody with the rhythm of the development section, and, indeed, starts a new development on its own. This second development section is, of course, one of the most characteristic features of classical sonata style from Haydn's *Russian* Quartets to the *Hammerklavier* Sonata, and it is almost always harmonically a reference to the larger development, as if the energy of the latter had not yet been dissipated, and was spilling over into what follows. The first of Mozart's mature concertos is no exception, and the passage opens with an unmistakable return to the climax of the previous development:

which is resolved after four measures of modulation with a return to the tonic quoted here to show how even the orchestration with the entrance of the oboe emphasizes the resolution of the F minor chord that has had such importance:

[1] For those ill-at-ease with perfection, I should add here that this short transitional phrase seems to me awkwardly contrived. There is nothing wrong with its thematic logic—it is derived both melodically and rhythmically from (3A) which immediately precedes it. But it is harmonically awkward in that its shape emphasizes the tonic while its function is to sustain a dominant, and I think the alternation of *p* and *f* is not convincingly motivated. But I advance this with a certain timidity, as the phrase is not ineffective, nor does it alter the dramatic force of what follows.

All of the transitions to the recapitulation in Mozart's piano concertos before K. 450 seem to me below the level of ease and power he was consistently to attain later. K. 414 in A major works best only by cutting the Gordian knot—it is dramatically abrupt, and there is no transition at all. K. 413 in F major merely repeats the entrance of the soloist without change, as it entered before on a dominant, and K. 415 in C major tries to gloss over this place with a little Adagio cadenza. K. 449 in E flat major has a sequential passage so weak that it makes pianists uncomfortable to play—one tries in vain to add dramatic interest by a *crescendo*, and the phrase will not bear the weight. But the analogous place in K. 450 (B flat major) is enchanting, logical, and completely natural. After this work, the return to the tonic is generally one of the most gracefully accomplished, and often one of the most memorable moments in Mozart's forms. The phrase that is so weak in K. 449 has a fairly close analogue in K. 456, for example; but there it is prepared harmonically and so strengthened by the orchestration that no awkwardness is left.

It may be said that the final resolution of the climax at measure 176 has been postponed until this point. Even though this passage is a new departure, it stands as a foil to the exactly analogous place in the solo exposition: there (1) is followed by (11), a development of (1*a*), and here (1) is followed by a development of (1*b*). This relation is underlined, as both (11) and (15) lead directly into (12).

In the recapitulation, along with some enchanting reorchestration, Mozart again contrives to make his most logical strokes seem surprising. The section of the soloist's exposition that was in the dominant is transposed almost exactly, although the brilliant passagework of (14) is largely rewritten with, naturally, a much heavier emphasis on the tonic chord; but the virtuosity is interrupted this time. The delightful phrase (2) cuts in, to be played this time twice, once by the orchestra and again by the soloist. Its surprising appearance here in the tonic is, nevertheless, a consequence and a resolution of its equally surprising appearance in the dominant between the solo exposition and the beginning of the development.

The extraordinary form of the end of the movement has the same rightness. After the piano has finished with the closing trill of (14), and the orchestra with (6) and (7) returns to the climax on the D♭, it is the piano, as before, that resolves it with the recitative-like phrase. Then the orchestra astonishingly enters with the fanfare of (1)—played yet again twice with its answer in the piano—and with one more climax in which the high D♭ is again prominent, there comes the traditional pause before the cadenza. In this way, like every other development section in the movement, the cadenza is preceded by the opening phrase played twice.

The last surprise is that the piano interrupts and accompanies the traditional orchestral conclusion with solo passagework, but the interruption is performed with a reasonableness that makes the humor only the more delightful. The cadenza is followed by the concluding phrases of the orchestral exposition (8) and (9), and the piano begins to play (10) in the middle of (9) exactly as it did before: this final licence is not licence at all, but strict recapitulation. Nothing is more logical with reference to the form of this individual movement, and nothing more eccentric with regard to the supposed traditional form of the concerto.[1]

What shall we term this manner of creation, freedom or submission to rules? Eccentricity or classical restraint? Licence or decorum? With a sense of proportion and dramatic fitness unsurpassed by any other composer, Mozart bound himself only by the rules he reset and reformulated anew for each work. His concertos are not ingenious combinations of traditional concerto-form with the more modern sonata allegro, but independent creations based on traditional expectations of the contrast between solo and orchestra reshaped with an eye to the dramatic possibilities of the genre, and governed by the proportions and tensions—not the patterns—of sonata style. We shall arrive only at a misunderstanding, more or less serious depending on the work, if we try to impose the form of a Mozart concerto from outside the work without considering the dramatic intention and the directional thrust of the material. Above all, we must remember that it is not the themes of the work—or the motifs—that form the material, but their ordering and their relation: a 'development' is not merely a development of themes, but takes into account, intensifies—'develops,' in short—the order and the sense of what has gone before. It is the exposition as a whole that is developed, not the individual motifs.

---

[1] The following diagram of one aspect of the form—the succession of themes—may make this fundamental logic perhaps more visible (the numerical labels are as above):

Orchestral exposition	Solo exposition	Development	Recapitulation	Coda
1(a–b)	1(a–b)	1(a–b)	1(a–b)	1(a–b)
2	11	11	15	Cadenza
3	12a–b	3	12b	[3]*
3A–B	3A–B	3A	3A–B	
4–5	4–5		4–5	[5]*
	13		13	
	14		14	
			2	
			14	
6	6		6	
7	7		7	
8	8			8
9	2			9
10				10
				Conclusion

* [Order from Mozart's own cadenza]

The equilibrium is even clearer if we remember that (2) is sequential and a combination of (1a) and (1b), (11) is a sequential development of (1b), (15) a sequential development of (1a), and the cadenza a development of whatever the soloist chooses.

How important this is for K. 271 may be seen not only in the recurrence of points of climax and resolution, but also in the way development already begins within the exposition at measure 69 (called (11)), a passage which returns and is extended within the development proper at measure 162, and in the way the tension of the development spills over into the recapitulation, starting a new development (15)—a few seconds after the opening of the recapitulation—harmonically related to the central one. This second development at the beginning of the recapitulation is the rule rather than the exception—in the works of Haydn, Mozart, and Beethoven—but it can only be understood as related to dramatic intent, not as part of a thematic order; it comes from a powerful sense of long-range harmonic dissonance, a conception not of the dissonant note in a chord, but of the long dissonant section in a tonally resolved work.

Heard with the same freedom from formal preconceptions, the other movements of K. 271 are no more problematic than the first. The slow movement is built very like the first, but more simply. As an expression of grief and despair, this movement stands, with the slow movements of the *Sinfonia Concertante* and of K. 488, almost alone among Mozart's concerto movements; not until the Andante con moto of Beethoven's G major Concerto is the same tragic power recaptured. The opening phrase of the orchestra is the introductory exposition: it is 16 measures long, but irregularly divided into 7 and 9 measures—a beautiful example of Mozart's irregular variation of a fundamental regularity. The piano enters and expands this phrase, decorating the 7-measure opening and modulating to the relative major with new but related material. It then enlarges the first measures of the 9-measure half into 16 measures (mm. 32–48), and closes with the last 6 measures, the whole oscillating between E flat major and minor, retaining the minor effect of the original even in transposition, but heightened by the dissonant major-minor clash.[1]

Both in the first and second movements, the solo exposition is essentially an expansion of the introductory exposition, or first ritornello; but in the first movement, the ritornello is itself the expansion of a short, initial motto. The opening phrase of the slow movement is both more complex and more complete, more self-sufficient—above all, less concise—than the opening of the first movement. As everything in the slow movement is derived from this long phrase, I give the first violin part, with fragments of the accompaniment:

---

[1] The expansion of this one orchestral phrase into the entire solo exposition that follows is shown in the following parallel measures:

1–7		7–10		11–16
17–23	24–31 modulation and new form of theme	31–34 in E flat major	35–47 extension	48–53

The relation of this to the other themes is too evident at first hearing to require analysis or comment:

as well as the relation to the first movement[1]:

What is most striking, however, about the opening phrase of the Andantino is its masterly architecture: the accents on the low A♭ (repeated in canon by the second violin) prepare the climax on an A♭ an octave higher in measure 4, and a second climax still another octave higher in measure 6; the level is sustained until the A♭ once again breaks out despairingly in measure 11 (harmonized by a D♭ chord to bring out its full power, and reinforced by the winds accompanying the muted strings) and is concluded (exactly as the exposition of the first movement) by a recitative (mm. 12–15). The whole phrase is like a great arch,[2] its classical rise and fall controlling and mastering the span of tragic grief from the canonic beginning to the climax and then to the halting, almost stammering end.

---

[1] The main theme of the finale is derived from the same mold.
[2] Measures 11–16 are a free mirror version of 1–4, and 7–11 clearly reflect 4–7.

The Concerto

The opening phrase's triple climax on an A♭ dominates the recapitulation within a framework analogous to the first movement's reiterated parallel moments of harmonic tension. Everything moves towards this moment and prepares for it, as the opening itself prepares for it on a smaller scale; after the cadenza it reappears again at the very end, and for the only time in the movement the strings take off their mutes and on the same climactic chord of measure 11 the full sound of the orchestra, *forte*, is heard at last.

The interplay between dramatic expression and abstract form that relates concerto to opera is strikingly shown by the return before the cadenza of the recitative that closed the first ritornello (mm. 12–15). This time it is heard in canon between the piano and the first violin (mm. 111–114), so that Mozart both makes a dialogue of great sadness between solo and orchestra in which the speech rhythms inescapably evoke the sound of words, and at the same time gives us the end of the ritornello in canon as a pendant to the canonic opening. It is rare for the demands of both symmetry and drama to be served so strikingly and in a way so true to the nature of a concerto.

The last movement is, in true classical style, the most relaxed in form. The main theme, ostensibly a brilliant but square rondo opening, is in reality very subtle in phrase structure. The most common way of beginning the finale of a concerto is for the main theme to be played first by the soloist (accompanied or unaccompanied) and then *forte* by the orchestra; all of Beethoven's concerto finales except that in the G major Concerto begin this way, and most of Mozart's. This is not so much tradition, as a necessity of style (although by the time of Brahms the weight of tradition was probably greater than the stylistic rationale). As the finale is itself a resolution of the entire work, and demands melodic material that will resist, rather than imply, development—in other words, a theme that gives the impression of squareness, regularity, and completeness—antiphonal treatment both brings out this character most clearly and colors it most effectively. In the few concerto finales where Mozart does not employ this effect at the opening he either reserves it for a later point in the movement (as in K. 451 and K. 503) or he writes a set of variations (K. 453, K. 491), in which the piano first appears more fittingly to decorate the first variation. The finale of K. 467 is a special case: the main theme, which begins in the orchestra, ends with a repetition of its first phrase, and this phrase, which now rounds off the melody, is surprisingly played, not by the orchestra, but by the piano; so the soloist both finishes what the orchestra began, and also begins exactly as the orchestra did. This is a pun based on the nature of concerto form: nothing could better illuminate the double-faced character of this phrase. In all of this, however, the principle of the alternation of orchestra and solo presenting a squarely cut theme is in no way vitiated.

The Presto finale of K. 271 is full of brio and an unflagging motor energy. The new subdominant theme that Mozart loves to place in the developments of his sonata rondos (or even in any finale in sonata form) here turns into a

213

full-scale minuet with rich, florid ornamentation enchantingly orchestrated; there is a chromatic, almost improvisatory coda leading to a transitional cadenza before the return of the Presto. The later E flat Concerto, K. 482, also has a similar minuet in the subdominant in the middle of its finale, less luxuriant this time, perhaps; it was evidently a device that Mozart judged a success.

In the end, very little of earlier concerto form was considered indispensable by Mozart. He always retained some kind of introductory orchestral exposition, part of which would recur to set off the solo divisions clearly and symmetrically, and he never abandoned the cadenza as a reinforcement of the final cadence. Brilliant passagework to close each solo section is not so much a tradition as a self-evident necessity of the genre: no composer gave this up until virtuoso display itself became distasteful to twentieth-century preciosity. Nor did Mozart invent the opening of the second solo section (the 'development') as a completely unaccompanied and extended solo: this device he did not, however, always employ. Methods of sonata form that had been worked out in chamber music and symphonic style were never applied for their own sake, but only in so far as they were the groundwork for the dramatic contrast of soloist and orchestra. This is the reason for the variety of forms in Mozart's concertos, and for their resistance to codification. Each one sets its own problems, and resolves them without using a pre-established pattern, although always with a classical feeling for proportion and drama.

Half a dozen years went by before Mozart wrote another solo piano concerto. Before K. 271, his concertos had naturally shown his melodic genius and his grace of expression, but they had not broken, except in small details, with the common sociable style of his contemporaries. The violin concertos, with all their charm, have none of the dramatic force of K. 271 and the later piano concertos. Soon after K. 271 came the two-piano Concerto K. 365, an amiable, brilliant, and unimportant piece, and the Concerto for Flute and Harp K. 299, which is hackwork: it is true that Mozart's hackwork is a lesser composer's inspiration, and his craftsmanship is significant even here, but it would be doing Mozart less than justice to discuss this work along with the great concertos. The horn concertos deserve more attention: slight and often perfunctory, they are full of splendid details, lacking only seriousness— which is not to say that the serious works lack humor. For a number of years the concerto form seems not to have interested Mozart greatly, with one remarkable exception, the *Sinfonia Concertante* in E flat major K. 364 for violin and viola.

In the same key as K. 271 and written two years later, this masterpiece is in some ways a companion to it; in particular the principal themes of the slow movements are similar in outline and have the same sorrowful, almost tragic quality. But the sonority of the *Sinfonia Concertante*, inspired by the solo viola part which Mozart probably wrote for himself to play, is unique. The very first chord—the divided violas playing double-stops as high as the first and second violins, the oboes and violins in their lowest register, the horns doubling the cellos and oboes—gives the characteristic sound, which is like the sonority of the viola translated into the language of the full orchestra. This first chord alone is a milestone in Mozart's career: for the first time he had created a sonority at once completely individual and logically related to the nature of the work.

The slow movement and finale of the *Sinfonia Concertante* are less ambitious in form than the corresponding movements of K. 271, if equally beautiful. As in that piano concerto, the slow movement makes important use of canonic imitation, but only for its closing theme; until then, the two soloists play antiphonally, each phrase seeming to outdo the previous one in depth of expression, and the successive phrases becoming shorter and more intense, but forming one long unbroken line. The form is the archaic sonata form, where the second part repeats the material of the first closely, modulating now from the dominant (here the relative major) to the tonic: a feeling of development is achieved as in the sonatas of Scarlatti through the detailed intensity of the modulation. The Presto finale has a form both simple and surprising: we might call it a sonata rondo without a development, which may seem paradoxical. The orchestra presents the main theme, and the soloists continue the exposition with a new series of related themes starting in the tonic and going to the dominant; then both soloists and orchestra return to the tonic and the main theme. If there is a development it is only four measures long, for after a surprise modulation, an exact note-for-note recapitulation starts as a second surprise with the soloists' opening theme in the subdominant (one of Schubert's favorite devices, but rare in Mozart). Everything exposed in the dominant is of course now neatly transformed into the tonic; and the only change is the insertion of a splendid tune for the horn from the opening ritornello. An exhilarating movement, full of invention, it manages to be almost absolutely symmetrical and astonishing at the same time.

The opening movement is perhaps the most significant of the three. The eloquent pathos of the semi-recitatives which open the development is only the most obvious of its unusual features. The material is as tightly linked as in K. 271, by the sonority as well as the melodic outline and the rhythm. The following succession of themes, all from the opening tutti, speaks for itself:

215

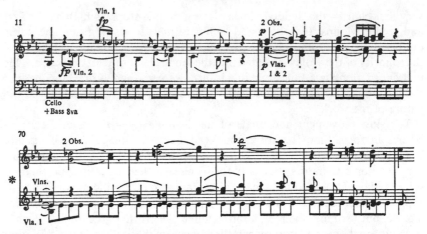

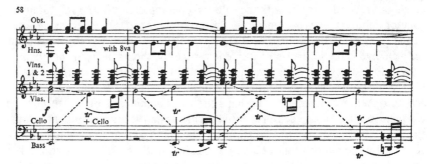

The last-quoted passage, perhaps the least obviously derived from the preceding one, is, however, felt by Mozart as being so close that it is used as a substitute for it in the recapitulation.

The logic of the discourse in this movement represents a great step forward in both maturity and subtlety. The sound of the viola, an instrument Mozart loved, gave him an opportunity to indulge in a richness of inner-part-writing that can only be called luscious. The discourse has a corresponding richness of movement; one passage must suffice here as an example, the extensive preparation for the first solo entry:

With their first two notes the soloists play all the main octave overtones of the E♭'s of the horns and orchestral violas: almost drowned in their sonority at first, the solo instruments—in part because they are doubling the octave overtones of the bass—vibrate intensely after the initial attack. The entrance of the soloists is defined only gradually as they sustain their first notes: the initial grace note—an upward swoop of an octave—blurs the sense of the beat, which has already been disrupted by the syncopations of the preceding measures. The harmonies of the two measures where the soloists hold the high E♭'s are dissonant to the bass that the soloists are doubling, and they continue to affirm their consonance with the bass until the dissonances melt away.

Equally extraordinary is the urgency given by the thematic relationship: the almost painfully expressive orchestral climax at measures 62–63, with the sudden drop to piano, is picked up again by the solo instruments. The relation between measures 62–63 and measure 74, for those with no auditory memory, is elucidated by the repetition of the scale motifs (a_1) and (a_2) four times by the oboes and violins. The miracle of Mozart's style was to make a clearly marked event, an action defined and set apart like the entrance of a character in an opera or the soloist in a concerto, seem to rise almost organically from the music, an integral part of the whole without losing a particle of its individuality or even its separateness. This conception of articulated continuity was a radical departure in the history of music.

By the beginning of 1783, Mozart had three new piano concertos for himself to play, all, however, less imposing than K. 271, and written for a small orchestra in such a way that the wind parts could be omitted and the works performed as piano quintets: this was an attempt to increase their attraction to amateurs, as even before publication manuscript copies of these works were sold to subscribers to Mozart's concerts. K. 413 in F major and K. 415 in C major remain somewhat slight in a style less advanced than that of K. 271 (the last movement of K. 413 even being a minuet, a finale better suited to contemporary chamber music with piano than concerto style), although both have a concision that Mozart could not have achieved easily before. The last movement of K. 415 is in a form that remains odd and complicated in spite of its logic and its workmanship: a sonata-rondo with a double exposition, the first entirely in the tonic (Mozart's normal practice with sonata expositions in concerto form), and a recapitulation that reverses the first and second themes (again not unusual in a Mozart rondo), the whole piece interrupted twice by a plaintive, florid, half-humorous Adagio in the tonic minor. The first interruption is between the two expositions (and justifies the pretension of the double exposition in so loose a form), and the second, quite naturally, as part of the recapitulation before the final appearance of the opening theme. Even in a light work in the popular style of a divertissement, Mozart's feeling for large symmetrical balance remains paramount.

The A major Concerto K. 414, however, is not only more lyric but more broadly conceived than its companions (in spite of K. 415's more brilliant orchestration and military character). The breadth of K. 414 comes from its wealth of melodic material in the first movement: without taking short motifs or transitional material into account, there are four long tunes in the ritornello alone (one of which is never heard again) along with a closing theme, and the piano adds two new ones. The entire development section as well is based on completely new material, and never refers at all to the exposition. This is not lavishness: Mozart uses melodies at once so complex and so complete that they do not bear the weight of development. All the tunes (for that is what they are) turn out to be completely regular: the eight-measure phrase is preserved intact in each one of them and the second phrase of all the melodies begins exactly like the first. Yet there is no feeling of squareness or monotony, and no lack of continuity: the transitions are masterly, and the sense of the weight of each melody and its place in the succession cannot be faulted. What gives this movement its dignity and keeps it from being light-weight is the richness and the continuously expressive quality of the melodies: in no other concerto first movement did Mozart so renounce the advantages of dramatic surprise or the tensions of resolved irregularity. It is, in its way, a *tour de force*, but it stands closer to the violin concertos than to the other more dramatically conceived piano concertos.

A year after these three works, Mozart returned to the grander conception of the concerto he had already shown with K. 271. In 1784 he began to experiment heavily with the form and wrote no less than six concertos, three of them specifically for himself to play at the subscription concerts he was giving in Vienna. The series of six, however, begins apparently somewhat timidly with the Concerto in E flat major K. 449, written for a pupil, Babette Ployer. Like the three concertos that preceded it, K. 449 may be played as a piano quintet, omitting the winds. But it is a more vivid work than any of these, even if written for accompaniment by a small orchestra as Mozart himself affirmed. The slow movement in B flat tries an interesting experiment of repeating the entire solo exposition with its modulation to the dominant in the key of the flatted leading tone or A flat: because of its remote key, this has the effect of a development, and yet the parallel modulation brings us reasonably to the more comfortable subdominant, to which Mozart adds a brief but very startling modulation to B minor before resolving the entire movement with the recapitulation.

The last movement of K. 449 recalls an earlier try at writing a contrapuntal finale to a concerto, K. 175; this time, however, the success is undeniable in a work of great complexity and subtlety with an outward appearance of witty ease. This success is due to the combination of contrapuntal art with *opera buffa* style, the one balancing the other so happily that the lightness and brilliance of a concerto finale are only enhanced by the weight of the more learned technique. The sonata-rondo form is used with great delicacy, and the possibility of an influence of Haydn (in the use of part of the second group in the tonic to effect the return to the main theme after the 'development,' so that the recapitulation actually has already started in the 'development') only emphasizes the originality of the work. Not one of the entrances of the main theme is the same, the comic-opera style and rhythm enabling Mozart not so much to decorate it as to transform and enliven it each time. The recapitulation, in particular, is marvelously subtle: a new theme introduced in C minor in the development is resolved in it, and after a long, electrifying modulation to D flat minor (the extension of a chromatic hint in the exposition), there is a fermata, and the first theme reappears in a new tempo and a new rhythm. We could safely label everything that follows a coda, except that it is used to recapitulate a theme from the 'second group' that had so far appeared only in the dominant. Every detail of this piece has been lovingly worked out, and, in spite of its modest appearance, K. 449 is a bold, even revolutionary concerto.

The two concertos that follow, K. 450 and 451, were written by Mozart for himself. K. 450 in B flat major is, as Mozart himself thought, technically the most difficult of his concertos up till then, and indeed, of those he wrote later. It is also the first to employ the winds with a complete sense of their color and their dramatic possibilities. The winds, in fact, boldly open the concerto on their own, as if to proclaim this new venture from the beginning:

This initial theme, which falls into the form

is the model for all the principal themes of this movement:

and for much of the episodic material as well. The use of winds for solo effects solves one problem for Mozart, that of giving interest to an extended ritornello entirely in the tonic so that the modulation can be reserved for the soloist. K. 449 with only accompanying winds had tried a ritornello which went to the dominant, and the result was a weakened interest in the second exposition. The two expositions of K. 450 are much more strongly differentiated; not only does the ritornello remain in the tonic, but one of its themes, perhaps its most striking one, is never replayed until the recapitulation. All three movements are equally masterly, and the enlarged orchestra that Mozart

220

used is deployed at the opening of the last movement in genuine symphonic style. The cadenzas that Mozart himself composed for this concerto are elaborate, and certainly the most brilliant and powerful he ever wrote out.

The Concerto in D major K. 451, written at the same time, is difficult for many listeners to appreciate today. All three movements, and the first in particular, are built with extremely conventional, impersonal material: an imposing, even brilliant, architecture is created, using this material in the form of blocks. What counts is the ordering, the brilliance, and, above all, the proportions: the significance, the resonance of the individual phrase has much less interest. This is not the Mozart we love, but he himself was proud of this work. We must be grateful for it, in any case: it was Mozart's experience in the handling of such harmonically conventional material that taught him the rhythmic control which he was able to apply in more expressive works. In K. 451 the relation of pure diatonic phrases to heavily (although still conventionally) chromatic ones is perfectly gauged, as is the outlining of large areas of both range of sound (the two-octave ascent from measure 1 to 10) and of rhythm (the introduction of syncopation along with the first chromatic phrase at measure 43). The Concerto in B flat major K. 456, written a little later in 1784, has something of the same quality: less brilliant and grandiose than K. 451, its charm and its melancholy also seem impersonal. But the handling of chromatics is even more far-reaching, and an experiment in combining chromaticism with syncopation is carried as far as Mozart's audacity would go, when a section in the distant key of B minor brings with it a clash of 2/4 against 6/8.

Written just before K. 456, the G major Concerto K. 453 (intended like K. 449 for Babette Ployer) contains innovations of much greater significance. In the first movement, perhaps the most graceful and colorful of all Mozart's military allegros, the ritornello stays in the tonic, but has a second theme so restless and so unstable harmonically that the monotony of a long stretch of the home key is forgotten:

221

(This device of a modulating second theme was shamelessly appropriated by Beethoven for his piano concerto in the same key.) The harmonic plan of K. 453 is also remarkable—a surprise descent to the flat submediant marks the climax of the opening ritornello:

the opening of the development (now descending from the dominant):

and the end of the recapitulation:

The first of these passages prepares the role that the minor mode is to play in the movement, and the others justify it. (Brahms was evidently so impressed by this effect that he absentmindedly put it in at the end of his cadenza for this concerto, where it makes harmonic nonsense.) It should be clear that these surprise cadences are not an intricate system of cross-references but a means of emphasizing and clarifying the inner proportions of the movement.

The C major slow movement is even bolder. In a number of his works in sonata form, Haydn makes no modulation proper to the dominant, only a pause and a bold leap. But there is no record of his trying this when the material before the leap lasts only a few seconds. This, however, is what Mozart does here. The first exposition, or ritornello, in the tonic is what makes the dramatic concision of the second exposition possible without smashing the tonal aesthetic on which Mozart depends. Even in the ritornello, the effect is already impressive and moving, without the use of modulation: a quiet, expressive, opening five-measure phrase in the strings, followed by a silence; then the orchestra softly begins an accompanied and unrelated oboe solo, as if the first phrase had never existed. The piano starts with the same opening phrase, with a *ritenuto*[1] before an even longer pause, and then plunges brutally into the dominant minor with a passionate new melody. No slow movement of Mozart had ever before attempted a dramatic stroke of such magnitude; even the turbulent development section in the second movement of the A minor Sonata K. 310 is arrived at gradually. In K. 453, however, this effect is used as a frame as well, so that its significance is as much formal as emotional: the development section starts with the same five-measure phrase followed by a silence, but this time in the dominant, and scored for solo winds alone. After the silence, the piano, again with an abrupt change, begins a series of chromatic modulations that reaches sequentially to C sharp minor. The return to the tonic is the boldest stroke yet and the logical outcome of all that has gone before. This return and the first seven measures of the recapitulation show how much dramatic movement can be compressed into a few measures:

---

[1] The added fermata may indicate not only a *ritenuto* but a very short expressive cadenza: to play a cadenza in the fermata over the rest is unthinkable. (See mm. 93–94, p. 224.)

In these eleven measures, the first four cut directly and powerfully from G sharp major and minor to C major, and from *pp* to *f*; the beautiful opening phrase returns and is played, this time with the barest minimum of added ornamentation.[1] Then after the silence, a new brusque attack, which will resolve the dominant minor of the first one (in the analogous place of the exposition at measure 35) into the tonic minor. The recapitulation reserves the closing theme of the exposition for a coda, after the soloist's cadenza. But before this closing theme, the initial phrase is used once more with magnificent effect. The woodwinds play it immediately following the cadenza; until now, each time it appeared it was left unresolved on the dominant—not only unresolved, but almost isolated, with a silence that separated it from all that followed. This last time, it melts into the succeeding phrase and is resolved in one of the most expressive, and yet perhaps most conventional, phrases that Mozart could have written:

---

[1] Here is the question of ornamentation in Mozart at its most problematic: if we have added anything to the phrase in its previous appearance, we must add still more here. Yet the music requires a marked simplicity for its full effect.

moving chromatically through the subdominant into the piano's cadence. This withholding of the resolution of the main theme until the very end of the movement, together with the silence that sets off each one of its appearances except the last, are only the most salient points of a work that is an important step in Mozart's transformation of a genre, making it capable of bearing the greatest musical weight.

The last movement of K. 453 also represents a new departure. Here Mozart first tries the variation form as a concerto finale.[1] The relaxed looseness of this form is not an unmitigated advantage in a finale. While it provides a resolution for the more dramatic and less decorative forms of the previous movements, it is hard to hold it together, or to give the repetitive pattern a clear architecture. The simplest and most common variation scheme throughout the whole eighteenth century is to arrive at a climax by decreasing the note-values (i.e., increasing the speed) with each successive variation. In the latter part of the century, brilliance was achieved by making the last two variations a florid Adagio with coloratura effects followed by a brilliant Allegro, a scheme that could be both loose and mechanical to the point of superficiality. Another scheme was to enforce unity by a return to the opening tempo after the acceleration: for the return to have its full effect, a basically slow tempo was needed, and while this could be used for the finales of intimate chamber works like Beethoven's Sonatas op. 109 and op. 111, it was unthinkable for the ending of the more sociable classical concerto.[2] A variation-finale in a quick tempo is much more difficult to write: the strain can be sensed in the last movement of the *Eroica* and even in the more impressive choral variations

---

1 Paul Badura-Skoda has pointed out to me that Mozart had previously replaced the finale of K. 175 by a variation movement (K. 382).
2 An attempt to combine both the return to the opening and a more brilliant finale can be found in Mozart's Violin Sonata in G major K. 379, where the original theme returns but at a faster tempo.

of the Ninth Symphony, and in the latter, the success of the form is due to Beethoven's widening of the frame.

Mozart's solution is a coda, Presto, in comic opera style. The theme of the variations is a bourrée of great popular charm. While the tempo remains the same, the note-values of the accompanying figures and decoration in the first three variations decrease from eighth-notes to triplets to sixteenth-notes. The fourth variation is in minor and so heavily chromatic that it has the modulatory effect of a 'development' section (the conception of variation-form being guided in Mozart's hands by the ideals of the sonata style); in this variation, too, we find Mozart's most remarkable use of wind doubling so far in any concerto:

where the first violin is doubled two octaves below, and the second violin an octave above; later in the variation, the piano is dramatically accompanied by an interjection of triple octaves in the wind. The last variation, half in military style and half like a cadenza from the piano—a remarkable conception—leads to the *opera buffa* coda, in which the main theme of the variations only reappears impertinently after almost half the Presto is over. Today, these variations are generally played too fast for Mozart's plan of gradual acceleration in the first four variations and the contrast with the Presto to be appreciated; most Allegrettos of the period were meant to be played more slowly than those written after the turn of the century.

The greatest of all Mozart's concerto finales is that of K. 459 in F major. The first two movements of this work are already heavy with Baroque sequences and contrapuntal imitation, as if to prepare for the final Allegro assai, for the last movement is a complex synthesis of fugue, sonata-rondo-finale, and *opera buffa* style. The weightiest and the lightest forms of music are fused here in a work of unimaginable brilliance and gaiety, going far beyond the finale of K. 449, with all its contrapuntal ingenuity. The light rondo theme is stated by the piano solo and each of its two phrases repeated by the woodwind alone. The full orchestra, *forte*, immediately starts a fugue on an entirely new theme which leads to a long symphonic development and cadence in the manner of an opera overture. Then the soloist begins his exposition which quickly modulates with a variant of the main theme, a new second theme, and the orchestral fugue theme for a dominant cadence. After a full return of the main theme, a second tutti starts without a break in D minor: this time it is a double fugue, with the original fugue-theme combined with the main rondo-theme. The piano does not enter until more than thirty measures of symphonic fugal development have gone by, and when it does come in, the writing remains still largely contrapuntal. The recapitulation is in mirror form, with the first theme last—held back, in fact, until after the cadenza. The movement finishes in a witty burst of *opera buffa* echo effects. The long contrapuntal tuttis give this movement the most symphonic sonority of any of the finales: even if the trumpet and drum parts, now lost, were replaced, the impression could not be any greater.[1] The form of this movement, at once concise and expansive, is the synthesis of Mozart's experience and of his ideals of form. Everything plays a role here—operatic style, pianistic virtuosity, Mozart's increasing knowledge of Baroque counterpoint and of Bach in particular, and the symmetrical balance and dramatic tensions of sonata style. The first movement, military but tranquilly dominated by its calm sequences, and the lyrical, restless, and poignant Allegretto 'slow' movement are equally sensitive. The whole concerto is one of Mozart's most original.

The principal lines of the classical piano concerto were laid down in 1776 by K. 271, but until the six great concertos of 1784, Mozart had never explored the technical range of the form. From this point on, there was no advance in skill; everything that follows is, in a sense, merely an expansion of what he had found out with these six concertos. What remained to be tried, however, was the emotional weight that the genre would bear. Mozart had not yet written a concerto in the minor mode. Nor had full symphonic grandeur been essayed: the brilliance of K. 451 (like that of K. 415) is the brilliance of the operatic overture compounded with virtuosity. In 1785, the year following, the range and the depth of Mozart's achievement were extended by two works written within a month of each other, the concertos K. 466 and 467.

With the D minor Concerto K. 466, in particular, we leave the history of

---

[1] Unless Mozart's memory failed him when he wrote his catalogue, and there never were any such parts.

the concerto as a specific form. It is not superior to the concertos that preceded it—the level reached earlier makes any such preference arbitrary, even though it was historically a more influential work. But the D minor Concerto cannot be considered only as a concerto, even as a supreme example of the form. With both K. 466 and K. 467, Mozart created works that belong as much to the history of the symphony and even the opera as the concerto, just as with *Figaro* we enter a world where opera and chamber music meet.

The D minor Concerto is almost as much myth as work of art: when listening to it, as to Beethoven's Fifth Symphony, it is difficult at times to say whether we are hearing the work or its reputation, our collective image of it. It is probably not the most played of Mozart concertos. But even at a time when Mozart's reputation was low—when his grace obscured his power—the estimation of this work remained high. It is not a work, of course, that is much discussed (it excites no controversy) or much imitated; nor is it the favorite Mozart concerto of many musicians, just as no one's favorite Leonardo is the *Mona Lisa*. Like the G minor Symphony and *Don Giovanni*, the D minor Concerto may be said to transcend its own excellences.

The historical importance of K. 466 is that it belongs to the series of works which made Mozart the supreme composer in most musicians' minds within ten years of his death. It represents the Mozart who was considered the greatest of 'romantic' composers, and it was the character of this work and a few others like it that pushed Haydn into the background for more than a century. It was the concerto that Beethoven played and wrote cadenzas for. It is one of the fullest realizations of that aspect of Mozart which the nineteenth century quite rightly named 'daemonic,' and which, for so long, made a balanced assessment of the rest of his work so difficult.

There is room here only for a brief discussion, and it is best to approach the work obliquely in order to get somewhere near its center. There is, as I have said, in the D minor concerto no progress in concerto technique proper, but it manifests an important advance in purely musical skill—the art of sustaining an increase in rhythmic motion, that is, the creation of excitement. In the classical style, this can only be done by discrete steps, but there are many such steps possible, and the art of controlling their relations—i.e. sustaining and intensifying a climax—is very complex. Let us look at the first important climax that concerns both the soloist and the orchestra:

Mozart

The increase of motion in this passage is induced in a great variety of ways:

1. In measure 93, the melody, which has been pulsating on one note, begins to move.

2. The piano, silent until measure 95, adds sixteenth-note motion to the syncopated quarters of the orchestra. The pattern of the right hand begins again every half-note.

3. Measure 97: the right-hand pattern now begins again every quarter note.

4. Measure 98: the horn entrance in the middle of the measure doubles the basic accent of the measure.[1]

5. Measure 99: the harmony, which has been changing every measure, now begins to change three times every two measures. There is an increase in a subordinate melodic rhythm, as the piano's sixteenth-notes all begin to have melodic significance, not merely harmonic. The syncopated quarter-note rhythm in the violins begins to change into eighth-notes every two beats.

6. Measure 100: the upper melodic voice in the piano moves every quarter-note, instead of every half-note.

7. Measure 102: The second wind entrance (bassoons, measure 101) was two and a half measures later than the first; the third entrance, here in the oboe, is only one measure and a half later.

8. Measure 104: The harmony changes four times a measure instead of twice a measure.

9. Measure 106: The motion of the violins and violas is doubled.

10. Measure 107: The upper melodic voice in the piano is quadrupled in motion, as by the end of the measure it has clearly taken over the sixteenth-note motion.

11. Measure 108: The melodic line of the bass begins to move twice as fast, and its rhythmic animation four times as fast.

12. Measure 110: The motion of the accompanying voices is increased by the entrance of the winds.

13. Measure 112: The speed of the melodic pattern is doubled and the harmony changes twice a measure instead of once. (Even the dotted figure in the winds now occurs twice a measure.)

This new range of sustained acceleration accounts in part for what might be called the 'romantic' excitement generated by this concerto.[2] The juggling with rhythmic counters—note-values proper, harmonic motion, melodic pattern—is done in so accomplished a way that when one of them disappears

---

[1] These measures are a repetition of the opening of the ritornello; at the corresponding place there, the horn enters on the *first* beat, while here the accent is put on the weaker beat.

[2] This excitement is reflected even in the orchestral color. There is an astonishing passage at measure 88 where the timpani alone (without the cellos) softly double the bass two octaves below the rest of the orchestra and the piano.

or slows down, another doubles or quadruples its speed, and it is always the accelerating part on which the weight of interest lies. Even the introduction of a faster rhythm, generally accomplished with such tact and, indeed, given here as so often in an accompanying part, is signalled by its being the entrance of the soloist. Everything concurs in this drive towards the climax: the whole shape of the passage is a gradual and passionate ascent (even the bass ascends with the upper voices for the first half) followed by an orchestrated crescendo. One aspect of the classical aesthetic can be seen here with particular lucidity: the dramatic manipulation of discrete and well-defined shapes to achieve an impression of continuity by finely graded transitions.

In addition, one of the limits of the classical style is reached: the first four measures of the example cited above (which are an exact repeat of the concerto's opening) go as far as the style will allow in the direction of rhythmic instability.[1] There is a similar figure at the opening of the *Prague* Symphony, but the syncopations cease once the voice takes on a melodic character: in K. 466 the syncopations continue and carry the burden of the initial theme. Combined with the menacing bass motif, these syncopations give a powerful impression of foreboding. When these measures are played *forte*, they have to be radically transformed (mm. 16 ff.) into something very like Don Giovanni's duel with the Commendatore; for the concerto starts (like K. 459, K. 467, and K. 491, along with so many sonatas of the period) with the complete theme played *piano* and then *forte*, but breaks the bonds of this symmetry. The energy of the music is such that it is difficult to hold it within the tonic for the entire opening ritornello: this recurrent formal problem is resolved here by a brilliant compromise. The modulation to the relative major begins, and goes too far—so far, in fact, that it turns back into the tonic in just the way it will later in the recapitulation. This reserves the larger action (the establishment of a secondary tonality) for the solo piano, but gives the opening tutti its share of dramatic movement. It also makes the recapitulation at this point both a faithful reflection of the first exposition and a resolution of the second.

No concerto before K. 466 exploits so well the latent pathetic nature of the form—the contrast and struggle of one individual voice against many. The most characteristic phrases of the solo and the orchestra are never interchanged without being rewritten and reshaped: the piano never plays the menacing opening in its syncopated form, but transforms it into something rhythmically more defined and more agitated; the orchestra never plays the recitative-like phrase with which the piano opens, and which it repeats throughout the development section. Yet the material of the concerto is remarkably homogeneous; so much of it is related with striking effect to the opening piano phrase, and always accompanied by the same parallel thirds:

---

[1] Except, of course, in a recitative, or an improvisatory cadenza-like style, where definition is not expected.

opening of first solo

opening of the "second group"

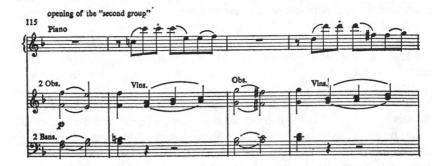

theme of "second group"

opening of finale

Finale: second theme of tonic group

234

The relations are almost too obvious; together with the chromatic phrase cited on p. 229–30 (mm. 99–102) and all its derivations,[1] the motif on which they are based and the continuous appearance of the parallel thirds dominate the sound of the concerto. For the first time the first and last movements of a concerto are so strikingly and openly related, although the *Sinfonia Concertante* K. 364 had already made a first gesture in that direction. This new openness of thematic relations, this parade of unity, arises from an inward dramatic necessity, the sustaining of a unified tone demanded by the tragic style. The power of this tragic character is such that it even spills over into the slow movement; if we isolated this movement, the Romanza, from the others, its dramatic middle section would be inexplicable. There is a similar eruption of violence in the slow movement of the great A minor Sonata K. 310, the first of Mozart's essays in the tragic vein. Although the exposition of that movement has already a pronouncedly dramatic character, the force of the development is there, too, almost unmotivated unless it is seen in relation to the opening movement. The even greater contrast of the D minor concerto is a mark of Mozart's greater ease of control. The most remarkable sign of this ease, however, it the supple phase structure of the first movement as well as the expressive transformations of its recapitulation.

In spite of its looser structure and the resolution in major of the coda, this tragic atmosphere permeates the finale to the point of turning the relative major into minor—the F minor theme at measure 93 is striking—and transforming the recapitulation of one of the secondary themes into an oscillation between major and minor that is a foreshadowing of Schubert's pathos. Almost all the modulations are brusque to the point of brutality, and the first orchestral tutti has a brilliant violence that Mozart had never employed in a symphony until then, much less in a concerto. The resemblances of this movement to the finale of the G minor Symphony K. 550 are more than thematic, but in the latter work Mozart was able to be even more uncompromising. However, I should not like this last remark to be taken as an expression of the usual disapproval, which I do not share, of the brilliance and gaiety of the coda of K. 466.

The pendant to the D minor Concerto, the Concerto in C major K. 467, is a work of symphonic majesty, and follows it as the *Jupiter* Symphony K. 551 does the G minor. The *Jupiter*, however, has a surface conventionality which is deceptive—it will not condescend to material which is too clearly

---

[1] The phrase first appears in measures 9–12, and from it come the themes at measures 44–47, 58–60; the relation to 28–30 is also obvious, and to all further appearances of these passages. The relations between the first movement and finale are also wider and deeper than I have exposed here.

striking. The C major Concerto makes no such pretense, although its main theme is similar to the opening of the *Jupiter*. This concerto is Mozart's first true essay in orchestral grandeur. Before this, the symphonies, even the *Linz*, K. 425, had striven more for brilliance than for majesty: with the rhythmic structure of the classical style it was a more easily attainable goal. It is the tranquil breadth of K. 467 that leads to the achievements of the *Prague* and the *Jupiter*. More than in any other previous work is Mozart's ability to work with large masses—to think in blocks and areas of sound—so in evidence.

The opening tutti masses the winds as a group against the strings with no solo wind effects except briefly at measure 28. The rhythmic breadth is particularly remarkable: while the excitement of K. 466 brought in a large number of short phrases in the opening ritornello, and several dramatic pauses, the beginning of K. 467 is continuous and massive, the tonic key laid out as a wide and firm base. The phrases are all a regular four measures in length (with one overlapping at measure 12) and, towards the end of the tutti, broader five-measure phrases (at measures 48, 60, and 64—the latter overlapping to preserve a four-measure rhythm and acting in the end like a *ritenuto* that holds back the final beat). Only just before the entrance of the soloist, as a preparation, does the rhythm become fragmented.

The piano part is particularly rich and inventive in new kinds of keyboard figuration, sometimes of a remarkable density. Most striking in this movement, too, is the long-range feeling for tonal areas and their stability. The modulation to the dominant is heavily reinforced by quickly turning to the dominant minor,[1] which I quote because of its extraordinary repercussions later in the piece:

---

[1] A dominant minor at this point of the exposition is both disruptive and stabilizing: it stabilizes the dominant major, and in so doing increases the tension with the tonic.

This passage never actually appears again except for measures 121–123; what happens in the recapitulation is the reappearance of the opening theme in the subdominant—a means of resolution that Mozart uses so frequently—and proceeds as follows:

It is not the *melodic* material of measures 110–120 that appears in the recapitulation, but its *harmonic* structure, which is there resolved by the turn to the subdominant minor, as can be seen from the identical ending of both passages. The primacy of harmony over melody in the recapitulation considered as resolution is clear: harmonic resolution is more important to the classical style than melodic symmetry.

The development section also is affected by the grandeur of style: it is entirely based on subsidiary material,[1] and it is not intended deliberately to recall the exposition, which has already given considerable development to the main theme. The tranquil introduction of what sounds like new material only adds to the breadth, and the richly passionate climax is in the tonic minor, so that the return of the main theme in the major brightens and clarifies with the greatest economy of motion. The tutti that follows is twice as long as the orchestral section opening the recapitulation of any other Mozart concerto; moreover, for nineteen of its twenty-two measures it is an unvaried replaying of the opening measures. This kind of expansive gesture is of a peculiarly symphonic nature: the concerto generally requires more embroidery, but the largeness and the freedom of Mozart's central conception here enable him to forego variation.

The same simplicity reigns in the Andante, an aria with muted strings and a pizzicato bass. Over a continuously throbbing accompaniment that never ceases except for one breathtaking moment, the soloist traces a series of long-breathed cantilenas of the greatest poignance: the only hint of virtuosity is exclusively vocal, an imitation of the long expressive leaps from one register to another in the operatic cavatina. If the form appears complicated to describe, it is only because it is so individual that we have no words with which to categorize it. The description is worth attempting: nowhere else are Mozart's freedom and his sensitivity to the emotional power of a structure more in evidence.

The opening twenty-two measures in the orchestra seem like one unbroken melody, but they are split by Mozart into three parts for the rest of the movement: *A* (mm. 2–7), *B* (8–11), and *C* (12–22) will make convenient labels.[2] After the ritornello the piano plays *A* and *B* in the tonic; ten measures later, *B* and *C* are played in the dominant (mm. 45–55). Since there is clearly developmental material at measures 55–61 and 65–72, and a recapitulation from 75 to the end, we could describe the form logically as a sonata—but that is not the way it sounds. For a new melody in the relative minor appears after a modulation at measure 38, and this is preceded by a strong tonic cadence and a long trill from the piano. The tonic close followed by the relaxed harmonic relationship of the relative minor and the strongly sectional phrasing are those of the da capo aria or the rondo, like the Romanza of the D minor Concerto. And in the middle of the development—again after

---

[1] Mainly that exposed in measures 170, 28, and 160.

[2] Quoted on facing page.

a cadential trill from the piano—yet another new melody is introduced (m. 62), this time in the subdominant, an even more relaxed key equally typical of the rondo. Still more characteristic of the rondo form (C.P.E. Bach's, in particular) is the recapitulation which begins in the flat mediant A flat major, after a modulation that is set apart—as if to emphasize how extraordinary it is—by its being the only moment in the entire movement when the accompanying triplets cease, and we can hear the slow melody of the winds alone (mm. 71–72). This modulation, the single moment of stillness, has the magical quality of some of Schubert's, and it is all the more unexpected as the passage just before has prepared an obvious return to the tonic. What we expect, in short, is to hear the original melody once again all the way through in the tonic. Mozart never completely fails to gratify a wish that he has himself aroused: after *A* in the flat mediant, *B* appears highly decorated in the tonic minor as a transition to *C* in its original tonic position; for a coda, *B* appears once more in the tonic major, and a new theme, only four measures long, concludes the work.

If a description is to correspond to what is actually heard, this is not a sonata movement at all, in spite of our being able to fit it neatly into that category. What we hear is almost like an improvisation, a series of melodies freely extended, softly floating over a pulsating accompaniment. Like a continuous flow of song, it seems the simplest, most naïve of forms: the simplicity is underlined by each new melody's being introduced by a straightforward change of key, as if there were no tight tonal pattern, and as if the continuity came only from the throbbing rhythm that passes from the strings to the winds to the piano, steadily and quietly supporting a stream of melody. Yet all of this is subtly guided—influenced rather than molded—by the ideals of the sonata style, nothing is arbitrary, and only when it is over does one realize with what a delicate balance everything has been weighed. The phrase structure seems as irregular, too, as an improvisation, yet the total shape has a regularity that defies belief. The principal melody, the opening ritornello, has the following shape: 3 + 3, 2 + 2, (1 + 1 + 1 + 1 + 1) or 5, 3 + 3; the climax is dead center, at the beginning of the five-measure phrase, and the symmetry of 3 + 3 at the beginning and the end is achieved without the last phrases being in any way a repetition of the first ones:

The quickening of the large rhythmic pattern comes in the change from 3-measure phrases to 2-measure phrases: the 5-measure phrase falls into units of single measures, thus continuing the increase of animation, and yet its greater length counters and balances this with a holding-back that is a transition to the final symmetry which resolves. The apparent irregularity gives us—as does the entire movement—that deeply moving impression of improvised song and formal design.

These two concertos, K. 466 and K. 467, written in 1785, cannot, in any sense, be called 'better' than many others Mozart had written and was to write. Nevertheless, they represent a liberation of the genre, a demonstration that the concerto could stand with equal dignity beside any other musical form, capable of expressing the same depth of feeling and of working out the most complex musical idea. What could follow these works might seem to be only further refinement, yet some great works were still to come, and they contain surprises.

In the winter of 1785–86, while working on *Figaro*, Mozart wrote three piano concertos for his subscription concerts. They are the first such works he had written with clarinets, his favorite wind instrument, in the orchestra. (At the end of this period, he also wrote the great Clarinet Trio K. 498.) The clarinets dominate the first of the three concertos, K. 482 in E flat major. The woodwinds altogether play a larger role than in any other concerto; even the bassoon has a considerable share of solo melodic work. Perhaps for this reason, this concerto places the greatest musical reliance on tone-color, which is, indeed, almost always ravishing. One lovely example of its sonorties comes near the beginning:

(Full score)

A few measures before, this same passage was scored an octave lower for horns and bassoons, and here we have the unusual sound of the violins' providing the bass for the solo clarinets. The simplicity of the sequence concentrates all our interest on tone-color, and what follows—a series of woodwind solos—keeps it there. The orchestration throughout, in fact, has a greater variety than Mozart had wished or needed to use before, and fits the brilliance, charm, and the somewhat superficial grace of the first movement and the finale. The slow movement in C minor is of a much deeper cast, but its pathos is elegant and even theatrical, above all accessible, and it does not abandon this new interest in pure color. Its form is close to Haydn's beloved double-variation scheme, being a rondo-variation set: the use of muted strings, long sections for woodwind alone, a duet for flute and bassoon, and menacing trills in unison strings all contribute to the orchestral palette; the movement was a great success at its first performance, being encored. Like K. 271, also in E flat major, the rondo-finale is interrupted by a minuet in A flat major, with the orchestration here, too, making a striking but less lavish use of pizzicato. If this minuet is not as impressive as the earlier one, that is in part because the high spirits of the last movement occasion much purely mechanical brilliance; the movement as a whole is an imitation of the finale of K. 450 without the latter's invention and freshness. The simplicity of the minuet is perhaps an advance on the heavily ornate style of K. 271, where expression still depends largely on luxuriance of detail. This new spareness does not come from Mozart's failure to fill out ornamentation, even though the concerto shows a few places incompletely written out (he composed it, after all, only for his own use). The melody appears equally unadorned in the orchestral parts, which double the solo, and while the solo part may need the addition of a few ornaments, most of the simplicity must be ascribed not to carelessness but largely to the development of Mozart's style.

One great suppleness of the concerto form—a freedom that it shares with no other—is illustrated in the happiest way by the Concerto in A major K. 488; that is, the placing of the end of the exposition, or—to give it a description that does not convey such a strong impression of a label—the placing of the last firm cadence on the dominant. There is naturally always a tutti or ritornello following the solo exposition, and the last cadence on the dominant may occur in one of three places: with the last solo phrase before the tutti, so that the orchestra begins the series of modulations called the development (as in K. 459 and K. 467); at the end of the tutti, so that the solo part begins in the dominant and initiates the new sense of movement (as in K. 456, K. 466, etc.); or in the middle of the tutti (K. 451, K. 482, among others). Mozart's first mature work in this form, K. 271, already played with this freedom by having the piano interrupt the tutti and so emphasize this ambiguity. Whatever is done, the opening of the tutti is always an affirmation of the dominant—a declaration, in short, of where we are and a reinforcement of the polarity of the exposition.

K. 488 takes advantage of this situation in a new way: after the pianist's closing trill on the dominant, the ritornello begins its cadential theme only to cut it off sharply and surprisingly after a brief six measures. Then, as we naturally expect a strong dominant cadence to resolve this, we are given something else, an entirely new theme (mm. 143–148):

The new theme has a cadential flavor, but a relatively weak one. The following development is entirely based on this theme (and another new one, much shorter, introduced by the piano). It was not unusual to begin a development section with new material; Mozart did it frequently in the sonatas, and a minor composer like Schroeter, whose work Mozart liked, frequently did it in concertos. What is rare and striking is that this beautiful theme is both an end and a beginning: a final cadence for the tutti, and the opening of the development—it acts as a kind of pun within the structure. Its double nature may be sufficiently indicated by the fact that Mozart evidently also considers it a part of the expository function of the movement, and replays it in the tonic in the middle of the recapitulation.

This is not a formal gesture for an effect of novelty, or a surprise for its own sake. Mozart returns in this work to the melancholy lyricism of the earlier A major Concerto K. 414; by withholding part of the exposition until the development, and by making this final theme as much a resolution of the transitional ritornello as the opening of a new section, he attains the uninterrupted melodic flow of the earlier work without its looseness of structure. The classical period worked almost entirely with separate, articulated units: vanquishing the overarticulate and sectional tendency of the style was the real mastery of Haydn and Mozart. Paradoxically, the clarity of function of the stylistic units made possible such effects of ambiguity as we have just seen: if the passage cited were not so clearly both a cadential resolution (and therefore the end of a section) and a new theme, Mozart would not be able to glide with such lyrical ease over what would ordinarily be a break of continuity.

Mozart's ability to draw the utmost poignance of expression from the simplest means is seen at its most striking in the Adagio that follows, and, above all, in the opening melody. The skeleton of the theme is a simple descending scale, accompanied by a parallel longer movement above it. Like so many of Bach's melodies, Mozart's single voice traces two polyphonic lines. In schematic form:

arranged so that every detail comes forth with the greatest possible pathos:

The harmonic suspension at the opening of measure 2 brings out the full expressive quality of the drop of the seventh in the melody: the displaced resolution of the suspension into the low E♯ of the bass only serves to make the second B in the right hand an expressive dissonance. The structure of the melody may be two regular parallels, but its beauty and its passionate melancholy lie in the irregularity of rhythm and variety of phrasing which reveal every possible expressive facet of the two simple descending lines. The difference in the outline of the sixth in each of the first three measures is an example of the richness of invention. Most remarkable, perhaps, is the withholding of the resolution of the D in the third measure of the melody until the sixth measure, and most expressive is the almost tragic retracing of the whole line in the seventh measure. I must content myself with those details, but this wonderful theme would repay more study than I have room for, particularly in its spacing of voices.

Before there is a misunderstanding, I hasten to add that I do not suppose that Mozart started with any such skeleton as I have given, and then embellished it. Reading a composer's mind, retracing the steps by which he worked, is not a viable critical method even when the composer is alive and one can ask him how he did it—he generally does not know. A composer's sketches are not as much help as is sometimes believed; Beethoven, the most prodigious sketcher of all time, expressly said that the sketches were only a kind of shorthand to remind him of the more complete ideas he carried in his head. How Mozart wrote the opening of the slow movement of K. 488—whether he started with the beginning or the middle, or whether it came forth from his brain as a fully-armed *Gestalt*—we shall never know. Although Mozart, too, made many sketches (more and more as he grew older), he could certainly carry in his head as much or more than any other composer in history.

The skeleton of the melody I have indicated is then, emphatically, not the 'musical idea.' Nor is it (although it is not irrelevant) what makes this theme so beautiful: when we admire the bone structure of a beautiful face, we are not really interested in osteology. But the tendency to think in terms of diatonic scale progressions is basic to late eighteenth-century composers, above all in the use of expressive dissonances and their resolution downwards. Mozart's genius lay in the understanding of how the expressive possibilities of such a simple progression could be used, and how it could give unity to a phrase, and to the movement between phrases, while the melodic line that traced and decorated the progression was as varied in rhythm and phrasing as the character of the music demanded.

Another device of unity—this time between larger sections—may be seen if we compare the opening phrase of the piano, the opening of the first tutti, and the opening of the next solo section:

in the third example, the piano begins its melody again, but combines it with the shape of the orchestra's phrase, so that the two are fused into one. This synthesis of musical elements which later extends to the second theme in A major enables Mozart to give the second theme the character both of a second subject and of the central section of an A B A form,[1] using certain elements of sonata style to dramatize an essentially looser structure.

The last of the three concertos is the greatest, the Concerto in C minor K. 491. Like K. 466, it is in the tragic vein: more intimate, it evades the theatricality of the earlier work. It is less operatic and closer to chamber music. What it loses in grandeur it makes up in refinement, and it achieves an equivalent breadth in a very different way. This concerto gave Mozart considerable trouble, not just in details, but in its proportions. There is a great deal of rewriting in the manuscript, and—what is uncommon for Mozart, who rarely made such large changes—there is an insertion of a new long section in the opening ritornello. The reason for this considerable change lies in the solo exposition. A full hundred measures after the piano has entered, we have:

---

[1] There is a direct expository movement from first to second theme, but no recapitulation of the second theme: however, the themes are closely related, and a recapitulation of the first ritornello is used as a substitute.

and yet, sixty measures later, we find the same cadence in the relative major, more expansively:

In other words, the exposition formally closes twice—the passage preceding the first cadence has, in fact, most of the signs of being the end of the exposition, with all the virtuosity and—almost—all the finality. If the opening ritornello were as short as it originally was before Mozart extended it, the relative proportions of solo exposition and ritornello would already be perfect at the first of these cadences—the solo exposition in all the concertos being the more expansive of the two.

What follows the first cadence, however, is not a cadential tutti but a new secondary theme and a new closing theme, both presented at length. Between them occurs a passage at first consideration even more extraordinary: the opening theme is replayed, beginning in the relative major—the normal practice of Haydn during the second half of an exposition, and not uncommon in Mozart—but quickly modulating within one measure to E flat minor and sustaining a series of modulations before returning to E flat major. Harmonically this has the character of a development section, and in this place it has a force and a passion that are unforgettable.

Mozart is experimenting once again, and this time more daringly, with the placing of the final dominant cadence of the exposition. There is, in a sense, a double exposition after the orchestral exposition, which therefore had to be enlarged to fit the wider proportions. None of this is experimentation for its own sake, or even for the sake of novelty and surprise: it comes from the character of the music and from the material.

The main theme has a terse, concentrated outline that is not often found in Mozart, and is much more typical of Haydn. The first movement of the C minor Concerto is, in fact, closely related to Haydn's Symphony no. 78 in the same key, written only four years before. The opening of the Haydn:

is recognizably like the beginning of the concerto, although Mozart's conception of phrase and period is much broader and less constrained:

The entrance of the oboes in measure 8 is that of an accompanying harmonic voice, but by measure 11 they have imperceptibly become the melodic part. This shift from accompanying to principal role is done with even greater smoothness than Haydn's similar procedure at the beginning of op. 33 no. 1.[1] Mozart needs all his subtlety to arrive at the high seriousness of tragedy with material essentially so shortwinded—in comparison with K. 466 and 467— and so angularly characterized. The irregularity of the phrase-structure sets the details in relief.

More than the opening of any previous concerto, these measures make us concentrate on their linear aspect, and not only because the first few bars are all played in unison. Above all, the nature of the melody, its angular

---

[1] Quoted and discussed on pages 115–117.

chromaticism, the phrasing, the sequences with rising sixths that follow each other staccato, give unusual importance to the intervallic relations. (On the first page of K. 466, for example, we are far more aware of the texture—the menacing rumble in the bass, the syncopated pulsations.) The beginning of K. 491 is almost oddly neutral for a few measures until its implications make themselves realized; there is a reserve, a restraint about this work that is absent in K. 466. In the earlier work, breadth is achieved easily by the regularity of the opening paragraph, all in four- and two-measure groups: the rise to the first climax is achieved smoothly. In the C minor Concerto, the material seems to have shrunk: the opening phrase stakes everything on a series of rising sixths and descending seconds. The first page of K. 466 is not really built out of much more, but there the regularity both of phrasing and of the opening ascent gives the listener a sense of paragraph and not of separate clauses; the irregularity of the opening of K. 491 sets the details rather than the larger movement in focus and we are inevitably more conscious of the individual units.

The 'double' solo exposition (making a triple exposition with the first ritornello) is a natural consequence of this—the fragmentation of the larger form corresponding to the inner divisions of the opening statement. This is not a mystical or holistic doctrine of correspondence between totality and part. When a classical composer wanted to use material that was melodically fragmented (as Beethoven, for example, did most of the time), where each detail appears *immediately* to have a significance that can only be understood beyond the phrase, he combined such material with extreme regularity of phrasing in the opening statement in order to overcome the divisive effect: the opening of a sonata may be a motto but not an epigram. It should be recalled that regularity of phrasing implies the imposition of a longer and slower beat over the main pulse, and the consciousness of a larger time scale. There are many works of Mozart with irregular phrase-lengths which enforce breadth by a largeness of statement and a symmetrical balance of the irregular elements as in the slow movement of K. 467 (the slow movement of the G minor Quintet is a more momentous example). But in the C minor Concerto, Mozart is dealing with a fragmentary melodic line that requires an irregularity of phrase. That is why there is a great variety of clearly defined although related themes in this movement, and yet each insistently repeats a fragment of itself, as if they were all constructed as a kind of mosaic:

These are the main secondary themes, and the insistent repetition of the smaller units is unusual for Mozart (although typical of Haydn). They are not themes that can be developed into long paragraphs at leisure, as the balanced opening statement of K. 467 can; yet to draw out the tragic implications of the material which can be so clearly sensed by the end of the first phrase, Mozart needs far grander proportions than the material will easily yield. This is why a new page was inserted into the opening tutti, and why, too, there is a 'double' solo exposition. If we half expect a development section instead of the second solo exposition, we are also half granted one within it by the far-reaching modulations of the main theme in E flat minor (from measure 220 on). Here the fragmentation of the harmonic movement of the exposition corresponds to the fragmentation of the structure (as well as to the melodic and rhythmic fragmentation of the material). The series of diminished chords in the opening statement of the main theme clearly presage and justify such a large-scale chromatic instability, and the exposition-as-development, subsequently brings a passion, even a kind of terror, that is central to the work. Although here Mozart works technically with the smaller units of Haydn, he still demands the much greater range of emotion that was always his own.

The recapitulation must sum up the three expositions. The two secondary themes (*b*) and (*c*) of the piano's expositions are played now one right after the other but with (*c*) before (*b*), and (*a*), the passage inserted in the opening tutti, is combined with a variant of (*d*) as a closing theme:

The piano interrupts the coda with a beautiful symmetry: a reworking of the last measures of the development. The end of the movement unites all the disparities.

The orchestration has a refinement and a fragmentation comparable to the structure: the inner part-writing is so detailed that the violas are often divided into two sections, and there are oboes as well as clarinets. The orchestral sound is not, however, colorful as in K. 482, but rich and somber. The use of the timpani and trumpets in soft passages is comparable in its strange, veiled quality to parts of K. 466 and *Don Giovanni*. With all its dramatic power, this concerto comes closer to the late chamber-music style of Mozart than any other, except for the last of all. The 'chamber' style of three earlier concertos—K. 413, K. 414, and K. 449—is only that of the serenades: with K. 491 we reach the inward-looking detail of the string quartets. Not only the despair of the music but its energy is introverted, turned away from all that was theatrical even in Mozart himself.

The other movements are less original in conception, although equally fine. The Larghetto is like the Romanza of K. 466 without its violent central section. The finale, Allegretto, is a set of variations in march-tempo. It is generally taken too fast under the delusion that a quick tempo will give it a power commensurate with the opening movement. Mozart, however, is not a composer whose defects have to be made good by his interpreters: if he had wanted that kind of power, he would have written it. The part-writing is as rich here as Mozart could make it, but the clarity of the theme is never obscured: it is always intended to be heard, and even the two transformations into major, while free on paper, sound strict to the ear. A classical finale, even when it can be categorized as a sonata, is always a looser form than a first movement, inevitably easier to grasp. With all its sobriety, nevertheless, this movement has enough of the passionate despair of the first movement for Beethoven to recall part of the coda in the finale of the *Appassionata*.

The Concerto

The Concerto in C major K. 503 has never been a favorite with the public. Completed at the end of 1786, eight months after the last of the group of three piano concertos with clarinets, it is a magnificent and—to many ears—a cold work. Yet it is the one that many musicians (historians and pianists alike) single out with special affection. The unattractiveness for the public comes from the almost neutral character of the material: in the first movement in particular this material is not even sufficiently characterized to be called banal. An opening phrase built as a series of blocks from an arpeggio:

cannot be called even a cliché. It is conventional, highly so, but in no pejorative sense: it is merely the basic material of late eighteenth-century tonality, the bedrock of the style. Even a later, more attractive theme in a military spirit is equally conventional in this sense: like bread, it cannot cloy.

The splendor of the work and the delight it can inspire come entirely from the handling of the material. There are other concertos of Mozart in which the material is almost wholly conventional—K. 451, for instance, of which Mozart was so proud, and K. 415—but none of them reveals the powers of K. 503. The different ideas in the first movement are treated in block fashion: in spite of the masterly transitions, we are conscious of the juxtaposition of large elements, and above all we are aware of their weight. Indeed, throughout this concerto, we are made to feel how much pressure the form itself can bring to bear even while using almost completely inexpressive ideas. To see this mastery, any join of the form will suffice. Here is the first entrance of the piano, nothing but a continuously repeated dominant seventh-tonic cadence:

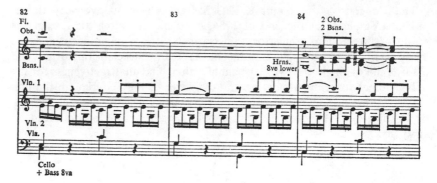

I have been obliged to cite extensively, because the sense of mass is important, and, above all, because so much depends on sheer repetition—and repetition of the most conventional harmonic sound in eighteenth-century music. The acceleration of measures 83–89 is handled with the technique that Mozart displayed at its most striking in K. 466, although he had the essentials within his grasp years before. The harmony of measure 88 moves four times as fast as before, and the last two beats of measure 89 double this once again. All this is now routine to Mozart (and only his ease in handling it was exceptional in the classical period). What is striking is that measure 90 is exactly enough of an end without being quite final: it is about two chords away from an absolutely final cadence. With the addition of one measure, in fact, this passage later serves as the last phrase of the movement: it is marvellous to see how Mozart is able to stop at the very edge here. It is, paradoxically, the pause that both provides a transition and extends the tension—a tension engendered rhythmically by a tonic cadence! This is the beginning of Beethoven's understanding of the exciting rhythmic power of pure repetition. We have, however, not yet done with the dominant seventh-tonic cadence: the orchestra starts it again, more slowly, like a resolution of the previous excitement, and the soloist enters. The cadence is played three times. We can identify the exact moment when the section we have been hearing ends: on the first beat of measure 96, which has the sound of a conclusion withheld before. Yet at this point the piano has already started a series of phrases which it continues—echoing the very same cadence three times more. In this way, the first beat of measure 96 is both the end of a section, and the middle of a statement from the piano; the overlapping device is the insistent repetition of one simple cadence. The conciliation of continuity with articulation—movement and clarity of shape—was never accomplished with more efficiency.

This economy of means is one of the first signs of the final development of Mozart's style. It is not, however, until the year of his death that the full significance of this tendency extends to all the elements of his music. In the

C major Concerto K. 503, the renunciation of harmonic color is already a marked characteristic: almost all the shadings arise from a simple alternation of major and minor. This can, of course, lead far: the use of C minor against C major brings up E flat major early in the work (m. 148), and, at its reappearance in the recapitulation, it calls up E flat minor; the dominant, G major, is introduced by G minor. But these are all major–minor and major–relative minor relations: that is, they are modulations that do not move, that leave the tonality unchanged.

It is not that in Mozart's late style the more dynamic modulations do not exist: on the contrary, there are no more brutal modulations than the ones in the finale of the G minor Symphony or the first movement of the last piano concerto. But their very brutality is a sign of the economy with which they are used, and of their dramatic purpose: they are not harmonic exoticisms, like the B minor in the last movement of the B flat major Piano Concerto K. 456. Nor does Mozart renounce the use of color, orchestral or harmonic, but each effect becomes more telling and more penetrating. *Die Zauberflöte* has the greatest variety of orchestral color that the eighteenth century was to know; the very lavishness, however, is paradoxically also an economy, as each effect is a concentrated one, each one—Papageno's whistle, the Queen of the Night's coloratura, the bells, Sarastro's trombones, even the farewell in Scene I for clarinets and pizzicato strings [1]—a single dramatic stroke.

The alternation of tonic major and minor is the dominant color of K. 503, and a prime element of the structure as well. We find it first hinted in measure 6 (quoted above, page 251) and more openly displayed a few measures later:

This alternation is more than consistent; it is almost obsessive. The fundamental rhythmic element of the piece is first introduced by the violins in measures 18–19 (cited above); at measure 26 it appears in the bass:

---

[1] Quoted on page 320.

A principal theme based on this rhythm

is immediately played in the tonic major a few measures after this appearance in minor. Another 'second' theme is first played in major and repeated half in minor[1] as its own second phrase:

---

[1] It should be noted that this is also a *tonic* major–minor, as G major is by now firmly established as the tonality of this part of the exposition (the use of a major and minor contrast within a subordinate chord would have the more purely coloristic effect of a chromatic harmony). In measure 175, all editions suggest a high A in the piano, as it is evident that Mozart used the lower one only because his keyboard stopped at F; the parallel place in the recapitulation shows that he would have kept the upward form of the melody both times as in measure 170. Unfortunately we cannot stop there; a comparison with the parallel place (measure 345) will show that if we change measure 175, we must also rewrite the next measure as follows:

as the high A would otherwise be left hanging. It is not as easy as editors think to rewrite even a detail of Mozart, which is why it is best as a general rule to print (and play) exactly what he wrote.

And finally, most Mozartean and most classical of all, after further alternation, the cadence ending the exposition is *both in major and minor at once:*

It is a summary, an example of classical resolution as synthesis.

The central and insistent opposition and synthesis of major and minor is remarkable for its long-range conception. It means that the bass generally remains absolutely stable against the continuous tensions of the harmony, often with the immobility of a pedal-point. Since the major–minor contrast occurs immediately within the opening phrases of the movement, its use in the structure on a larger scale follows naturally.[1] This grandiose ambiguity of stability and tension—a characteristic sound, massive and yet disquieting —is the key to this work's tranquil power.

All the elements of the piece contribute to this effect of mass. The use of obstinate repetition, as we have seen above, is marked throughout: this work not only recalls Beethoven to us, it is probable that Beethoven remembered it himself when he wrote his Fourth Piano Concerto. The beginning of the development section has the piano make a surprising shift of tonality by softly taking over the orchestra's rhythm:

---

[1] For example, the opening ritornello goes directly to the dominant G major (mm. 30– 50) but immediately returns to the tonic *minor*: the solo exposition uses this gravitation towards C minor to make the move to the dominant more expressive, as the music goes by way of E flat major (established by now with ease) and G minor (mm. 140–165). The profoundly expressive quality of the music here comes almost entirely from the structure and not from the material. The parallel place in the recapitulation (mm. 320–340) is harmonically more startling, although equally logical within the framework (the E flat major turns into E flat minor and chromatically back to a C minor-major) and even more deeply expressive.

and Beethoven uses exactly the same rhythm with the same dynamic contrast at the same place of the G major Concerto; even the function of the phrase is the same—a surprising modulation. (Beethoven, however, strengthens the effect by having the modulation appear a more remote one, and by having the piano interrupt the orchestra.)[1] The rhythm is thrown into relief in both cases by being a repetition of one note; in both the repetition is thematic. Beethoven's version is more dramatic and more striking but it is perhaps Mozart who achieves the greater impression of ease and power. The final triumph of the massive power of K. 503 is the second half of the development section which—in addition to the piano's figuration—is in full six-part polyphony, with imitative writing almost strict enough to be called canonic, a *tour de force* of classical counterpoint comparable to the finale of the *Jupiter* Symphony or the ball scene in *Don Giovanni*.

In general, the lyricism of Mozart's works lies in the details, and the larger structure is an organizing force; in K. 503, the details are largely conventional, and the most striking expressive force comes from the larger formal elements, even to the point of pervading a heavily symphonic style with melancholy and tenderness. For the most part, too, this melancholy arises miraculously from the simplest of changes from major to minor, often leaving a tonic chord in root position: the resulting impression of tranquil

---

[1] Quoted on pages 391–2.

power and lyricism is unique in music before Beethoven.[1] The emotion is less poignant than in some of the other concertos, but it is the combination of breadth and subtlety that has made this work so admired.

The slow movement is a beautiful combination of simplicity and lavish decoration (with a great variety and contrast of rhythms), which it would be a pity to spoil by decorating the leaner phrases. I have myself added ornaments to a few measures when playing this work, and am sorry for it now. The finale is also colored, like the first movement, by frequent changes from the major to the minor mode, and has Mozart's favorite rondo devices of a recapitulation in reverse order (main theme last). Written at the same time as the *Prague* Symphony and the String Quintets in C major and G minor, K. 503 stands well in this company of the grandest works.

After this, Mozart's interest in the concerto almost ceased completely. From 1784 to 1786 he had written a dozen works in this form; during the last five years of his life he was to write only three. All three works stand somewhat apart in character as well. Perhaps the strangest of them is the so-called *Coronation* Concerto in D major K. 537. Musicians and historians alike have been very hard on it. The most popular of all Mozart's concertos throughout the nineteenth and much of the twentieth centuries, the music deserves more respect: it is historically the most 'progressive' of all Mozart's works, the closest to the early or proto-Romantic style of Hummel and Weber. It is even the closest in its style of virtuosity to the early concertos of Beethoven. We have only to compare

with Beethoven's first piano concerto

to see one detail among many. One might say that this is the concerto that Hummel would have written if he had had not only a remarkable talent but genius.

---

[1] Beethoven's violin concerto, in its first movement, uses a similar emphasis on the root of the tonic triad and a series of changes from major to minor, for its expansive effect of power and tenderness.

The Concerto

In one important respect, this concerto is a revolutionary work, as it shifts the balance between the harmonic and melodic aspects so that the structure now depends largely on melodic succession. This is already evident in the opening ritornello, which has long transitional athematic passages, setting off one section from another:

or, even more remarkably:

where the beginning of the melody in the next-to-last measure cited (m. 59) is itself like an up-beat, and therefore like a continuation of the transition as well as a beginning. These transitional phrases, generally reserved for the solo exposition as expansions and here already in the initial orchestral statement, serve to loosen the structure. The melodic aspect of the themes is emphasized over their harmonic function, and over their place in the directional flow. It should be noted that neither of these transitional phrases is a resolution; they come after a resolving cadence, and they are, therefore, pure suspensions of movement, filled silences. Their only purpose is beautifully to make us wait for a melody to begin.

This loosening of the harmonic and rhythmic structure requires that the resultant weakening of tension be compensated from somewhere else. There is a consequent luxuriance of virtuoso figuration. At the end of an exposition, the use of such figuration had been, in Mozart's previous concertos, only the enhancement of already established tension; now it is used actually to create excitement. The increase of brilliance and intricacy is natural:

259

This is not weighty or majestic as in K. 467 or dramatic as in K. 466 (the two concertos with the most brilliant piano figuration before this), but complicatedly rich and a little more difficult for the ear to follow: it has an interest of its own almost out of relation to the other material of the movement.

Both the loose melodic structure and the reliance on figuration for tension are characteristics of the early Romantic style, as in the concertos of Hummel and Chopin. It was not Beethoven but Mozart who showed how the classical style might be destroyed. To appreciate K. 537 we cannot listen to it with the same expectations that we have for the other works. It demands to be judged by later standards: viewed in this light, it can be seen as the greatest of early Romantic piano concertos. The brilliant rondo has the same character as the opening movement, but the Larghetto is a foretaste of Mozart's last development. It is so simple in character that if it were not a masterpiece, it would be merely pretty. Already it is an example of that popular, lean, almost *faux-naïf* grace that is the glory of *Die Zauberflöte*.

In the last year of his life, Mozart wrote two concertos which depend more upon the delicate interplay of chamber music than upon the dramatic interplay of concerto style. The Clarinet Concerto in A major K. 622 is very close in its lyricism and even in the shape of its themes and their harmonic content to the A major Piano Concertos, K. 414 and K. 488. The last Piano Concerto, K. 595 in B flat major, written six months before, also has the same freely lyrical quality, here gradually permeated by an expressive, even painful chromaticism that dominates everything by the beginning of the development section. Both concertos give the sensation of an inexhaustible and continuous melodic line, somehow both seamless and yet clearly articulated. The structure, nevertheless, is neither a loose succession of melodies (as in K. 537) nor an unvaried flow.

Mozart uses a system of overlapping phrase-rhythms in these two late works, and puts it unobtrusively at the service of a lyrical invention which pours forth unimpeded, yet without losing either tension or poignance. In the Clarinet Concerto, for example:

a new phrase starts somewhere between measures 102 and 105 without—at the moment of hearing—its being clear just at what point. Hindsight tells us (by the time we hear measure 106) that the new phrase began at the first beat of measure 104, yet when we had heard that measure we were aware only of the continuity of movement. In this way, Mozart has both the clear articulation and the uninterrupted flow at the same time. This example may be called the articulation of continuity: the complementary process—the integration of an interrupted movement—may be seen a few pages before:

measures 76–77 are both an end to the cadence at measure 75 and the beginning of a new phrase; 78–79 repeat the harmonies of 76–77 changed into
minor, and the exact parallelism of the orchestral accompaniment makes
them an answer to 76–77 and the end of a four-measure phrase; yet at the
same time measure 78 is the beginning of a new phrase in the clarinet which
goes to measure 80 and even beyond. Similar examples could be multiplied
indefinitely. Neither the dovetailed articulation nor the double significance
of a phrase facing both ways—a completion and a fresh start—are new in
Mozart, but I do not think he had ever developed them with the subtlety
and the constant invention he displays in his last two concertos. This balance
between clarity of shape and continuity makes the first movement of the
clarinet concerto seem like an endless song—not a spinning-out of one idea,
but a series of melodies that flow one into the other without a break.

The opening Allegro of the last piano concerto, K. 595, is more complex,
but leaves the same impression of continuous melody. The means of attaining
lyrical continuity are even more delicate here. It is a temptation to quote one
of the loveliest passages in the work:

The beginning of the phrase that starts at measure 29 is given the most subtle urgency by our having to wait a split second for the resolution of the viola and second violin line coming out of measure 28: the harmony overlaps across the eighth-note rest, an added link between two phrases already tied together by the first violin line of measures 28–29. The phrase is repeated at measure 33, and the unity with what precedes is now far more emphatic, as the beautiful bass line in the cellos and basses starts in measure 32 and goes uninterruptedly until measure 35.

In this same passage, the sweetness of Mozart's dissonance is at its most powerful: the clash in measure 33 between a D♮ in the first violins and a D♭ three and four octaves below in the cellos and basses is one of the most painful in tonal music. The brutality of this clash is neatly sidestepped in the shortest possible time, and a more acceptable dissonance is substituted, yet our ear and our memory supply all the expressive force, above all because the first violins rise so suddenly to the D♮ (doubling the D in the bass just before it moves to D♭). In this way, on the third beat of the measure there is the unplayed but audibly imagined harshness of a minor ninth (D–D♭) along with the major seventh (D♭–C), which gives the effect of the most dissonant and most expressive harmony without the harshness of actually playing it. Throughout the work the most painful dissonances are evoked and yet softened. This passage is an important moment in the concerto, the first appearance of the minor mode and of the chromaticism that plays such a crucial role, the first sign of the work's limitless melancholy. The development section, where the key changes almost every two measures, carries classical tonality as far as it can go; the chromaticism becomes iridescent, and the orchestration and spacing transparent: the emotion, with all its anguish, never disturbs the grace of the melodic line.

Both the last piano concerto and the Clarinet Concerto are private statements: the form is never exploited for exterior effect, the tone is always one of intimacy. The slow movements aspire and attain to a condition of absolute simplicity: the slightest irregularity in the phrase structure of their themes would have appeared like an intrusion. The melodies accept the reduction to an almost perfect symmetry and triumph over all its dangers. It is fitting that Mozart, who perfected as he created the form of the classical concerto, should have made his last use of it so completely personal.

2

String Quintet

By general consent, Mozart's greatest achievement in chamber music is the group of string quintets with two violas. The viola was his favorite string instrument, the one he habitually chose when playing quartets; in the *Sinfonia Concertante* K. 364 it was probably the viola solo he played and not the violin. His partiality may have come not only from the instrument's sonority but from his love for rich inner part-writing: in his music there was a fulness of sound and a complexity in the inner voices that had disappeared from music since the death of Bach. 'Too many notes' was the reproach cast at Mozart as it had been at Bach: it was not a sonority fashionable after about 1730, and the later eighteenth century preferred a drier and leaner sound. In spite of this taste, the string quintet was already a popular form when Mozart took it up, as the enormous number of insipid but agreeable works in this form by Boccherini attest. Before Mozart, however, the heavier sonority was avoided largely by treating the form as a duet between two soloists— first violin and first viola—with accompaniment. This concertante element is not entirely absent from Mozart, particularly in his immature first essay, K. 174 in B flat major, but this approach translates the form into a kind of divertimento, taking away all serious possibilities: it allows neither the dramatic contrast of the concerto between a large force and a soloist, nor the complex intimacy of chamber music. Only with the eccentric and rhapsodic style of the late Haydn trios was a kind of concertante chamber music to reach real profundity, and then the full resources of the keyboard were needed as well. The concertante string quintet is a lazy extension of the habit of treating the string quartet superficially as an accompanied solo for the first violin: if this kind of quintet has greater variety, it is not essentially more interesting.

At three different times in his life, Mozart turned to the string quintet, and always directly after having written a series of quartets, as if the experience of composing for only four instruments prompted him to take up the richer medium. His first quintet was composed when he was only seventeen years old. In 1772, having recently come into contact with Haydn's Quartets op. 20, and inspired by the new conception of chamber music he found there, he wrote six quartets in which his struggle to assimilate Haydn's language results in a constant alternation of awkwardness with his more natural grace. The Quintet K. 174 followed a year later, a less constrained and more conventionally ambitious work. It is, of course, filled with remarkable things, most of them Haydnesque: a witty play on a two-note figure in the minuet that is almost worthy of the older master, a genuine false reprise in the finale, and an unusually dramatic use of silence in the exterior movements. More typically Mozartean is the exploitation of the special sonority of the medium, with the echo effects in the trio of the minuet, and the constant use of doubling (at the octave or the third) and antiphonal exchanges between the higher and lower instruments. The most original moment is perhaps the beginning of the slow movement, with its use, muted, of an accompanying figure *unisono* for its expressive quality as a melody:

In a passage like this, a witty ambiguity—a grammatical pun, in fact—is so much a part of the style that it cannot disturb the intensity, but remains only as a trace of good manners in the expression of sentiment.

What is most astonishing about this early work is the breadth of conception, which goes far beyond any of the string quartets he had written just previously. The classical feeling for balance demanded that the fuller and richer sonority of the quintet be given a larger framework—within the context of Mozart's own style of the moment—than was fitting for the string quartet. The concertante element may have been instrumental in creating this added breadth, but, in fact, the new grandeur is most striking in K. 174 when the concertante style is completely absent. The finale is the most complex contrapuntal work that Mozart was to write for many years to come, far more intricate than the fugal movements of the early string quartets; the opening movement, along with its solo passages and antiphonal effects, has moments of an expansively dramatic character unattempted by Mozart as yet in the string quartet. The immediate model for this work is not at all Michael Haydn, as has been thought, much less Boccherini, but the *Sun* Quartets of Joseph Haydn. The experiment of adapting Haydn's technique to the richer sound and more relaxed pace demanded by the string quintet is, however, only partially successful; the changes of texture are often more startling than convincing. Still, Mozart's instinctive understanding at the age of seventeen of the fundamental difference between quintet and quartet is remarkable. Beethoven, too, reached the same conclusion in his first and only work in this form: the Quintet op. 29 was written in 1801, the same year that he finished the six quartets op. 18, and it has a breadth and a tranquil expansiveness possessed by none of them; but then he had Mozart's great series of quintets to point the way.

It was fourteen years before Mozart came back to the string quintet. After 1773 he abandoned the string quartet as well for almost a decade; his return to chamber music was again inspired by Haydn: the appearance of the revolutionary *Scherzi* Quartets op. 33. Mozart's six quartets of the years 1782–85 were once more in emulation of the elder composer, and in tribute to him, though now with a full mastery and a new originality; and a year after they were finished, he wrote the beautiful and completely personal *Hoffmeister* Quartet. He then returned to the string quintet in 1787, and wrote two works grander in scope than anything that Haydn had ever conceived even for the orchestra. Nevertheless, he had still the memory of Haydn's op. 33 echoing in his ears. The opening of the C major Quintet K. 515:

inevitably recalls the first measures of Haydn's op. 33 no. 3, the *Bird* (cited on p. 65): there is the same mounting phrase in the cello, the same inner accompanying motion, the same placing of the first violin. Yet Haydn's nervous rhythm is avoided; in place of his independent six-measure phrases —the motion broken abruptly between them—Mozart has a linked series of five-measure phrases with absolutely uninterrupted continuity. In other words, a larger period is imposed on Haydn's system of phrasing: the twenty measures of the first paragraph are divided into 5, 5, 5, 4 plus 1 (the last being a measure of rest—even Haydn's remarkable use of silence in op. 33 no. 3 is turned to account here, but in a grander sense in the context of the larger period). The irregular phrase-length helps to assure the feeling of continuity, and the symmetrical arrangement gives it balance. The transition from the third to the fourth phrase of the paragraph is imperceptible; it is almost impossible to say where the new phrase begins as the violin and cello overlap: while the violin finishes the echo of the first phrases, the cello enters (m. 15) —without waiting the expected two measures—on a new harmony, a dissonance that is given poignance and even sweetness in a spacing that covers four octaves. The symmetrical articulation dissolves at the end, and the measure of rest is all the more dramatic. The second large paragraph begins with a symmetrical repetition, reversing the violin and cello roles, and starting brutally in the tonic minor, a surprise that is all the more effective for being at once so solid as well as so unexpected.

This tonal solidity is the principal source of the breadth and majesty of this work. For a longer time than in any work he had written until then, Mozart avoids a real movement away from the tonic: he transforms it into minor, he alters it chromatically, but he returns to it decisively again and again before moving to the dominant. His powers of expansion—the delay of cadence, the widening of the center of the phrase—are called into play on a scale he had never before known. When the movement to the dominant finally comes, it, too, like the tonic, is established with tranquil firmness: there are three complete themes in the 'second group,' and each one is played twice. This 'second group' has a majestic symmetry of its own: its first theme begins with an emphatic pedal on G, now become the tonic, and an expressively serpentine phrase above it:

and is repeated with a counter-subject. The second theme has a syncopated rhythm in the first violin, and its diminution in the other instruments:

After the expressive instability of this cadence, the pedal-point returns:

with a phrase above it that gradually alludes more and more to the winding chromatic phrase quoted before. The expressive syncopations are thus framed by two similar pedal points; and the immobility of the bass for such long sections of the 'second group' is the balance to the concentration on the tonic and the length of the 'first group.' I have emphasized these proportions because, although the C major Quintet is accepted as one of Mozart's greatest works, it is not generally recognized as perhaps the most daring of all.

The first movement of the C major Quintet is the largest 'sonata allegro' before Beethoven, longer than any other Mozart ever wrote, or any that Haydn had written or was to write. Even the Allegro of the *Prague* Symphony is shorter, and the whole first movement of that work attains the dimensions of the C major Quintet only by virtue of its Adagio introduction. In the quintet, Mozart's principal expansion of the form takes place in the exposition, which is, astonishingly, longer than any first-movement exposition of Beethoven, I believe, except that of the Ninth Symphony, which it equals. Even the exposition of the *Eroica* is shorter.

Size, by itself, of course, means little; pacing and proportion are everything. What is extraordinary in this exposition is that Mozart has discovered the secret of Beethoven's dimensions. First, there is the marked hierarchy of periodic movement—phrase, paragraph, and section. It is for this reason that Mozart does not begin the movement with a clearly defined melody, but with motivic fragments, following Haydn's more usual practice, and anticipating Beethoven's use of these motifs in a continuous unbroken motion within the paragraph. Not only does Mozart abandon melody, he also renounces much of the seductive harmonic color that appears in the first measures of almost all his other works which reach the expressive intensity of this quintet.[1] He postpones, as he so rarely did, the use of the supertonic, the submediant, and the subdominant: for fourteen measures he defines nothing but pure tonic and dominant. In this, too, he anticipates Beethoven, the openings of whose grandest works more often than not outline only the tonic chord. The tonal areas of Mozart's expositions generally have a tranquil solidity absent from Haydn's more nervous and more openly dynamic forms: when this solidity was combined, as it is here, with Haydn's motivic technique of exposition and expansion integrated within a subtle and clearly marked feeling for a large periodic structure, the majestic proportions of this movement became possible, without weakening the lyric intensity that diffuses itself throughout the work.

In expanding that small but resilient symmetrical structure derived from the dance that was later called 'sonata form,' the problem was always how and where to add weight without undoing the proportions and wrecking the unity. The simplest solution was the addition of a long, slow introduction, as in the *Prague* and the E flat symphonies, or in the splendid G major Sonata for Piano and Violin K. 379: but this always remained an exterior device—an additive concept, rather than a synthetic one, until Mozart's D major Quintet and the Haydn symphonies of the 1790s, which reveal new relationships between the introductions and the following allegros. In expanding the form itself, Haydn generally enlarged the second half—not only widening the 'development' but often continuing it throughout the recapitulation. To increase the length of the first half is both difficult and dangerous: the exposition of a sonata is based on only one action, the establishment of one polarity; to delay its arrival too long is to diffuse all the energy, to risk chaos; once it has arrived, everything remaining in the first half tends to have a purely cadential function. In a concerto, the with-

---

[1] There is a similar concentration on simple tonic and dominant at the opening of works, like the first movement of the *Jupiter* and the earlier C major Symphony K. 338, but they have none of this intensity and intend only grandeur or brilliance.

holding of this cadence is the simplest and most justifiable procedure, the occasion for virtuoso passagework from the soloist: cadential virtuosity is, after all, the origin of the 'improvised' cadenza at the end of the movement. This kind of brilliance, which would be empty in a piano sonata,[1] is a dramatic necessity in a concerto: it gives the solo instrument an equivalent for the weight of the full orchestra, and allows a satisfactory equilibrium to be reached. (Only when, as in some works of the nineteenth and twentieth centuries, the virtuosity reaches such proportions that the orchestra is itself overwhelmed, does the brilliance become tasteless.) In any case, this recourse is not open to the 'sonata form' outside the special case of the concerto.

In the C major Quintet, Mozart chose the most difficult and most satisfactory way of increasing the range of the first half of the sonata—the expansion of the opening tonic section, or 'first group.' This meant the dramatization not of an action, but of a refusal to act, the creation of tension while remaining at the extreme point of resolution. To achieve this dramatization, Mozart uses a beautiful variety of means. He withholds all chromatic color from the opening, introducing it more and more as the section proceeds. He employs what was a traditional means of going to the dominant, the counterstatement (i.e., repeating the opening phrases of the movement and beginning the modulation before the repetition has been completed), but radically alters its aspect and its function: the opening phrases are repeated, but in the tonic minor—giving the illusion of harmonic motion while staying essentially in the same place, making the tonic unstable without actually denying it.

This is followed by one of the most extraordinary expansions of a progression; a simple plagal phrase IV–I

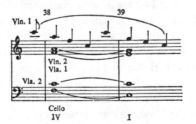

is decorated:

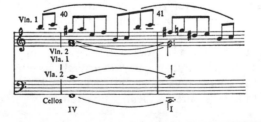

---

[1] The finale of the B flat Sonata K. 333 achieves it only by a witty and frank imitation of a concerto rondo.

The F major starts once again and then is turned into F minor, and the cadence is lengthened, and made deceptive:

and finally and most magnificently this phrase is repeated with the A♭ of the F minor chord made the basis of an extraordinary inner expansion, still outlining essentially the same cadence:

in which the five previous measures have become ten, and the harmonic resonance is immensely widened without really leaving the tonic. (In the recapitulation, this phrase is even longer, and goes as far as C sharp minor, without otherwise changing its fundamental shape or purpose.) Following this, and for the first time, the chromatic movement becomes at last truly directional:

although still returning to the tonic once more with the same IV–I cadence before the movement to the dominant begins. The unprecedented majesty of this work comes from the long immobility and the firm tonic harmony, its lyric poignance from the chromatic alterations that made the proportions conceivable.

It should be remarked in passing that Beethoven expands the 'first group' in quite different ways when he elected—infrequently—to do so. In a number of works (op. 10 no. 3 and op. 2 no. 3, for example), he goes to another secondary key with a new theme before establishing the dominant, which has occasionally given rise to foolish discussions as to which was the 'real' second theme: musicology sometimes considers odd metaphysical questions. In the Sonata op. 111, following the finale of the *Jupiter* Symphony, he expands the tonic area with a fugal development before modulating to the submediant, which serves him as a dominant. The Ninth Symphony has an exceptionally subtle device: Beethoven replays the main theme on B flat major, the submediant (which he will again use as a dominant), but in such a way that it still sounds as if the tonality had not left the tonic D minor: in this way he lengthens the first group, strikingly and dramatically widens the significance of the tonic, and prepares his modulation—all with one stroke. It is typical of Beethoven that his largest works should be also the most economical.

If listeners measured their experiences by the clock, the development section of the C major Quintet would seem too short; but complexity and intensity are a more than adequate substitute for length. The development is one of Mozart's richest: the climax is a double canon in four voices with a free counterpoint in the fifth (second viola):

and almost the whole development is in minor, making the return to C major grand and luminous. (This minor coloring also entails the elimination in the return of the first group of the counter-statement in the tonic minor, which would be pleonastic here.) The coda, demanded by the dimensions of what precedes, is masterly: the closing theme, which in the exposition was a tonic pedal on G,[1] starts once again as a pedal on G, becoming thereby a dominant pedal instead of a tonic:

the beginning of a gigantic cadence of 47 measures, essentially the simplest of all cadences in its outline, although brilliantly enlivened in its detail:

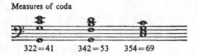

The simplicity of the structure is a proof of the life of the style: when the 'sonata' became academic, it had to be expanded by the continuous injection of new material and sequential development, but Mozart is still able to heap on the form all the weight—in terms of both expression and mass—that he wishes it to bear.

The same spaciousness is found in the other movements of the quintet. Both the slow movement and the finale are sonata movements without development sections, with the expositions laid out on a grand scale: both begin leisurely with a succession of two clearly separate themes in the tonic. The slow movement is an operatic duet for the first violin and first viola: there is even a written-out but well-defined cadenza for them towards the end. The finale, though organized like the slow movement, has, appropriately, some characteristics of the rondo: the squarely articulated themes, the loose transitions, the sectional structure. The 'secondary development' of the sonata (between the first and second groups of the recapitulation) is expanded, and emphasizes the subdominant, as it traditionally does; but this is also exactly the place that the 'development' of the 'sonata rondo' occurs, and we often find there, too, a new theme in the subdominant. In this movement we can see, as it were, the sonata rondo latent in the sonata finale, and we can understand the reasons—not historical but aesthetic—for its existence. The necessary looseness of a finale and its less dramatic character allow for

---

[1] Quoted on page 268.

Mozart's great melodic abundance: in the 'second group' there are three complete new melodies, a fourth clearly derived from one of them, and a fifth developed from the opening theme, the last being perhaps the most striking, if not the most gracious of them:

The first violin plays the opening theme here in its original form, but the first viola has already inverted part of it with a shift of rhythm. With an exposition as rich and complex as this in a finale, it is easy to understand why Mozart chose to dispense with a principal development section, or a new theme after the return of the opening—thus avoiding both the full sonata and the full rondo form. The finale of the G minor Quintet K. 516 is cast in much the same mold, including two generous themes in the tonic at the beginning, but it takes two steps further towards the rondo: a new theme in the subdominant after the recapitulation of the first theme, and a fragmentary reappearance of both opening themes at the end as a coda.

The finale of the G minor Quintet raises the problem of the classical finale in all its complexity, real and imagined. It is a movement that has often disappointed. It is, indeed, almost always played with less understanding than the other movements but this only challenges us to explain why it inspires such heartless performances. The role of a finale in the late eighteenth century needs to be disentangled from a later age's conception of an effective ending. The G minor Quintet is one of the great tragic works, but it is not Mozart's fault if, for that very reason, many listeners today would openly or secretly prefer an ending with the frank pathos of Tchaikovsky's *Symphonie Pathétique*. Things change very little with Beethoven: the coda to the finale of the Quartet op. 95 has often seemed irrelevant, if not positively frivolous, and objections to the finale of the Ninth Symphony are common enough to cause no surprise, even when they come from those who should know better.

The problem of the finale is naturally one of weight, of sufficient seriousness and dignity to balance the opening movement, but there would be no problem at all if it were not for the classical conception of the finale as a resolution of the entire work. There was, after all, nothing except his sensibility to prevent Mozart from writing a last movement as complex and closely knit as a first movement, like the finale of Brahms's Third Symphony, for example. Beethoven was capable of a choral work as tightly organized as the *Gloria* from the Mass in D, and he must have felt that the looser shape of the choral finale to the Ninth Symphony was necessary in its place. A finale demanded a simpler and less complex form than an opening movement: that is why it is generally a rondo, or a set of variations (as in Mozart's G major Concerto, or the *Eroica* and Ninth Symphonies of Beethoven). If it is a 'sonata,' then it is necessarily a squarer and simpler version of that form; sometimes the structure is loosened as in Beethoven's Fifth Symphony by a change of tempo in the development (the return of the Scherzo), or a new theme at the same place in the subdominant as in Mozart's F major Sonata K. 332. But, in any case, the thematic material of a finale is always rhythmically squarer than that of a first movement,[1] the cadences heavily emphasized, the phrases well-defined, and the first theme completely rounded off before any harmonic movement can take place. (In the finale of Beethoven's Eighth Symphony, for example, the cadences are hammered brutally, and there is even a brief pause when the theme is over (at the tonic cadence in measure 28), while, on the other hand, the opening theme of the first movement, simple as it appears, moves directly into what follows.) If the finale was to be a slow movement, a complex form (as in Mahler's Ninth) was out of the question: in this case the only formal possibility was a set of variations[2] or a slow minuet.

The limit of dramatic complexity in a classical finale is reached with Mozart's G minor Symphony: despairing and impassioned, it is also rhythmically one of the simplest and squarest pieces that Mozart ever wrote. The main theme is absolutely regular, in two equal halves, each half rounded off with the same tonic cadence and each played twice. Except for an electrifying second at the opening of the development (even there integrated within two four-measure phrases, followed by a regular two-measure transition), the rhythm impels gloriously but does not surprise. All the harmonic daring is concentrated in the development section, while the exposition, although it has a few chromatic passages, has nothing to parallel the harmonic ambiguity

---

[1] The only exception to this squareness is the contrapuntal finale, as in many of the Haydn quartets, the Mozart G major Quartet K. 387, the *Jupiter* Symphony, and the equally famous essays of Beethoven. These form a special case, first because they are all to some extent revivals of an earlier style—the composers themselves felt these works an anachronism, or better, a modernizing of the past; second, because they are all to some extent displays of technique—they were to the eighteenth-century composer what the virtuoso finale is to the soloist. The emotional complexity is, therefore, always less than that of the other movements: even the Great Fugue of Beethoven is structurally looser and simpler than the opening of op. 130, in spite of its complex texture.

[2] The Adagio last movement of Haydn's Quartet op. 54 no. 2, a strange work in every way, while appearing to be a loose ternary form, is set of free variations.

of such a passage in the first movement's exposition as the one at measures 58–62. The phrasing, too, is absolutely straightforward: all the dove-tailing, all the syncopations and suspensions of the opening movement have disappeared. This is not to deny the dramatic tensions within this finale, but essentially it resolves, grounds, and settles. This is perhaps only a hidden tautology, a way of saying that a finale ends and completes, but the classical composer took the idea of finale literally, and had no inkling of the 'open' effects, the attempts to break down the feeling for a frame that were to come with the first Romantic generation.

A finale in major to a work in minor was naturally nothing more than a *tierce de Picardie* in larger terms; in eighteenth-century tonality a major chord still had less tension than a minor one, and gave a more satisfactory resolution. Haydn's abandonment of minor endings in his later work is not an outbreak of cheerfulness in middle age, but a development of the classical taste for resolution. In the late trios, where he can use the minuet form as a finale, he allows himself the deeply moving last movement in minor of the F sharp minor trio. The turn to major at the end was anything but a concession to the public: the second, Viennese version of *Don Giovanni* makes more concessions to outside pressure than the original production in Prague, and it is this version which deletes a great part of the original D major ending. On the rare occasions when Mozart chose to end in minor—that is, with some of the harmonic tension still echoing in the mind when the music is over—he always compensated for this by an added simplicity of phrasing and articulation, as in the E minor Sonata for Piano and Violin K. 304 and the A minor and C minor Sonatas for piano, K. 310 and K. 457, or by the sectional variation-form as in the D minor Quartet K. 421 and the C minor Piano Concerto K. 491. And none of these immediately follows music as complex and as anguished as the first three movements and the introduction to the finale of the G minor Quintet.

Not that the problem of weight in a finale was not a real one for Mozart, as we can see from the manuscript of the A major Sonata for Piano and Violin, K. 526. Like those of the C major and G minor Quintets, the last movement opens with two successive and distinct melodies in the tonic. Mozart could not at first decide whether to round off the second theme in the tonic before modulating, as in the G minor Quintet, or to use it as a springboard to the dominant before it seemed complete, as in the C major Quintet. The problem here was essentially how much looseness of form and squareness of periodic rhythm would be desirable. He eventually decided on the less sectional form, and then proceeded with a 'sonata rondo' in which the development section combines two resolving harmonic forces: a new theme in the relative minor, and a recapitulation that starts in the subdominant. The loose structure of the finale admitted as much variety of mood and technique as the more 'organically' conceived opening movement. (It must be admitted that these relaxed forms could sometimes produce finales that seem inadequate even when judged by classical standards, as in Beethoven's *Kreutzer* Sonata or the G major Sonata for Piano and Violin K. 379 of Mozart, where the variations, lovely as they are, substitute an ornamental stylishness and brilliance for the raging power that preceded them.)

It is evident from the G minor Quintet that the greatly increased dimensions of its companion C major Quintet are not an isolated and eccentric experiment in Mozart's development. The enlargement remains part of his conception of the genre. The increase of space demanded by the sonority entails an increase not so much in the span of time as in tonal mass. The first movement of the G minor Quintet, like that of the C major, concentrates on the tonic area far beyond the limits that Mozart allowed himself in any quartet. This makes possible an opening page of a chromatic bitterness and insistence that can still shock by the naked force of its anguish. It is an opening that was unique for the last quarter of the eighteenth century in presenting directly so deeply troubled an emotion, reaching a point of tension by the twentieth measure that all other works hold in reserve until much later.

Yet the mastery and the control are as serene as ever: a new theme is brought forward in the tonic, used as a bridge to the relative major, and then played again, profoundly intensified. Its two forms are:

In this way, any feeling of anti-climax and of slackening after the storm of the opening is evaded by the later more complex and agitated form of this new theme, and, at the same time, the 'first group' is enlarged as in the C major Quintet so that the dimensions correspond to the intensity. The tragedy is allowed to expand freely, which is why this work, like the G minor Symphony, has an emotional force as objective as it is personal. (Later composers need procedures almost diametrically opposed: Chopin, Liszt, and Schumann constrict the expressive elements so that they can be cut off at the moment of their greatest intensity, a technique that Wagner attempted to diffuse through a longer time-span, and that Brahms tried to reconcile with classical form; this constriction is particularly evident in works of neo-Romantic composers like Mahler and Berg.) The essence of Mozart's 'classicism' is the equilibrium between the intensity of the expression and the tonal stability which fixes the dimensions of each work. That is why the larger implications of the sonority of five instruments allow him, as the quartet did not, both the massive, tranquil grandeur of the C major and the limitless anguish of the G minor quintets. There is a freedom to resolve dissonance in the widest sense, not only the immediate clashes, but the far-reaching tensions. The form is always a closed one, and we are left with the memory of a struggle resolved and not with its contradictions alone.

The other movements reach towards the same expressive limits. It is difficult to go further than the opening of the minuet without destroying the contemporary musical language:

the syncopated contrasts of texture and accent in measures 4 and 6 are surely extreme for the time. As the quintet proceeds, it moves as a complete whole within the framework—in terms of intensity and phrasing—of the sonata aesthetic, as if the entire work were conceived as one sonata movement. In spite of its violence, the minuet in second place, right after the first movement, has the decisive simplicity and concision of the closing theme of an exposition. The slow movement, like a development[1] rhythmically the most complex point of the entire quintet, breaks up its material more strikingly than any other movement. Already at measure 5, we find the kind of fragmentation characteristic of a development section:

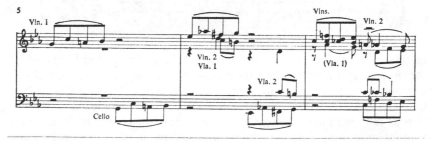

---

[1] It is interesting to note that in Mozart's works in a minor key, if the slow movement has a marked expressive complexity, it tends to be in the submediant major (i.e. Sonata for Piano in A minor K. 310, G minor Symphony, Concerto in D minor K. 466), while the simpler movements are in the less remote relative major (Concerto in C minor K. 491, D minor Quartet, K. 421, C minor Sonata K. 457).

And the four-note motif developed here is used a few measures later in a remarkable disruption of the rhythm and phrase:

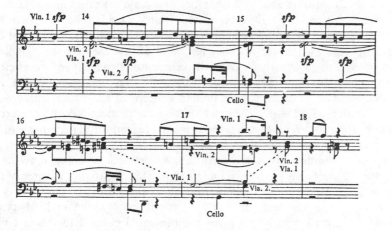

The motif, expanded, is already implied in measure 14 by the first violin, but in measures 16 and 17 it is simply inverted with an astonishing shift of accent. The phrase lengths, which change throughout (here they are a measure and a half long), indicate the continuous alteration of the pulse which moves from *alla breve* as in the first quotation to common time in the second, and becomes eight in the measure at a later point. The harmony is correspondingly intricate.

The finale acts as a recapitulation; its Adagio introduction gives it the weight to meet the rest of the quintet on equal terms, and divides the functions of recollection and resolution. The introduction even surpasses the other movements in its open use of direct expressive symbolism: the sobbing rhythm in the inner strings, the sighing appoggiaturas, the harsh expressive dissonances, the aria at once sustained without end and continuously broken, the *parlando* insistence on one note, the unceasing chromatic movement. Nothing closer to an ultimate despair has ever been imagined: recalling the first movement in tonality and in mood, it exceeds it in emotional turbulence. To have followed this movement with an Allegro of any dramatic complexity would have been an outrage: the final Allegro is a necessary reconciliation as well as a resolution. The device of breaking off the separate clauses of the main themes at their final appearance in the coda, soon to become so familiar

279

in Beethoven and Schubert, and already used, generally with comic effect, by Haydn, has here an air of sadness and resignation. Like the last movement of the B flat Concerto K. 595, it cannot be played for brilliance without trivializing it. It makes its effect by the spaciousness and breadth of its structure, and by its alternation of passages of great simplicity with others contrapuntally richer and more openly expressive.

Placing the minuet second instead of third in the order of the movements throws the expressive weight of a quartet or quintet towards its latter half. It is an order that Haydn used frequently in his quartets until 1785, after which he almost entirely abandoned it[1] (except for op. 64 nos. 1 and 4, and op. 77 no. 2). Mozart used it in chamber music almost as often as the more usual order. When the slow movement in third place is followed, as in the G minor Quintet, by a long Adagio introduction to the finale, the shift of the center of gravity within the work is even more perceptible. Not that the place of the minuet was so clearly fixed: the divertimento often had two—one before and one after the slow movement. But it seems clear that both Mozart and Haydn, working towards a more unified concept of the whole work, were experimenting with the possibility of shifting the proportions and the order of the movements. With Mozart, the principal reason for placing the minuet in second place may have been the desire to separate an exceptionally complex slow movement from the traditionally dramatic opening movement. (He does this not only in the two Quintets, K. 515 and 516, but in three of the *Haydn* Quartets and in the *Hoffmeister*, all works with slow movements of unusually serious character or, as in the variations of the A major Quartet K. 464, of great length.) This gives a more equal balance to the first and second halves of the work. Beethoven, who generally followed the more traditional order, at the end of his life rediscovered or reinvented Mozart's proportions and put the scherzo before the slow movement in his two most massive works,[2] the *Hammerklavier* Sonata and the Ninth Symphony; in both, the scherzo is conceived partly as a parody of the first movement, but the order serves again as a more equal distribution of the expressive weight. The late works of Beethoven in many respects show a marked return to the ideals of Mozart and Haydn within a very different emotional context.

In 1788, the year after completing the two great quintets, Mozart wrote no chamber music for strings except the Divertimento K. 563 for string trio. An essay in contrapuntal and harmonic richness, with a surface ease of man-

---

[1] Considerably greater importance was given to the scherzo after that, however.

[2] In the quartets, Beethoven also chose this order for his first attempt in a new broad style: op. 59 no. 1. The A major Quartet op. 18 no. 5 is a movement-for-movement imitation of the Mozart A major Quartet, and this order prevails there, too, with the slow variation movement in third place. The slow variations of op. 135 are similarly placed after the scherzo. The order of the movements of the last quartets cannot be described in summary fashion, but the B flat Quartet op. 130 clearly belongs with the *Hammerklavier* and the Ninth Symphony in this respect.

ner that makes light of its ingenuity, this work is a distillation of Mozart's technique and experience. The mastery of the normative technique of writing for four instruments in the seven quartets of the years 1782 to 1786, and the immense expansion of scope in the two quintets of 1787 are now concentrated within the limits of the string trio. No other composer of the eighteenth and nineteenth centuries ever understood the demands of writing for three voices as Mozart did, except for Bach in his six trio-sonatas for double manual and pedal keyboard. As a string trio, this one of Mozart's stands alone, far above all other works in that form. It is also an interesting precursor of the last quartets of Beethoven, in its transference of the divertimento form, with two dance movements and two slow movements (one a set of variations), into the realm of serious chamber music, making purely intimate what had been public, and, as Beethoven was to do in so many of the short, interior movements of his late chamber works, transfiguring the 'popular' element without losing sight of its provenance. In Mozart's Divertimento the synthesis of a learned display of three-part writing and a popular genre is accomplished without ambiguity or constraint.

In 1789 he began the series of three quartets, which were to be his last; they were composed for the King of Prussia, who carried on the musical tradition of his family as an amateur cellist. The great increase of solo writing in these quartets is generally ascribed to Mozart's wish to please the king; balancing the solo passages for the cello with solos for the other instruments saved the integrity of the style. The assumption is that brilliance for its own sake was offensive to the classical mind. Nevertheless, every great composer has loved brilliance for itself, and a high value was put upon it by Mozart. It is a way of increasing emphasis without thickening mass, or a way of expanding the frame when the stylistic concentration is so intense (as it was with Mozart in the *Haydn* Quartets and the two great quintets that followed) that further development would have endangered the equilibrium of tension and resolution. Throughout Mozart's career, the oscillation between soloistic elements and ensemble technique is a rising spiral: the solo style stimulating a richer ensemble form, and then the new synthesis in chamber or symphonic style becoming still further expanded by virtuosity.

A few months after finishing the *Prussian* Quartets, Mozart wrote two more string quintets: his recent experiments with solo writing in chamber style are evident in the first of the two, K. 593. The brilliance of the individual instruments is more remarkable here than in the previous quintets, and each is often pitted against the other four; there are fewer duets and less antiphonal writing (except in the alternation of solo and ensemble). There are passages which demand an exceptionally bright sound of virtuosity: the trio of the minuet displays both the first and second violins (and the cello) as soloists in the most striking way. The famous correction of the main theme of the finale is not by Mozart at all, but probably the emendation of a fiddle-player who found the original and more characteristic chromatic form too difficult to play. The recent discovery that the change in the manuscript is not in Mozart's hand is particularly gratifying as there are several passages —above all one starting twenty-five measures before the end—which are only odd in the 'corrected' version, but directly and intimately derived from the main theme in the original.

The opening movement essays a remarkable integration of introduction and Allegro in a way that looks forward to Haydn's *Drum-Roll* Symphony, and Beethoven's *Pathétique* Sonata and E flat Piano Trio op. 70 no. 2. The themes of both the Larghetto introduction and Allegro

outline a shape similar enough for the listener to sense their closeness at once. The Larghetto reappears as a coda, but not as part of a static frame; the Allegro comes back once more at the very end. Indeed, the opening eight measures of the Allegro are wittily tailored so that they are both a beginning and a final cadence: their return at the end is absolutely unaltered. The return of the Larghetto is also a resolution of its more dynamic first appearance: it is a true recapitulation in sonata style, not a variant of da capo form.

The conception of an opening slow section rewritten as a resolution at the end (i.e., with the original closing dominant cadence replaced by a tonic, all that precedes taking on a new form) is not an original idea. One finds it as far back as the Baroque overture, Bach's French Overture in B minor being only one example. But we are dealing here with two kinds of cadence on the dominant: the French Overture's opening slow section has the cadence of the regular dance form, and therefore of the sonata exposition—a movement to the dominant in a pattern which implies symmetrical resolution. The cadence of the opening Larghetto of the D major Quintet is *on* the dominant but without leaving the tonic: it is a true introduction, it accomplishes no action, it only presages, foreshadows, hints at what is to come. That is the reason the Larghetto turns immediately to the tonic minor, troubling the tonality with a darker color without weakening it (an introduction acts as an extended dominant chord within a tonic area—the latter sometimes, as in the C major Quartet K. 465 but not in the Quintet, defined only gradually and clarified little by little). To treat this as a more than local event, as a tension to be resolved not only by the following Allegro but much later at the end of the movement—as if it were part of the exposition—is original, even radical for its time. The concept of exposition is widened, and we are forced to hear the tensions in a larger temporal sense than we are accustomed to.

Even more radical is the relation between the coda and the Allegro: not the thematic similarity, a common enough device (a way of ensuring the unity of separate pieces at least as old as the late medieval *chanson* mass), but the interaction of texture and harmony. The end of the Allegro takes on more and more the minor coloring of the introduction, the texture so thinning out that the quiet sound of the cello alone, as at the opening of the work, seems too natural and inevitable to surprise.[1] In this way, the Allegro blends into the return of the introduction, and the contrast of tempi is not only rhythmic, but inheres in the harmonic development as well. The most masterly stroke of all is the return of the first phrase of the Allegro at the very end, not only bringing a witty symmetry, but retaining for the slow coda its still essential quality of introduction, and weaving the two tempi together in an even more intricate unity.

The D major Quintet exploits a scheme of descending thirds throughout. The harmonic pattern of the main theme of the first movement is:

---

[1] The very last measures of the recapitulation are the same as those at the end of the exposition, since the second part of the Allegro is also meant to be repeated, and the thin texture is common to them both, but the gradually increased minor coloring is largely new in the closing section of the recapitulation.

The descending thirds, one of the simplest of all progressions, are implicit. This shape also inspires the large outline for the thirty-six measure long principal theme of the finale. The pattern is not essentially melodic, however, but a way of constructing sequences, a motor impulse, in short. How it is used can be seen from the first violin part that follows the principal theme of the first movement. The harmonic sequence of the opening theme is used here to construct the modulation to A major, and makes the pattern explicit:

In the minuet the descent in thirds takes over all aspects of the work, and everything is derived from it:

At the end of the minuet the capacity of such a progression to render the writing of a canon childishly simple is fully demonstrated. When a melody descends in regular thirds, a canon is almost automatic:

String Quintet

The minuet here only exposes and simplifies what was latent and complex in the other movements.

The most exceptional use of the descending sequence is in the slow movement from the climax of the development through the return to the tonic:

In the sequence at the opening of this passage, each new phrase takes up the descending thirds where the previous one left off, even where there is a half-cadential pause between. The climax is the sudden creation of a void: a cadence, built up powerfully and with the fierce energy that the cumulated descent can arouse, is, in measure 52, *not* played—not only postponed but permanently withheld. Instead of the cadence, all motion ceases, and with a sudden *piano* only the soft throbbing of the two violas is left. As the other instruments enter with a new sequence that leads directly back to the main theme, we find four completely different kinds of rhythm superimposed in a contrapuntal texture at once complex and deeply touching. The exchange of lines in measure 56 between first and second violins is a last refinement and prepares the entrance of the main theme after a *crescendo*. The sequence and the superimposition of rhythmic textures achieve a condition of stillness after the vigorous descent of thirds: everything is resolved quietly and inevitably, suspended motionless almost without breath after the arrest of impulse by the daring non-cadence.

The Quintet in E flat major K. 614 is a tribute to Haydn: it is Mozart's last work of chamber music. Along with the previous one in D major, it is said to have been written for Johann Tost: the imitation of Haydn may have been due at least partly to Tost's friendship with the elder composer, who had only recently written twelve quartets for him. Did Mozart's commission perhaps come through Haydn? The musical debt to Haydn, in any case, is as considerable in this work as in the first String Quintet K. 174. The finale of K. 614, written in 1791, is derived from the finale of one of the quartets that Haydn dedicated to Tost in 1790, op. 64 no. 6:

The slow movement is very close to the slow movement of Haydn's Symphony no. 85, *La Reine*, written in 1786; while the rustic drone bass trio of the minuet is surely influenced by the similarly conceived trio in Haydn's Symphony no. 88 of 1787. The imitation of technique is more relevant than melodic reference. The finale is Haydnesque throughout, even to the point of a comic inversion of the theme at the end. This work, which—in its outer movements—combines a detailed treatment in Haydn's fashion of the dynamic qualities of the tiniest motifs with a typically Mozartean sonorous and complex inner part-writing, makes a few musicians uncomfortable, perhaps because it lacks the expansive freedom of the other quintets, and seems to concentrate its richness. In the first movement, only the leisurely opening of the 'second group' has Mozart's typical generosity. The contrapuntal complexity of the finale, too, seems antagonistic to its asserted jollity. But these are only defects if we expect, not more, but something else than this splendidly conceived work is prepared to give. It is only fitting, after all, that, in his last chamber work, Mozart should once again appear to submit to Haydn's instruction. It was Haydn who created this chamber style, made it viable, and endowed it with the power to bear dramatic and expressive weight without flying apart. In the quintets Mozart expanded the range of the form beyond Haydn's range, and attained a massiveness that Beethoven himself never surpassed. The fundamental and imaginative vision, of chamber music as dramatic action, however, was Haydn's; and his conception and his innovations were a living presence in every work of this kind that Mozart wrote.

3

Comic Opera

On November 12, 1778, Mozart wrote to his father from Mannheim about a new kind of drama with music that was being produced there, and about the invitation extended to him by the producer to compose one: 'I have always wanted to write a drama of this kind. I cannot remember whether I told you anything about this type of drama the first time I was here? On that occasion I saw a piece of this sort performed twice and was absolutely delighted. Indeed, nothing has ever surprised me so much, for I had always imagined that such a piece would be quite ineffective. You know, of course, that there is no singing in it, only recitation, to which the music is like a sort of obbligato accompaniment to a recitative. Now and then words are spoken while the music goes on, and this produces the finest effect. . . . Do you know what I think? I think that most operative recitatives should be treated in this way— and only sung occasionally, when the words *can be perfectly expressed by the music.*'[1] The letter ought not, perhaps, to be taken at face value: Mozart's attempt to conquer the musical world of Paris had failed miserably, and he now faced what he most hated and dreaded, a return to Salzburg and the Archbishop's service once again. How much of his enthusiasm is genuine, and how much only an effort at persuading his father, who was waiting impatiently in Salzburg, that it was practical to put off the return for the moment, and that there were other prospects in view? Nevertheless, Mozart's attitude, his experimental approach, is revealing. He is delighted with the possibilities of what is called 'melodrama' (spoken dialogue accompanied by music), and his feeling for theatrical effect is by no means centered upon vocal music. On the contrary, he assumes a clear distinction between music that is an equivalent for dramatic action and music that is the perfect expression of the words.[2] It is the first concept that has priority, and he is willing to abandon sung words for spoken ones when the action can be made more telling this way.

Zaïde has some splendid effects of melodrama which look forward to the second act of *Fidelio*, but we have lost everything else that Mozart wrote in

---

[1] Mozart's own emphasis, cited from the *Letters of Mozart and his family*, ed. Emily Anderson, London, 1966.
[2] In a letter of November 8, 1780, he objected to the idea of an aside in an aria: 'In a dialogue all these things are quite natural, for a few words can be spoken aside hurriedly; but in an aria where the words have to be repeated, it has a bad effect, *and even if this were not the case I should prefer an uninterrupted aria*' [my emphasis, C. R.], *ibid.*, p. 659.

this form that so interested him for a moment, unless one counts the interruptions of Pedrillo's serenade and Osmin's song by spoken dialogue in *Die Entführung*, or the moment in *Die Zauberflöte* when Papageno counts three before preparing to commit suicide. Yet Mozart never lost his desire to experiment or his sense that, in opera, music as dramatic action takes precedence over music as expression. This is not to deny Mozart's skill at writing for the voice, or his love for elaborate vocal coloratura. Nevertheless he was not always tender with the vanity of singers who wished to show off the beauty of their voices. Particularly in ensembles, like the great quartet in *Idomeneo*, he insisted that the words should be more spoken than sung.[1] Mozart's brief interest in 'melodrama' while in Mannheim is the enthusiasm of a young composer who has just discovered that music on the stage can do more than meet the requirements of singers or express sentiment, but can become one with plot and intrigue as well. This was an idea that he had only half understood when writing the beautiful and little-known *La Finta Giardiniera*.

The style of the early eighteenth century had been equal to any demands that words alone could make. The operatic music of Handel and Rameau could transfigure the sentiment and the situation at each moment, but it left untouched the action and the movement—anything that was not static, in short. To say that the sonata style provided an ideal framework for the rendering of what was most dynamic on the stage is to oversimplify only insofar as it does not take account of the important role that opera itself played in the development of the sonata style. *Opera buffa*, in particular, was influential, and the classical style moves with the least strain in its depiction of comic intrigue and comic gesture.

The three points that made the new style so apt for dramatic action were: first, the articulation of phrase and form which give a work the character of a series of distinct events; second, the greater polarization of tonic and dominant, which allowed for a much clearer rise in tension in the center of each work (as well as more specifically characterizing the significance of related harmonies, which could then also serve a dramatic meaning); and third, by no means the least important, the use of rhythmic transition, which permitted the texture to change with the action on the stage without endangering the purely musical unity in any way. All these stylistic characteristics belong to the 'anonymous' style of the period; they were the common currency of music by 1775. There is no question, however, that Mozart was the first composer to comprehend, in any systematic way, their implications for opera. In one sense, Gluck was a more original composer than Mozart, his style was much more personally forged by a stubborn act of will rather than by an acceptance of the traditions of his age. But this very originality barred the way to that ease and facility with which Mozart mastered the relation of music to drama.

---

[1] Letter of December 27, 1780, *ibid.*, p. 699.

The adaptability of the sonata style to opera can be seen in its least complex and most perfect form in Mozart's own favorite among the individual numbers of *Figaro*, the great sextet of recognition in the third act, which is in slow-movement sonata form (i.e., without a development section, but with a recapitulation starting in the tonic—although the 'second group' of the exposition is sufficiently heightened and intensified here as to provide some of the effect of a development). The sextet begins with Marcellina's expression of joy at finding that Figaro is her long-lost son (*a*):

The tonic section has three main themes, of which this is the first. The second (*b*) appears after Doctor Bartolo has sung a variant of (*a*); Don Curzio and the Count express their irritation:

290

the third (*c*), an ecstatic one based on a diminished fifth, is divided between
Marcellina, Figaro, and Doctor Bartolo:

The painful dissonance outlined by this melody gives it its passionate character. The section ends on a semi-conclusive dominant cadence as Susanna
enters with the money, no longer necessary, to buy Figaro out of his contract
of marriage with Marcellina:

This is the beginning of what is respectably called the 'bridge passage' in a sonata exposition, and the added tension that comes with the change to the dominant is admirably calculated to parallel Susanna's ignorance of what has been happening and her inevitable misunderstanding. As at the beginning of the second group of most of Haydn's sonatas and many of Mozart's, part of the first group reappears:

It is (*c*) that is repeated, as Marcellina, Figaro, and Bartolo are still lost in their discovery. A dissonant sonority appears with a turn to the dominant minor and Susanna's rage at seeing Figaro kissing Marcellina (*d*):

While Figaro tries to appease her, a new caressing motif appears in the violins:

but it is derived from the violin part in (*a*), and has the same sensuous swell as (*c*). The exposition continues with a motif (*e*) derived from it and combining with it—which expresses Susanna's indignation:

and closes with a firm cadence on the dominant, as every exposition did then.

Only the recapitulation of a sonata requires any ingenuity in being adapted to the stage; an exposition is, as it stands, a model for an intrigue that becomes more complex and more tense with the introduction of new elements and new events. For a recapitulation, on the other hand, the classical composer had to find the elements of symmetry and resolution in the situation and in the very words of the libretto. It need hardly be emphasized that this is not a playful or pedantic adaptation of a fixed form to a dramatic genre; the symmetry and resolution of the sonata were permanent needs of the classical composer, not dispensable elements of form.

The resolution in the sextet begins when the situation is carefully explained to the furious Susanna; accordingly the tonic returns, and the recapitulation begins with (*a*) once more:

The words, of course, will no longer fit the opening melody, so it is the winds of the orchestra that play the melody (*a*) here, and Marcellina who decorates it.

Susanna is bewildered, and her confusion is expressed by a variant of (*b*), used in the exposition for the consternation of the Count and Don Curzio, quoted above:

Finally, there is a concluding section in which all express their joy, except, of course, the Count and Don Curzio:

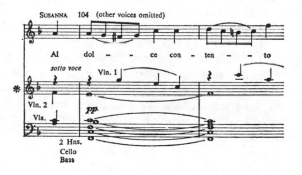

which recalls, above all, the deeply expressive character of (c). There is even a move towards F minor (mm. 110–117) which parallels the C minor of (d). We are given a fine example of the priorities of classical form: the harmonic structure and the proportions outweigh the letter of the melodic pattern here, just as they do in so many of Haydn's and Mozart's abstract works.

In fact, no description of sonata form can be given that will fit the Haydn quartets but not the majority of forms in a Mozart opera. This coincidence between abstract and dramatic pattern is significant in many ways, particularly in the insight it provides into the nature of late eighteenth-century form. There are no fixed 'rules,' although there are successful patterns imitated and even aped, and unconscious habits. The abstract forms, no more than the theatrical ones, do not make their effects by breaking 'rules,' as is so often thought: the element of surprise in the string quartets and the operas does not depend upon a deviation from some imagined musical norm outside the individual work. It is the work itself (once its language is understood) that provides its own expectations, disappoints and finally fulfils them: the tensions are implied more by the music and very little by the specific experience and prejudices of the listener, although he must have an educated ear to know what to listen for, educated in the stylistic language and not just in its superficial formalities. One must accept the essentially innovatory nature of the style, like that of any language, its built-in possibility of creating original combinations. In other words, such rules as the classical style genuinely developed—the need for resolution, the sense of proportion and of a closed and framed pattern—are never broken at all. They are its means of communication, and it could say astonishing things without violating its own grammar. As for the conventional patterns that so many composers used unthinkingly, they were not rules of grammar but clichés: they were turned into rules when the musical language changed, and the pressures and the forces that had produced the classical style (along with its idioms and formulas) were exhausted and died.

When the dramatic situation will not lend itself easily to a symmetrical resolution and recapitulation, the sonata aesthetic still remains valid in Mozart's operas. Its use is only superficially more complex: there is the same need for resolution, the same sense of proportion. The second act sextet of *Don Giovanni* has a form as clear but far less openly symmetrical than the sextet of *Figaro*, yet it satisfies the same aesthetic demands. The dramatic complexity—the gradual introduction of new characters, the surprising changes of situation—requires an immense expansion of the 'development section,' and much new material: the resolution is equally immense and emphatic. The opening in E flat major, a small sonata exposition, is short and succinct: like the exposition of Haydn's *Oxford* Symphony, it gives no hint of the enormous consequences that await. At the beginning, Donna Elvira and Leporello (whom she believes to be Don Giovanni) are lost in the dark. Donna Elvira is frightened at being abandoned and her shudder of fear is rendered by the orchestra with a motif (*a*) which will appear later:

The music moves to the dominant as Leporello gropes for the door; as he finds it, he sings the typically regular closing theme and cadence of a sonata exposition. Then there is a most extraordinary moment, as Donna Anna and Don Ottavio appear dressed in mourning. The oboes hold their final notes of the dominant cadence, then with a soft drum-roll the music luminously moves to the remote key of D, and as Don Ottavio begins to sing, the transitional phrase is wonderfully repeated as a counterpoint. The overlapping enforces both continuity and articulation:

297

The tonal relations here entail an important paradox. D is a remote key in a work in E flat, but it is the basic key of the whole opera. The significance of this moment of modulation is therefore an ambiguous one, and it is· no wonder that every listener senses its mysterious quality. The trumpets and drums, appearing in the sextet for the first time here, set the moment into sharp relief. The connection with the opening of the opera and the conviction that we have reached the central key are made strikingly evident in two ways. First Don Ottavio even recalls the main theme of the overture in the measures that follow:

This is by no means a thematic allusion: it only comes because the conception of the key of D is so emphatically a unity throughout the opera and calls up the same associations. Then, when Donna Anna replies to Don Ottavio, the music shifts to the D minor mode of the opening of the overture and the Commendatore's murder. The change is once again marked by mysterious soft drum-rolls:

Until this point of the opera, whenever Donna Anna appeared, it was always with the fundamental key of D, except in the large ensemble numbers. Her first duet with Don Ottavio after the death of her father is in D, and the opening recalls her phrase in the sextet:

Her great aria 'Or sai chi l'onore' is also in D.[1] Moreover, when Donna Anna and her masked companions, Don Ottavio and Donna Elvira, appear for the first time in the finale of Act I, they bring the key of D minor with them:

The opening motif (given to Donna Elvira) is again close to the one in the sextet. These are not thematic references, but the result of a total conception of the opera in which everything is related to a central tonality, which itself has, not only a symbolic reference, but an individual sonority that it seems to evoke. The fact alone of having one singer so closely associated with the tonality lends it an immediately recognizable sound. Whatever key the individual section may be in, the appearance of D minor unequivocally calls up the death of the Commendatore.[2]

One does not, therefore, need perfect pitch to hear a reference to the tonic of the entire opera at this point in the sextet. Nevertheless, even in a non-operatic work an eighteenth-century composer's sensitivity to such long-range relations may have been greater than some critics, Tovey in particular, have been willing to admit. No composer, of course, has ever made his crucial effects depend on such perception: even if he expects his most subtle points to be appreciated only by connoisseurs, he does not write the entire work calculatedly above the head of the average listener. But there is at least one person who is sure to recognize the reappearance of a tonic even without thematic reference: the performer. It is for this reason that subtle effects based on tonal relations are much more likely to occur in a string quartet or a sonata, written as much for the performers as for the listeners, than in an opera or a symphony, more coarsely if more elaborately designed. The

---

[1] Her later aria, 'Non mi dir,' is in the relative major of D minor, F major, and it is preceded by an accompanied recitative largely dominated by D minor.

[2] Even the ghostly voice of the statue in the cemetery starts his first phrase with a D minor chord, while his final appearance in the last act is the signal, not only for the most emphatic return to D minor, but for an explicit recapitulation of much of the overture.

last sonatas of Haydn play with distant tonal relations, for example, in a way that he never attempts in the *London* Symphonies. Mozart, however, as we have seen, has dramatic ways of making these relations clearly felt in the operas.

The entrance of Don Ottavio and Donna Anna in the E flat major sextet, and the strange modulation that heralds it, make D into a second dominant in some ways more powerful than B flat major. (The search for a substitute dominant became very important later with Beethoven, but only once, at the end of his life, with the Sonata op. 110, did he attempt anything as harmonically daring as the key of the leading-tone. Mozart's success, however, depends as much on dramatic considerations that receive their harmonic justification outside the sextet as on the inner logic.) The D major and minor, in spite of the breadth with which they are established and drawn out, are therefore unstable and lead to a modulation to C minor, which by its immediate relation to E flat major reduces the highly charged atmosphere, but still moves as within a 'development section.' An important new theme for Donna Elvira (*b*) is introduced, built of sobs:

and Leporello, trying to leave, repeats his concluding theme and is stopped by the entrance of Zerlina and Masetto.

The discovery of Leporello brings back the little motif (*a*) that previously represented Donna Elvira's terror:

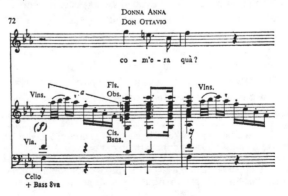

300

and then a long development of the sobbing phrase (*b*) begins, as Donna Elvira begs mercy for the man she believes to be Don Giovanni, and the music stays for many measures in G minor, which serves both to resolve the D major partially and to bring us closer to the tonic E flat major. Leporello, almost weeping, begins his plea, followed and seconded by a whining chromatic scale from all the winds: there is a marvelously witty passage at measures 108–109, where his phrase grows more impassioned and desperate, and the winds cannot wait to let him finish and impose their phrase contrapuntally over his. The development ends on a chord of G major, made doubly unstable by the sequences that have just preceded it. The signal for these sequences is the discovery that the terrified captive is Leporello, not Don Giovanni; they begin with a surprise cadence, and could be called a 'bridge' to the recapitulation, except that they do not lead directly to E flat major, but only serve to weaken the firm G minor of Leporello's plaint and to make it evident that the dissonant tonality is about to be resolved.

At this point, dramatic exigency has required that an 'exposition' of twenty-seven measures be succeeded by a 'development' of 113 measures: the resolution that will follow is properly grandiose. Everything that happens in the final section (mm. 131–277) is nothing more than a series of (V-I) tonic cadences on E flat, dramatized, decorated, expanded, and fantastically enlivened. The fundamental harmony does not really move: no matter how remote the chords or how complicated the harmony, there is no true modulation. The rhythmic motion, precipitate and furious, is all on the surface. This whole section, marked 'Molto allegro,' sticks even closer to the tonic than any abstract sonata recapitulation would dare to do; there is an E flat major triad in almost half the measures. The Molto allegro resolves as a recapitulation does, and its relative proportions are those of a sonata, given the greatly enlarged 'development' that preceded: the 140-odd measures of the Molto allegro go about twice as fast as the rest of the sextet, so that its length is equivalent to seventy of the preceding measures and its heavy concentration on the tonic make an adequate classical balance and resolution for all the harmonic tensions of the sextet. The climactic points of the sextet are, too, at the same places and have the same character as in a sonata: the startling change at the opening of the development when Donna Anna and Don Ottavio enter, and the long drawn-out tension at the end of it when Leporello reveals who he is. The last section Molto allegro may be said to follow the sonata aesthetic almost in spite of the words, as 'Mille torbidi pensieri' hardly implies so rigid an attachment to the tonic.

The sextet should not be considered as an abstract musical form; it is responsive to other than purely musical pressures. Nevertheless, the proportions and ideals that help to shape it are the same as those which created the sonata form. Mozart explicitly said that the words must be the servant of the music, but he also emphasized the parity of the dramatic and musical conceptions. In his operas, the intrigue and the musical forms are indissoluble. The capacity of the sonata style to fuse with a dramatic conception as no other previous style had done was Mozart's historical opportunity. Without this complementary relation between musical style and dramatic conception, the greatest music cannot make an opera viable; with it, the most foolish libretto can barely undo one.

This sextet is conceived fundamentally as an *opera buffa* 'finale,' and for the development of this form Mozart owed little to his predecessors: he may be considered as at once the creator and the only master of it. Formally defined, the finale consists of all the music between the last *secco* recitative and the end of the act, and it may have as many as ten numbers or as little as one. Mozart appears to have been the first composer to conceive of the more complex finale as a tonal unity. It cannot have been a theoretical principle of the age; the finales of his earlier operas (*La Finta Giardiniera*, for example) begin and end in different keys. From *Die Entführung* on, however, the finale of every act of every opera ends in the key it started with, and the tonal relationships within them (and they are often very complex) are so conceived as to produce a harmonic equilibrium in terms of sonata style. Contemporaries of Mozart are either so inconsistent that we may consider the occasional finale that appears to be shaped around a tonic as an accident, or else (like those by Piccinni) they venture so little from their original key that the tonal relationships are unified only by remaining unvaried.

For the more complex finales, Mozart needed a libretto that provided him with a series of events so arranged that the music could both clarify and dramatize the order. He was prepared to insist upon transferring the beginning of one act to the end of the previous one if it would give him the situation and the order he wanted, even if it also entailed a less reasonably distributed action and forced the librettist to invent unnecessary complications to fill the gap. The supreme example of a librettist's achievement in constructing a finale is generally considered the reworking of Beaumarchais by da Ponte in the second act of *Figaro*, where the successive addition of new characters constantly enriches the sonority, and the growing complication of the plot is the ideal foil to the increased brilliance and animation of the music: it is a finale worked out with the musical style in mind.

Unity in late eighteenth-century music is imposed chiefly by framing devices, and the more strongly the outer frame is defined as part of the work, the greater will be the tendency to set off individual sections within a larger whole by analogous framing. The opening scene of *Don Giovanni* starts in F major with Leporello alone on the stage, and the music ends before the first *secco* recitative (after the death of the Commendatore) in F minor. This long scene, however, is contained within a larger grouping, a fact emphasized by a slight dissolution or blurring of the inner frame at both ends: the orchestra modulates from the overture directly into Leporello's F major, and there is no full close at the end of the F minor, but rather a terrifyingly effective shading into the whispered recitative. The larger grouping is framed by the overture and the scene between Donna Anna and Don Ottavio, both of them in D, a tonality emphasized by its return in the central section of the group for the duel. This handling of the half-frame within a frame serves to establish D as the fundamental tonality of the opera, a function rigorously demonstrated when the next scene also ends in D major with Leporello's brilliant and comic catalogue aria, so that the D minor of the larger group (as well as of the smaller one of the overture alone) has a traditional D major resolution.[1]

The Mozart finale is made up of separate numbers, but many of them run directly one into another, and they are intended to be heard as a unit. Those large groupings represent the closest that Mozart came to the conception of large-scale continuity. The separate large divisions correspond to the inner articulation of the classical phrase; Beethoven, who tried (in the *Missa Solemnis*, in particular) for continuity on a greater scale than Mozart ever attempted, still relies on this kind of sectional form as the basis for a longer one (and there are even clear traces of it in Wagner). The importance of the Mozart finale within the operas as a whole cannot be placed too high: they gather together the disparate threads of both the drama and the musical form and give them a continuity that the opera had never before known. The arias, beautiful as they are, serve in part only as a preparation for the finale of the act, which is the set piece of the occasion.

It is not surprising that the development of the finale as a unified conception had, as one effect, the reduction of the musical importance of the *secco* recitative. Not that there is any less of it quantitatively in the later operas, but they are both less daring and less expressive. There is little *secco* recitative in Mozart after *La Finta Giardiniera* that can parallel the chromaticism of this passage from that early work:

---

[1] I have remarked above (pp. 94–5) on the similar framing of part of a larger whole in the finale to Act I of *Don Giovanni*.

Starting with *Idomeneo*, the *secco* recitatives are more workaday in their harmonic conception, although there are several interesting dramatic interruptions, particularly in *Figaro*. The *secco* recitatives now provide a truly dry contrast to the more expressively conceived large structures.

The sense of form in the finales is very similar to that in the symphonies and chamber music; the dramatic exigencies of eighteenth-century comedy and musical style have no difficulty walking in step. In the penultimate number of the second act finale of *Figaro*, the Countess reveals herself with the most gracious of transitions back to the tonic major: a sudden turn to the tonic minor represents the Count's shamed surprise as a secondary development section, and he turns back to the tonic major to ask forgiveness in a long resolving passage. The recapitulation of a string quartet has a dramatic shape that is not very different, and it would be a misunderstanding of Mozart's chamber music style to miss this point. Within the larger context of the whole finale, this penultimate number as a whole has a significance as ordered and as direct: it is in the subdominant (G major) of the basic D major tonality of the whole opera, and serves, as within an even larger recapitulation, to reinforce the final symmetry and resolution.

A finale is an opera in miniature: the same tonal unity that reigns there may be found—more loosely understood as is appropriate to its greater length—within the opera as a whole. Once again Mozart appears to stand alone among his contemporaries in his insistence on this integrity. It is also a mature development: only after the age of twenty did Mozart invariably finish an opera in the key of the overture. Was this theory or developing instinct? This is not a question that can be fruitfully pursued, but in any case it would be absurd to consider Mozart's working habits as a form of somnambulism.

Where instinct surely played a role is in the constitution of classical proportions within the harmonic structure of the opera as a whole. The most highly organized and the most brilliant of the finales is never the last (or second of the two large ones) but the first: it is, like a development section, the extreme point of tension within the work. It is also placed harmonically as far away from the tonic of the whole opera as Mozart could go. The first finale of *Figaro* (actually in the second act of four) is in E flat major against the entire opera's tonic of D, and the other works follow the same pattern: D to C major for *Così fan tutte*, C to E flat major for *Die Zauberflöte*, C major to D minor/major for *Don Giovanni*. These central finales are indeed the heart of each work, and they are worked out with an elaboration and a complexity that Mozart reaches nowhere else. To many people, this has made the second finales of the operas, particularly those of *Figaro* and *Così*, disappointing.

The classical sense of an ending is the element of the style most antipathetic to modern taste, yet it is as essential to the style as the more organized textures of the opening and central sections of a work. In every one of the opera finales, without exception, the last number does not modulate, but remains firmly fixed on the tonic. It serves as a cadence to the finale as a whole, an expanded dominant-tonic (V–I), just as the last finale serves as a cadence to the entire opera. The last number of a finale is a harmonic resolution of all the preceding dissonance like the recapitulation of a sonata.

The looseness and even squareness, inseparable from the classical rondo-form so often used for the last movement of a sonata or symphony, is rendered in a striking way by the second act finale of *Don Giovanni*, which begins with an orchestra on the stage playing a medley of popular operatic tunes of the day. There is here a determined attempt to break down the dramatic concentration of the opera, and even to weaken the continuity. A similar looseness is evident in the fourth and last act of *Figaro* when it is performed uncut, with the arias of Basilio and Marcellina included. Even if these numbers were only provided because the singers had a right to at least one aria apiece, it is evident that both composer and librettist felt that the disruption of dramatic continuity would be most suitable in the last act. The finale of the second and last act of *Così fan tutte* has a modulatory structure that is bewilderingly rapid and sectional with none of the intensity and concentration of the first one; the inspiration and the mastery are, however, fully as consistent.

The solidity and clarity of the classical ending, above all the harmonic resolution of all the long-range dissonance, gave a new form to the operatic aria. With the finales and the sextet from *Don Giovanni* in mind as a model, we can understand the role of the final short allegros of arias like 'Non mi dir' and 'Battì, battì, bel Masetto.' An aria in moderate tempo with a faster concluding section is often found in operas of the last quarter of the eighteenth century, and the final section is not a coda or an independent movement, like the second part of Bellini's 'Casta diva,' but a harmonic resolution of the previous tensions. The slower first part of almost all these arias is outwardly an *ABA* form which has nothing to do with the da capo aria, or with normal ternary form: the *B* goes always to the dominant, and has the character of a 'second group' in a sonata (followed sometimes by a development). The faster concluding section that follows the return of the opening theme substitutes harmonically for the recapitulation of *B*, or the 'second group': like the end of the sextet in *Don Giovanni*, this section never leaves the tonic, except for a glance at the subdominant, even in such long examples as the final Allegro moderato of ' Per pietà, ben mio' from *Così fan tutte*.[1] The Countess's aria 'Dove sono' in *Figaro* acknowledges this incomplete form of the first slow section by breaking off the return of the opening melody in the middle of a phrase: the Allegro that follows both resolves the phrase and the whole piece. This form of aria (Andante (tonic—dominant—tonic)—Allegro (tonic)) conforms to the harmonic ideal of the sonata by moving first towards the dominant, and by devoting at least the entire last quarter of its length to a firm tonic resolution; the harmonic climax is placed at the center, and the resolution is sustained by virtuosity as in the concerto.[2]

With the growth of his experience as a composer of operas, however, Mozart's conception of the aria became more imaginative. The sonata patterns of most of the arias in the earlier operas—*La Finta Giardiniera*, *Zaïde*, *Idomeneo*—are relatively simple and straightforward, the melodic symmetries clearly and literally marked. Many of them could be used as ideal textbook examples for the most rigid and most narrow definitions of sonata allegro. Even those arias with the most surprising innovations are relatively direct. Several times in *Idomeneo*, Mozart attempted a fusion of sonata and da capo forms (nos. 19, 27, and 31). The arias begin with a regular tonic-dominant sonata exposition, and they all have recapitulations which resolve

---

[1] Like his feeling for the tonal unity of an opera, this feeling for tonal proportion is a later development of Mozart's style, starting in this case with the *Entführung*. It is not true, for example, of the E major trio 'O selige Wonne' in *Zaïde*, which follows an unresolved sonata exposition with a complete sonata form.

[2] The duet 'Là, ci darem la mano' from *Don Giovanni* begins with a clear slow-movement sonata form (without a development section) with a full recapitulation; the faster section (in 6/8) that follows is an extended cadence, and it never leaves the tonic. It may be called a genuine coda, as its emphasis on the tonic has none of the urgency of the final section of the arias previously cited. With no formal need for resolution, the luxury of such an indulgence in the most consonant of harmonies, developed with the lilting dance rhythm of a siciliana, is a reflection of Zerlina's delighted surrender.

the 'second group' in the tonic (no. 27, 'Nò, la morte,' even shows the older dominant-tonic form of recapitulation). The middle section is in a different and contrasting tempo, which sometimes begins with the relaxed air of the trio of a minuet and then begins to show the more dramatic character of a 'development' section leading directly back to the opening. These examples are experiments in Mozart's career, and ideally none of them should be considered apart from their dramatic function, the words, and their place in the opera as a whole. One example of an unusual formal device must suffice for all, Electra's 'Tutto nel cor' (*Idomeneo*, no. 4), where a D minor exposition has a recapitulation that begins for 12 measures in C minor, the key of the flat leading tone—as far removed from resolution as one could imagine. It is, of course, a departure that Mozart justifies dramatically and formally, as a perfect equivalent for the violence and rage of Electra's character; the same harmonic instability is revealed in her other arias. But it is equally noteworthy that this D minor aria is followed without interruption by a stormy chorus in C minor, describing the shipwreck: the abnormal opening in C minor of the recapitulation of the aria prepares this without lessening its dramatic effect. This recapitulation, in turn, is itself prepared by the exposition, which goes from D minor to F minor as much as to F major. The C minor seems natural when it appears as it arises from the F minor; only the realization that it is the true beginning of a complete recapitulation, and not a development, is a surprise. The return of the *tonic* paradoxically provides the real shock, an effect typically concise and powerful.

To some readers these considerations may appear unnecessarily finicky: still others may find such large-scale tonal significances simplistic. Yet there is no question that Mozart himself thought in exactly such terms, as is shown by the often-quoted letter to his father about *Die Entführung*, where he explains the choice of A minor to finish an aria of Osmin that begins in F major. There is, one must add, an element of self-justification in the letter: he is explaining one of his more surprising harmonic effects—indeed, almost explaining it away: 'as music, even in the most terrible situations, must never offend the ear, but must please the listener, or in other words must never cease to be *music*, so I have not chosen a key remote from F (in which the aria is written) but one related to it—not the nearest, D minor, but the more remote A minor.' This is, no doubt, the expression of a deeply classical taste, one which had repudiated the mannerism of the previous generation; but it is also an attempt to reassure a father always afraid his son will write clever, *avant-garde* music unintelligible to the general public, and not make any money—which is, of course, more or less what happened. The change of key in the aria of Osmin in question (no. 3 of the *Entführung*)[1] does not in any way invalidate Mozart's insistence on unity of key, as the different sections

---

[1] It is a relationship that symmetrically reappears (once again to illustrate Osmin's rage) in the *vaudeville* at the end of the opera, but is there resolved within a larger frame.

are clearly, if briefly, separated by spoken dialogue; a naïve device, perhaps, but the tonal patterns of the *Entführung* are not yet as sophisticated as those of the later operas. The whole of the letter to his father, however, makes it clear that a definite symbolic meaning was to be attached to a change of key.

The arias in the later operas are much more subtle and infinitely more varied. The more common symmetries of sonata form, as manifold as they were, are no longer used so directly and simply, although they remain the guiding principles: the harmonic and rhythmic energies of the sonata style are combined with the dramatic situation in ever more imaginative ways. Susanna's 'Deh vieni, non tardar' seems, at first hearing, to be pure song, untrammeled by any strict conception of form. It is, however, in what I have called sonata-minuet form, in which a more animated combined 'second-group'-and-'development' starts in the dominant after the first double-bar. In 'Deh vieni' the recapitulation is a half-disguised variation of the opening:

The final form interchanges and expands both halves of the opening, and in this way the first measure of the melody is turned into the lyrical expansion of a cadence. There are many sketches for this exquisite and subtle aria, and its perfection was not easily arrived at.

Figaro's cavatina 'Se vuol ballare' is an even more remarkable example of a freedom supported by a strict sense of proportion and balance. It begins as a monothematic sonata, the opening melody reappearing at the dominant, and a modulation to D minor acting as a clear development section. The Presto that follows is a variation of the opening theme; it stays entirely in the tonic and functions as a resolution and recapitulation, but it admirably represents Figaro's menacing sense of triumph as he contemplates the future ruin of the Count's plans. The opening must be compared with the Presto, to see how powerful the transformation is in its change of rhythm and speed, and yet how the original outline remains unaltered:

L'ar-te scher - men-do, l'arte a - do - pran-do, di quà pu - gnen-do, di là scher - zan-do, tut - te le ma-chi-ne ro - ve-scie - rò, ro - ve - scie rò.

The wittiest stroke is to have the basic melodic elements move twice as fast in a phrase which sums up the whole aria at top speed:

tut - te le ma - chi-ne ro - ve-scie - rò, tut - te le ma-chi - ne ro - ve - scie - rò,

The original tempo is brought back at the end before a very short final burst of Presto to make the relation more telling and the balance more dramatic. Mozart's recapitulations in all the operas after the *Entführung* became less and less literal, but his sense of harmonic proportion and symmetry never wavered.

The economy of a Mozart aria is exactly that of a Haydn quartet. The little phrase 'signor contino'

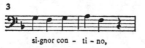

si-gnor con - ti - no,

becomes a triumphant assertion of victory with 'le suonerò sì,'

le suo-ne - rò sì

merely by transposing the final note up an octave, and the motif that makes this change possible runs through all the transformations of the melodic outline in the cavatina. This kind of dynamically conceived motivic development derives, as a technique, from Haydn, but its dramatic propriety is incontestable. The changing forms of a motif not only give a logical coherence to the music, but allow it to express not a fixed sentiment, but an emotion that changes before our eyes from menace to triumph. Here, as elsewhere, the classical style achieves unity and continuity with the use of discrete, separable elements.

The coincidence of musical and dramatic events is the glory of Mozart's operatic style. In an essay defending the complexity of Mozart's operatic music, E. T. A. Hoffmann describes a moment from *Don Giovanni*:

When in *Don Giovanni* the statue of the Commendatore sounds his terrible 'Si' on the tonic E, but the composer now takes this E as the third

of C and thus modulates to C major, which tonality is seized upon by Leporello, no layman in musical matters will be able to understand the technical structure of this transition, but in the depths of his being he will tremble with Leporello; similarly the musician who has attained the highest level of culture will, in the moment of this most profound emotion, give as little thought to this structure, because the construction has long since occurred to him and so he has come round again to the layman's position.

The descent admired by Hoffmann is only one of a series in this E major duet, and forms part of a 'sonata' symmetry. There are four such descents, two from the dominant (B major) to a G♮, and then two—as a recapitulation—from the tonic to C♮. The first occurs when Don Giovanni threatens to kill Leporello if he refuses to approach the statue:

the second when the statue terrifyingly nods its head:

obviously recalling the first. The two descents from the tonic to C♮ are more elaborate,[1] first when Don Giovanni steps forward to command the statue to speak:

---

[1] The descent to C♮ in measure 49 has a different harmonic sense, as it is immediately preceded by the drop to G♮ just cited, and it is in the context of the dominant key of B major.

(again clearly recalling the earlier examples), and immediately following this, with the most dramatic sudden accents as the statue sings his one word of acceptance:

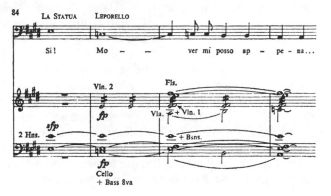

There is no better example of the ease with which Mozart's style offers a true equivalent for stage action and not only an expression of it: the symmetries he needed were not a hindrance but an inspiration.

Not only the new classical style made this equivalence of drama and music possible. There was also a corresponding revolution of dramatic technique in the eighteenth century, most significantly in the development of the rhythm of comic intrigue. The comedy of character was dethroned, and the comedy of situation took its place. The comedy of situation had, of course, always existed: *Twelfth Night* and the *Comedy of Errors* are only the most famous English examples of a genre that goes back to Menander. But comedy based on character was the dominant mode, and it was considered the higher form by most critics, Lessing being the most authoritative German dramatist to proclaim its superiority. By the end of the eighteenth century, however, Herder was to insist that the comedy of character was dead, and that the only plays of Molière which could still hold the stage were those based on situation, like the *Médecin malgré lui.* In an article, 'Das Lustspiel,' Herder reversed the usual critical commonplace and insisted that characters (like Tartuffe and Harpagon) dated and changed from era to era, while situations—comic intrigue and the dramatic upsets and reversals of comic plots—remained eternally valid and ever fresh.

Character, of course, is as eternal—and no more so—than situation, but the eighteenth-century preference went very deep. The pre-eminence of the comedy of situation did not come from its novelty, as it was hardly new, but from the development of dramatic rhythm. The eighteenth century created a new kind of art from the sheer mechanism of stage management; what was new was not the awkward discovery, the inopportune arrival, the disguise unconsciously revealed, but the speed, controlled and accelerated, with which these events occurred. Already at the end of the seventeenth century, the successors of Molière (Dancourt and Le Sage, in particular) had begun to develop this art of rhythm, and to neglect the powerful psychological typology of Molière. The greatest masters by the middle of the eighteenth century were Beaumarchais and Goldoni; in spite of the latter's continuation of the comedy of picturesque characters and of local manners, he wrote several masterpieces of pure comedy of situation like *Il Ventaglio,* where the interest centers almost exclusively upon the rhythm of the intrigue.

By the end of the nineteenth century, the genre finally attained an almost abstract form, the comedy of adultery, in which there is no sensuality at all, and illicit sexual relations are only strings that pull the puppets and make them run. The comedies of Feydeau are the greatest examples: character has disappeared, and there is a mathematical poetry drawn from the manipulation of a formidable number of adulterous liaisons and cross-liaisons in and out of the doors of several hotel rooms. But this is the old age of the form, and in the eighteenth century we have only its first moment of maturity. The origin is the improvised theater—the *commedia dell'arte*, the *Théâtre de la Foire*, for which many of the greatest writers of the eighteenth century wrote scenarios. Mozart came along at the exact moment when the improvisation had been replaced by a fixed and literary art, when the sketched scenarios of a series of comic situations became plays and librettos, developing the new rhythm of intrigue learnt from the popular, improvising troupes. It was an opportune time for Mozart, and we must be grateful that it coincided so neatly with the new dramatic possibilities of the sonata style. The arts do not always run so smoothly in harness, but eighteenth-century theater had developed the same feeling as music for an articulated series of events and for controlled rhythmic transitions. This conjunction made it possible for Mozart's genius to be deployed with such ease in his operas: he had the feeling lacking in Haydn for large-scale dramatic movement, and he had a control of the sonata style that only Haydn, of all his contemporaries, could equal. From the point of view of large-scale rhythmic movement, *Figaro* is his masterpiece, and for this Beaumarchais and da Ponte must share in the credit. It is the supreme musical example of the comedy of intrigue.

The development of the rhythm of comic intrigue was facilitated by a changing conception of personality in the eighteenth century, based on a new, although still primitive interest in experimental psychology. Earlier centuries produced a more striking and more individual conception of personality: Molière's Harpagon, to take only one example from so many in his plays, is neither an average miser nor an allegorical personification of avarice but a man possessed by avarice as if by a demon; Alceste, in *Le Misanthrope*, struggles against the misanthropy which controls him, and ends by yielding to it with delight. This conception of personality is reflected throughout the seventeenth century in the interest of the animal in man, the fables of La Fontaine, the studies by Della Porta and Le Brun of facial resemblances between animals and men, and it is closely related to the idea of human personality dominated by the humors. All men are different, each can be set off from his fellows, characterized by the abstract forces that govern his individual nature. The eighteenth-century view, by contrast, was a more leveling one: all men are the same, all dominated by the same motifs; *così fan tutti:* they all behave the same way; the differences between Fiordiligi and Dorabella are only superficial, the one like the other will end in the arms of a new suitor. One of the most revealing moments in *Le Nozze di Figaro* is when the valet, misled by Susanna, becomes as blind with jealousy as his master. Eighteenth-century comedy springs from the tradition of masked players, but it made the mimes drop the masks as the century went on, as if the fixed grimace were irrelevant to the blander, more mobile, real face underneath.

The relation of eighteenth-century comedy to the popular improvised theater cannot be overestimated, but it can be misunderstood. All the great comedies of the time are in some way related to this tradition, yet none of them allow for improvisation—in fact, they destroyed it. The *opéra-comique* arose from a scenario where only the songs were written out, but it was not long before the dialogue was set down as well. Even Gozzi, who promoted the improvised, masked theater in opposition to Goldoni, wrote out all the dialogue after the success of his first scenario, *The Love for Three Oranges*. The stylization of the masked troupes fitted in very well with eighteenth-century psychology: the outward personality is a mask, what is real is the *tabula rasa* underneath upon which experience writes. For the seventeenth century, beneath the mask lie features even more strikingly characterized, more individual; beneath the eighteenth-century mask is only human nature. In comparison to the individualized characters of the sixteenth- and seventeenth-century stages, the personages of the eighteenth century are almost blanks; their reactions can be controlled and manipulated by the intelligent rascal and the clever valet—except that they, too, can be caught in their own plot when the complexity escapes them. The reliance of the popular theater upon stylized characters and upon the comedy of situation—the development of intrigue—was an inspiration to the eighteenth-century playwright, but the theater did not remain popular for long under his hands. It was for the masked troupe of the Italian Comedians that Marivaux developed his highly sophisticated plays and created a genre that may be called the comedy of experimental psychology, a kind of play that was quickly taken up in Italy and Germany. These are not 'thesis' plays but 'demonstration' plays: there is never anything controversial about their ideas. They demonstrate—prove by acting out—psychological ideas and 'laws' that everyone accepted, and they are almost scientific in the way they show precisely how these laws work in practice.

Così fan tutte belongs in the center of this tradition: if the book is less profoundly conceived than the finest of Marivaux, it is still, because of its music, the greatest example of its kind. The interest in such a play lies chiefly in the psychological steps by which the characters move to an end known in advance: as in Marivaux' *Le Jeu de l'Amour et du Hasard*, how a young girl disguised as a maid and a young man disguised as a valet will overcome their feelings of class and, first, become aware that they are in love and, then, openly admit it. There must be a disguise, or the play would be not a psychological comedy, but a social drama about marrying outside one's class; and it must be a double disguise, so that both lovers may be guinea-pigs. In plays where only the man is disguised, the valet-scientist must fool him so that he, too, will become a part of the experiment, and weep real tears. In *Così fan tutte*, we know in advance that the girls will be unfaithful, but we expect a demonstration of how they will yield: step by step, it must be true to the eighteenth-century laws of psychology. It is necessary that the new lovers be the old ones disguised, or we would have a *comédie larmoyante* of the returning soldier who finds the girl he left behind in the arms of another; but it is necessary, too, that the disguised lovers each take the other's former girl, or the girls would be unconsciously faithful, and the play would prove quite a different psychological theorem.

In short, what is essential is a closed system. No outside influences may be allowed to enter: the atmosphere of the rest of life is sealed off. There are only victims and scientists; and the two young men, who start by thinking they are among the scientists, learn, to their rage, that they are numbered among the victims. That is why in *Così fan tutte* Guglielmo cannot join in the beautiful A flat major canon at the wedding but mutters that he hopes they are drinking poison. In order to isolate the experiment, the scientists play all the necessary roles: the notary and the doctor are both Despina disguised. The libretto has been condemned as absurd and cynically immoral, and oddly defended as realistic (by W. J. Turner): it is none of these. It constructs an artificial and completely traditional world in which a psychological demonstration may be acted out, and it is true, not to life, which never intrudes here, but to the eighteenth-century view of human nature. The psychological viewpoint was one that the nineteenth century found outdated, and yet so recently overthrown as to be distasteful: the opera was, in fact, the very end of a tradition and had to deal with a changed atmosphere from the start. Soon after its first performance it was already being censured as immoral and trivial, and for the next hundred years only exceptional critics, like E. T. A. Hoffmann, understood the warmth and irony that the libretto enabled Mozart to achieve.

The music follows the psychological progression with great sensitivity. Fiordiligi's two famous arias strikingly reflect the individual psychological moment: the first, proclaiming her fidelity 'like a rock,' is magnificently comic, with her display of virtue accompanied by two trumpets, and with vocal leaps as enormous and as ludicrous as the words. At moments, pride is mocked by the gaiety of the music as it forces the singer into an ungrateful register:

que - sto e - sem - pio di   co - stan-za,

In the second aria 'Per pietà, ben mio,' however, Fiordiligi is deeply troubled by the realization that her fidelity was, not a sham, but the most fragile of constructions. The two trumpets are replaced by two horns, the long leaps are no longer ridiculous but deeply expressive, the phrasing more complex.

From the point of view of the opera, when Fiordiligi yields to Ferrando (in the great A major duet 'Per gli amplessi') she becomes more herself as she becomes more like every woman: after the mock grandeur of her first aria and the real grandeur of the second, the music of the duet is correspondingly more human. The relation of musical style to operatic psychology is ambiguous at best, and always indirect, but in this duet Mozart abandons the immediately perceptible formal clarity that he commanded so readily, although the final resolution and the proportions are as satisfying as ever. The normal movement to the dominant E major has only begun when it is cut short by the entrance of Ferrando, and a surprising modulation to C major establishes this key (the flat mediant) as a new 'dominant' or secondary key. This is another anticipation of Beethoven's use of a substitute dominant, that is, a chord sufficiently akin to the dominant to be reasonably set against the tonic, and yet remote enough to give a chromatically expressive, large-scale dissonance to the structure: its purpose here is symbolic, but dramatically and not only expressively so. Fiordiligi's music expresses real anguish, but her most despairing cry, 'Ah non son, non son più forte':

is the conventional operatic representation of tears, nonetheless deeply touching: she is at her most desperate as the music obviously moves (from C major to A minor) towards a return of the tonic. We know how near Fiordiligi is to admitting her love, as we become aware how close the sound of A major is. When it finally comes, we sense that Ferrando has won, and he begins his final plea in a new tempo (Andante), full of confidence. Fiordiligi's answer—her defeat—is the most exquisite of cadences:

in which it is no longer the vocal line that carries the dramatic meaning, but the long-drawn-out and finally resolved phrase of the oboe. The classical realization of the cadence as an articulate dramatic event finds its triumph here.

It should not be concluded that the music becomes more sincere as the characters drop their pretenses. Mozart is as direct—and as pretentious—in the one instance as in the other. The irony of the opera depends on its tact; it is a masterpiece of 'tone,' this most civilized of all aesthetic qualities. There is no way of knowing in what proportions mockery and sympathy are blended in Mozart's music and how seriously he took his puppets, just as we cannot know how seriously Ariosto took his tales of ancient chivalry or La Fontaine the morals of the fables he versified. Even to ask is to miss the point: the art in these matters is to tell one's story without being foolishly taken in by it and yet without a trace of disdain for its apparent simplicity. It is an art which can become profound only when the attitude of superiority never implies withdrawal, when objectivity and acceptance are indistinguishable. Those who think that Mozart wrote profound music for a trivial libretto misunderstand his achievement almost as radically as those who, like Wagner, felt that with *Così fan tutte* he had put empty music to a foolish book.

The farewell quintet in the first act ('Write to me every day,'—'Twice a day') is a touchstone of Mozart's success: heartbreaking without ever for a moment approaching tragedy, and delightful without a trace of explicit mockery in the music, it seems to hold laughter and sympathy in a beautiful equilibrium. Even the parody of the operatic sob is done with great delicacy (as it is in Stravinsky's parody of, and homage to, this quintet, the chorus of sentimental prostitutes in *The Rake's Progress*).

This virtuosity of tone is everywhere visible in the score. One of its most remarkable manifestations is in the finale of the first act: as the two men, supposedly dying of poison, lie stretched out on the ground, and the ladies examine them with more tenderness than before ('What an interesting face!'), the orchestra plays what would be a long double fugue—except that there is only one voice at a time, and almost no accompaniment. The music becomes genuinely and richly polyphonic after this long passage, but the surprising combination of baroque contrapuntal movement and the thinnest of *opera buffa* textures once again holds the finest of balances between seriousness and comedy.

The operas of Mozart are international in style, and borrow eclectically from all the important contemporary dramatic traditions of Europe. Even the *Singspiel* has not much more specific local character for Mozart than the Italian operas. The background of French culture, for example, is perceptible throughout *Die Entführung*, not least in its vaudeville ending. The 'seraglio' comedy, in fact, was developed with more grace and wit in France by Favart than by any of the Italian playwrights. The only dramatic form in eighteenth-century Europe not to have affected Mozart's work at all is the serious German comedy that found its first great exponents in Lessing and Lenz and its masterpiece later in *Der zerbrochene Krug* of Kleist. This tradition, the most original of all the German contributions to comedy, seems not to have existed for Mozart. Otherwise he took his material wherever he found it: Beaumarchais, Wieland, Favart, Metastasio, Molière, Goldoni. The essentially Viennese transformation of the Italian clown into the Hans Wurst figure is, of course, important for *Die Zauberflöte*, but even in this supposedly most Viennese of Viennese operas, the model and the inspiration for the form comes essentially from Italy through the work of a Venetian, Carlo Gozzi, and his influence on the Viennese comedy of magic.

Turandot and *The Love for Three Oranges* still keep Gozzi's name alive today. Enormously popular in Germany during the last quarter of the eighteenth century, he provided a challenge and an alternative to the rational, bourgeois comedy of his arch-enemy Goldoni, who was influenced heavily by the French tradition. Gozzi called his own works dramatic fables, and what he says about them (in his *Memoirs of a Useless Man*) reads like a hand-tailored description of *Die Zauberflöte*:

> the dramatic genre of the fable . . . is the most difficult of all . . . it should have an imposing grandeur, a fascinating and majestic mystery, arresting novelty of spectacle, intoxicating eloquence, sentiments of moral philosophy, the sophisticated wit (*sali urbani*) of nourishing criticism, dialogue that springs from the heart, and above all the great magic of seduction that creates an enchanting illusion of making the impossible appear as truth to the mind and spirit of the spectators.[1]

The impossible fabulous fairy-tale plot made to seem real, the spectacle, the mystery, the didacticism, the critical approach, the heartfelt sentiments—all this strangely mixed together can be found in *Die Zauberflöte*. In addition, the incongruous juxtaposition of vulgar traditional clowning and political and religious allegory so characteristic of *Die Zauberflöte* was already at the heart of Gozzi's first play.

The theater that Gozzi partly invented, partly revived, was both aristocratic and popular, fiercely reactionary in philosophy and brilliantly innovatory in its mixing of previous genres. Essentially it was based on a combination of fairy-tale adventure of great nobility with the farcical tradition of the *commedia dell'arte*; originally an attempt to revive the inspired improvisatory style of the discredited *commedia dell'arte* troupes, it quickly turned into something new, fully written out and heavily charged with ideological content. Perhaps only through the Viennese *Singspiel* could this hybrid inspiration—this monstrous child of farce, philosophy, dialect comedy, fairy-tale and Spanish tragedy—be transformed into musical theater. The *opera buffa* was too well-defined a tradition to tolerate such a metamorphosis, but the *Singspiel* remained as yet undeveloped and malleable.

Mozart's correspondence testifies to his interest in Gozzi's work, and Schikaneder, the librettist of *Die Zauberflöte*, was producing plays of Gozzi with his troupe in Salzburg at a time when Mozart was still there. What Gozzi provided was a structure—a systematic conception of drama and even stagecraft—that enabled Mozart to unite and to fuse the most popular and the most complex and learned forms of art. The action of *Die Zauberflöte* ranges (as in Gozzi's dramatic fables) from the popular farce of Papageno (partly

---

[1] Bari, 1910, vol. I, p. 267.

improvised by Schikaneder at the first performances, it appears) to fairy-tale illusionism and spectacle and even to religious ritual. Sensitive people are sometimes made uncomfortable by the vulgar diction of *Die Zauberflöte*, but the conception, flawed as it is by inconsistencies, is among the noblest on the operatic stage. The music correspondingly goes from the simplest of tunes and the most farcical of patter-effects to the fugue and even the chorale prelude (a revival of this very special Baroque form that was to remain unique in the classical style until Beethoven's Quartet op. 132 with its working of *Veni Creator, Spiritus*). In *Die Zauberflöte*, too, Mozart was able to create the first genuinely classical religious style that could be placed with honor beside his imitations of the Baroque religious forms and textures.

With the role of Sarastro and the chorus of priests, the classical hymn makes its first appearance; it is a texture rather than a specific form, and one that was to be of central importance in Beethoven's development. It attains gravity while deliberately avoiding the rich and complicated movement of inner voices of the Baroque. Above all, it avoids the Baroque harmonic dissonance, and replaces the continuously expressive suspensions almost entirely by pure triadic sonority. Harmonically, therefore, it is partly a return to sixteenth-century sound, above all that of Palestrina, whose music remained alive and performed throughout the eighteenth century. The melodic line, however, is the classical one, expressively shaped, symmetrical, and with a sharply marked climax; the articulation is equally sharp and the phrases lack not only the rich continuity of the Baroque, but the delicacy of the sixteenth-century divisions as well. The appearance of this texture in the classical style was not unprecedented in *Die Zauberflöte*; it affects the same harmonic simplicity as one finds in many passages of Gluck. The neoclassical ideal finds in passages of *Die Zauberflöte* a most remarkable incarnation. The immediate origin of the classical 'hymn,' however, is to be found in some of the symphonic slow movements of Haydn: the idea of applying it within a religious context belongs to Mozart. The renunciation of his favorite appoggiaturas, which invariably emphasize dissonance, and the reliance on the undecorated shape of the melodic line alone are managed by Mozart with exquisite virtuosity.

Die Zauberflöte develops, as a corollary to the hymn, a conception of music as a vehicle for simple moral truths: in this work, the expressive range of music is decisively enlarged in an intellectual direction. There is no question, of course, of music as a substitute for verbal expression, but of the creation of a viable setting for the exposition of ideas. 'What shall we say to Sarastro?' Papageno whimpers, and as Pamina cries 'The truth,' the music takes on an heroic radiance unheard in opera before then. The morality of *Die Zauberflöte* is sentientious, and the music often assumes a squareness rare in Mozart, along with a narrowness of range and an emphasis on a few notes very close together that beautifully illuminate the middle-class philosophy of the text:

Nur der Freundschaft Har – mo – nie mil – dert die Be – schwer – den; oh – ne die – se

Sym – pa – thie ist kein Glück auf Er – den

Mozart's *Gemütlichkeit* here is as much intellectual as sensuous, and it is characteristic that in responding to the bourgeois, sentimental world of *Die Zauberflöte*, with its self-satisfied farcical comedy and its easy Masonic mysticism, his sonorities become purer, less chromatic in detail than in any other work. Sometimes this purity is clearly symbolic, as in the march of the trial by fire, where the majestic dwelling on the tonic, varied only by a dominant-seventh chord, is the musical equivalent for the steadfastness of the Masonic initiate:

The bare, strange sonority, entirely of flute, brass, and timpani, reflects and enhances the absolute simplicity here. The transparency, however, is often its own justification:

320

Comic Opera

This is Mozart's late style developed as far as he carried it: the purity and the bareness are almost exotic, so extreme have they become, and this almost wilful leanness is only emphasized by the exquisite orchestration. Each of the mature operas of Mozart has its characteristic sonority, but in none is this sonority so much to the fore, so direct in its action and so fundamental, as in *Die Zauberflöte*.

Gozzi's 'fable' was a two-edged weapon: with its reliance upon old-fashioned popular farce and tales of magical enchantment for the conveyance of philosophical and political ideas, he hoped to combat the nefarious influence of the French Enlightenment and to reinforce the waning prestige of the aristocracy. In the hands of Mozart and Schikaneder, it became an arm of middle-class liberalism, a covert attack on the government, and a splendid work of propaganda for the Freemasons. Gozzi's aristocratic bias remains implicit in the form, however, in the contrast between the princely, idealistic Tamino and the materialistic Papageno, a figure made complex only by the venerable farcical tradition in which he exists, and which he implicitly recalls. Gozzi's work was, in the most profound way, an attack on contemporary rationalism, and his mixed forms released new springs of imagination. His influence on Mozart cannot be confined to *Die Zauberflöte*: the dramatic current that he set in motion had its effect on *Don Giovanni* as well. To some extent the text of da Ponte follows, not Molière, but the version of Gozzi's arch-enemy Goldoni, who had, however, sensibly removed from the story the childish devices of the stone statue that walked and talked, and the descent into hell—in his play, Don Giovanni was more reasonably struck by lightning. Childish popular traditions of this kind were, however, the very stuff of Gozzi's conception of drama—they gave the chance for elaborate spectacle, and most of all they represented the old order, the old way of things, they preserved the traditions by which the aristocratic life could survive. Gozzi's was not the first, nor the last, romantic alliance of the aristocracy and the lower-class against the bourgeoisie. With all da Ponte's and Mozart's dependance on Goldoni, their conception of the Don Juan story was essentially Gozzian in taste and outlook: the statue and the descent into hell are restored, and it is these Punch-and-Judy elements and the clowning of Leporello that have the greatest share in the imaginative and philosophical depth of the opera.

The comic side of *Don Giovanni* has given rise to the kind of controversy that, by its very nature, does not admit of a straightforward solution. Is *Don Giovanni* tragic or comic? Phrased this way, the question makes any answer right, but this would be to mistake the importance of the genre in eighteenth-century operatic practice. Is *Don Giovanni opera seria* or *buffa*? In the passion of the argument, intelligent men have lost their heads over even this innocuous technical point. Dent claimed that none of the characters of the opera had anything to do with *opera seria*, which is patently extravagant.

The structure and pacing of *Don Giovanni* are those of *opera buffa*, but it is evident that at least one of the characters, Donna Anna, comes directly from the world of *seria*, and Donna Elvira and Don Ottavio and even Don Giovanni himself mediate in varying degrees between the two worlds. This is not to imply that Donna Anna, too, is not contaminated at some points by the more fundamental *buffa* atmosphere, particularly in the ensembles. Nevertheless, the range of style of *opera buffa* is considerably broadened: Donna Elvira's aria 'Ah fuggil traditor' is a parody of old-fashioned *seria*, while Donna Anna's 'Or sai chi l'onore' is pure *seria* in its noblest form. The pathos of *Don Giovanni* is no greater than that of *Idomeneo*, but it is at moments as elevated and far more concentrated. The speed of the *opera buffa*'s large-scale rhythm and its emphasis on action in place of the dignified expression of *opera seria* enable the work to move at a dazzling pace from aria to ensemble: the moments of terror and pity are all the sharper in such surroundings. The first minutes of the opera set the tone, and establish the contrast, as the comic complaint of Leporello leads swiftly to the duel, and the pianissimo trio of horror as the Commendatore dies. No *opera seria* moves with this velocity. The comic pacing is essential to the effect, yet the result is anything but comic. This range of tone is, of course, not confined to *Don Giovanni*; the nobility of Fiordiligi or the Countess equally depends on the surrounding *opera buffa* structure for its full significance. The fusion is so perfect in *Don Giovanni* that the mixture of genres is no longer noticed today, but it was decidedly remarked upon and often condemned at the end of the eighteenth century.

The mixed genre in the eighteenth century is a sign of indecorum, and *Don Giovanni*, in more ways than one, is decidedly indecorous. In acknowledgement of this, da Ponte and Mozart called it not an *opera buffa*, but a *dramma giocoso*. Like *Così fan tutte* it was attacked from the beginning: it was immoral, shocking, out-of-date, and childish. The artistry of the music was naturally recognized, if its complexity was often bitterly resented. (The first Italian production had to be given up in despair after many rehearsals because of the difficulty of the score.) It was a frequent complaint of the time that Mozart's style was too learned to speak directly to the heart, but his enormous skill was never questioned. The dramatic conception, however, by no means always found favor. A critic of the first Berlin production wrote that the ear was enchanted while virtue was trampled underfoot.

The scandalous side of *Don Giovanni* had political, as well as artistic, overtones. It will not do to overstate this, but an element of liberal revolutionary aspiration is decidedly, if unsystematically, present in the work. No one in 1787 (the year when the meeting of the Estates-General echoed over all of Europe) could have missed the significance of Mozart's triumphantly overemphatic setting of 'Viva la libertà'[1], or of the wicked exploitation of

---

[1] See above, pp. 94–5, for the structural role of this passage in the first act finale.

peasant innocence for dissolute aristocratic vice. The novels and political pamphlets of the time were filled with references to such matters. Mozart's ideological bias is clear in all the late operas, except for *La Clemenza di Tito* and *Così fan tutte*, which exist in abstract worlds of their own. The cartoon-like attack on the Catholic Establishment of Austria is not a negligible part of *Die Zauberflöte*; it has been denied that the identification of Maria Theresa with the Queen of the Night was intended, but it was made from the beginning, and Schikaneder and Mozart would have had to be astonishingly obtuse not to have foreseen this in a work so heavily charged with Masonic doctrine and ritual (Freemasonry was the principal outlet in Austria at that time for bourgeois revolutionary ideals). In *Figaro*, too, the omission of the more overtly political passages of Beaumarchais' play can have made little difference to a public which, for the most part, knew quite clearly what was being left out; and in any case the call for the renunciation of unjust aristocratic privilege is sufficiently underlined in the opera as it stands. *Don Giovanni*, however, goes beyond all of this in its deliberate picture of a complete world disrupted by aristocratic immorality. The great ball scene in the first act is not mere musical virtuosity with all its three separate orchestras on the stage, and the complicated cross-rhythms of the dances. Each of the social classes—peasantry, bourgeoisie, and aristocracy—has its own dance, and the total independence of every rhythm is a reflection of the social hierarchy; it is this order and harmony that is destroyed by the attempted rape of Zerlina off-stage.[1]

The political ambiance of *Don Giovanni* is given greater weight by the close relation in the eighteenth century between revolutionary thought and eroticism. I have no wish to draw a consistent doctrine from the work, but only to set in relief the significance of some of its aspects. Political and sexual liberalism were intimately connected in the 1780s; even for the most respectable citizens the idea took the shape of a governing fear that republicanism implied complete sexual license. The Marquis de Sade, in his pamphlet *One More Step* did, indeed, claim the most extravagant sexual freedom as a logical corollary of political liberty; his ideas were current everywhere in a milder form, and were the end of an already considerable amount of eighteenth-century speculation. Mozart's early and devoutly Catholic horror at French liberal thought must surely have abated considerably when he became a Freemason, but in any case his personal beliefs have little importance in this connection. The political connotations of sexual liberty were very much alive at the première of *Don Giovanni*, and they would have been inescapable. Part of the outrage and the attraction that this work inspired for years to come must be understood in this context. After 1790, the repudiation of sexual liberty and the extreme puritanism of the revolutionary government

---

[1] Don Giovanni lowers himself and raises Zerlina as he dances with her to the music for the bourgeoisie, meeting her halfway, as it were.

of France (and of the counter-revolutionary governments elsewhere as well) are a reaction to the intellectual climate that produced *Don Giovanni*, and are reflected in Beethoven's rejection of Mozart's libretti as unworthy of being set to music.

This sense of outrage connected with the opera—and it is implicit in Kierkegaard's view of *Don Giovanni* as the only work that perfectly embodies the essentially erotic nature of music, and in E. T. A. Hoffmann's stressing of what he called its 'romanticism'—this sense of *Don Giovanni* as an attack, at once frontal and oblique, upon aesthetic and moral values is more useful for understanding the opera, and Mozart's music in general, than the common-sense view which shrugs off this aspect impatiently. Music is the most abstract of all the arts only in the sense that it is the least representational: it is, however, the least abstract in its direct physical assault on the listeners' nerves, in the immediacy of effect that its patterns gain from the apparently almost total reduction of mediating symbolism, of all ideas that seem to call for decoding and interpretation, and so to stand between music and listener. (If, as a matter of fact, the reduction is very far from total, and the listener must expend considerable labor decoding the symbolic relationships set before him, his activity is less conscious, less verbalized, than in any other art.) When this physical immediacy of music is stressed, then its erotic aspect stands well to the fore. Perhaps no composer used the seductive physical power of music with the intensity and the range of Mozart. The flesh is corrupt and corrupting. Behind Kierkegaard's essay on *Don Giovanni* stands the idea that music is a sin: it seems fundamentally sound that he should have chosen Mozart as the most sinful composer of all. What is most extraordinary about Mozart's style is the combination of physical delight—a sensuous play of sonority, an indulgence in the most luscious harmonic sequences—with a purity and economy of line and form that render the seduction all the more efficient.

A more prosaic and more conventionally respectable view of Mozart comes not from the sober perspective of the twentieth century but from the height of Romantic enthusiasm: in the G minor Symphony, a work of passion, violence, and grief for those who love Mozart most, Schumann saw nothing but lightness, grace, and charm. It should be said at once that to reduce a work to the expression of sentiments, however powerful, is to trivialize it in any case: the G minor Symphony is not much more profound conceived as a tragic cry from the heart than as a work of exquisite charm. Nevertheless, Schumann's attitude to Mozart ends by destroying his vitality as it canonizes him. It is only through recognizing the violence and the sensuality at the center of Mozart's work that we can make a start towards a comprehension of his structures and an insight into his magnificence. In a paradoxical way, however, Schumann's superficial characterization of the G minor Symphony can help us to see Mozart's daemon more steadily. In all of Mozart's supreme expressions of suffering and terror—the G minor Symphony, *Don Giovanni*, the G minor Quintet, Pamina's aria in *Die Zauberflöte*—there is something shockingly voluptuous. Nor does this detract from its power or effectiveness: the grief and the sensuality strengthen each other, and end by becoming indivisible, indistinguishable one from the other. (Tchaikovsky's grief, for example, has an equal lubricity, but his diffuse and wasteful technique of composition makes him far less dangerous.) In his corruption of sentimental values, Mozart is a subversive artist.

Almost all art is subversive: it attacks established values, and replaces them with those of its own creation; it substitutes its own order for that of society. The disconcertingly suggestive aspects—moral and political—of Mozart's operas are only a surface appearance of this aggression. His works are in many ways an assault upon the musical language that he helped to create: the powerful chromaticism that he could employ with such ease comes near at moments to destroying the tonal clarity that was essential to the significance of his own forms, and it was this chromaticism that had a real influence upon the Romantic style, on Chopin and Wagner in particular. The artistic personality that Haydn created for himself (related to, but not to be confused with, the face he wore for everyday purposes) prevented, by its assumption of an easy-going geniality, the full development of the subversive and revolutionary aspect of his art: his music, as E. T. A. Hoffmann wrote, appears to have been composed before original sin. Beethoven's attack was naked, no art was less accommodating in its refusal to accept any other conditions than its own. Mozart was as unaccommodating as Beethoven, and the sheer physical beauty, prettiness, even, of so much of what he composed masks the uncompromising character of his art. It cannot be fully appreciated without recalling the uneasiness and even dismay that it so often evoked in its time, and without recreating in our own minds the conditions in which it could still seem dangerous.

Part VI
HAYDN AFTER THE DEATH OF MOZART

1

The Popular Style

_____

By 1790, Haydn had created and mastered a deliberately popular style. The immensity of his success is reflected in the volume of his production in the next ten years, the decade after the death of Mozart: fourteen string quartets, three piano sonatas, fourteen piano trios, six masses, the _Sinfonia Concertante_, the _Creation_, the _Seasons_, twelve symphonies, and a great number of minor works. Today, when Haydn is almost a connoisseur's composer whose music cannot compete at the box office with that of Mozart or Beethoven, this atmosphere of enormous popular success must be borne in mind in order to understand the late works, above all the symphonies and the oratorios. There have been composers who were as much admired and others whose tunes were as much whistled and sung during their lifetimes, but none who so completely won at the same time the unquestioned and generous respect of the musical community and the ungrudging acclaim of the public.

A relationship between Haydn's late style and folk music is evident, but the nature of that relationship questionable and even slippery. There is a story, surely apocryphal but worth telling in this context, about the professor who went to do field research on Haydn among the peasants of that ethnically indecisive section of the Austro-Hungarian Empire where Haydn spent part of his childhood. The professor's method of investigation was to sing some of the better tunes of Haydn to the peasants, and ask if they recognized them. The peasants, with an earthy shrewdness even older and more traditional than folk music, quickly discovered that they were given a bigger tip when they recognized a melody than when they failed to do so, and their memories accordingly became richly accommodating. And to this day, the story ends, the peasants of that little Danubian region sing the songs that the professor taught them.

The folk songs that Haydn actually used on occasion are largely indistinguishable from many of the undoubtedly original melodies of his late years. To discuss the influence of folk music on Haydn's style is to set the matter on its head. The use of folk music or the invention of folk-like material becomes increasingly important in Haydn's works from 1785 on: there had always been some allusions to popular tunes, hunting-calls, yodels, and dance-rhythms in his music as in the music of most composers from Machaut to Schoenberg, but before the _Paris_ and _London_ Symphonies these had remained in the margin of his style. It will not do to sentimentalize over the elderly composer turning more and more to the songs he heard as a child. Mozart

329

similarly developed a style close to folk music with *Die Zauberflöte* at the same time as Haydn, and the age of thirty-five is hardly advanced enough for Mozart to have been impelled by a similar nostalgia. The movement towards a 'popular' style must certainly be related to the republican enthusiasm of the latter part of the eighteenth century, as well as to the growth of national sentiment and the consciousness of particular national cultures. Nevertheless, an autonomous development of the musical language must be admitted to a role at least partially decisive here, as the interest in folk music had a long history already by the time it took on such significance for Haydn and Mozart, but it is only in the late 1780s that the classical style was able thoroughly to assimilate and to create elements of folk style at will.

The assimilation is the crux of the matter, and it is entirely new in eighteenth-century music. When Bach uses folk songs, as he does on rare occasions, either they lose their folk characteristics, or appear as quotations from a foreign language: both processes can be seen in the Quodlibet from the *Goldberg* Variations and in the *Peasant* Cantata. In Haydn, however, the opening of the finale of the Symphony no. 104.

is at once a folk song (and sounds it), and a perfectly normal Haydn rondo subject; even its rusticity is not unusual.

Even more illuminating is a comparison with the Baroque treatment of chorale-tunes, which, if not folk music, had become folk property long before Bach. The chorales are, indeed, completely assimilable into the Baroque style, but only because their original rhythms had, in time, been thoroughly flattened into an almost totally uniform movement. Not only the original dance rhythms have been destroyed in the early eighteenth-century chorale, but even the inflections of speech have largely disappeared. The opening phrase of *Ein feste Burg* in its original and its eighteenth-century forms[1] show this progressive regimentation:

It was only at this price that the tunes could be received by the homogeneous rhythmic structures of the High Baroque. In the process their popular character is almost entirely lost.

Haydn, too, rarely accepts a melody without altering it, but often the

---

[1] Cited from Schweitzer, *J. S. Bach*, London, 1945, vol. I, pp. 23–24.

alteration only serves to reinforce the popular character. The slow movement of the *Drum-Roll* Symphony no. 103 is a double variation set in which both themes are based on folk melodies. The two themes resemble each other closely:

The F♯ in the second theme is not in the original folk song, however, which goes:[1]

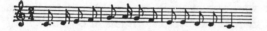

Rosemary Hughes remarks that the added F♯ makes the major melody recall the minor one. The addition of the trill and its downward close also brings the second theme in closer relation to the first, as they now outline the same shape (Haydn's double variation sets are almost never intended to sound as if they contain two distinct themes; the second melody appears as a free variation of the first, and the form is that of a monothematic rondo). But the F♯ also strengthens the popular character of the theme, which, in its original form, was evidently not folk-like enough for Haydn. The rustic, modal dissonance that is Haydn's invention belongs of course, to a world of pseudo-folklore, a world like that in Perrault's tales: it is the world of eighteenth-century pastoral.

For this reason it makes not the slightest difference whether Haydn invented his folk tunes or remembered them. The melody in the major of the *Drum-Roll* Symphony's slow movement, for example, is very like several dozen other folk tunes, among them the mock serenade that Bach used in the *Goldberg* Variations:

and it was as easy to invent variants as to find them. We know that Haydn was interested in collecting folk tunes, and that, as a young man, he gained experience in the popular music of street serenading. Nevertheless, the technique of thematic elaboration and the balanced and articulated symmetry of his style were worked out and perfected before the folk themes were used in

---

[1] Cited from Rosemary Hughes, *Haydn*, London, 1950, p. 131.

his music in any way except that of incidental quotation and external humor. In any collision between his style and the folk tune, it was always the tune that had to give way, and for this reason if for no other it would be difficult to allow the folk melodies a formative influence. Both melodies cited from the *Drum-Roll* Symphony are radically altered before the end of the first phrase, so that they each form miniature sonata patterns, with developments and recapitulations all in place.

There are composers (Bartók is perhaps the most famous of them) who have used research into folk music for the specific purpose of forming a style. Even in such cases, the development is a little mysterious and by no means straightforward. Bartók treats the folk music of entirely different cultures very much alike: his arrangement of Rumanian, Hungarian, and Czechoslovakian folk songs do not differ from each other in any way that can be easily related to the original qualities of the songs. They provided him with non-diatonic modes, which was what he was looking for in the first place. The composer who employs folk material for patriotic reasons is also a familiar figure, and, as the Negro spirituals in Dvořák's music can testify, it does not seem to matter which folk material he chooses. But none of this has any relation to the folk material in the works of Haydn and Mozart, who used it only when needed within an already formed style, and who were perfectly ready to invent it when they found it necessary.

The procedures of Haydn and Mozart must be understood in a larger context, that of the creation of a popular style which abandons none of the pretensions of high art. Their achievement is perhaps unique in Western music: Beethoven attempted a similar synthesis with the last movement of the Ninth Symphony, and his triumph, which seems to me incontestable, has nevertheless been contested. This solitary success in the history of musical style should make us wary of critics who reproach the *avant-garde* composer for an uncompromisingly hermetic style, or the popular composer (like Offenbach or Gershwin) for low ideals; that is like blaming a man for not having blue eyes or for not having been born in Vienna. The most esoteric composer would welcome the popularity of Mozart in Prague, where people whistled 'Non più andrai' in the streets, if he could achieve it as Mozart did without sacrificing a jot of his refinement or even his 'difficulty.' Only for one brief historical period in the operas of Mozart, the late symphonies of Haydn, and some of the Schubert songs, has the utmost sophistication and complexity of musical technique existed alongside—or better, fused with—the virtues of the street song.

It is, of course, not the mere use of popular elements of style that achieves this fusion. The *chanson* masses of the Renaissance used popular as well as art songs, but the melodies were subjected to a treatment which removed their most characteristic qualities. The folk elements in Mahler—Ländler rhythms and turns of phrase now even more urban than pastoral—are deliberately left unassimilated, unfused with the strikingly advanced orchestral style in which they are embedded. It is their unmitigated banality—vulgarity, even—upon which so much of the tragic irony in Mahler depends. The fusion of popular and high art depends on a delicate equilibrium: Verdi's popular style goes hand in hand with a technique that proclaims its naïveté, for all his genius, and greater sophistication is gained at the end of his life only with a progressive abandonment of the most characteristically popular effects. The style of Mozart in *Die Zauberflöte* and Haydn in the *Paris* and *London* Symphonies, however, became not less, but more learned, as it became more popular.

For this achievement of the classical style, comparable to the brief glory of late Elizabethan drama, a new social situation had to coincide with a powerful stylistic development. The situation is easy enough to identify: it is the rising aspirations of the commercial class throughout the eighteenth century and their growing interest in music as an element of aristocratic culture and a proof of social distinction; the increase in amateur musicians (and the increase in population) provided a new and affluent public. In short, secular high art became public. The unexpected discovery of the existence in the 1730s of a commercial public for religious music gave Handel his immense success, but he had only a limited use for specifically popular stylistic elements in winning it. Public symphonic concerts and comic opera became the new forces behind the historical development of style in the later part of the century.

The freshness of this new mass appeal of high art has never been recaptured. It was, at least socially, bound to disappoint: the snob value of music has never been taken off the market but it has also rarely paid the dividends hoped for. There was also an inevitable conflict of interest among music as science, music as expression, and music as public spectacle: it was not to be expected that the synthesis of the Mozart piano concerto could occur again. Beethoven's Fourth and Fifth Concertos are something of a miracle; one should not underrate the difficulty of calculating the relation of social forces to individual genius.

What made this achievement possible, the process by which learned and popular elements were wedded, must be looked for within the musical language itself. The melodies with a marked popular flavor are most striking in three places of Haydn's symphonies and quartets (and, to a lesser extent, of Mozart's): towards the close of the expositions of the first movements, the openings of the finales, and the trios of the minuets. The first movement is generally the most complex and the most dramatic, and the problem of integrating a 'folk' melody (whether borrowed or invented need not concern us here) is at its most delicate. The use of an obviously popular tune at the beginning had its dangers, as any opening theme that seemed to exist for its own sake would have failed to provide the dynamic impulse for the whole movement. Mozart could overcome the danger of opening his expositions with a long and well-rounded melody by disturbing the surface from the outset by a restless motion and a gradually increasing harmonic intensity (as in the G minor Symphony) or by the more subtle disturbance of an ambiguity of accent, as in the Symphony in E flat K. 543:

where the feminine endings and the imitation in the horn throw the accent onto the third and fifth measures, while, on the other hand, the pause and the syncopation in the melodic line turn it towards the second and fourth measures. Haydn's most complex ideas are initially more straightforward and he rarely tries for this shadowy interplay between resonance and significance.

The themes near the end of the expositions of the Symphonies nos. 99 and 100 are less complex than the opening themes, and they both serve a similar purpose:

that is, they ground the tension previously generated. The full measures of introductory accompaniment common to both is revealing: nothing else would bring out so well the atmosphere of a popular band while anchoring the music so firmly in place. The squareness of the tune that follows, and which gives it the air of unbuttoned, unsophisticated relaxation, does the rest. These 'popular' tunes are used as cadential forces, to round off and to articulate the form.

They have consequently the same function as the virtuosity in a Mozart concerto, which is, as we have seen, always most in evidence towards the end of the exposition. Mozart uses tunes of the same character at the same place in his symphonies, as the end of the exposition of the *Jupiter* shows:

and the accompaniment also starts before the melody after a pause as in the examples from Haydn. This sort of melody is rarely used in the opening movements of the piano concertos, as it is displaced there by brilliance in the solo part. In short, the 'popular' tune is used for its squareness and symmetry as a substitute for the banal cadence formulas, for the 'filling' that would otherwise have been needed in its place.

In Haydn's brilliant D major Quartet op. 71 no. 2, the main theme is a rich and complex contrapuntal elaboration of an octave leap:

while the closing melody of the exposition has the popular squareness of the closing themes of the symphonies:

and further examples of this contrast could be added with ease. It should be noted that when the opening theme has a markedly regular character, the closing theme is generally made even more decisively popular in style. The first theme of the Quartet in G major op. 76 no. 1 is, on the surface, as jolly and square as one could wish:

but the end of the exposition outdoes it with ease:

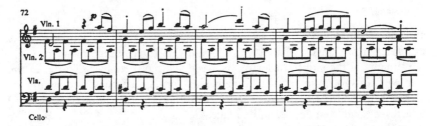

and the stable bass and introductory accompaniment figure appear here once more. The main theme of the *Drum-Roll* Symphony has a dance-like character:

but it is nothing to the Ländler rhythm and frankly popular dance accompaniment of the later theme:

336

In sum, the popular tune could be integrated into high art as a means of clarifying the form (I need hardly add that this was only the method of integration and not the reason for it).

The opening themes of the finales have almost always the same symmetrical regularity of rhythm that indicates the popular style. The argument may seem circular: the identification of 'folk' music with regularity and squareness of rhythm is neither evident nor, indeed, true. However, most people expect of a tune exactly the regularity of phrase-length always divisible by four and partial symmetry of outline which the classical composer took from the dance and from folk music. It was their recurrent symmetries that interested him, and he conditioned most listeners to expect them for more than a century. What is meant when Beethoven and Stravinsky are denied the title of great melodists is not that the linear patterns in their music are not beautiful, a contention only too clearly ridiculous, but that these patterns do not often fall into the symmetrical forms and four-measure lengths of Schubert and Prokofiev, for example. A great deal of folk music, some of it surely known to Haydn, is strongly asymmetrical and rhythmically irregular, but that is not what interested Haydn. He could provide all the rhythmic irregularity one needed (although it has perhaps not been sufficiently emphasized in the literature about him to what an extent his irregular and unexpected rhythmic effects are tightly controlled after 1780 within a large-scale system of symmetries, with an eight-measure phrase pattern dominating, and the odd-numbered phrase lengths balanced by appearing in pairs). The folk style has significance in Haydn's music mainly as an element of popular style in general and this, as it appears in Haydn's music, is used largely for its stabilizing effect. That is why it so often comes in the form of a drone bass as in the finales of the Symphonies no. 82 (the *Bear*) and 104 and the D major Quartet op. 76 no. 5.

The clear, well-defined, eminently detachable shape of the finale-theme is the basis for one of Haydn's best-loved and most dramatic effects: the surprise return. A great deal of ingenuity is expended upon the return of the theme, almost always with rollicking effect: the trick is to keep suggesting the return but to delay it until the listener no longer knows when to expect it—although if he keeps his sense of long-range symmetry he can generally make a good guess. A theme with an upbeat is most useful, as the upbeat can be played over and over, as in the finale of the *Surprise*:

Consequently most of the finales of the late symphonies start with an upbeat. Those with two upbeats work even better, and the result in Symphony no. 88 is incomparably funny:

while the same witty effect is raised to the point of comic magnificence in Symphony no. 93:

with its powerful contrast between the full orchestra with timpani and one solitary cello. The most subtle returns are, however, those in the rare finales where the theme has no upbeat, and Haydn must seek other inspiration for his humor. The return in the finale of the *Clock* is a pianissimo fugato, and the return of the last movement of Symphony no. 104 is an effect of such delicacy that it would have to be quoted at great length for its radiant poetry and wit to be appreciated.

Haydn needed *three* upbeats to write the finale with the most outrageous rhythmic effects, that of the Quartet in E flat major, op. 76 no. 6, which surpasses even the duplicity of the minuet of the *Oxford* Symphony in fooling the listener as to the place of the downbeat. The opening, indeed, sounds clearly not like three upbeats, but like *five*:

and the development section disrupts what rhythmic equilibrium the listener has retained by an apparently random distribution of accents:

339

although the entire development (from measures 66 to 118) is controlled by a completely rational system of four-measure phrases reinforced by a regular harmonic movement. The beginning of the recapitulation is calculated to throw off even the quartet-players:

The *sforzando* in measure 118 is Haydn's charity, otherwise we should never recognize the first note of the theme at all. The brief double canon at measures 111 to 114 was not hard to write (anyone can make a canon out of a descending scale), but the comic rhythmic complexity is a true display of virtuoso invention.

The melodies of marked popular character in the trios of the minuets (and sometimes in the minuets themselves, which became more boisterous as Haydn grew older) are the most striking examples of Haydn's pastoral style. It is above all at these moments that the traditionally aristocratic form is made democratic—or at least available to the new audience. They make an unabashed appeal to popular taste (although we must remember that in London it was most often the slow movements of Haydn's symphonies that were encored at their first performance). The minuets, however, do not patronize the folk style as Rousseau's *Devin du Village* or Gay's *Beggar's Opera* did, or present it as exotic; they transfigure it musically and integrate it with the whole work. No doubt the ostentatious presence of the rhythms and turns of phrase of the popular dance-forms are heard as a frank extramusical reference—the irruption of the ideals of the non-aristocratic classes into the world of high art; but the style that Haydn had elaborated was, by 1790, one of such power that it could accommodate these ideals without loss of its own integrity. Haydn's technique of thematic development was able to accept almost any material, and absorb it: the simplest yodel phrase is transformed by the instrumentation, and a subtle alteration of its rhythm allows it to bear the weight of a modulation, as in the minuet of the *Drumroll* Symphony:

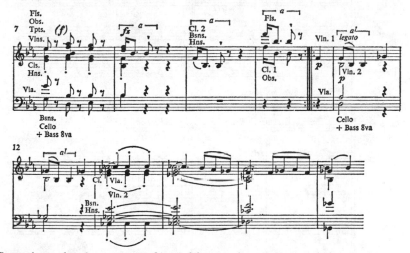

Sometimes the element transformed is even less elaborate, being nothing but a rhythmic scrap.

The popular material retains its character exactly because Haydn's technique isolates what it intends to develop. The identity of each element had to be clarified before it could enter into the larger continuity of the work. This enabled Haydn to exploit the most characteristically popular side of his material while using it as the basis for the most sophisticated structures, provided only that the material had a strong tonal orientation. (Yodelling is so obsessively triadic that it might easily have been invented by the classical style if it had not already existed, and it is difficult to take seriously the formative stylistic influence of something structurally so inevitable and so logical.) This isolating tendency of the classical style preserved the integrity of both the style and the material.

The orchestration of Haydn's minuets is often enchanting: Mozart was rarely so ingenious. The most memorable passages are those where the combination of different orchestral colors remains deliberately heterogeneous, totally unlike the more solidified textures of Beethoven and Mozart even when these contrast woodwinds and strings. In the following passage from the minuet of Symphony no. 97:

we can see why Rimsky-Korsakov declared Haydn to be the greatest of all masters of orchestration. The oom-pah-pah of a German dance band is rendered with the utmost refinement, amazingly by kettledrums and trumpets pianissimo, and the rustic *glissando* (a sort of glottal stop on the first beats) is given a finicky elegance by the grace notes in the horns as well as by the doubling of the melody an octave higher with the solo violin. These details are not intended to blend, but to be set in relief: they are individually exquisite.

This minuet is admittedly extraordinary with all of its repeats written out to allow for changes of instrumentation and dynamics, but the preciosity of orchestration is by no means exceptional in Haydn. The extensive writing for the strings on the bridge of their instruments in the slow movement of the same work is only another example. In the following passage near the beginning of the exposition of the first movement of Symphony no. 93, the instrumental color is used to reinforce a rhythmic tension:

The three measures 40 to 42 expand by repetition, sustaining like a fermata not over the preceding note but over the whole of the preceding measure: the change of wind doubling from flute to bassoon to oboe is not intended to blend with the violins but to stand out sharply from it. (These measures are a beautiful model both of the classical isolation of a motif, and of the charging of a tonic chord with tension almost by rhythm alone.) In his conception of orchestration Haydn is often far closer than either Beethoven or Mozart to the coloristic ideals of much twentieth-century music; the use of solo instruments isolated within the mass of the orchestra, and the employment of trumpets and timpani in many of the slow movements as pure tone-color recall the orchestration of Mahler more than anything else in the eighteenth or nineteenth centuries.

What would once have been called the high seriousness of this deliberately popular style needs to be seen clearly: the artistic personality of 'Papa Haydn' that the composer created—surely as much in response to his own needs as to those of his public—had more than its jocular, genial side. The moments of sentimental poetry are far more frequent than the grossly humorous effects, although both are tempered by wit, and the care for dramatic line is constant. The increased weight of Haydn's style can be felt in his transformation of two formal structures, the introduction, and the traditional ternary *ABA* form. The metamorphosis of the ternary form is part of the logical development of the classical style: the middle section becomes, not a relaxation of tension, but a move towards a climax, and the return of the first part is consequently a genuine harmonic resolution. The opening movement of the D major Quartet op. 76 no. 5, for example, begins with a long symmetrical melody that resolves firmly on the tonic, and the second section opens, like many trios, in the minor mode: however, it quickly takes on the sequential modulations and the melodic fragmentation of a development section. After the return of the first section in a decorated form like a da capo aria, a long coda provides an astonishing second development. The loose da capo or ternary form could no longer satisfy Haydn, and he now often conceived the middle section so far as possible as a true classical development. The most significant result of his new approach are the dramatic dance-finales (minuets and German peasant dances) of the late piano trios.

Haydn turned the introduction into a dramatic gesture. Before his late works it had been largely a way for him to indicate a solemn mood while fixing the tonality; basically it did nothing but add importance.[1] An introduction implies a sense of expectancy: in more technical language, it is rhythmically an expansion of an upbeat, and if it extends to any length, it must end as an unresolved dominant chord without having modulated. Examples from the early part of the century include accompanied recitatives before an air, as in the Bach cantatas, and of a certain number of preludes, but the means used are always more diffuse than in the classical period, which concentrated the harmonic sense and gave the rhythmic beat greater definition. (The slow opening section of a Baroque work like a French overture is not introductory at all, but modulates to the dominant and is a beginning in its own right.)

The new dramatic role of the introduction can be seen at its most laconic in the opening of Haydn's Quartet op. 71 no. 3:

---

[1] For the difference between the classical introduction and the opening section of a Baroque work like a French overture see page 282.

The introduction has here become a single, brusque chord. As before, this creates expectancy (the lengthened, unmeasured silence in the second bar would see to that); it adds importance to the light comic theme that follows; and it defines E flat major with a rare economy. But it also has a new dramatic interest of its own. After the pause in the second bar, we are aware that the first chord was not a true beginning of the discourse. It was only a gesture, in the literal sense of a physical movement that conveys a meaning.

Beethoven may have remembered this opening when he wrote the *Eroica*, which begins with a similarly spaced E flat chord played twice, but Haydn did something like this often enough for the procedure, rather than a particular instance of it, to have been the influence. All six of Haydn's Quartets op. 71 and op. 74 play with this idea, which goes from one or two chords (there are three in op. 76 no. 1) to a fanfare (op. 74 no. 2), and finally, in op. 74 no. 3, to a first theme that is made to sound like an introduction:

The two-measure pause gives the opening phrase the air of an introductory motto, and this phrase is not replayed in the recapitulation; nevertheless it is an integral part of the exposition, to be repeated with it, and dominates the development section; the second theme is directly derived from it. Haydn was not a good opera composer, but his sense of a dramatic musical gesture intimately linked with the general action was exceedingly sharp.

The slow introductions of the *London* Symphonies (eleven out of the twelve begin with one[1]) are more elaborate, but none of them overstep the limits of being only a stepping-stone to a movement of more pronounced character. These opening symphonic Adagios have a longer history in Haydn's work than his experiments with brief introductions to the quartets of 1793. Slow introductions appear very early in his orchestral works; the finest examples

---

[1] The Symphony no. 95 is the only exception, and it is also the only one in the minor mode, which guarantees its seriousness even without the added weight of an introduction.

before 1787 are all in D major: no. 57 of 1774, nos. 73 (*La Chasse*) and 75 of 1781, and no. 86 of 1786. Some of the dramatic character of the later works appears as early as 1774.

In 1786, Mozart wrote the *Prague* Symphony (also in D major, a key that inspired brilliance perhaps because it provided a full sonority for both brass and string instruments), a work with perhaps the richest and most complex introduction before Beethoven's Seventh Symphony. It has a breadth of movement that none of Haydn's ever attains, and a wealth of contrapuntal and chromatic detail that Haydn rarely attempted. Yet Mozart, in the *Prague*, makes no attempt to emulate Haydn's system of thematic transition between the introduction and the Allegro (and his later use of it in the E flat Symphony K. 543 of 1788, while subtle and lovely, does not carry the conviction it almost always has in Haydn).[1]

These thematic relationships in Haydn always respect the character of the introduction, and are based upon a profound psychological understanding of its nature. When we hear the related theme in the Allegro, we recognize immediately (and generally with delight at the witty presentation) the kinship with the introduction. But when it had appeared first in the introduction itself, it did not sound like a theme. The essential character of an introduction (Mozart's as well as Haydn's) is a lack of precise definition; if it does not retain enough of this nebulous quality, it risks sounding like the true opening in itself.[2] That is why these close thematic relationships can be dangerous within the scheme of the classical introduction. Haydn's handling of the problem is one of his greatest triumphs. The theme which is to reappear in the Allegro generally makes its first entrance unobtrusively in the introduction, sometimes as part of the accompaniment (in *La Chasse*) and sometimes almost unnoticed as part of a conventional formula for a cadence. When it has a shape that cannot be so hidden, it is played so slowly that it seems, not a melody, but the majestic outline of a harmony, as in Symphony no. 98. The *Military* Symphony opens with a theme

that is a half-formed premonition of the main theme of the Allegro

and the Symphony no. 102 presents the same effect of the melody taking shape out of the not quite fully formed material of the introduction.

---

[1] To these two introductions of Mozart, one should add the openings of the *Linz* Symphony, of the magnificent four-hand Sonata in F major (for *one* piano) K. 497, completely symphonic in style, and above all, the Quartet in C major K. 465.
[2] The introduction of the Symphony no. 104 has more clarity than most, but the melodic cells (and they are very small here) remain fragments.

Perhaps most remarkable in this respect are the Symphonies nos. 97 and 103. In the former the introduction both opens and closes with a simple but expressive cadence, which appears later as the cadence of the Allegro exposition itself, there written out in longer note-values so that the tempo is approximately the same as the opening Adagio. This way of recalling an introduction was vivid enough to inspire Beethoven to employ it in the E flat Trio for Piano and Strings op. 70 no. 2. In Symphony no. 103, the *Drum-Roll*, the rhythm of the opening phrase is completely uniform:

the very slow tempo makes it seem to have no rhythmic definition. The opening theme of the Vivace (cited above p. 336) is clearly but very freely drawn from it (as in the *Military* Symphony), but it also returns with its sequence of pitches intact, and a new and highly characteristic rhythm:

and further makes a startling reappearance at its original very slow tempo near the end of the movement.

When this slow, rhythmically almost shapeless, theme rises in the bass out of the long opening drum-roll (and if the new edition is surely unwise to accept the *fortissimo* attack suggested by the piano quintet arrangement of 1797, it is certain that the timpanist should make this a very long and effective roll), we have the impression of the gradual molding of form from indeterminate matter itself. The technique behind the writing of these slow introductions made it possible for Haydn to conceive the famous depiction of chaos in the *Creation*.

Harmonically these symphonic introductions have little directional force. The most frequent pattern is a simple one: a fixing of the tonic major, and a move to the minor so the major can begin again with the Allegro. There are a few which start, like Mozart's C major Quartet K. 465, directly with the minor mode. The extensive chromaticism that appears in almost all of them serves the same purpose as the minor mode: a disturbance of the sense of harmonic stability that, nevertheless, lies only on the surface of the fundamental harmonic structure. These introductions are, of course, delaying actions.

The Popular Style

The significance of any work of late eighteenth-century music depends on the establishment of the tonic: to delay this process is essentially to widen the proportions and the range of possible action. The expansion is one not merely of the time-scale, but of the scale of dramatic and expressive significance as well, as the brusque introductions to the quartets of 1793 have shown.

The classical introduction also enlarged the thematic possibilities of the style, in two complementary ways. First, they enabled the composer to use as a principal theme of the following Allegro a melody too light to serve as the opening of the entire work. The *Drum-Roll* Symphony is one of Haydn's largest achievements, but the beginning of the Vivace would be too trivial by itself to initiate a work of such magnitude: it gains weight by being at once a contrast to the slow introduction and a clearly recognizable derivation from its material. In the same way, the massive introduction to Beethoven's Seventh Symphony frees the dance-like theme that opens the Vivace from the responsibility of establishing the dimensions of the whole movement. The introduction opened up a new range of themes that could otherwise have been used only in far more modest frameworks.

The second and perhaps more interesting expansion of the thematic possibilities is the radical change of significance of the first theme enforced by the preceding introduction. The opening theme of the Allegro becomes an answer to the resolved tension of the introduction. In Mozart's Symphony in E flat major K. 543, the melody of the Allegro literally extends the unfinished cadence of the Adagio:

as the violin moves to take up the line left suspended by the flute. The opening phrase is therefore an end as well as a beginning. Haydn made extensive use

349

of this effect and never neglected its importance, but the most subtle example is probably in Beethoven. The two brusque chords with which the *Eroica* Symphony begins change the rhythmic sense of the theme that follows. If we play the theme alone, it begins on a bar which carries the strong accent of the pulse. The two opening bars of concise introduction shift the accent away from the first note of the theme and place it two bars further on, and so add a rhythmic impulse that moves forward with an energy the theme could not achieve by itself.

Once again, it was Beethoven who carried these possibilities to the outer limits beyond which the language itself would have had to change. How little the actual duration in measured time has to do with the range of expression is shown in the beautiful opening of his F sharp major Sonata op. 78:

One step beyond this lies the Romantic introduction, with a melody so well-rounded, so complete that it can be attached only with difficulty to the movement that follows (as in Schumann's F sharp minor Sonata or the famous opening section of Tchaikovsky's B flat minor Concerto). Beethoven stops just in time: his melody remains only a fragment. The immovable F♯ in the bass defines the tonic with the clarity of Haydn and denies real harmonic movement to the melodic line; the fermata in the fourth measure ensures the same feeling of expectancy as the introductions of the *London* Symphonies. For the hesitant phrasing and carefully undefined movement of Haydn's symphonic introductions, or the brusque, dramatic opening chords of Haydn's quartets, Beethoven substitutes a simple phrase that finishes on the tonic, but seems not to end. The fragmentary character is indispensable: the classical introduction is an 'open' effect in a system which demanded a closed form, and which exacted a price for each expansion of the language.

2

Piano Trio

Haydn's piano trios are a third great series of works to set beside the symphonies and the quartets, but they are the least known of the three groups for reasons which have nothing to do with their musical worth. They are not chamber music in the usual sense, but works for solo piano, solo violin, and accompanying cello. For the most part the cello serves only to double the piano's bass, although in a very few places it is briefly independent. Under Haydn's influence, the string quartet developed from a work for solo violin and accompanying instruments to one in which all instruments have independent importance (although the first violin remained dominant until the twentieth century, and still retains much of its former prestige). Haydn's failure to develop a similar independence for the cello in the piano trio, and to balance the roles of the piano and the violin is generally a heavy charge laid against these trios. They may be splendid pieces, but they are unprogressive, backward in style, and should have been written differently. Even Tovey, who admired them, rewrote one to give greater prominence to the cello. Part of the prejudice against the trios comes from a snobbish preference of many musicians (mostly amateur) for chamber music over other forms (opera, for example, is sometimes considered a particularly degrading form of art). Some of this snobbery is a reaction, a righteous and rightful one, against the mass public for its lack of interest in chamber music. (Logically, why should the public take an interest, when chamber music is by definition not public? It was never intended to be a success, as Monteux has said of Debussy's *Pelléas*.) Another cause for neglect is a purely practical one: if Haydn's trios are essentially solo piano works with added solo violin passages, then the proper place for them is at piano recitals, where the hiring of extra musicians is not economically attractive.

No doubt Haydn was working against history when he wrote these trios, but there is no reason to judge them any the worse for that. Almost all of them were written late in Haydn's life when he knew perfectly well what he was about. Before many of them were written, Mozart had already produced several piano trios in which greater independence is given to the cello, works which Haydn surely knew; but, with the exception of the great E major and B flat major Trios, all of Mozart's are thinner in style and less interesting than the best dozen or sixteen of Haydn's. The brilliance of Haydn's piano writing in these works is surprising to one who knows only the sonatas; there are even some wrist-breaking octave passages (those in the C major Trio H. 27 were

351

certainly intended as *glissandi*). They are, in fact, along with the Mozart concertos the most brilliant piano works before Beethoven. Nor does virtuosity imply a loss of profundity: it has harmed these works no more than the Mozart concertos or the Beethoven sonatas. A string quartet written with an overdominating first violin part does, indeed, lose in musical value, but that is because of the nature of the medium, which in this case would entail a loss of contrapuntal richness and thematic significance in the other parts. No such corresponding loss is implied by the dominance of a piano—the only instrument, after all, capable of both complex polyphony and dynamic inflection.

The fact that these trios are essentially solo works makes possible their greatest quality, a feeling of improvisation almost unique in Haydn's work, and, indeed, rarely found in any of the three great classic composers. Haydn was a composer who needed the piano in order to write music; these trios seem to give us Haydn at work. They have a spontaneous quality that the composer rarely sought elsewhere; their inspiration seems relaxed and unforced, at times almost disorganized, when compared with the quartets and symphonies. The forms are also more relaxed: a great many of the trios have dance finales—minuets or German peasant dances—and some of the first movements are among Haydn's finest double-variation sets.

Piano trios in the eighteenth century were written for the best amateurs, although the gap between amateur and professional at that time appears to have been very small. They were not serious pieces, like quartets, written chiefly for connoisseurs, and a display of compositional virtuosity would have been out of place: a fugue, for example, was possible in a string quartet, but unthinkable in a piano trio. The performer's virtuosity, on the other hand, was very much in place. We should do wrong to despise the inspiration of virtuosity in late eighteenth-century composition. Without it we should not have Mozart's operas or piano concertos or even the finale of Haydn's *Lark* Quartet. In Beethoven's piano music, the virtuosity has become so integral an element of the style that it is impossible to detach it for analysis: it is taken for granted in every one of the great sonatas. However, the virtuosity demanded by Haydn's trios is of a special nature: if they are not chamber music in the sense of compositions for several instruments of more or less equal importance, they are chamber music in the most literal sense, that of not being public. To the extent that they are display pieces, they are for private display. The violin also takes part in the display, and is not used only as a doubling instrument like the cello. Even when a modern concert piano is used, the cello is still necessary in these pieces, although it plays few notes that the piano does not also play. I have found that cellists, when they are persuaded to play one of the trios, are surprised to discover their part a fascinating one, more interesting, in fact, than in the Mozart trios, where relative independence is bought at the price of a great many patches of silence.

If the trios needed any justification, it would be found in a consideration of the pianoforte of Haydn's day. The bass was thin and weak, the sustaining power was poor. The piano trio was the solution to all the mechanical difficulties, with the cello reinforcing the bass and the melodies that most needed singing power given to the violin. In this way, Haydn's fantasy was set free, and the performer, too, had the chance at virtuoso effects impossible for a piano alone; the orchestra did the same thing for Mozart in his concertos that the violin and cello did for Haydn.

The contemporary piano was incapable alone of the powerful effects that Haydn and Mozart needed for their most imaginative works. By the beginning of the nineteenth century, pianos were being built that were more adequate to the demands made by composers. For this reason, the most congenial instruments for many works are not the ones for which they were written but those that were built twenty years later in response to the music. The piano was still in an experimental stage at the end of the eighteenth century, and its development was stimulated by the music of the period, which demanded greater possibilities of dynamic inflection. Both Haydn and Mozart sought instruments of greater power and response, and with a few magnificent exceptions their works for piano alone tend to be more inhibited and less rich than the compositions for piano with accompanying instruments. The use of one or more stringed instruments released their imaginations through the combination of an instrument that could sustain and sing together with the contrapuntal resources of the piano.

Instrumental changes since the eighteenth century have made a problem out of the balance of sound in Haydn's piano trios, and, in fact, in all chamber music with piano. Violin necks (including, of course, even those of all the Stradivariuses and Guarneris) have been lengthened, making the strings tauter: the bows are used today with hairs considerably more tight as well. The sound is a good deal more brilliant, fatter, and more penetrating. A less selective use of vibrato has added to the contrast. The piano, in turn, has become louder, richer, even mushier in sound, and, above all, less wiry and metallic. This change makes nonsense out of all those passages in eighteenth-century music where the violin and the piano play the same melody in thirds, with the violin *below* the piano. Both the piano and the violin are now louder, but the piano is less piercing, the violin more. Violinists today have to make an effort of self-sacrifice to allow the piano to sing out softly; to do so is as much an exercise in virtue as in musicianship. The thinner sound of the violin in Haydn's day blended more easily with the metallic sonority of the contemporary piano and made it possible for each to accompany the other without strain.

All this applies to violin sonatas as well as to trios. It is sometimes claimed that Mozart and Beethoven did not fully understand the problem of balancing a piano and a violin, and that we can congratulate ourselves on the progress in composition since then. It is true that they did not grasp the nature of the future piano and violin as well as might be hoped, but they more than adequately understood the instruments of their own time. Changes in sonority, it should be added, call for a different phrasing, and it is impossible on modern instruments completely to achieve the kind of inflections and the dynamics these pieces call for. (But this does not imply that it is not, after all, better to play them on instruments of our own day than to turn a performance into an historical reconstruction.)

The use of the cello essentially to double the piano bass has been called a hangover from an earlier style; it comes, in short, from the *basso continuo*, and in this specific sense Haydn's trios may be called stylistically regressive. This is historically correct, but trivial: the doubling of keyboard basses by a cello does, indeed, come from an earlier period, but it would only be stylistically reactionary if it were unnecessary. No one who had heard the sound of the cello doubling in the slow movement of Haydn's great E flat major Trio, the last one he wrote, would doubt the necessity; that magnificent line (quoted below, p. 364) spanning almost two octaves in two measures has its full poignancy only with the cello. The piano alone will not do—nor will the cello alone, as the piano is needed to tie the music together and give it a unified texture. Like Haydn's quartets this is music that rarely makes use of a contrast of instruments: or, rather, it makes use of the individual qualities of the different instruments without seeming to exploit them. The piano plays what suits it best, and the violin takes over what the piano cannot properly make effective—the long sustained melodies. Much of the time the two instruments double each other.

It is odd to have to defend some of the greatest music ever written. In any case, the Haydn trios are doomed. Only pianists will ever want to play them, and the modern piano recital is no place for them. The following pages are a brief guide written for the pleasure of music-lovers who will read the trios at their pianos, while imagining the violin and cello parts.

Haydn's imagination is particularly luxuriant in these trios. Unconstrained by considerations of public effect, as in the symphonies, or by impressive refinements of style as in the quartets, Haydn wrote them for the sheer pleasure of the solo instrumentalists. There are twenty-six such trios; the thirty-one usually published under his name include two by other composers (one by Michael Haydn, which Joseph Haydn evidently thought he had composed himself as he put it into a catalogue of his own works); and three for flute, piano, and cello, pleasant works of no great interest. (One of these, too, is probably by brother Michael.) Two trios are very early (before 1769), one before 1780, nine between 1784 and 1790, and fourteen masterpieces written between 1793 and 1796—six of them right after the first *London* symphonies, and eight after the second set. To say with Tovey that 'the works cover Haydn's whole career' is to obscure the concentration at the end of his life, twenty-three of the twenty-six being written after Haydn was fifty years old, fourteen of them after he was sixty. It would be best to speak of them largely as products of his latest and most mature style.

The first Trio in G minor H. 1, however, is already a lovely piece, with a first movement almost completely in the French Baroque style in harmony, melody, ornamentation and rhythm—in everything, in fact, except its more fully articulated phrasing. Of the nine written in the 1780s, three should be singled out as among Haydn's greatest achievements. The Trio in C minor H. 13 has a double-variation first movement, where the main theme in minor is transformed into major for the second theme with such glorious effect that Haydn hardly varies the third appearance of the version in major. It is one of the finest examples of Haydn's ability to create an emotion that was completely his own and that no other composer, not even Mozart, could duplicate—a feeling of ecstasy that is completely unsensual, almost amiable. There is no recipe for producing this effect, but it depends in part on a preference for melodies that reach their climax (not necessarily their highest note) on the upper tonic as in the Austrian national anthem, rather than on the sixth, ninth, or fourth as Mozart's most often do; and, above all, from the use of harmonies in root position under very expressive melodies and an avoidance of complex past-writing. How this harmonic effect is employed can be seen in the opening of the slow movement of another trio, H. 14, from the late 1780s:

A melody of such uncomplicated beauty, it could be used at a funeral to be absolutely certain of a few tears. Part of the direct intensity of the chromatic progression in the last four measures comes from the fact that every chord is in root position, while the inner parts are as simple as possible.

In the finale of this trio, the recapitulation is introduced by this extraordinary passage:

where Haydn disrupts the sense of tonality—only as a joke, of course—partly by the octave displacement, partly by the chromatic alteration. For a moment the B♮ sounds like nonsense, and only when the melody starts do we understand it. The last trio of the 1780s that cries out for special mention is the great E minor H. 12, where the first movement, one of Haydn's most dramatic, ends still in minor instead of turning to the major as he generally did by then. The slow movement is in fully developed sonata style, and the finale is a brilliant symphonic rondo, full of surprises.

The trios of the 1790s fall into four triads (each dedicated to a different lady) with two separate trios at the end. The two sets of 1793 are dedicated to the Esterházy princesses. The three for Princess Nicholas Esterházy (for whom Haydn had already written three sonatas), are powerful, imaginative works (H. 21–23), the one in D minor having the most brilliant finale full of rhythmic ingenuity (including a passage in the recapitulation where Haydn goes into 4/4 without changing the 3/4 time signature), and the one in E flat the most imposing first movement. The opening measures of the latter are immediately transformed in a way that is worth quoting not only for its own sake, but also because it shows what Haydn could do more easily in the piano trio than in any other form. The first four measures

become

This feeling of spacious, relaxed, almost improvised expansion is almost never found in the symphonies, and rarely in the quartets. This is why the tempo mark for the majority of opening sonata movements in the trios is Allegro moderato, occurring almost twice as often as Allegro. Not only is the organization looser than that of the quartets, but also the effects are broader, with a brilliance and a massiveness that the sonatas for piano solo never reach and only approach in the early C minor H. 20 of 1770 and the two very late ones in E flat major.

The three works for the wife of the elder Prince, Princess Anton Esterházy, are even more interesting than those dedicated to her daughter-in-law. The Trio in B flat major H. 20 follows a first movement in brilliant virtuoso style with a set of variations in which the theme is played by the piano as a solo for the left hand alone, an example of the bare two-part counterpoint beloved by Haydn. The unusual first movement of H. 19 in G minor is discussed above (pp. 83–7). The finale of the A major Trio H. 18 shows Haydn's rondo form at its most original: it is a dance movement which begins with a two-part theme, both parts repeated, with the light air which generally implies the old-fashioned *ABA* form. What succeeds, however, is in the dominant, a second group of a sonata using (as Haydn mostly does) material based on the opening theme. A development does not follow, but rather a reprise of the opening in the tonic, giving us what appears to be an *ABA* form, after all—except that this, too, is followed by a recapitulation of the second group in the tonic, with large interpolations of development. To call this last part a coda would be a misnomer: it does not sound like a coda, but like a recapitulation and development combined, satisfying all our instincts for adventure and for resolution. Nothing shows better the fluidity of forms of the period: it has affinities with the sonata rondo, and if there were a few more examples we should have a name for it. It is a comic, high-spirited piece, full of syncopations.

Almost three years later, after his second and last visit to London, Haydn wrote two more sets of three Trios. One set was dedicated to Theresa Jansen, the wife of the engraver Bartolozzi; at about the same time, he wrote for her his last three piano sonatas. These Trios H. 27–29 are the most difficult Haydn ever wrote, and are a formidable musical and intellectual achievement. Mrs. Bartolozzi must have been a more than ordinary pianist: the C major Trio in particular is a compliment to her technique. The first movement, at once brilliant and leisurely, has a profusion of motifs unusual for Haydn, and a wealth of rhythmic contrast that would have made a work of the 1770s fall to pieces. The faster rhythms are gradually introduced one by one with the ease of apparent improvisation (real improvisation is much more lumpy), and the movement never loses its flow except for a dramatic silence in the contrapuntal development. The slow movements of these trios are all surprising: here, after a lyric opening section that is at once ingenuous and intricate, the minor section starts as a shock with a *forte* in the middle of a measure and continues with a dramatic power that is close to brutality. The finale, Presto, is a symphonic rondo, possibly the most humorous piece that Haydn wrote. Everything about the movement is unexpected: the opening theme is an enchanting joke, with the harmony changing to make accents on off-beats, an angular melody that appears at times in the wrong register, and a scherzando rhythm that allows the melody to start when one is least ready for it. The style of writing for the piano in this movement is, at times, close to the Beethoven of op. 31 no. 1.

The E major Trio is even more extraordinary, in some ways the strangest of all Haydn's late works. In part, many of the eccentricities of the compositions of this period may be considered a return to an earlier style, and affinities with the mannerist qualities of 1750 to 1775 can be found above all in the late trios. In this sense they could be said to be reactionary works if it were not for the transformation that the mannerism undergoes here. The control of the classical style is everywhere apparent: not for a moment does the large rhythmic movement fall to pieces or develop the effect of nervous indecision that occurs at least once in any work of Haydn's before 1775. It is true that Haydn does not often try for the impression of perfect regularity that Mozart preferred: Haydn's irregularity is more overt; dramatic silence and the fermata play a greater role in his music than in Mozart's, even including the operas. But in Haydn's later works, the silence is in every case a preparation for something crucial. The E major Trio, for example, has a close relationship with an earlier E major Piano Sonata H. 31 written probably in 1776; there are resemblances between all three movements of each work, particularly the two second movements. The first movement of the sonata comes to rest for a full measure in the development: the effect is one of exhaustion, and it starts up again only to resume its previous motion. There is a parallel moment in the development section of the trio where the music dies away: what follows is electrifying—the main theme, played *forte* for the first and only time, in the remote key of A flat major, in full rich harmony, and *arco* instead of pizzicato as it is elsewhere. This is, in fact, the climax of the whole movement: everything before leads up to it, everything afterwards resolves it. Pianistically this is one of Haydn's most imaginative works: the opening theme is scored for piano in such a way that it, too, sounds as if it were playing everything pizzicato except the sustained melody notes, even without the pizzicato accompaniment of the two stringed instruments.

The sonority of the second movement, an Allegretto in E minor, is peculiar to Haydn, written for the most part in a bare, harsh two-part counterpoint with the voices often three to four octaves apart. The relationship of the classical style to the preceding Baroque and to the Romantic that was to come is posed by this piece; one of the most startling creations of Haydn, it is a passacaglia like no other. It is Baroque in formal character, in the unchanging, relentless rhythm of the bass maintained until the final cadence, in its 'terraced' dynamics, in its superimposition of one rhythm on another with each remaining absolutely distinct, and in its use of a sequential pattern as a generating force within the main theme itself and not only in its development. The music is classical, however, in its firmly established movement to the relative major, articulated by the introduction of new melodic material, and in its wealth of dynamic accents serving to vary the pulse. Finally, it is Romantic in its tension, keyed to a steadily higher pitch than most eighteenth-century works could bear, in its dynamics which give the impression not only of a step-by-step ascent but of continuous *crescendo*, and, above all, in the fact that the final cadence after a fermata serves, not to resolve the excitement as a Baroque ending generally does, but to increase it through a series of brusque but elaborate flourishes that offer a resolution only with the violent final chord. To the extent that Romantic style meant the reintroduction of Baroque procedures and textures modified by a classical sense of climax, the movement may be said to be already Romantic. This work is a warning against too unified and dogmatic a view of style, and reminds us how elements may remain dormant ready to reappear at any moment as an artist goes back to the day before yesterday to find something newer and more progressive.

In the third and last trio for Mrs. Jansen, in E flat major, the opening movement shows what a personal turn Haydn gave at the end of his life to a simple *ABA* form. *B* is a dramatic development in the minor of *A*'s thematic material. The second appearance of *A* becomes a variation, and there is a further dramatization of the material in a lengthy coda. In this way the decorative form of the variation is given a dramatic framework more in keeping with the whole tendency of Haydn's style. The slow movement (*innocentamente*) is a slow-moving modulation from B major to E flat major by means of a plain two-part melody, another way of dramatizing a less complex form: here a simplicity of melody and a dramatic form combine to produce a sweetness rare in Haydn (or in any music, indeed). The last movement, Allemande Presto assai, is a German dance in rustic style with a grossly comic evocation of a village band; it is a difficult virtuoso piece for the piano as well as a form of low comedy for which the trio, more intimate than the symphony and less highfalutin than the string quartet, is particularly suited.

The three trios for Rebecca Schroeter are musically as distinguished but technically less demanding. She was a young widow in London who copied Haydn's music for him, and whose letters to Haydn express an affection which the sixty-year-old composer apparently returned. The Trio in G major H. 25 ends with the famous *Rondo all'Ongarese*, a real work of love for a pianist—brilliant, exciting, and sounding harder to play than it really is.

The Trios in D major H. 24 and F sharp minor H. 26 are both lyric works. The latter is the more exceptional, and not only in its somber tone which it keeps to the end. The full form of one of the closing themes in the exposition is not heard (or exposed) until the recapitulation, where it is also played much nearer the opening material. The development is short, but its harmonic range is unusually wide. The other movements intensify the seriousness of the first. The slow movement derives from that of Symphony no. 102 (unless the trio is the original). Without Haydn's varied orchestral sonority, the melody seems more personal and unrolls like an improvisation:

The skeleton is very simple, with the melody defining an ornamental and expressive arabesque and a descent down the notes of the scale from D♯ back to the tonic note. Yet it not only sounds eccentric but appears to accelerate. The acceleration is real: the first beat of the second measure plays the arabesque twice as fast. The irregularity is part of the acceleration: the high note of each measure is successively closer to the first beat, and the arabesque occurs twice in the third measure, where the movement is slowed by making the last appearance almost a written-out *ritenuto*. Even with a melody of such personal emotion, there are all the signs of a controlled energy. The minuet-finale has the same intimate gravity, and it has, too, the dramatic power of the minuet from Mozart's G minor Symphony without departing so far from the character of the dance. It is this movement better than any other, perhaps, that shows the superiority of the piano trio to the solo sonata for Haydn: of all the dance movements with which so many of the sonatas end, none even tries to attain the power and the depth of feeling of this work. What Haydn has done is to dramatize the minuet (that is, make it more like a sonata) while never losing the elegance of its rhythm. The trio, like the piano sonata, was for

Haydn a form light enough for the dance-finale to be possible as it was not for the symphony and only rarely for the quartet: with the finale of the F sharp minor Trio, the genre is transformed by a melancholy so intense it is indistinguishable from the tragic.

After these four great sets, Haydn wrote only two individual trios. One in E flat minor in two movements H. 31 is the only piece of Haydn's I can think of in that key. The first movement is a deeply expressive slow rondo-variation-set; the second theme, in the major, begins as an inversion of the first, and a third is surprisingly added—a long high soaring melody for the violin, one of Haydn's finest solos. The finale is Allegro ben moderato, a German dance in elaborate and sophisticated style, where the accompaniment is so important it becomes a counter-theme. The whole movement appears to be built out of fragments, almost without melody of any kind, yet the continuity and the lilt of the dance are always there. This is the kind of work that can only come at the end of a long career. The return of the main section is fantastically varied—the original form of the following five measures:

is changed into:

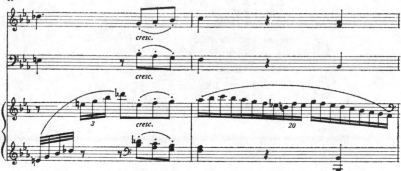

In this difficult movement, the violin collaborates on an equal, if less brilliant, footing, although the cello still remains principally a reinforcing instrument.

The last Trio in E flat major H. 30 is a work on a larger scale. One of the most massive of all Haydn's movements, its opening Allegro moderato is expansive, almost leisurely, and has a Mozartean wealth of themes. The succession of melodies comes in a continuous flow with little development in the exposition proper, which is unified, however, by passing allusions to the opening measures; the melodies grow one from the other, each continuing an aspect of the previous one, and their interdependence is such that they seem to well from one source in a fusion of power, lyricism, and logic. The slow movement alone would make this the most unjustly neglected masterpiece in all of Haydn's works. The opening bass line immediately brings forward a deeply expressive wide chromatic space:

and continues in a way that anticipates passages of *Tristan*:

and

364

The return of the opening melody is combined in decorated form with the rhythmic pattern of a middle section, at once a trio which does service both as the central part of a large ternary form (or *B* of an *ABA* form) and as an extension of the opening section. Haydn then makes the return into a sonata recapitulation by resolving in the tonic a theme of the middle section that had appeared in the dominant. As grand and as complete as the form of this movement feels, it does not actually end, but after a surprise cadence modulates mysteriously to prepare for the last movement. This is another German dance, Presto, Beethoven-like in its boisterous humor and in the dramatic development that acts as a bridge between the middle section in minor and the return of the opening. The coda is brilliant and difficult. In this last work, Haydn's achievement in the field of the piano trio is resumed: accepting the virtuosity of a light and informal genre, and without greatly altering its character, he made it the vehicle of some of his most imaginative and inspired conceptions.

3

Church Music

The classical style is at its most problematic in religious music. This was a genre beset with difficulties that could not trouble the secular field. Each composer met with a special and different kind of ill luck. Mozart's two greatest religious works remained only half-finished: the C minor Mass of 1783, K. 427, and the Requiem that he was working on when he died. Joseph Haydn's masses were already under attack for their unsuitable character during the composer's lifetime. He himself thought his brother Michael's church music superior to his own. Beethoven's first Mass in C major was responsible for his most humiliating public failure, the contemptuous reception given it by the Prince Esterházy for whom it was written. His *Missa Solemnis* in D major can still seem a difficult work today. As for the oratorio, *The Mount of Olives*, it is unique in Beethoven's entire output for its total lack of interest: it almost never rises above the merely competent, or falls below it.

The hostility of the Catholic Church to instrumental music throughout the eighteenth century was a factor in these difficulties. The use of instruments in church was even restricted by order of the Austrian government during the 1780s, a time of great creative activity for both Haydn and Mozart. In most periods the Church has not encouraged stylistic innovation: it disliked the heavily chromatic music of many Renaissance composers just as it refused to accept the centralized church preferred by most Renaissance architects. There are many works even of Palestrina that would not pass the church's test for orthodoxy in music style. A conservative taste is not illogical in an institution that relies so fundamentally on continuity of tradition. Nevertheless, the dislike of instrumental music is more deeply motivated: vocal music has always been considered more apt for a religious service, and the reputation for purity that is attached to *a capella* writing has symbolic value. At least with purely vocal music the words of the service make their presence felt. The classical style, however, was in all essentials an instrumental one.

In addition, there was an important conflict of musical ideology. Was the music there to glorify the mass or to illustrate its words? Is the function of music expressive or celebrative? Art has other uses but they were only obscurely formulated in the eighteenth century. Since the Renaissance the concept of music as an expressive art has dominated, and this was the principal source of much of the discomfort. The problems were, naturally, greater within a Catholic context: the Protestant sense of religion as personal and even individual expression made a happier partner with eighteenth-century aesthetics.

An uneasy relation between art and religion is not confined to the eighteenth century. In music, the contradiction is felt at its most acute in the opening and closing sections of the mass: if music is essentially celebrative, these sections should be brilliant and imposing; if expressive, then quiet and pleading in character. The celebrative tradition is the older one, but while it remained a powerful force in practice, it had long ceased to influence aesthetic theory by the 1700s; the eighteenth century is filled with complaints of unnaturally brilliant and inaptly jolly settings of the *Kyrie* and the *Agnus Dei*. If music is to express the sentiment implied by the words 'Kyrie eleison' ('Lord have mercy upon us'), most of the masses of the century would have to be judged as defective by this standard. Composers were largely obstinate in their refusal to yield to the expressive aesthetic, and Bach stands out in his achievement of a *Kyrie* at once grandiose and supplicatory.

Things were not improved after 1770 by a style firmly rooted in the rhythmic techniques of Italian comic opera. This produced settings of the mass which appear strikingly irrelevant to the text—not only to us today but to contemporaries as well and even, it appears, to the composers themselves. Some of the coloratura passages of a Mozart mass are as intrinsically absurd as the nineteenth-century adaptations of Donizetti arias to Latin texts—although the absurdity only shows its head if a demand for relevance is made, a demand which was itself irrelevant if the music was there only to glorify and to decorate. Nevertheless, given the nature of classical texture and rhythm, it was more difficult than in the early part of the century to encompass an imposing and lengthy opening movement of an emotional neutrality—avoiding the twin traps of the amiable gaiety or, more rarely, the dramatic ferocity of the classical Allegro. Not until the *Creation* of Haydn does classical rhythm have enough weight for a long slow opening movement that pretends to more than introductory status. The style of the High Baroque, with a heavy contrapuntal texture and the almost indefinitely extensible phrase, can provide some of this weight. One avenue open to the classical composer of religious music is, therefore, archaism. An imitation of High Baroque style, a moribund but not buried tradition by the 1780s, had the advantage that a reference to the past always has in religion: using the contrapuntal style was like continuing to address God as 'Thou,' and brought by itself a satisfaction that a more modern style could never have provided.

Mozart was the greatest of parodists. His works in Baroque style are not, it is true, quite perfect as period-style: Lowinsky has pointed out a squareness and clarity of phrasing in the fugues that is most un-Baroque in spirit. It is difficult, as well, to imagine Bach agreeing with Mozart's dictum that fugues must be played slowly so that the entrances of the theme are always heard: many of the entrances of Bach's fugues are securely hidden, tied to the previous notes, and the listener can only be gradually and belatedly aware of the theme. Nevertheless, Mozart's mastery of the older style is unquestionable. It would take a sharp ear and a considerable amount of hindsight to distinguish stylistically between the great double fugue in the *Requiem* and one of Handel's, and if some of the chromaticism is not Handelian, it was not beyond the reach of Bach. Mozart's knowledge of both composers and of Hasse was profound if not extensive: he certainly knew *Israel in Egypt* and the *Messiah,* and he studied the *Art of Fugue* and the *Well-Tempered Keyboard.* The 'Qui tollis' of the unfinished Mass in C minor comes almost directly from *Israel in Egypt,* but with a more personal use of both chromaticism and syncopation. The opening *Kyrie* of this mass, unrelievedly Baroque in its harmonic sequences and its homogeneous rhythmic texture, has an austerity of feeling that contrasts surprisingly with the beautiful Rococo decoration of the solo soprano 'Christe,' which is its middle section.

These successes of parody are personal victories, triumphs of virtuosity: they do not belong to the history of style, except as the *Requiem* influenced the revival of Baroque technique that became so important after the death of Beethoven. To some extent Mozart preserved what life still remained in the heritage of Bach and Handel until it became so important to Chopin and Schumann. But most of his church music remains perfunctory, less profound and even less carefully written than the great secular works. The arias in the masses, fine as some few of them are, are almost indistinguishable from their operatic counterparts except by their slightly more sedate motion, and not even that decorum was always considered. Only in the Masonic works, transfigured in *Die Zauberflöte,* does an original spirit become apparent. One other exception is the ensemble for solo voices (the greatest example being the 'Quoniam' from the C minor Mass), where Mozart combines a continuously rich and expressive contrapuntal motion with a sweetness of line and a large-scale pacing that he derived directly from his operatic experience. On the other hand, Mozart's use of the chorus differs from Handel's only in being less imaginative. Nevertheless, the most impressive part of Mozart's achievement in the composition of religious music remains a deliberate exercise in an old-fashioned style.

Haydn had little of Mozart's talent for mimicry, and his music, although influenced by Handel, remained almost unmarked by that of Johann Sebastian Bach. Haydn could write an old-fashioned fugue, but it always retained much of the modern instrumental style. The discomfort that his religious style caused his contemporaries was ruefully acknowledged by Haydn with the magnificently disingenuous remark that whenever he thought about God it made him feel cheerful. Disingenuous but surely true: Haydn's religious faith was, from all evidence, simple, direct, and popular in character. I emphasize this only because of the naïve notion that stylistic development is directly related to the strength and sincerity of the artist's beliefs. Haydn's comparative failure as a composer of liturgical music cannot be related to his own faith, and only very indirectly and tenuously to the general tenor of eighteenth-century religious development. In addition, it cannot be set down to lack of interest, as Haydn's concentration on church music was considerable at the end of his life: after the *London* Symphonies he virtually abandoned pure instrumental music except for the string quartet, and the principal works of his old age are six masses and two oratorios.

The masses are, of course, full of admirable details and contain much writing of great power. They remain, however, uncomfortable compromises. The *Kyrie* of the *Mass in Time of War* opens with an expressive Largo introduction, but the Allegro moderato that follows has passages that can only have sounded as trivial to Haydn's contemporaries as they do to us today:

Haydn's symphonic style transfigures scraps like these: in ecclesiastical music, however, he cannot do without them, but he does not dare to do much with them.

Parts of the text of the mass are handled very easily within the classical style. The opening section of the *Gloria* can be accommodated by a symphonic Allegro of normal character. The more dramatic sections also present no problems, and there are passages in Haydn's masses, particularly the magnificent *Kyrie* of the *Windband* Mass and the 'Crucifixus' of the *Theresa* Mass, which are among the most affecting that Haydn ever wrote. Yet even at such places the incoherence of the late eighteenth-century's tradition of religious music and the lack of a stable and acceptable framework for liturgical settings can lead to effects of peculiar irrelevancy: the long sentimental cello solo of the *Mass in Time of War* has great sweetness, but to be accepted as an adequate setting of *Qui tollis peccata mundi* it requires more tolerance than the most emotional religiosity of eighteenth-century painting, which had at least a coherent symbolic organization and a visual harmony with the architecture that surrounded it.

The most immediate weakness of Haydn's religious style appears naturally enough in the settings of the Nicene Creed. A naïve aesthetics of expression was of little help in facing a text of pure doctrine except in its single moments of narrative drama: the Incarnation, Crucifixion, and Resurrection. These represented opportunities that every composer seized, but how was the rest to be turned into music? Expressive relevance could be abandoned, as it so often was, but even then decorum prevented a style that relied so heavily on irony and wit from creating works of much character. As a result, when Haydn and Mozart are not attempting the grandeur of the Handelian style as a stop-gap, their religious music, while never falling below the competent, is graceful (in Mozart's case often enough) or brilliant, but rarely compelling or, indeed, interesting. The setting of the first part of the *Credo* in the *Theresa* Mass of Haydn, for example, has vigor and some power, but one would have to look far in Haydn's music to find another rhythmic structure equally turgid and unimaginative.

Haydn's escape was through his beloved pastoral. In neither the *Creation* nor the *Seasons* is the high level of writing always as successfully and as continuously sustained as in the great symphonies and quartets (although the less admired *Seasons* seems to me more successful in this respect), but they are among the greatest works of the century, and music of specifically religious character settles with ease in a framework that allows it to escape from liturgical constraints. Above all, the pastoral tradition provided unequivocal solutions to the problem of setting a text which the late eighteenth-century religious style, corrupted by logical contradictions, was no longer capable of giving. In particular, the pastoral accommodated itself without misgivings to the shape of the 'sonata,' which it had, after all, helped to create.

The famous depiction of chaos at the opening of the *Creation* is in 'slow-movement sonata form,': nothing could show better how, for Haydn, the 'sonata' is not a form at all, but an integral part of the musical language, and even a necessary minimum for any large statement that can be made within that language. The themes are here reduced to very small fragments, as are the musical paragraphs, but the proportions of a sonata movement without an isolated development section but with articulated exposition and symmetrical recapitulation (both with two regular groups of themes) is as present as ever in Haydn's slow movements. The opening theme:

is as much dynamic marking as a series of pitches, and it is later enriched by a staccato arpeggio as the movement becomes more complex. The second theme, in the relative major:

(actually an inversion of an earlier phrase) has an even more characteristic outline. The beginning of the recapitulation could not be more easily identifiable:

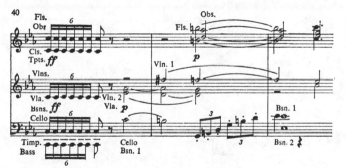

and the most unusual formal device is only that the second theme is recapitulated and resolved at the tonic with the first theme in counterpoint:

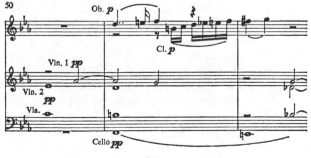

371

where the clarinet's ascending motif is a decorative form of the opening notes in the first violins quoted above.

By what, then, is chaos represented, and how can Haydn's musical language express this and still remain language? Simply by the absence of clear articulation in the large phrase-groups, which merge and blend with each other, and by the witholding of clear and definite cadences. The progression to the relative major is at first as clear as in any sonata movement in a minor tonality, but there is a sudden evasion to a surprisingly remote VII♭:

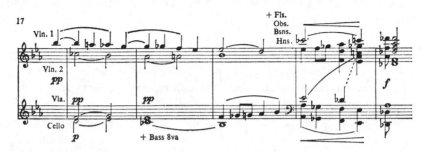

and the return to the more normal E flat major, while effected almost immediately, is never granted an ending in root position:

so that the second theme begins without the firmness of the usual cadence. The extremely slow tempo, the syncopated string chords and the irregular phrase-lengths do the rest; in spite of the breadth of feeling, the facture is concentrated on movement in the miniature, and everything depends on detail.

With the two oratorio texts, the pastoral tradition at last allowed Haydn a structure which enabled him to sum up his technique and his life's work: they were to him what the *Art of Fugue* was to Bach, and the *Diabelli* Variations to Beethoven. The *Seasons* and the *Creation* are descriptions of the entire universe as Haydn knew it. The imposed simplicity of the pastoral style was the condition which made it possible to grasp subjects of such immensity: without the pretense of naïveté in the deepest sense of the spontaneous and unaffected response of the child's eye to the world, these works could not exist at all. The subject of pastoral is not Nature itself, but man's relation to nature and to what is 'natural': this is the reason for the extreme stylization of Haydn's descriptive writing in the oratorios. He did not like the purely programmatic parts of his texts, and called them 'French trash,' but they were an essential part of the tradition, which had, indeed, become largely French during the eighteenth century.

The greatness of the two oratorios lies in their range of expression, and for once Haydn equalled Mozart's breadth if not his control. The *Seasons* makes an unabashed appeal for popular favor; as early as the fourth number, Haydn shrewdly quotes the tune from the *Surprise* Symphony that had become so popular. But this is not the only allusion to Haydn's previous works[1]: the *Seasons* contains references to Haydn's music from years back. When he finished it, he was written out. The last years of Haydn's life, with all his success, comfort, and celebrity, are among the saddest in music. More moving than the false pathos of a pauper's grave for Mozart (who was only buried there because Baron Van Swieten advised the economy to Constanza) is the figure of Haydn filled with musical ideas which were struggling to escape, as he himself said; he was too old and weak to go to the piano and submit to the discipline of working them out.

It was left to Beethoven to reconcile the liturgical tradition with the classical style, and paradoxically by evading the problem altogether; both his masses are frankly concert pieces, and more effective outside than inside a church. Yet the evasion is compensated by an evocation of ecclesiastical atmosphere attempted in no work of Haydn or Mozart. The care taken to that end is heard at once in the opening measures of the C major Mass op. 86 of 1807:

[1] The closeness of 'Sei nun gnädig' (no. 6) to the slow movement of Symphony no. 98 is almost as candid as the quotation from the *Surprise*.

The first two notes are for the basses of the chorus alone without orchestral accompaniment, a deliberate and brief allusion to the ancient *a capella* style which becomes even more marked a few pages later:

The sixteenth-century Italian liturgical style, theoretically *a capella* if not practically so, had never died out: Palestrina was still performed, if seldom. Michael Haydn already made heavy use of the style. In writing his masses, Beethoven made a deliberate study of the older forms of religious music, and with many of his contemporaries he believed that they were more suitable for religious texts than the more modern style. His assimilation of the older style never takes the form of pastiche, still less that of quotation, even in the famous 'Et incarnatus est' of the D major Mass. There are also more than a few Handelian references in the C major Mass, but in general the texture is as symphonic and as personal as ever. The *Kyrie* of the C major Mass integrates its references to the older contrapuntal style within a sonata form with a short development section, and, like the *Waldstein* Sonata, uses the mediant E major as a dominant.

This opening solves the problem of pacing as if it had never existed, but

374

nevertheless Beethoven was more than usually preoccupied with the tempo-mark; the manuscript has no tempo indication and a later copy has *Andante con moto*, but when Beethoven came to publish the work, it had become *Andante con moto assai vivace quasi allegretto ma non troppo*, where concern has become almost comic. Nevertheless, as the magnificent breadth and steady, unfolding line of the opening measures rises to a *forte* in the ninth measure, the conciliation of the contradictory stylistic forces in the setting of the mass is accomplished for the first time in European music since Bach.

The *Missa Solemnis* in D is perhaps Beethoven's most considerable single achievement. With it he developed a manner so intellectually powerful as to be completely adequate even for the purely doctrinal sections of the mass. The Mass in D provides a musical equivalent for almost every word of the Creed: the music is no longer just a framework, a setting, against which the words are to be understood. Not even the greatest difficulties are shirked. The magnificent and seemingly endless series of crossing scales at the end of the *Credo*, which seem to go ever higher and lower like a Jacob's ladder as the complexity of sound hides the new beginnings, must be accepted as Beethoven's audible image of eternity, and they are the equivalent of the words, 'I believe in the life to come, world without end, amen.'

The two masses of Beethoven present each of the five great parts of the Mass as almost completely unified movements, in place of the undisguisedly sectional treatment of earlier composers. In this respect the *Gloria* of the D major Mass is perhaps most remarkable by its use of a recurrent texture to organize the form, and by the reappearance of the opening words, now Presto, at the end. Even the relations between the large sections are closely knit: the *Credo* opens with a brilliant and rapid modulation to the new key, a modulation which becomes itself a thematic element. The unification of each of the separate parts of the Mass derives from Beethoven's tendency, at the end of his life, to combine a four-movement work within the frame of a first-movement sonata. Basically, however, he relies on the technique of Mozart's operatic finales both for the unity and the sense of pace, and the greatest achievements of the classical style in liturgical music are related as closely as ever to the *opera buffa* which helped to shape the style.

Part VII

BEETHOVEN

———

Es pflegt manchem seltsam und lächerlich aufzufallen, wenn die Musiker von den Gedanken in ihren Kompositionen reden; und oft mag es auch so geschehen, daß man wahrnimmt, sie haben mehr Gedanken in ihrer Musik als über dieselbe. Wer aber Sinn für die wunderbaren Affinitäten aller Künste und Wissenschaften hat, wird die Sache wenigstens nicht aus dem platten Gesichtspunkt der sogenannten Natürlichkeit betrachten, nach welcher die Musik nur die Sprache der Empfindung sein soll, und eine gewisse Tendenz aller reinen Instrumentalmusik zur Philosophie an sich nicht unmöglich finden. Muß die reine Instrumentalmusik sich nicht selbst einen Text erschaffen? und wird das Thema in ihr nicht so entwickelt, bestätigt, variiert und kontrastiert wie der Gegenstand der Meditation in einer philosophischen Ideenreihe?

Friedrich Schlegel, (*Fragment* 444) *Athenäum*, 1798

[*It generally strikes many people as strange and ridiculous if musicians talk about the thoughts (= themes) in their compositions; and often it may even happen that we perceive that they have more thought* in *their music than* about *it. Who has a feeling, however, for the wonderful affinity of all the arts and sciences will at least not consider the matter from the flat and so-called "natural" point of view, according to which music should be nothing more than the language of sentiment, and he will find a certain tendency of all pure instrumental music to philosophy not inherently impossible. Must not pure instrumental music itself create its own text? And is not the theme in it developed, confirmed, varied, and contrasted in the same way as the object of meditation in a philosophical series of ideas?*]

Beethoven

In 1822, five years before his death, Beethoven felt himself almost completely isolated from the musical life in Vienna. 'You will hear nothing of me here,' he said to a visitor from Leipzig. 'What should you hear? *Fidelio?* They cannot give it, nor do they want to listen to it. The symphonies? They have no time for them. My concertos? Everyone grinds out only the stuff he himself has made. The solo pieces? They went out of fashion long ago, and here fashion is everything. At most Schuppanzigh occasionally digs up a quartet.'[1] The ageing artist, unappreciated and half-forgotten, is a familiar figure, and the neglect is as often imagined as real, yet Beethoven's visitor, the editor of Leipzig's musical journal, if he felt that Beethoven exaggerated, did not remain unconvinced. At the end of his life, Beethoven was most decidedly out of fashion.

That he was, at the same time, universally accepted as the greatest living composer, did not in any way alter his increasing isolation. Not only musical fashion but musical history had turned away from Beethoven. In the music of his younger contemporaries (with the exception of Schubert) and of the generation that followed his death, his work, while admired and loved, is hardly a vital force; not until Brahms and the later operas of Wagner will it play a significant role. The prestige of his music blinds us to this fact, in the same way, indeed, that it blinded the musicians of the first half of the nineteenth century. Only *An die ferne Geliebte*, a sport among his forms, played an important part in the musical development of the 1830s and 40s. The rest of his achievement was not an inspiration but a dead weight in the style of those who immediately followed him.

The prestige, however, was immense. Perhaps only Chopin, coming from a provincial musical culture, succeeded in being completely free from its spell.[2] For the other composers, Beethoven's achievement provoked an emulation which led, and could have led, only to disaster. Both Mendelssohn and Brahms imitated the *Hammerklavier* with singularly awkward results. The sonatas and symphonies of Schumann are constantly embarrassed by the example of Beethoven: their splendor breaks through his influence, but never starts from it. All that is most interesting in the next generation is a reaction against Beethoven, or an attempt to ignore him, a turning away into new directions: all that is weakest submits to his power and pays him the emptiest and most sincere of homages.

---

[1] Thayer, vol. II, p. 801.

[2] It is not astonishing to find the most Philistine of all comments on Beethoven's music on Chopin's lips. In Delacroix' Diary, he is reported as saying, 'Beethoven turned his back on eternal principles.'

Beethoven

The antagonism between generations, and the swing of fashion between one generation and the next are well-known phenomena in the history of styles. Too much weight is sometimes placed on them. The changes effected by reaction alone are rarely profound. With all Beethoven's declared independence from preceding influences, and his evident resentment of Haydn, there was in his career no radical movement away from the style of Mozart and Haydn comparable to the break with the past made by the generation of Schumann and Chopin. As for Mozart and Haydn, the antagonism between succeeding generations hardly existed even on a personal level. The changes of fashion between generations are really only pretexts, at worst, and, at best, reinforcements in the strategy of revolutionaries. Beethoven transformed the musical tradition he was born into, but he never challenged its validity. If he resented Haydn's patronage and even his help and support, he never abandoned Haydn's forms and the greater part of his technique, nor, musically, did he ever express anything but veneration for Mozart even when he condemned the frivolous moral outlook of the opera libretti.

In fact, with age, Beethoven drew closer to the forms and proportions of Haydn and Mozart. In his youthful works, the imitation of his two great precursors is largely exterior: in technique and even in spirit, he is at the beginning of his career often closer to Hummel, Weber, and to the later works of Clementi than to Haydn and Mozart.[1] The first movement of the Piano Sonata, op. 2 no. 3, has a rigid sectional structure and, above all, a wealth of connecting material that is never found in the opening movement of a work of Haydn or Mozart, with the exception of the latter's *Coronation* Concerto. The equilibrium between harmonic and thematic development so characteristic of Haydn and Mozart is often lost in early Beethoven, where thematic contrast and transformation seem to outweigh all other interests. Beethoven, indeed, started as a true member of his generation, writing now in a proto-Romantic style and now in a late and somewhat attenuated version of the classical style, with an insistence on the kind of broad, square melodic structure that was to find its true justification later in the Romantic period of the 1830s. The early song *Adelaïde* is as much Italian Romantic opera as anything else: its long, winding melody, symmetrical and passionate, its colorful modulations and aggressively simple accompaniment could come easily from an early work of Bellini. Many of the slow movements of the early sonatas, too, foreshadow the easy-going, sprawling long-range rhythmic sense of Weber's piano music and of much of Schubert. (Later both Schubert and Weber were to start by disapproving of what they considered Beethoven's wilful eccentricity, and Weber became for a time one of his most vicious

---

[1] The earliest of his works (the sonatas published when he was only thirteen, in 1783) start clearly from Haydn's work of the late sixties: we tend to forget that Beethoven's early musical education antedated any knowledge (in Bonn, at least) of the works of Haydn and Mozart in the fully developed classical style—the works by which they are best known. Bonn was less advanced than Vienna.

critics. Schubert made amends by a respect that amounted almost to idolatry, and by a consistent use of Beethoven's forms as models.) The Septet, the work that became so embarrassingly popular that Beethoven in later years winced when it was mentioned, and the Quintet for Piano and Winds may be called 'classicizing' rather than 'classic' in style, like the works of Hummel: they are reproductions of classical forms—Mozart's in particular—based upon the exterior models, the results of the classical impulse, and not upon the impulse itself. 'Classicizing' works have a beauty that is often unappreciated: these early pieces of Beethoven have an easy freshness and serenity that redeem their awkward lack of unity. His technical mastery of the 'reproductive' style has often been underestimated; as a young man he was already the greatest of its practitioners. In his A major Quartet op. 18 no. 5, modeled faithfully on Mozart's quartet in the same key, he produces a fine and yet original example of one of Mozart's most refined effects, difficult to achieve in a manner that is neither tasteless nor perfunctory: the phrase that can turn either to the tonic or the dominant depending upon what has preceded it. It cannot have been easy for Beethoven to abandon such facility for a more experimental approach. Only gradually did he return to more definitely classical conceptions: but with the *Appassionata* he set himself firmly against the squarely organized and yet loose and apparently improvisatory structures of late classicism and early Romanticism, and returned decisively to the closed, concise, and dramatic forms of Haydn and Mozart, expanding these forms and heightening their power without betraying their proportions.

The question of Beethoven's position as a 'classical' or 'Romantic' composer is generally ill-defined, additionally complicated by the fact that Haydn and Mozart in the early nineteenth century were called 'Romantic' composers as often as anything else. It is not a question that would have had any meaning during Beethoven's own lifetime, and it is difficult to give it a precise significance today. Nor is it a helpful tautology that a man belongs to his own time: historical time in this sense is not bounded by dates. Every period of time is traversed by forces both reactionary and progressive: Beethoven's music is filled with memories and predictions. Instead of affixing a label, it would be better to consider in what context and against what background Beethoven may be most richly understood.

To begin with what may appear the larger issues—the spiritual content, the emotional ambiance of the music—would be to lame discussion from the start. It would be to risk confounding personal expression with general stylistic changes, and inevitably to muddle the different significance of similar expressive devices within disparate systems. That Haydn and Beethoven, or Schumann and Beethoven, used the same details or worked within forms that resemble each other, implies no sort of musical kinship if the details have entirely different meanings or if the forms function in different ways and for different ends. Meaningless resemblances between composers can be found wherever sought for. Until we know how the details work and to what purpose, comprehension can only be, not simply provisional (for that is what it is at best), but illusory. It is, of course, difficult to avoid assuming a knowledge of the larger context in advance, regimenting the details accordingly: Beethoven often appears to speak too directly for us to admit the possibility that we have misunderstood him. A little methodological false humility in criticism, however, may go a long way towards revealing a genuine ignorance.

For example, in his frequent evasion of strict dominant-tonic relations within a single movement, Beethoven may seem to be closer to Schumann, Chopin, and Liszt in their most successful, least academic forms than to Haydn and Mozart. In almost any work of Haydn and Mozart, the twin poles of tonic and dominant are firmly maintained: an increase of tension at the opening almost always implies the imminent establishment of the dominant as a secondary tonality; the more remote harmonies are played, not only against the tonic, but against the polarity of tonic-dominant as a continual area of reference; resolution always goes to the tonic through the dominant. This polarity has a much less fundamental role in the work of the first generation of Romantic composers, and sometimes disappears completely: the A flat Ballade of Chopin never employs E flat major, and the F minor Ballade has little to do with either C major (or minor) or A flat major; only an already reactionary and high-principled view of sonata form imprisoned Schumann at times within a tonic-dominant relationship which was evidently largely uncongenial to him, if one is to judge by the more imaginative works: *Davidsbündlertänze*, the *Carnaval*, the C major Fantasy, and the great song cycles.

Almost from the beginning of his career as a composer, Beethoven attempted to find substitutes for the dominant in the classical tonic-dominant polar relation. His first efforts were prudent, not to say timid: he does, indeed, go to the dominant by the end of the exposition of his early sonatas, but often before doing so, he establishes a more remote key first: in op. 2 no. 3, the dominant minor; in op. 10 no. 3, the submediant minor. The establishment of a succession of tonalities is typical of the early style of Beethoven, and illustrates its closeness to the loose, additive forms of his contemporaries. He turned back later from this coloristic use of keys towards a more cohesive scheme. By op. 31 no. 1 he ventures to dispense with the dominant as a secondary tonality altogether: from G major he goes to the mediant B, and oscillates between its major and minor forms. A short time before this work, he had experimented in a similar way with a largely minor submediant in the String Quintet with two violas, op. 29. Here the continual swing back and forth between the major and minor is even more essential as the submediant minor is the relative minor of the tonic and implies a relaxation of tension, a subdominant relation, in fact; the submediant major, however, counteracts this by its orientation towards the dominant. It was not a relationship that Beethoven ever attempted in a sonata movement again, even with an alternation of major and minor to safeguard the dramatic character.

After the *Waldstein* Sonata, Beethoven is almost as likely to use the more remote mediant and submediant keys as to employ a straightforward dominant. The logical possibilities of these keys within a diatonically conceived aesthetic may be said to be exhausted in his works: only chromaticism could further enlarge the field. More astonishing than their frequency are the imaginative resources which Beethoven calls upon in the use of these substitute dominants and the variety of ways of arriving at them. Their effects cannot be easily subsumed in any simple formula: sonata movements like those of the *Waldstein*, the *Hammerklavier*, the op. 111, the Ninth Symphony, and the Quartets op. 127 and op. 130 all use a mediant or submediant key for very different expressive purposes.

It is tempting to think of Beethoven's substitute dominants as having something in common with the harmonic structures of the Romantic period, but his harmonic freedom is of a different order and nature. When the Romantic composer is not following an academic theory of form—that is, when he is not writing what he felt should be called a 'sonata'—his secondary tonalities are not dominants at all, but subdominants: they represent a diminishing tension and a less complex state of feeling, and not the greater tension and imperative need for resolution implied by all of Beethoven's secondary tonalities. Each of the three movements of Schumann's C major Fantasy goes clearly to the subdominant, and all its material is directed towards this modulation. For much of the F minor Ballade, Chopin avoids establishing a secondary key with any degree of clarity: when one arrives, it is astonishingly B flat major. These are two of the most remarkable works of the period, and they are only two instances out of many.

No comparable subdominant relationship can be found in any work of Beethoven (except, of course, those based on a ternary *ABA*, or minuet and trio form, which has no relation to the unified dramatic forms of Schumann and Chopin cited in this context). His expansion of the large-scale harmonic range took place within the limits of the classical language, and never infringed on the tonic-dominant polarity or the classical movement towards a greater tension away from the tonic. These secondary tonalities to his work, mediants and submediants, function within the large structure as true dominants. They create a long-range dissonance against the tonic and so provide the necessary tension for a move towards a central climax. In addition, Beethoven always prepares their appearance so that they seem almost as closely related to the tonic as the dominant is, so that the modulation creates a dissonance of greater power and excitement than the more usual dominant without disturbing the harmonic unity and tearing the structure apart. Within a tonal system this naturally imposes an inner contradiction, but a secondary tonality already exists as such a contradiction in its own right. Beethoven's harmonic practice only serves to heighten the effect of a style which depends for its dramatic expressiveness upon exactly this contradiction and its harmonious resolution. Beethoven, indeed, here enlarged the limits of the classical style beyond all previous conceptions,[1] but he never changed its essential structure or abandoned it, as did the composers who followed him. In the other fundamental aspects of his musical language, as well as in the key relations within a single movement, Beethoven may be said to have remained within the classical framework, even while using it in startlingly radical and original ways.

The foregoing naturally does not imply that the tonic-dominant relationship disappeared during the Romantic period—it is still with us to some extent today. But to Schumann and his contemporaries it was no longer the exclusive central principle of long-range harmonic movement. It is significant, however, that they used it, as far as I can remember, in all their movements in 'sonata-allegro' form. In other words, with all their harmonic daring and exploration in other forms, when it came to the 'sonata' they were far more conservative than Beethoven. Their greatest harmonic conceptions could not be applied to the sonata without making nonsense of it, whereas all of Beethoven's most startling innovations took place easily and comfortably within the sonata style.

We cannot even claim that Beethoven's harmonic licence within the classical style was a step towards the greater freedom of the Romantic generation, or that his magnificent stretching of the tonic-dominant polarity made it possible for those who followed to supersede it, or at least to bypass it. If Beethoven's daring had provided an example of such consequence, the Romantics would hardly have produced such uniformly conservative 'sonata' forms. The great harmonic innovations of the Romantics do not come from Beethoven at all, and have nothing to do either with his technique or his spirit. They arise from Hummel, Weber, Field, and Schubert (without taking into account Schubert's acquisition and mastery of classical procedure in the last years of his life), and, too, from Italian opera. They are made possible, in other words, not by an aesthetic in which the tonic-dominant polarity has been expounded to the limits of its effective power, but by one in which it has been loosened and weakened, where the orientation towards a powerful tonic area at the beginning and end has been threatened by a new and pervasive chromaticism, and by a more lyric and less dramatic conception of form. It was, for example, Schubert—in the last movement of the *Trout* Quintet—who first wrote an exposition which went to the subdominant. In the early works of Schubert, as in the music of Weber and Hummel, there is the first large development of a truly melodic form, one in which the classical harmonic tension is replaced by a relaxed and expansive succession of melodies. A new conception of harmonic tension was later developed by

---

[1] The use of the mediant or submediant as a dominant is, however, only an extension of Haydn's emphasis on them within the sonata exposition in his late works.

Schumann, Mendelssohn, and, above all, by Chopin, but they could not start from the classical style at its most highly organized, and Beethoven was of no use to them. The Romantic style did not come from Beethoven, in spite of the great admiration that was felt for him, but from his lesser contemporaries and from Bach.

It is worth noting, in this respect, the extremely limited influence of the music of Bach in Beethoven's works, in spite of the fact that his knowledge of Bach was considerable. He had been brought up on the *Well-Tempered Keyboard*, made his reputation as a child prodigy by playing it in its entirety, and continued to play it all his life. He copied out passages of Bach while making sketches for the last movement of the *Hammerklavier* as well as for the Fugue for String Quintet in D major. He had a copy of the Inventions, and two copies of the *Art of Fugue*, and he certainly knew the *Goldberg* Variations. Yet, except for an obvious and touching reference to the *Goldberg* in the conception of the final variations of the *Diabelli* set, the use he made of all his familiarity is very small, almost negligible in comparison to the continuous reference to Bach in the music of Mendelssohn, Chopin, and Schumann. The classical style had already absorbed all that it could of Bach as seen through the eyes of Mozart in the early 1780s, and as Beethoven continued to work within these limits, his love for Bach remained always in the margin of his creative activity.

That Beethoven's musical language remained essentially classical—or, better, that he started with a late and diluted version of classicism and gradually returned to the stricter and more concise form of Haydn and Mozart—does not mean that he stood outside his time, or that his conception of classical form was the expression of an outlook identical to the late eighteenth century's. To cite only one trait, his music often has a sententious moral earnestness that many people have found repellent, and which is presented with an enthusiasm far more typical of Europe after the French Revolution than of the *douceur de vivre* that preceded it. Much of his music, too, is autobiographical, sometimes openly so, in a way that is unthinkable before 1790 if not presented playfully; it is embarrassing when historians read into the music of Haydn and Mozart[1] the kind of directly personal significance appropriate to Beethoven and other nineteenth-century composers. Yet it is certain that Beethoven assumed a position not only contrary to the fashion of his time, but also in many ways against the direction that musical history was to take. He was perhaps the first composer in history to write deliberately difficult music for a great part of his life. Not that he ever set his face against popular success, or lost hope of achieving it despite the uncompromising difficulty of his work. The fame and the love that his music inspired during his lifetime were, in any case, considerable; but the ovations

---

[1] Even Chopin resented this approach to his music, but it is deliberately provoked by certain aspects of Schumann's.

he received at the premieres of the Ninth Symphony and *Missa Solemnis*—works apparently difficult enough to understand even today and which must have been almost disastrously executed when first played, to judge by the reports—are more a testimony to the respect in which the elderly composer was held than to a genuine acceptance of the music itself. No composer before Beethoven ever disregarded the capacities of both his performers and his audience with such ruthlessness. The first of his truly 'difficult' works, his stumbling blocks for critics, were written soon after the first signs of deafness, while the earliest works—even when they were found startlingly original or eccentric—won an almost immediate acceptance. He was already known throughout Europe as one of the greatest living composers by 1803, before he had written the *Eroica*, *Fidelio*, or the *Waldstein* Sonata. Whether the solitary path that he chose in music and his increasing physical isolation from the world are connected can remain a matter only for speculation.

Once having turned back to the language of Haydn and Mozart, Beethoven showed an almost wilfully tepid appreciation of most of his contemporaries: Handel appears to have interested him more than any of them. His special contempt was reserved for Rossini: one can easily see why. To have written even the greatest of Rossini's masterpieces before the *Le Comte Ory* only genius was necessary: intellect or hard work hardly entered into it. Rossini's reputation as the laziest of composers was not undeserved. (There should be no mystery about the reasons for his virtual retirement from music at the age of thirty-five: it is the age when the most fluent composer begins to lose the ease of inspiration he once possessed, when even Mozart had to make sketches and to revise.) For Beethoven, whose own compositions were the result of a meditation and a labor almost unparalleled elsewhere in music, the magnificent thoughtlessness of Rossini's work must have been as exasperating to him as Rossini's public triumph in Vienna with a genuine popular success that Beethoven could never equal. 'He needs only as many weeks as the Germans need years to write an opera,' he remarked, with what must have been envy as well as scorn.[1]

Of all his contemporaries Beethoven seems to have preferred one of the most conservative and classicizing of all, Cherubini. When asked who was the greatest living composer after himself, he is said to have replied Cherubini, but not too much weight should be placed on this judgment, as he appears to have had some difficulty in thinking of any name. However, he is known to have greatly admired Cherubini's (and Méhul's) success in writing serious opera: his own struggles and revisions of *Fidelio* made him set a high price upon this achievement. He also respected both Weber and Schubert, the former somewhat unwillingly: at least, he is known to have spoken disdainfully of Weber, and his more admiring comments are reported chiefly by Weber's son. Beethoven's enthusiasm for Schubert is also not well

---

[1] Thayer, vol. II, p. 804.

attested, as the evidence comes chiefly from Schindler in a polemical article defending his own admiration, and Schindler was not only inaccurate but prone to invention when his passions were roused.

None of this need surprise: few composers past a certain age are genuinely interested in anybody's music except their own, unless they find an invention, an idea, or even only a texture that they can use themselves, as Beethoven could use Handel, and Mozart learn from Bach. The most revealing remark of Beethoven's, however, about another composer—revealing about himself, that is—is his crushing verdict on Spohr: 'He is too rich in dissonances, pleasure in his music is marred by his chromatic melody.'[1] If this is exactly what Beethoven said—it was reported in memoirs published only many years later—it shows how deep was his lack of sympathy with the newly arising Romantic style. No one today could find Spohr more dissonant than Beethoven if by dissonance is meant harshness, or even if the more technical sense of an unresolved interval or chord is taken: Beethoven is as rich as any composer in emphatic dissonance of both kinds. What was 'dissonant' in Spohr to Beethoven's ear was evidently a new chromaticism, left insufficiently integrated within a diatonic framework; and it was just this kind of chromaticism which became so essential a part of the music of the 1830s. There are moments when Beethoven is as chromatic as any composer before late Wagner, including Chopin, but the chromaticism is always resolved and blended into a background which ends by leaving the tonic triad absolute master.

It is, in fact, with this fundamental triad that Beethoven attains his most remarkable and characteristic effects. At one point in the G major Piano Concerto, he achieves the seemingly impossible with it and turns this most consonant of chords (into which all dissonance must be, by definition, resolved by the end of the piece) itself into a dissonance. In the following measures, almost by rhythmic means alone and without modulating from G major, the tonic chord of G major *in root position* clearly requires a resolution into the dominant:

---

[1] Thayer, II, p. 956.

The majesty and the excitement combined in measure 27 come from the fact that it is the fundamental chord of the piece that is being held for a full measure after being rendered unstable by the steadily repeated (and increasingly animated) movement into a D major chord.

Withholding the D major chord in measure 27, however, is the source of its power: not only does the G major tonic chord sound unresolved, but reining in its resolution for so long even forces the beautiful resolution in the next measure beyond the D major chord to an A minor triad. The grandeur of the sonority comes from the use only of root positions for all the chords in measures 26 to 28 and the consequent purity and stability of sound[1] in a phrase of extreme instability.

The sudden and complete halt in measure 27 is an act of will. It implies an almost muscular effort that justifies the relaxation of what follows. To encompass this, the animation of the previous measures is essential. The acceleration and the *ritenuto* are completely articulated: the movement of the pattern:

occurs once per measure in 23, twice in 24 and 25, and four times in 26; but in 27 and 28, it is now spread over two measures. The classical conception of increased animation in discrete units of 1, 2, 4, 8, etc., is given its most exemplary form. It is hard to see how the system could have been carried further than Beethoven does here. The Romantic composer rejected it, with some malaise, in favor of a more fluid conception, but Beethoven was absolute master over the classical articulation of rhythmic forces. The occasions when he, too, attempted to go beyond it were very rare.

---

[1] The spacing of the chord and its instrumentation (to discuss one is inevitably to consider the other) serve to reinforce what is said here.

Beethoven

It should be remarked that if, in this passage, the integration of melodic, rhythmic, and harmonic forces is such that they seem indissoluble, the material is not only simple but could not possibly be simpler. The two alternating tonic and dominant chords are the basic chords of any tonal work. The passage quoted is, of course, a transitional one, and serves to introduce the new theme that begins in measure 29. It is also, however, not only the first climactic moment of the work but has thematic significance as well. The two chords are the opening chords of the movement:

heard very shortly before. In short, the climax—the written-out and measured fermata of measure 27—is the opening chord of the work now rendered unstable, or, in other words, transformed into a dynamic element. This is very close to Haydn's practice of charging the openings of his movements with directional force, but no one before Beethoven was able to do this so powerfully with the simple tonic chord in its most fundamental position. And no one since Beethoven could repeat this dramatic effect without weakening the tonic; the fact that the tonic is as powerful as ever—in short, that it remains within the classical language—is proved by the majestic breadth of this whole section.

The use of the simplest elements of the tonal system as themes lay at the heart of Beethoven's personal style from the beginning. It was only little by little, however, that he realized its implications. The traditional division of his music into three periods is not untenable, but it can be as misleading as it is useful. There is no line that can be drawn between the first and second periods, and if there is a clear break in the continuity of his work around the beginning of what is called the third period, the works that contain many of the characteristic new developments belong just before the break as well as after it. When the division into three periods is retained, it should be clear that it is a fiction for the purposes of analysis, a convenience for understanding, and not a biographical reality. The steady development discernible in Beethoven's career is as important as its discontinuities even if these are easier to describe. It is only in comparing works several years apart that the discontinuities assume a demonstrable and persuasive sense.

Beethoven's return to classical principles may be measured by such a discontinuity if one compares the Third Piano Concerto in C minor of 1800 with the Fourth in G major of 1808. Both works rely heavily on Mozart but in entirely different ways. The C minor is full of Mozartean reminiscences,

389

in particular of the concerto in the same key, K. 491, which Beethoven is known to have admired. Most striking is the imitation of the coda of K. 491, with its exceptional use of the solo instrument playing arpeggios at the end of the first movement. Beethoven omits a final ritornello after the cadenza and leaps directly to the coda; the Mozartean arpeggios are made almost melodramatic with timpani playing part of the main theme. In this superbly effective coda, only the arpeggios are not thematic, and this makes their borrowed character all the more apparent. In the development section, a curiously beautiful non-thematic passage also turns out to be inspired by Mozart, this time the B flat Piano Concerto K. 450. But it is the C minor K. 491 again which dominates many of the thematic details, at least of the first movement.

There is, however, nothing genuinely Mozartean about this movement except for the borrowings and the perhaps unconscious reminders. The orchestral tutti which opens the movement is set off from what follows by a full halt and a dramatic fermata; it is almost a complete work by itself, appearing thoroughly self-sufficient. This exaggerated separation, which makes for a relaxed looseness of structure, tends to make the solo exposition a decorated form of the tutti instead of a new and more dramatic conception of the material as in Mozart.[1] It is, in fact, the form of the first two piano concertos as well, and of the concertos of Hummel and the other post-classic composers (including the two concertos of Chopin, both composed before he was twenty). The completely separate introductory orchestral exposition is a characteristic of all these works, and this became an embarrassment when the loose and rambling manner was no longer acceptable to the taste of the early Romantic composers. The response of Schumann and others was to fuse both these expositions into one.

The diffuse forms of the early nineteenth century had clearly become unacceptable to Beethoven as well by 1808, but his solution was a resurrection of Mozart's practice. The Fourth Piano Concerto in G major contains few direct imitations of Mozart in the classicizing, almost academic manner of the earlier works, but the principles of large-scale construction have now become Mozart's, transformed and rendered more fluid. The double sonata exposition of the first three concertos is renounced in favor of the Mozartean ideal of a double presentation, static and dynamic, of the material—the orchestral one introductory and stable, the soloist's in a more dramatic sonata exposition. As in many of Mozart's first movements, the two presentations are welded together, the second interrupting the first with a cadenza-like version of the opening thematic elements. The orchestral exposition remains in the tonic throughout: its only secondary theme has a series of surface modulations

---

[1] Mozart has many opening tutti in the concertos which round themselves off with a cadence, but these tutti have only the completeness of the introduction to an aria, and never of a full sonata exposition.

so rapid that it is difficult to realize that we have never really left G major. As Mozart does in the G major Concerto K. 453, Beethoven obscures what might be too monotonous a unity of key for several pages and then lets the soloist make the decisive move.

Most important of all, Beethoven takes up the conception of the dramatic entrances of the soloist where Mozart had left it, and so realizes some of his own most imaginative ideas. Two of the most original effects in the Fourth Piano Concerto are paradoxically occasions for the only direct references in the work to Mozart. The entrance of the piano in the first measure of the work immediately brings to mind the opening of K. 271, where Mozart has the piano enter in the second measure in direct answer to the opening orchestral motif. Beethoven's opening, at once poetically resonant and reticent, recalls Mozart's only conceptually, but they both result from a similar logic or way of thought. The *Emperor* Concerto also brings in the piano at the opening, but with very different effect, as does the unfinished sketch for a sixth piano concerto in D major: in both these works the soloist enters with a cadenza, postponed in the unfinished concerto until after the first statement in the orchestra of the main theme—an interesting foreshadowing of Brahms. The device obviously interested Beethoven but he never permitted it to alter the classical relation between orchestral and solo expositions.

The second reference to Mozart amounts almost to a quotation: the entrance of the piano at the beginning of the development is directly modeled on the same moment in Mozart's C major Concerto K. 503, quoted on page 257, except that Beethoven closes the slight gap between orchestra and soloist and makes the entrance the occasion for an abrupt change of key, so sudden that it is not immediately intelligible and becomes so only some measures later:

391

The difference between Beethoven and a classicizing composer like Hummel is that Beethoven, particularly after 1804, is inspired by Mozart's most imaginative and most radical conceptions, while Hummel starts from the most normative ones.

The finale of the G major Concerto makes masterful use of the Haydn-esque device of appearing to start in the wrong key, and with all its virtuosity it is closer to Haydn's symphonic finales than to any of the concerto finales of the early 1800s. The episodic rondo form has been tightened and unified, rather than loosened, as it was by other composers of that time. Even the slow movement, perhaps the most dramatically conceived ever written, has its roots in the late eighteenth century: only some of Haydn's slow movements in the quartets and the trios and the slow introduction to the last movement of Mozart's G minor Quintet are so uncompromisingly theatrical. (The second movement of Beethoven's first Concerto in C major is a far more typical example of the common style of the first quarter of the nineteenth century.) The slow movement of the G major Concerto is, in another respect, comparable to the Adagio introduction to the finale of the G minor Quintet: it stays so close to the tonic E minor that it is to be conceived almost as an expanded E minor chord, and is not an independent piece but must be played, by Beethoven's own direction, without a pause before the last movement. Its only short modulation is not to its own dominant but to VII, D major, which is the dominant of the finale. The beginning of the finale *pp* on a chord of C major transcends the Haydnesque idea of a 'false' opening, makes it far more cogent, as it is now a modulation directly out of the E minor of the previous movement back to the G major of the concerto as a whole. Much of the poetry of this slow movement derives from its incomplete nature: it defines and establishes, not itself, but something to come.

The first of Beethoven's immense expansions of classical form is the *Eroica* Symphony, finished in 1804, the same year that produced the *Waldstein* Sonata. The symphony, much longer than any work in that form that preceded it, provoked some displeasure at its first public performance. The critics complained of its inordinate length, and protested against the lack of unity in this most unified of works. This unity is so intense that a cello–oboe duet which is almost always called a new theme in the development is directly derived from the main theme. It is the oboe line that is later dropped, and the cello's motif remains and is transferred to the winds. The relation between the cello line and the main theme is very close:

This is not merely a relationship on paper, but one that is clearly audible if the conductor observes the *sforzandi* as genuine accents and not, as is so often the case, as expressive swells. This small detail is significant here because, while there is an unusual richness of motifs in the first movement, almost every one with a specific melodic character is directly linked to the opening measures. Everyone is immediately aware of the relation to the first theme of the following motifs:

along with many other similar motifs too numerous to cite; but these relationships are far less remarkable than the extraordinary continuity into which they are woven. Partly because of the variety and number of episodes, the exposition does not fall into as simple a sectional form as in the two symphonies that preceded it, and this helped to make the music more painful to grasp at first.

The public, indeed, seems to have been ill-natured at the first performance and the work immediately divided its hearers into two furiously opposed factions. Not only the bitterness of the criticism, but its nature remind one of more recent attacks on what is thought to be the *avant garde*: one critic wrote that Beethoven's 'music could soon reach the point where one would derive no pleasure from it unless well trained in the rules and difficulties of the art, but rather would leave the concert hall . . . crushed by a mass of unconnected and overloaded ideas and a continuing tumult by all the instruments.' It is understandable that the symphony was found so difficult, as the extension of the range of hearing in time is remarkable: the dissonant C♯ in the seventh measure finds its full meaning only much later at the opening of the recapitulation, when it becomes a D♭ and leads to an F major horn solo; yet the unprecedented scope of modulation in the development is carried out without the slightest diffusion of the sense of tonal unity; above all, the proportions are firmly defined.

It is clear that such an increase in size without altering the fundamental classical proportions (the placing of the climax, the ratio of harmonic tension to resolution) could not start from the long, regular and complete melodies of Mozart, but had to base itself on Haydn's treatment of tiny motifs.[1] The short motifs could easily form a tissue of periods essentially much larger than Haydn's with a correspondingly slower harmonic motion, while complete melodies—in order to keep the proportions of period to the whole—would have to be made much longer. This presents a problem for any symphonic style that is to move at a faster pace than Bruckner. For this reason Beethoven is sometimes called a weak melodist, although it is difficult to see how that could ever have been said about the composer of the second movement of the Piano Sonata op. 90, or the minuet of op. 31 no. 3, to mention only two of Beethoven's many long and beautifully regular melodies. Musical ideas that form a complete whole in themselves—tunes, in short—were rarely of any use to Beethoven in his dramatic expansions of Mozart's forms, although Mozart's proportions were most relevant. In the relation of development to recapitulation he more often follows Mozart than Haydn, and his large codas are less an imitation of Haydn, as Tovey thought, than the restoration of a Mozartean balance.

Haydn's codas, at least in his later years, are inextricably fused, even tangled with his recapitulations: Beethoven's, like Mozart's, are often separate, articulated entities. They are generally preceded by tonic cadences, and their most immediate analogues are the last numbers of a Mozart opera finale: like them, they saturate the ear with the tonic chord. The astonishingly long coda to the first movement of the *Eroica* (astonishing by previous standards, although completely logical and expected by its own) serves to ground the extreme tension of the development, which was not only long but far-ranging harmonically; the coda, in fact, balances the development. Starting with the initial tension of juxtaposing powerfully spaced and orchestrated chords of D flat major and C major, without any explanatory modulation, he soon goes briefly through a series of keys of basically subdominant character, the relative minor in particular. From there we arrive at one of the longest tonic cadences ever written, pages of nothing but V–I repeated over and over. It is certain that the lyrical alterations at the opening of the recapitulation along with its traditional move to the tonic were not sufficient to counteract the climax of the development, and that this enormous tonic cadence in the coda is necessary to give the movement a satisfactorily closed form.

---

[1] Except for the songs, the early works of Schubert (like all the piano music of Weber and Hummel) start from the long Mozartean melody while greatly expanding the size of Mozart's forms, with the result of a breakdown in rhythmic tension never found in Beethoven.

The length of the movement being so unusual, Beethoven briefly thought of omitting the repeat of the exposition: he finally decided the repeat was essential. Without it, as we still sometimes hear the symphony played, the exposition is dwarfed by what follows. The question of repeats is often grasped by the wrong end of the stick: that of contemporary practice. Unfortunately no distinction is generally made between what was approved and what one could get away with—the distinction between morality and law, in fact, and it is a pity in such matters to decide legalistically. It might be said that there is almost no possible desecration of a classical work that is not sanctified by a tradition dating back to the composer's lifetime. Beethoven's friends indignantly reported to him a performance of the Fifth Symphony which went from the C major Trio of the scherzo directly into the pedal point of the transition to the finale.

A better basis for decision would be the question of significance (and in the classical style, proportions are an essential part of meaning); even if it becomes longer, a work can only gain in interest if it makes more sense. There is no rule: some repeats are dispensable, others absolutely necessary; some succeed in clarifying what is only half-intelligible without them. The development sections of the Sonatas op. 31 nos. 1 and 2 both begin with the opening measures of the exposition: if the repeat of the exposition is carried out, and the circular form heard in its entirety, the new turning of the development after a few measures becomes only more effective. The use of repeats is, in fact, transformed during the classical period, and is carried by Beethoven far beyond the point to which Mozart and Haydn had brought it.

The repeat during the Baroque period is a way of accenting the regularity of a dance-form; repeating an entire piece as a unit only serves to continue the dance, but repeating each half separately emphasizes its symmetry. In Bach, particularly in the *Goldberg* Variations, the end of each section—moving back to the beginning or forward to the second (or concluding) half—is the occasion of much subtlety. In the third quarter of the eighteenth century, the repeat was above all the opportunity for expressive ornamentation, for the display of sentiment or virtuosity (they are more closely related than is sometimes thought, and both of them were realized through traditional decorative figures). It is largely in the music of Haydn and Mozart after 1775 that structure replaced ornamentation as the principal vehicle of expression. The repeats (particularly in the first movements, the slow movements always retaining some of their ornamental character) then became above all an essential part of the proportions, the balance of tonal areas, and of the interplay of harmonic tensions. It makes a great deal of difference to the effect of the last movement of Mozart's G minor Symphony if the second and more dramatic half is repeated (as it so rarely is in performance today) as well as the expository first half. In Haydn, where the direction of tonal movement is perhaps even more important than its weight, a repeat will entirely change the significance of a section: many of Haydn's opening phrases have a new sound, a different force when they are heard returning from a dominant cadence. Beethoven, who after 1804 dispensed with the traditional repeats as often as not, used them when he did in such a way that they add significance and weight (as in Haydn and Mozart), and yet concentrated and extended their effect so that their omission either falsifies the sense of what follows, as in the Sonatas op. 31 nos. 1 and 3, or even, as in the *Hammerklavier*, makes the transition to the development illogical.

A similar concentration and, at the same time, expansion of Haydn's way of letting the music grow dynamically from a small kernel, or central idea, is found increasingly in Beethoven's music. It is even more tempting in Beethoven's case to think of this central idea in exclusively linear terms and even more dangerous: this often works magnificently on paper and strays far from what can actually be heard. For example, all the themes of the first movement of the *Waldstein* Sonata without exception can be related easily in linear terms, as they all move in stepwise fashion, are all based on scale progressions. Some of these linear relationships are indeed audible because they have been made so by Beethoven, and are a part of the discursive logic of the surface. Nevertheless, the music hardly ever moves in a purely linear fashion, and listening with a totally innocent ear is no worse than accepting a theory which obscures more than it enlightens.

The first movement of the *Waldstein* Sonata has a characteristic sound, not only unlike the music of other composers, but unlike any other work of Beethoven, an energetic hardness, dissonant and yet curiously plain, expressive without richness. It is the consistent harmonic interpretations of the stepwise progressions that give this movement its specific character. In each phrase of the themes, every second chord is a dominant seventh:

a)

Beethoven

b)

c)

d)

The dominant seventh is the plainest, the most neutral of dissonances; its relentless alternation in scale progression with pure triads invests this movement with its particular sonority and invades every phrase. It immediately provides the first climax from measure 9 on, with a spacing of the hands that brutally emphasizes its character. (A work of Mozart or Haydn has a sonority as characteristic as one of Beethoven's, but rarely so concisely and so concentratedly individual.) I do not mean that the central idea of the *Waldstein* can be entirely reduced to this simple but pervasive alternation of triads and dominant sevenths, but it is enough to show that the idea cannot be described in purely linear terms.

The *Waldstein* also establishes its themes in a genetic order; that is, they appear to be born one from another even more than in Haydn's technique of thematic derivation, although the method is not very different. The descending fifth outlined in the fourth measure (itself an expanded echo of the third

397

measure) produces the right hand of what will become the fourth or closing theme[1] quoted above:

It is only on paper, however, that we can identify this with the descending fifth outlined more slowly by the opening of the 'second group' (mm. 35–36): they are only distantly related, as the descent of the second theme is more directly presented as an inversion of the rising motion of the first three measures of the movement. This relationship is forced on our attention by the transition to the second theme:

where the rising third of the opening theme is used as the beginning of an ascending scale in the bass, of which the new theme, *dolce e molto ligato*, is an inversion and a clear balancing movement. (The descending fifth in the first theme (measure 4) is also an answer and a balance to the rising motion of the first three measures, so the indirect relationship is nevertheless one that contributes to the unity of conception in this movement.)

The pulsating energy in this work is perhaps its most remarkable innovation. Description in purely rhythmic terms, however, will not do. Part of the energy comes from the immediate recourse to modulation in the second measure. There is not the slightest obscurity about key and the effect has nothing in common with Haydn's 'false' starts. What the widening of the

---

[1] The left hand of this fourth theme comes directly and obviously from the second theme.

harmonic range at the outset enables Beethoven to do is to expand the time-scale of his music as well. To establish a key in almost all music from 1700 to 1800 is to present the tonic and dominant in their proper relationship to each other, that is, by at least an implied or passing resolution on the tonic. In spite of the fact that there is no tonal ambiguity, it takes the entire first thirteen measures of the *Waldstein* Sonata to define the key of C major. Except in cases where a deliberate mystification is intended (as in Haydn's pun at the opening of op. 33 no. 1) or where there is an introduction (which often retards a decisive resolution on the tonic by resolving towards the dominant as an harmonic up-beat), no work of Haydn or Mozart can delay tonic stability for so long. The greater breadth of Beethoven's harmonic movement and the larger scale on which he worked provides the steady energy and excitement of the opening rhythm with a controlling framework. What this entails is combining Haydn's technique of dynamic growth from the smallest details with Mozart's feeling for large harmonic masses and for tonal areas. This is why Beethoven can so often appear at once more dramatic and more stable than Haydn.

The development by Beethoven of a unity of conception, rhythmic and harmonic as well as thematic, very close to the concepts of Haydn and Mozart although on a larger scale takes shape during the years 1804–6. In 1803, the *Kreutzer* Sonata has a first movement unequalled in formal clarity, grandeur, and dramatic force by anything that Beethoven had yet written; the beautiful slow movement, however, a set of variations in F major, belongs to a totally different style, elegant, brilliant, ornamental, and a little precious, the style of the F major Variations for Piano, op. 34, without the latter's original harmonic scheme and dramatic contrasts, but with a more artistic care for detail; the finale, a light and brilliant tarantella, was written for another sonata altogether. Beethoven never again presented such a hybrid as one work. For the slow movement of the *Waldstein*, in 1804, he had originally written a rondo in a style very similar to the variations of the *Kreutzer*, but replaced it with the far more suitable half-slow-movement half-introduction-to-the-finale that now stands there. The next year, 1805, with the *Appassionata*, he finally arrived at a conception of a sonata where all three movements have been formulated as one. (The tradition of playing a Beethoven sonata without pausing between the movements is an old one, at least as old as von Bülow, and whether it is correct or not,[1] it is a response to an important element in Beethoven's style.) The years 1804–6 represent a growth in artistic conscience for Beethoven. They were years of consolidation in all fields: the first version of *Fidelio* and the Quartets op. 59 were written then, as well as the *Eroica*, the Fourth Piano Concerto, the *Waldstein* and the *Appassionata*.

It might be said that the *Appassionata*, the most concise of all these, is a

---

[1] I am not, of course, discussing the cases where Beethoven expressly directs that no pause be made.

cautious work in one important respect: the opening movement is almost rigidly symmetrical in spite of its violence, as if only the simplest and most unyielding of frames could contain such power. This kind of prudence is typical of the most revolutionary works: suppleness comes only when experiment has succeeded. The first movement of the *Appassionata* falls into four clear sections: all of them (exposition, development, recapitulation, and coda) begin with the main theme; the recapitulation follows the thematic pattern of the exposition with the minimum of alteration necessary to return the second group in the tonic; both the development and the coda conform to this pattern by playing the thematic material they select in the order set forth in the exposition; in addition, the development and the coda have very similar structures, except for the final Più allegro at the end.

The violence is achieved simply and efficiently. The most original and remarkable moment is another of Beethoven's uses of the tonic chord: the harmony at the beginning of the recapitulation is naturally a tonic chord, but in six-four position—that is, with a dominant pedal pulsating continuously, which turns an important moment of resolution into a long-sustained, menacing dissonance. The pathetic harmonies of the Neapolitan chord are used with great fierceness throughout, pervading all the thematic material, and culminating in the harsh pedal blurring of the minor second D♭–C at the climax just before the Più allegro. The rising bass of the development, as Tovey pointed out, creates an excitement unknown in music before then. The control of complex rhythmic effect is more impressive than ever before. The exposition moves from the disjunctive phrases of the opening, balancing rhythmic and harmonic tension as the movement grows more animated until the harsh and turbulent closing theme, which is not in the relative major but decisively in the minor of the relative major. Almost all of Mozart's and Haydn's works in minor color the relative major of the second group with this minor mode, but neither of them had gone so far as to close an exposition with it: once again, in this work, Beethoven extended classical harmonic language without violating its spirit. It is evident that, in 1805, the classical style was not yet exhausted, and that its framework was still serviceable. Only in this sense do styles appear to develop according to a logic of their own, but it is useless to ask if the conclusions waiting to be developed would have been so without Beethoven. It would also be a mistake to ignore other pressures on Beethoven's development, in spite of their lesser importance.

Three examples of these different pressures of musical style and taste may be mentioned: the Thirty-two Variations in C minor, *Wellington's Victory*, and *An die ferne Geliebte*. The C minor Variations for Piano, written in 1806, quickly became popular. As the only set to take up the Baroque form again, it stands apart from all Beethoven's other variations. It is, stylistically, a remarkably prescient work as well, a forecast of the revival of Baroque rhythmic development and harmonic movement that was to produce

Romanticism, or its musical form. The piece was to become the basis for Mendelssohn's *Variations Sérieuses*. Beethoven's set follows Handel's passacaglia form closely, imposing only a classically articulated sense of climax within the phrase and over the series of variations, as the first generation of Romantic composers were to do. Its immediate popularity testifies to the direction in which music and taste was moving. Beethoven was not happy about this essay in early Romanticism, professing later to be ashamed of it.

Wellington's Victory of 1813 is so frankly a potboiler that shame would have been of little comfort, and Beethoven, reproached for it during his lifetime, indignantly put the best possible face on it. It is in large part not by him at all, but by Mälzel, who was responsible for the structure, many of the ideas, and even, it seems, some of the actual writing. It was, in fact, originally written for Mälzel's mechanical organ and only later, again at Mälzel's suggestion, orchestrated and performed. Descriptive pieces of this kind were not new; their history goes back several centuries, at least to Jannequin. Yet the combination of descriptive realism in music with the stimulation of enthusiasm and excitement (in this case, of the patriotic variety) begins to be important in music after the French Revolution. The persuasive excitement envisaged by Beethoven's potpourri is, perhaps, more progressive than its realism, and leads in the direction of what was to become one of the most important Romantic genres, the programmatic symphony. Beethoven's contribution lacks the serious pretentiousness or the incorporation of ideology of Mendelssohn's *Reformation Symphony*, or of Berlioz' *Symphonie Funèbre et Triomphale*, but it is only the less interesting for its modesty. It was, ironically, the composer's greatest popular success.

The kind of evocative and nervous realism in *Wellington's Victory* should not be equated with the descriptive effects of the Sixth Symphony, which, as Beethoven himself wrote, is 'a matter more of feeling than of painting in sounds.' The *Pastoral* is, for the most part, a true classical symphony strongly influenced by the then fashionable doctrine of art as the painting of feelings or sentiments, a philosophy better suited to the music of the 1760s (and before) than to the dramatic style that succeeded it. An aesthetic doctrine is more often unconsciously a codification or even a rear-guard action than a reflection of current practice: the works precede the doctrine. Beethoven's *Pastoral*, however, has not only a certain ambiguity, but a decided split in its expressive position: the moments of outspoken realism are naïve rather than evocative (the birds and the thunder and lightning, for example, go far beyond anything Haydn had ever written in his descriptive effects), and they intrude rather than blend with the mood-painting. It cannot be said that this contradiction affects the beauty of the work: the mood-painting is contained easily within a classical symphonic structure organized as dramatically as ever; even the realistic bird-calls are presented as a solo cadenza, almost a final trill, so that their heterogeneous relation to the rest of the movement passes as easily as the 'improvised' cadenza of a concerto. Nevertheless, there is a loss of unity of tone; if one compares Beethoven's Sixth with the more obviously 'pastoral' works of Haydn (the symphony *The Bear*, for instance, or *The Seasons*), one sees that the less stylized realism, the substitution of nature for rusticity, and the more obvious mood-painting in Beethoven have both coarsened and sentimentalized a genre, and that the loss of a delicate balance is only compensated for by Beethoven's magnificently lyric energy. The five-movement structure is sometimes noted as a forecast of later Romantic experiments (like Berlioz' *Symphonie Fantastique*), but this is an illusion; Beethoven's fourth movement has no independent existence, but is treated as an expanded introduction to the finale as in Mozart's G minor Quintet. Nothing in the language or the structure of the *Pastoral* can be related in any meaningful way to the later programmatic works concerning outdoor life of Raff, Goldmark, and Richard Strauss,

An die ferne Geliebte, however, is a work which not only steps outside the classical aesthetic, but which also had a deep and genuine influence upon the music of the generation immediately after Beethoven's death. In this cycle of songs, it is astonishing that Beethoven goes even beyond Schubert to the open and circular form of Schumann. The last phrase of the cycle is the only ending in Beethoven so inconclusive, so obviously implying a continuation. Since this last phrase is also the opening phrase of the cycle, the effect of open, unending form is only the more compelling:

There are many lengthy songs by Schubert which are more a string of separate *Lieder* than one single work, but the problems of continuity and articulation among the different sections are very loosely handled; and Schubert's large cycles are sets of independent songs each one of which makes sense by itself and can stand alone, even if it gains in depth from being placed in context. The individual songs of *An die ferne Geliebte*, however, like many of those in Schumann's cycles, cannot stand by themselves; at several points Beethoven has tried to blend the rhythms of one with those of the next song and make the transition almost imperceptible. Schumann's conception is at once simpler and more subtle; although each song of his cycles appears to be complete in itself, many are impossible to conceive outside their setting, and cannot be heard as significantly independent pieces. In this way, Schumann arrives at a series of genuinely open forms, and by seeming to accept the divisions annuls them, as Beethoven never succeeds in doing. Nevertheless, Beethoven's set stands as the first example of what was the most original and perhaps the most important of Romantic forms.

An die ferne Geliebte was written in 1816, towards the end of a crisis in Beethoven's musical development; since 1812 he had composed nothing of importance except the sonatas for cello op. 102 nos. 1 and 2, and for piano op. 90 and op. 101. The revision of *Fidelio* and the composition of a fine *pièce d'occasion*, the Overture *Zur Namensfeier*, also took place during this time, but the rest amounts to a handful of canons and other short pieces. This is not a poor harvest, but it seems meager compared to that of the years both before and after this period. The slim production of this time cannot be ascribed to the usual slowing-down due to age, as the prodigality of the years from 1818 on would then be difficult to explain. It is possible that this crisis was accompanied by one in Beethoven's personal life (the famous letter to the unknown Immortal Beloved can be dated 1812), but a biographical explanation of this kind does nothing to elucidate the rare musical experiments that broke the silence of the period. Not only *An die ferne Geliebte*, but also the cello sonatas and the Sonata for Piano op. 101, show a development towards openly cyclic form, a tendency that was abandoned later.[1] In addition, the Piano Sonata op. 101 begins as if in the middle of a musical paragraph; in other words, here is an essay in, or at least a movement towards, the open forms of the Romantic period, even if the harmonic language retains the firmly closed nature of the classical style. The harmonic structure of the finale of op. 101 has an unclassical looseness that brings it close to many works of Mendelssohn. The exposition is as classical as any other of Beethoven's, but the development consists entirely of a fugue, its opening is completely detached from what precedes, and it remains in the tonic minor throughout. This is a way of evading classical tension (harmonically here) and reaching the relaxed expansion of large Romantic forms. This is also true of the Sonata op. 90, where, after a despairing and impassioned first movement, laconic almost to the point of reticence, a moderately slow, *cantabile* rondo follows, symmetrical, relaxed, and with an exquisitely beautiful, squarely regular theme that is repeated many times without the slightest abridgement and is varied only at the end by placing the melody in another register. This loose, melodically centered structure was to become a standard Schubertian form,[2] and it is, indeed, typical of the post-classical style from

---

[1] The passages which return from earlier movements in the finale of the Ninth Symphony are not only presented as quotations, but completely isolated within a new context, while the return of the opening in op. 101 and the song cycle are much more integrated into the discourse. (The reference to the first movement in the finale of the Quartet op. 131, is neither a return in cyclic form nor a quotation, but a result of a new conception of the unity of the musical material in a work in several movements.)

[2] This is not the only foreshadowing of Schubert in Beethoven, the Minuet of the Trio op. 70 no. 2 in E flat major being even more remarkable, but the rondo of op. 90 is the only work of Beethoven after 1804 to use this loose and melodically based large form.

1800 on, but such a degree of squareness is very rare in Beethoven, and in no other piece does he rely on the unaltered repetition of a long melody to bear so much of the expressive weight.

During this time when it was so difficult for him to complete a work, it was as if the classical sense of form appeared bankrupt to him, spurring him to search for a new system of expression. In the preceding years from 1807 to 1812, he had written four symphonies (5 through 8), the Mass in C, the Piano Trios op. 70 nos. 1 and 2, and op. 97, the Cello Sonata op. 69, the Quartets op. 74 and 95, and the *Emperor* Concerto. These works are a formidable series which may well have seemed to exhaust beyond renewal the style and the tradition he worked in; it may be only an accident that this musical crisis coincided with a personal one, or we may even surmise that it was artistic exhaustion and despair that provoked the turmoil in his personal life. 'Art demands always something new from us,' he once said to an admirer of an early work. Except for *An die ferne Geliebte*, the Romantic experiments are only tentative: neither classical tonality nor classical proportions are really abandoned except in details. Yet it is in the rare works of this period that Beethoven is closest to the generation that followed his death.

The decision to continue with the more purely classical forms was, in its way, heroic. The act of will was marked by the composition of the *Hammerklavier* Sonata, which took him the two years of 1817 and 1818. He declared that it was to be his greatest. It is not, however, a work that sums up a lifetime of experience, a compendium of art, like the late works of Bach, but a demonstration of power, a gesture. By contemporary standards, it was monstrously long and scandalously difficult: Czerny wrote in Beethoven's conversational scrapbook that a lady in Vienna who had been practicing for months complained that she still could not play the beginning of the sonata. With this work, the emancipation of piano music from the demands of the amateur musician was made official, with a consequent loss of responsibility and a greater freedom for the imagination. Even so, Beethoven said later that he felt constricted by the limitations of the piano, although there is no reason for the claim (now happily out of fashion) that he ever calculated without those limits when writing for the keyboard. The opening of the *Hammerklavier*, which sounds so feeble and ineffective in any orchestral transcription, is gigantic on the piano.

The new, almost obsessive, clarity of this work released the fertility of imagination which had been held back for so long; if no important new work followed immediately, that was only because Beethoven had begun work on the *Missa Solemnis*, which he hoped, vainly, to finish in time for Archduke Rudolph's installation as cardinal-archbishop. Between 1819 and 1824, he completed three immense works (the D major Mass, the *Diabelli* Variations, and the Ninth Symphony) along with the three last piano sonatas; in the remaining two years of his life he composed five string quartets. The *Hammer-*

klavier had pointed the way to this renewed activity, and in the severity of its treatment it put an end to experiments with more loosely constructed, open patterns. The apparently freely expanded forms of the late quartets are closely tied to the severity of the *Hammerklavier* and to its clarity of definition. They start from its principles, transforming and reworking them, rather than from the experimental works of 1813–16, although it would be a mistake to set these completely apart from what followed (the D major Cello Sonata, for example, adumbrates many ideas that reach maturity only in the op. 106). The last works are most precisely related to the *Hammerklavier* above all in their extreme concentration of material.

The sets of bagatelles that Beethoven wrote in the early 1820s are sometimes considered as rejected sketches for larger works, ideas too simple to be developed. In reality, the fundamental material of many of the bagatelles is more complex, even at times richly so, than the material of the larger works. It may almost be stated as a rule in Beethoven that the longer the work the simpler the material that goes into it. Both the range and the length of the *Diabelli* Variations were made possible by the existence of a theme with primitive virtues (which is not to say that they are not indeed virtues). The forms of late Beethoven descend clearly and directly from Haydn's technique of allowing the music to grow out of a small kernel, the simplest, most condensed of musical thoughts announced, generally, at the very opening. During what is called his 'third period,' Beethoven extended this technique far beyond any limits that could previously have been imagined.

To what an extent a composer can describe his working habits is more dependent on chance, the right interviewer, or an irrelevant talent with words than upon any distinction between reason and instinct. On at least one occasion, nevertheless, Beethoven put into words something about the interplay between the central musical idea and the total form of his works. Speaking to a young musician from Darmstadt, Louis Schlösser, he is supposed to have said: 'The working-out in breadth, length, height and depth begins in my head, and since I am conscious of what I want, the basic idea never leaves me. It rises, grows upward, and I hear and see the picture as a whole take shape and stand forth before me as though cast in a single piece, so that all that is left is the work of writing it down.'[1] These words were published more than fifty years after they may have been spoken; it is perhaps unwise to put too much faith in the exactitude of the reporting. The suggestion that a work was finished in his head before he began to write certainly does not tally with what we know of Beethoven's voluminous sketches through all stages of a piece, but it is by no means certain that he would not so have represented his methods of composing to a young visitor. In any case, the phrase about conceiving the work in several dimensions, working it out 'in

---

[1] Thayer, vol. II, p. 851. (The conversation took place during the period when Beethoven was working on the Ninth Symphony.)

breadth, length, height and depth,' is striking enough to make it likely that this was really a phrase of Beethoven's that would remain in the memory.

The conception of a work as a whole, and in a way that brought the details and the larger structure together more intimately than in the music of any other composer, is reflected in Beethoven's working procedures. He not only sketched extensively and exhaustively, but (as Lewis Lockwood has shown[1]) he began to make a sketch in full score of an orchestral piece— laying out all the measures, writing out the subsidiary details as well—even before the thematic material had reached its final state. This was a manner of working that he used at least by 1815, if not consistently. In Beethoven's music, one can literally speak of the basic material and the final shape being worked out together, in constant interdependence.

This growth from a central idea had been used by Beethoven before 1817 to determine, not only the entire thematic development of a movement, but also (to a much greater extent than in Haydn or Mozart) the texture of a work, its rhythm, spacing, thickness—as the *Waldstein* is dominated by the constant dominant seventh chords, the pulsating rhythms, and the descending scale a fifth long, the *Appassionata* by its insistent rhythms, its Neapolitan harmonies, and its repeated climaxes on a D♭.

Beethoven's power of thematic transformation, his ability to make much of little, was already astonishing. For example, both halves of the second theme of the Fifth Symphony are constructed out of the same small pattern:

so that the second half is a decorated form of the first, with the appoggiaturas making a contrast out of a unity. The four-note pattern that lies at the basis of this theme is already itself only an augmentation (in intervalic range, not in time) of the four-note pattern of the opening

so that what originally covers a fourth is stretched out over an octave. (Every composer before serialism played with the shapes of his themes, abstracting them from the exact pitches; only during the first three decades of twelve-tone music did pitch exert so absolute a tyranny that it deprived shape of its importance.)

---

[1] 'On Beethoven's Sketches and Autographs: Some Problems of Definition and Interpretation,' *Acta Musicologica* Vol. XLII, 1970, Fasc. II-I, Januar–Juni, Basel.

Beethoven

Starting with the *Hammerklavier*, Beethoven extended Haydn's technique to large-scale harmonic structure. Not only the development of the tensions implicit in the musical ideas, but also the actual course of their resolution is now more fully determined by the material itself. Put less teleologically, not only the discursive melodic shape but the large harmonic forms as well have become thematic, and derive from a central and unifying idea.

In the *Hammerklavier*, the use of descending thirds is almost obsessive, ultimately affecting every detail in the work. Chains of descending thirds (and their twins, ascending sixths) are, of course, common throughout tonal music: Brahms' Fourth Symphony is based on such a chain, and I have given examples above (pp. 283–5) of the importance of similar sequences in Mozart's D major Quintet. There is a relentless succession of descending thirds and rising sixths near the end of the first movement of Mozart's *Hunt* Quartet K. 458:

and the chain continues for some measures in ever greater contrapuntal complexity. Examples could be multiplied indefinitely. It is interesting to note that the opening of Beethoven's Fifth Symphony was originally sketched as such a chain of descending thirds.[1]

---

[1] Cited in Thayer, vol. I, p. 431.

The use of these chains in the language of tonality is many-sided. They are central in that they start by defining a triad.[1] In addition, as the example from Mozart shows, they provide the easiest way of writing a canon, and of thickening the contrapuntal texture, as every note in such a group forms a consonance with the two preceding, and the two following, notes. Haydn uses a very long chain of them at the climax of the finale of the Symphony no. 88. The counterpoint is child's play, but the energy is masterly:

---

[1] A triad is made up of a major and a minor third, and this asymmetry of classical harmony considerably enlarges the possibilities of a string of descending thirds. Our ear accepts, as part of the conventions of the language, a semi-identification of a major and a minor third in such a series, but also accepts a descent of minor thirds alone, which outline a dissonance and can be used to initiate a modulation.

and this example also reveals another useful characteristic of descending thirds, the possibility of forming a variety of harmonic sequences.

The kind of sequence achieved depends upon the placing of the rising sixth within the series of descending thirds: in the example above, Haydn gets magnificent rhythmic surprises by varying the grouping—a rhythmic device which has no name in musical terminology, and which we may call the rhythm of melodic pattern. The beginning of the excerpt from Haydn, however, groups the descending thirds in threes and creates a rising sequence, since the lowest note of each group continues to rise. To group them by fours, as Mozart begins above, is a way of producing a descending harmonic sequence of a common Baroque character: Verdi, in the 'Libera Me' from the *Requiem*, has a fugue which starts with descending thirds,

and the soprano soloist enters with a derived, falling sequence of thirds almost exactly the same as Mozart's Baroque progression:

Both the rising and falling sequences based on descending thirds are important in the *Hammerklavier*, and with them Beethoven realizes opposed kinds of motion with almost identical material.[1]

The development section[2] of the *Hammerklavier* uses sequences of descending thirds as almost its only method of construction, and concentrates on them with a determination and a fury previously unheard in music:

---

[1] Chains of rising thirds are much less frequent than descending thirds in tonal music. They would seem to be useful since they also define triads, but grouping them in threes sounds like parallel fifths and in fours like parallel sevenths: this is because the first note of a rising series continues to function as a bass for what follows it, and influences the fundamental harmony even after its release.

[2] The structure of the first movement may be summarized as follows:

Establishment of B flat major by the single rising and falling thirds of the opening theme and by definition of the octave space B♭–B♭.

G major (second group): chain of descending thirds in thematic form, and opposition of B♭–B♮ affirmed.

E flat major (development): complete exposition of sequence of falling thirds and modulation to B major.

Resolution by modulating through the subdominant direction (G flat major as flat submediant) to B minor, and reduction of B♭–B♮ and F♯–F♮ oppositions to the murmur of a trill.

The development has taken over the major task of exposition, which is why I begin this analysis with it. The progressive revelation of the material is the basis for the musical drama. (The second movement also follows this form.) The structure was a major innovation for Beethoven: when he had finished the *Hammerklavier* he said about it, 'Now I know how to write music.'

410

411

What determines the energy is not only the melodic rhythm or the changes of harmonic rhythm (with the enormous harmonic *ritenuto* towards the end of the passage), but also the rate of speed at which the thirds descend, and the change in their movement at cadences. The sequence of thirds starts as an interacting double sequence; that is why the answer of the fugato opening is at the subdominant, so that one sequence of descending thirds makes a descending sequence in canon with the other, while both retain their integrity. The double chain of thirds becomes a more complex and more exciting quadruple chain in measure 156 and even more emphatically in measure 167. The movement of thirds becomes very slow in measure 177, as does the harmonic rhythm, and comes to a dead halt at measure 191 with a pedal point on D that lasts a full ten measures.

The last descent of a third from D to B at measures 200–201 is the most important of all; after the long pause on D, this descent changes the key, and modulates—enharmonically, without warning and with a magical sonority—to B major. This is perhaps Beethoven's greatest innovation in structure; the large modulations are built from the same material as the smallest detail, and set off in such a way that their kinship is immediately audible. After the endless sequences of thirds, the slower movement and the pause, this modulation appears only as the last and inevitable step of the process; the pause before it only sets it in relief, and signifies that it is a descending third of a different nature, one which changes the tonal framework. We can see why one seems to *hear* structure in the late works of Beethoven as in the music of no other composer.

This modulation is only one step of the large structure of the first movement, and every major structural event is a descent of a third. The changes of key signature correspond exactly to the successive events:

B flat major	Opening themes	} Exposition
G major	'Second group'	
E flat major	Opening of development	
B major	End of development	

which is a triple descent by thirds to a point tonally remote from the tonic. The opposition between B♭ and B♮ arrived at in such a way creates an immense tension that can be resolved in the recapitulation only by extraordinary means.

The return to B flat major at the beginning of the recapitulation is so brutally abrupt as to resolve none of the tension at all. There is an almost immediate descent of another third to G flat major, which is related to B flat major as a key of subdominant character, and balances and resolves the G major of the exposition. But G flat (F sharp) major is also the dominant of B major, which is the heart of the unresolved tension. After a page in G flat major, the magnetic force of the still unresolved tension of B♮ on G♭ (F♯) is finally realized by an explosion:

and this time it is *B minor* (!), even more remote from B flat major than the B major of the development, which had at least the relation of a pathetic Neapolitan chromaticism. After this climax, there is an exhausted descent (by thirds) to F, the dominant of B flat, and the rest of the movement continues firmly in the tonic. This is the greatest example of a climax placed after, instead of just before, the beginning of the recapitulation; it is only in a work of considerable dramatic ambition that it can be so effective.

This large structure is derived from the thematic material (or the themes are derived from the structure—Beethoven's method of composition makes both formulations equally valid). The descending thirds and the resultant clash between B♭ and B♮ are the governing factors. The beginning of the 'second group' is derived from the falling thirds:

The continuity of the series of descending thirds is emphasized here by Beethoven: the ascending sixths are always doubled at the octave below by the descending third, so that the equivalence is stressed and the movement uninterrupted. (This form of doubling produces an ascending harmonic sequence that rises much faster than the grouping by threes cited above.) The harmonic movement here is once again obsessive, except for the interruption of a cadence after which the melody starts again. The thirds shift from the melody to the bass; at the moment of the shift the direction of the harmonic sequence changes from a rising to a falling motion as the familiar Baroque

415

progression appears. The ascending sequence balanced by the succeeding downward harmonic movement gives this melody its familiar classical symmetry. The two indications of *rubato* (*poco ritard.*) mark the articulation of the structure (the first at the interruption of the chain of thirds, and the second at the shift from the melody to the bass line) and show the expressive sensitivity of the sequence. The sudden doubling of the speed of the thirds at the end carries the line over into what follows.

The most important of the themes at the end of the exposition derives from the clash between B♭ and B♮:[1]

---

[1] When this theme appears in the recapitulation, the B♭–B♮ becomes D♭–D♮, but Beethoven is less interested in the major–minor sound than the B♭–B♮ clash, and he accordingly changes the inner voice here to bring it out:

and the clash here inspires an analogous one between E♭ and E♮ in the two phrases. This contrast has already been prepared a few bars before in a magnificent arabesque at the end of the theme quoted above:

and Beethoven's accents make certain we hear this clash. In these two passages, the major–minor (or flat–natural) opposition engenders a true pathos that appears rarely elsewhere in the movement.

The main theme, with a dynamic opposition of *forte* and *piano* that is a standard classical opening, defines the interval of a third in both a rising and then descending form over the whole range of the piano:

so that all the principal themes of the movement are related closely to the larger plan. Measures 5 to 8, indeed, outline exactly the same thematic shape as the two heroic fanfares of the first four measures, but this shape is now softened, conciliated, and united in a gradual swell. The rhythmic unity of the movement appears in this softer version, which already announces the rhythm ♫ | ♩♩♩ of the first G major theme cited above, page 415. A significant element in these measures is the gradual introduction of the accidentals of the B major to come (B♮, F♯, and E♮) into the tonic B flat major. The long-range clash of B♭–B♮ is prepared from the beginning.

To reinforce the framework of this opposition and hold it firmly, the next phrase melodically defines an octave from B♭ to B♭, and ranges from the highest to the lowest B♭ on Beethoven's keyboard:

while the long, sinuous bass line still insists on the F# (or G♭). It is the power-ful and insistently diatonic sound of B flat major against the harsh, chromatic and non-pathetic alterations of B major that gives this movement a sonority unlike any other, and it dominates every page. The following phrase shows how far the ordinary progressions of a normally diatonic B flat major are already contaminated by the B major which still lies in the future:

This is less a preparation than an overflow from the later tension into every corner of the work.

The modulation down a third to G major is as abrupt and rapid as possible:

and is tempered only by graceful strings of descending thirds:

where the left hand now develops the opening third of the main theme rhythmically.

G major already has the B♮ that clashes with the B♭, and the ending of the exposition exploits this to the full:

To hear this ambiguity, the repeat of the exposition is essential. When the B♭ is heard in the first ending's context of G major (measure 121), it is a shock. The B♮ of the second ending is an equal, or even greater shock, but only if the first ending has already made its mark. Not only does this effect incomparably clarify the structure, but it has a dramatic force that no pianist should wish to miss.

This harsh opposition dominates the coda, from the dissonant inner trill of its opening:

(where the B♮ is written as C♭) to the later and even harsher written-out bass trills of F♯/G♭–F♮, which combines with fragments of the opening theme:

and which continue till the end of the movement. The sonority created is dissonant but without pathos, and that is why many people, even musicians, have found the *Hammerklavier* disagreeable. Nevertheless, the characteristic sound is charged with an immense vitality.

The pervasive sonority and the structure that creates it can remove two stumbling blocks in discussions of the movement; the metronome marking, and the famous A♯/A♮ of the transition to the recapitulation:

I used to believe that the A♯ of measure 225 was correct, but I now think that Beethoven probably forgot to add a natural. Tovey also believed that it should be A♮, but that the misprint was a stroke of genius! He was surely right; the A♯ would fit the sound of the movement better, and I suspect that Beethoven's musical subconscious caused the error. Critics are always going on about the importance of instinct in composition, and a slip of the pen would be the most convincing proof of its operation and guidance.

The textual evidence for the A♮ is not, however, as strong as some writers would have us believe; the sketch by Beethoven proves nothing, as he made far more radical changes between sketch and final version. I have heard it asserted by a fine pianist that the A♮ is necessary for the climax, as its sonority provides the brightness of a bare fifth with the E rather than the tritone given by the A♯. But it is neither necessary nor possible to make much noise; the real climax does not occur here but pages later with the sonorous return to B minor, marked by a fermata. The unmeasured pauses in this movement are beautifully placed, and they mark the most significant steps in the tonal structure, the modulations to G major, E flat major and B minor; they should be held with a full sense of their necessary breadth, as they are the successive end points of each energetic onslaught of the music.

The metronome mark is ♩ = 138, which is very fast. There is nothing sacred about any metronome mark, and Beethoven was, after all, deaf and unable to test the justice of his suggestions. What can be heard clearly by the imagination may often be blurred and muddy in actual performance. Tempo indications, however, must be taken very seriously indeed, because they reveal the character of the work, and Beethoven was very careful about his markings. The tempo of the first movement of the *Hammerklavier* is Allegro, which for Beethoven was always a fast tempo. He never wrote a simple 'Allegro' when he meant 'Allegro maestoso' or 'Allegro ma non troppo.' It does not matter what metronome marking a pianist chooses for this movement providing it *sounds* Allegro; there is no excuse, textual or musical, for making it sound majestic, like Allegro maestoso, and such an effect is a betrayal of the music. It is often done, because it mitigates the harshness of the work, but this harshness is clearly essential to it. A majestic tempo also saps the rhythmic vitality on which the movement depends.[1] As we have seen,

---

[1] A metronome mark of from 126 to 132 to the half-note seems to me the most reasonable, but one must reckon with the sound of different pianos and different halls. It should also be emphasized that passages marked *espressivo* are meant to be played with a slight *ritenuto* in late Beethoven, as, for example, the theme cited above, page 416, marked *cantabile dolce ed espressivo*. As Beethoven himself said, you cannot put a metronome mark to sentiment.

the actual material of the work is neither rich nor particularly expressive; it only lives up to its reputation for greatness if its rhythmic power is concentrated. And it is meant to be difficult to listen to.

Insofar as a musical idea can be circumscribed by words, it should be obvious that even in a purely formal description, the central idea of the opening movement of the *Hammerklavier* is not merely a series of descending thirds, but the relation of the large tonal structure (with its powerfully dissonant long-range clash of B flat major and B major) to the rhythmic and harmonic energy of the sequences formed by the falling thirds. From this relation between far-flung dissonance and the impetuous force of the details comes not only the sonority peculiar to the work but also the combination of stern brilliance and transitory pathos.

The change in Beethoven's methods of composition can be measured by comparing the *Hammerklavier* with the early B flat major Piano Sonata, op. 22. There are interesting coincidences, as certain tonalities seem to develop different and individual qualities for almost every composer, and Beethoven's treatment of B flat major throughout his life is almost as characteristic as his emphasis on Neapolitan harmonies whenever he wrote in F minor. The Sonata op. 22 begins as if the *Hammerklavier*'s first theme were on a miniature scale:

and has. a second theme that is also basically our series of descending thirds:

but nothing in the large-scale structure is derived from this material, which is used concisely, but with a less urgent logic than Haydn or Mozart brought to the form in their last years.

The other movements of the *Hammerklavier* follow the pattern of the first very closely, but, as always in a classical sonata, with a gradual loosening of the formal tensions. The scherzo is a parody of the first movement; even its main theme is like a humorous form of the main theme of the first:

and the structure of descending thirds is even more in evidence. The main theme of the trio (in B flat minor) begins like the major theme, and throughout the scherzo there is the same detailed insistence on B♮ that we found in the first movement:

At the end the B♮ finally explodes again, in a mocking parallel to the climax of the first movement, a brutal joke that is as much sinister and dramatic as good-humored:

The elaborate structure of the first movement is missing here, but reflections of its dramatic shape and its sonority are heard as if in a distorted echo.

The slow movement is in F sharp minor, a key which is a third down from the B flat major of the first two movements. Its opening theme has the series of descending thirds, and Beethoven added in proof an opening measure which gives the rising third with which the first two movements and the theme of the last begin, and which serves as a transition from the scherzo:

The structure of descending thirds is not audibly prominent here in its shift from treble to bass, but it is set very much in relief when the theme is repeated at the opening of the development (which, *like the development of the first movement,* continues the sequence of thirds remorselessly to the end of the section):

Beethoven

A quotation from Brahms' Fourth Symphony would seem to be inevitable in a work built out of similar material.

There are both literal, untransposed echoes throughout this movement of the earlier B♭–B♮ ambiguity, and an analogous opposition of F sharp minor and G major. The major–minor opposition here, although again that of tonic and flatted supertonic, is intended for pathos, and the deep expression of grief is one of Beethoven's most moving achievements. Much of the writing (marked *con grand'espressione*, a rare indication in Beethoven) is in arabesques of a Chopinesque grace and chromatic poignance. The rich decoration of the return of the main theme has few parallels in the rest of Beethoven's music.

Although in 'first-movement sonata form,' the exposition of this Adagio goes, not to the relative major, but down a third to D major; as in the two preceding movements, the principal climax is withheld until after the recapitulation. It is again a climax on the supertonic, but the symmetry of the relations does not prevent a less formal emotional ambiance of an entirely different order. It is obvious that the sequence of descending thirds and all it implied, almost identifiable with the actual content of the music in the first movement, have here been relegated to the formal structure; the expressive interest of the slow movement is now centered above all on the almost operatically expressive and decorative line of the melody, and on a chromatic texture which has little in common with the dissonant and harshly diatonic sonority of the other movements.

What follows is less an introduction to the fugal finale than a transition from the slow movement, and to be understood it must be played without pause after the Adagio.[1] The transition begins with the drop of a minor second from the last measures of the slow movement: the long series of soft F sharp major chords is followed by a soft arpeggio, *dolce*, of every F♮ on Beethoven's keyboard:

---

[1] Beethoven's letter to Ries for the English edition suggesting cuts and rearrangements of the movements if Ries felt the work was too difficult for English taste has no value as evidence of his artistic intentions. He was concerned only with a good sale in England, and the sonata was being correctly printed in Vienna.

Beethoven

This mysterious, unharmonized and therefore unexplained F♮ is the dominant of B flat major, and into the soft ending in F sharp major a hint is given of what is to come, without a complete resolution into the new tonality. This is a device almost exactly repeated in the Ninth Symphony, there with a terrifying dissonance, as Beethoven takes the last B flat chord of the slow movement and places under it the dominant A♮ of the next movement.

In the *Hammerklavier*, however, the music first returns immediately to the F sharp major of the Adagio. The transition sets up an improvisatory motion, partly without barlines, and is the most interesting of all the concentrations of descending thirds. It is the bass that outlines the thirds, moving down them and supporting a succession of soft, hesitant chords: the series of thirds is interrupted every so often by an interlude, each one a little more brilliant in character. The first interlude is based on falling thirds as well, so that there is a small set within the large one:

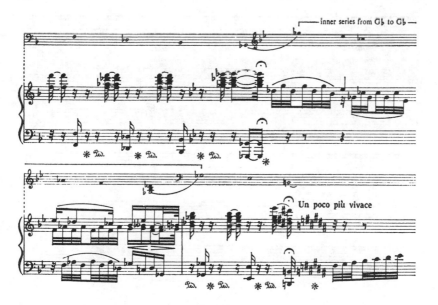

427

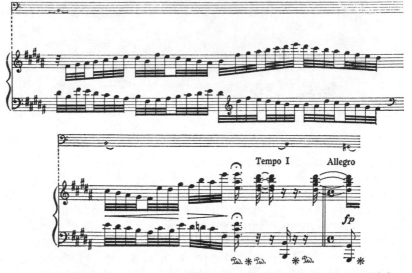

When the falling bass has reached G♯, the third interlude is a pastiche of Baroque counterpoint, and the sketches for this movement show that Beethoven copied out little phrases of Bach's *Well-Tempered Keyboard* along with his work on the themes. It is evident that he wished here for an effect of the gradual creation of a new contrapuntal style, arising from the improvisatory structure of the transition.

After the interlude in Baroque style, the thirds begin again, and reach an organ point on A♮, to which the opening arpeggio on F♮ is now transposed:

This long-range succession of F and A is the first hint of the theme of the fugue. The thirds in the bass begin to descend again faster and faster until at *Prestissimo* they return to A once more, at which Beethoven hammers away. Slowing down, there is a final descent of a third, *pianissimo*, to F♮:

so that we have now returned to the F with which these pages began, yet with a new significance and with a new firmness.[1] This transitional page is one of the most astonishing in the history of music. No other work until then, to my knowledge, combined the effect of almost uncontrolled improvisatory movement with such a totally systematic structure. Even the notation is revolutionary, as the syncopated spacing of the chords serves to enforce less a hesitant rhythm than a delicate, uninsistent tone-quality. We have the sense of a contrapuntal texture taking shape, and growing organically out of unformed material.

When the bass reaches F♮, we have arrived at the tonic key of B flat major, and the left hand hints again at the opening F–A of the fugue theme:

---

[1] The last descent before the A at *Prestissimo* is not a third but a fourth (D to A): in Beethoven's sketches the series was originally to continue on in thirds (D, B, G, E, C, A) back to A, but this entailed harmonic and rhythmic problems; consistency was abandoned without much loss as the descent in this passage is only an interior set from A to A, and not part of the larger movement.

and in its leap of a tenth from the bass, we can hear its relation to the opening of the first movement.

Where the first movement makes little distinction between thirds and transpositions of a third to a tenth and even to a seventeenth, using them almost interchangeably, the finale insists upon keeping the integrity of the tenth as fundamental and thematic. The fugue theme states its opening tenth leap followed by a trill, and then goes at once through the series of descending thirds that dominates the work:

The last two measures bring up the dissonant B♮ that plays such an important role throughout. Arranged in a new pattern and with a radically different character, the elements of the fugue-theme are exactly the same as those of the first movement.[1]

The plan of the fugue is also a descent in thirds similar to that of the first movement, but leaning more heavily upon the subdominant and minor keys, and so retaining one of the traditional features of the classical finale. This movement resolves not only by its harmonic character but also by its looser organization, a decided articulation into sections midway between a rondo and a set of continuous variations, both forms typical of the finale as conceived in the late eighteenth century.

The fugue-theme is transformed by its context throughout the movement. At each entirely new form or treatment of the theme, there is a modulation which is, as one might expect, always the descent of a third. (The return of the theme in a previously heard form provides subsidiary modulations.) The first half of the form falls into the following sections:

1. B flat major   Exposition; re-exposition with a shift of accent (D flat major)
2. G flat major   Episode (variant of the theme)[2]
3. E flat minor   Theme in augmentation; return of episode (A flat major)
4. B minor   Theme in contrary motion with new counter-theme; return of original form of theme (D major)
5. G major   Theme in the inversion

[1] Even the trill is derived from the figure of a descending second at the end of the first measure of the opening movement.

[2] The episode is based only on a decorated form of the opening leap of a tenth of the fugue theme which appears as

430

At this point a descent by thirds back to the tonic would entail five more sections, and Beethoven uses instead a descent of a minor second that is found at so many crucial points of the work: B major to B flat major at the beginning of the recapitulation of the first movement, and once again in the middle of the recapitulation; B major–minor to B flat major at the end of the scherzo, G major to F sharp minor at the end of the slow movement, and F sharp to F at the opening of the transition to the last movement. The modulation by minor second is neither makeshift nor short-cut. All of these descents of a minor second are the larger counterpart of the B♭–B♮ clash from which the most pathetic and lyrical moments of the work derive. Ultimately, they must be related to the complex harmonic situation entailed by the modulations of descending thirds, which substitutes tonic-mediant relations for tonic-dominant. This is, in fact, the principal reason for the 'difficult' sound of the *Hammerklavier*, as the ear is traditionally used to the dominant-tonic resolution implied by the language, and Beethoven withholds such resolutions fairly consistently throughout the work. Almost all the large resolutions are uncompromising juxtapositions of minor seconds (which arise directly from the descent by thirds of B♭, G, E♭, B♮ and the return from B♮ to B♭), and they sound and even echo long after as 'enharmonic.' But they are the main source of the work's expressive and dramatic tension.

The fugue therefore continues from the G major inversion of the theme without a break by a descent of a third to:

6. E flat major   Short development and stretto ending with a brilliant cascade built from the opening tenth leap and descending harmonically by thirds:

which modulate down a minor second to:

7. D major   Second episode (variant of the theme)

This new and delicately lyrical episode (which begins with the ubiquitous descent by thirds) is formed freely from the main theme:

and, as the end of the section can show, it is constructed with the harmonic sequences that characterize the rest of the work:

The modulation at the end of this passage (mm. 277–8), one of the most moving in all music, and in which the chromatic detail has a purity of sound within the diatonic frame that it would never find again in the nineteenth century, is the last inner change of tonality in the work: it returns (by a drop of a third) to the tonic B flat major.

8. Establishment of B flat major   Transition: combination of second episode with fragments of the main theme.

The establishment of the tonic here is once more by a sequence of thirds:

432

and the final section, like the last number of a Mozart operatic finale, stays close to the tonic for all of its very considerable length.

9. B. flat major   Theme inverted and in original form simultaneously, followed by stretto and coda.

In this final section, Beethoven unleashes a demonic energy and a torrent of dissonance that make the harmonic progressions, basically simple, very difficult to hear.

In passing, it may be mentioned that the descent in thirds was so important to Beethoven that in his sketches he tried to turn the opening of the *inversion* of the fugue into a descent by thirds. However, this made for an uninteresting melodic form, and he quickly dropped it. There was a compensation, however. The counter-subject of the theme in its original form descends by thirds:

In the inversion, it should, of course, ascend. Instead, while the main theme is inverted (and rises by thirds), the counter subject continues to descend:

so that the basic character of the harmonic movement is retained.

The fugue of the *Hammerklavier* is essentially a dramatic set of variations; each new form of the theme is an event, emphasized and set in relief. With this movement, the fugue is at last transformed into a classical shape. The analogies of its structure with that of the preceding movements are obvious; like the first, it descends by thirds from B flat major to the remote B minor, and the harmonic detail is largely identical. What is new in the movement (and indeed in the history of music) is the treatment of the trill on the second note of the theme, employed with a violence that deprives it of any decorative character: Beethoven's trill is not an ornament, but plays a role as thematic as the opening measures of the Fifth Symphony.

433

The *Hammerklavier* is not typical of Beethoven, and does not sound it; it is not even typical of his last period. It is an extreme point of his style. He never again wrote so obsessively concentrated a work. In part, it must have been an attempt to break out of the impasse in which he found himself. Much longer than any piano sonata he (or anyone else, I believe) had written until then, it was an attempt to produce a new and original work of un-compromising greatness, and Beethoven himself talked of it in those terms. It is just this extreme character which makes it a statement of such clarity, and allows us to see, as almost no other piece does, the principles by which he worked, particularly at the end of his life; through it we can understand how the total structure as well as the details of a work of Beethoven have such an audible power.

It is also a work which extends (and even, to some extent, strains) the relation of musical form and content in a specific way. The content—the subject-matter—of the *Hammerklavier* is the nature of the contemporary musical language. The work of art which is literally about its own technique is almost too familiar by now: the poem about poetry itself (like most of those by Mallarmé), the film in which the principal subject-matter is cinematic technique and the cross-references to other films, the painting which actually attempts to depict the process of projecting space upon a flat surface or which refers, not outside itself, but directly to the medium of paint. This paradoxical interchange of form and content is a normal process of any art, which naturally tends to displace the weight of significance away from that which is signified towards the sign. But music, where denotation is at once precise and totally unspecific, presents a special problem. If we omit the occasional imitative effects (from bird-song in Jannequin to insect noises in Bartók) and the direct conventions of pathos, we can deny neither that music has significance nor that it signifies most clearly and most often itself.

Beethoven sharpens the focus of this self-reference, as the introduction to the fugue of the *Hammerklavier* makes peculiarly explicit. Out of an undefined rhythm and a harmony which evades a fixed context, there are a series of gestures towards a polyphonic form. The third of these gestures is an exercise in Baroque style, which is not only left unfinished like the first two, but broken off abruptly in the middle as if emphatically cut off and rejected. The search is resumed, the arpeggio on A echoes the opening one on F, and out of this succession F–A is born the theme of the fugue after the whirlwind descent of thirds which attains prestissimo. A more open and direct statement about classical counterpoint and its historical relations to the preceding style could not be made within a strictly musical language. Yet the language of the other movements is no less immediate for being implicit. The subject-matter of the *Hammerklavier*, the first movement in particular, is the nature of one aspect of tonality, but it makes no statement which can be given purely verbal form, and Beethoven's art is here as sensuous as a Schubert song.

Beethoven

Throughout his life, Beethoven increasingly relied directly upon the fundamental tonal relationships for material. His continuous attempt to strip away, at some point in each large work, all decorative and even expressive elements from the musical material—so that part of the structure of tonality is made to appear for a moment naked and immediate, and its presence in the rest of the work as a dynamic and temporal force suddenly becomes radiant—this ever greater use of the simplest blocks and elements of the tonal language gives his development, seen as a whole, an undeniable consistency. It is interesting that the harshness of much of his music, his ruthless disregard of the desires and even of the needs of both public and performer, and the loneliness of the stand he took were proof for most of his contemporaries of his wilfulness, and his eccentricity. For us, as for E. T. A. Hoffmann, they are a sign of his selflessness and his 'sobriety'—his logic, in short. This logic is most manifest in his transformation of the only two forms which had, in the hands of Mozart and Haydn, still managed to retain part of their Baroque nature: the fugue and the variation. By the end of his life Beethoven had succeeded in turning these last survivals of an earlier style into fully classical forms, with a dramatic shape and an articulation of the larger proportions analogous to the sonata, and that are, in fact, based on sonata style.

Haydn had already attempted a new approach to variation-form in his double variation-sets with contrasting themes. It was, however, a static contrast that he reached; in addition, his approach to the actual writing of variations remained always decorative, except in his essentially personal disinclination to allow decorative patterns to continue and develop with any regularity. Beethoven's patterns are (like Mozart's) more regular, but the structure of his variation sets undergoes radical change: what takes place is a drastic simplification.

How much of any given melody must be immanent in a variation, how much of the shape is essential, is largely a matter of stylistic definition. The whole of the theme is almost always completely recognizable in any of Mozart's or Haydn's variations. Beethoven, however, made the requirements absolutely minimal—only the barest skeleton of the melodic and harmonic shape is necessary, after which, of course, the superfluous elements of the theme can be used both dramatically and decoratively. What Beethoven did to *Rule, Britannia* is as good an illustration of the extremity of his methods as anything in the larger and more famous sets. The first four measures of the theme

are, in Beethoven's first variation, reduced to:

The only part left of the theme is the barest minimum of its shape:

and this shape is then broken up by being transposed into different registers.

The wide difference between this kind of simplification and that of, say, Bach's *Goldberg* Variations cannot be overemphasized. Bach's method is to isolate one element of the original theme, the bass, and to build upon that. Beethoven's system is to make an abstract of the total shape of the theme; the form implied by his first variation, a form which supports the variation and relates it to what follows, is not the melodic shape alone (as is shown by the use of the first measure entirely as a bass) nor the bass alone, but a representation of the theme as a whole. The classical attack on the independence of voices made the linear approach of the Baroque variation-form no longer satisfactory, or even feasible except as pastiche. Beethoven's conception of the action in a sonata as arising from material as concentrated as Haydn's but even simpler in nature enabled him to effect a comparable simplification of material within the variation-form, and this, in turn, released an imagination that would otherwise have been bound to the decoration of an already complex line.

This sense of a supporting non-linear musical scaffold informs all of Beethoven's large variation sets (even the oddly Baroque C minor Variations, although this stands naturally somewhat apart). For this reason, although no two themes sound superficially more disparate than Diabelli's waltz and the Arietta of the Sonata op. 111, the last page of one appears to quote the last page of the other textually at one point: a descending fourth underlies the otherwise so different openings of both themes, and the coincidence of the later development is an almost inevitable result of Beethoven's way of looking at a musical idea.

In many of the late variation sets (opp. 109, 111, 127, etc.) there is a progressive simplification as the variations proceed—not of the texture but of the conception of the underlying theme. That part of its shape to which the variations allude becomes gradually more and more skeletal in nature. There is also a progressive isolation of different aspects of the theme, as if they were being illuminated one by one. It is true that we need less to be reminded of what is gradually becoming more familiar by repetition, but in any case Beethoven tends to simplify as the texture becomes more complex. For this reason, his late variations give the impression that they are not so much decorating the theme as discovering its essence.

The development of the large structure made for changes that are still more profound. Essentially static and decorative, almost always in one key so that the interplay between harmonic tension and general texture could only be on the level of small details, variations presented a problem to the dramatically conceived classical style. Even the rigidly fixed proportions of the form were alien to it. Relatively early in his career, Beethoven made a striking attempt to overcome the harmonically static nature of the form: in the Variations on an Original Theme in F Major, op. 34, he set up a sequence of descending thirds, each variation starting a third lower than the preceding. The sequence is, however, resolved with unusual prudence: the penultimate variation is in C, and the finale's immediate return to F restores a dominant-tonic relation. The succession of tonalities in this work, moreover, is basically coloristic, not structural. There is nothing in the theme, or, for the most part, in the variations themselves that implies such treatment. The florid writing, operatic in its decoration, corresponds in texture to the coloristic harmonic structure: in no other work is Beethoven closer to the ornamental style of Hummel, a style in which Chopin was to find his beginning and which he never entirely renounced. These F major Variations, therefore, in spite of their great charm and an unusual lyric fullness, represent a purely exterior attempt to break out of the decorative formula imposed by the variation form. Yet at the end of his life in the choral finale of the Ninth Symphony, Beethoven returned to the scheme of changing the key by descending thirds for successive variations, now modified and justified both formally and dramatically.

The *Eroica* Variations, in both the orchestral and the piano versions, are also an exterior solution, but of a different kind, in which the form is dramatized by the separation of the bass and treble elements of the theme, and by the delayed introduction of the latter. The theme is, as it were, anatomized at the opening, and reconstituted. The bass alone makes a theme that is bare to the point of being grossly humorous, and nothing is more typical of Beethoven's comedy than his insistence on it. The emphatic awkwardness of the bass and its violent dynamic and rhythmic contrasts prevent the appearance of any suggestion of the Baroque passacaglia. Nevertheless, such a split conception of bass and melody as independent fits less well with the later work of Beethoven than with the first generation of Romantic composers, who tended to combine a melodically centered structure with a Baroque sequential bass. The opening of the *Eroica* Variations was, indeed, directly imitated by Schumann in the early *Impromptus on a Theme of Clara Wieck*, a work whose high inspiration is almost matched by its maladresse, and which Schumann marred without pity in rewriting it for a second edition.

The *Eroica* Variations (particularly the version for piano) also take the first step towards a classical dramatization of the variation-finale. The typical late eighteenth-century set of variations generally followed a French scheme, in which the penultimate variation, a very slow one filled with brilliantly florid coloratura, was followed by a fast and extended virtuoso finale like a fantasy on the theme. In the *Eroica* set, the Largo, florid enough for any taste, is introduced by a minor variation, remarkably restrained and delicate in its chromatic expression; these two form a clear slow movement, set off all the more by the harsh virtuosity of the preceding variation, which provides a clear close to all that has gone before. The finale itself is a brilliant fugue which leads directly to a replaying of the theme—a written out da capo, decorated and transformed by trills. Once again at this time we find Beethoven trying to enlarge the forms of the late eighteenth century by referring to earlier eighteenth-century models—the fugal finale to a set of variations (as in Bach's Passacaglia and Fugue in C minor) and the da capo return of the theme—and once again the form attained was one even more suitable for a later period, as in Brahms' later imitation of many of its features in the *Handel* Variations.

We tend to consider a composer's development as if it were the most gradual of approaches towards a satisfactory form, a completely integrated ideal; yet when this form actually appears, it is often with a surprising discontinuity, with a novelty and simplicity of conception that is difficult to relate to what has preceded. The slow-movement variations of the *Appassionata* are a classical solution in the most inward sense: without any attempt at significant innovation of form, they reach the proportions of the sonata style, the dramatic shape and the placing of tension and resolution. Moreover, they attain this with the minimal use of harmonic tension, without modulation, and almost by rhythm and melodic texture alone. The complete stillness of the hymn which is its theme makes the slightest increase of motion deeply telling: its static harmony—almost an unmoving upper pedal on A flat— gives the least chromatic alteration the larger significance of a modulation. Most important, perhaps, is the restriction of register within each variation: the successive rise step by step from the low bass to the treble is the clearest articulation of the form. The acceleration of note-values and the increased syncopations are the main vehicle of expression and build the most powerful of climaxes, so that the return of the theme in the low register comes to seem not like a da capo but like a true sonata recapitulation[1] (it is even rewritten to include a reminiscence of the obbligato bass line of the second variation). The most extraordinary part of the achievement is the feeling of release that comes with the return of the theme in its original form, and the resolving force of this 'recapitulation.' Through this, the variation form loses

---

[1] This effect of resolution upon the return to the original shape of the theme in variation sets was already attempted by Haydn (the *Surprise* Symphony is as good an example as any), but with far less cogency. Nevertheless, Beethoven is, in effect, returning here to Haydn's principles after the more 'advanced' experiments of a few years before.

its additive character, and conforms to the dramatic and almost spatially conceived figures of sonata style.

With this movement it is possible at last to say that the variation set has become a classical form: the forces that created the sonata, the same feeling for event and for proportion, move here unrestricted within a form that they have themselves shaped. It is from this model that the slow movements in variation form of the later works are taken. The most subtle is the set in the last quartet, op. 135, where the change to minor which brings a strong move to the mediant major has the effect of a genuine modulation without actually moving, and the return to the tonic major, like a decorated recapitulation, is all the more touching. The resolving character of the last variation is essential to this conception: by means as delicate as they are powerful, Beethoven succeeds in giving harmonic tension to a work that does not move from the tonic. Only in this way can the essential classical preference for recapitulation over da capo be satisfied, and the symmetry of the return be conceived not as a frame but as a dramatic resolution.

The idea of the finale of the *Eroica* Variations reappears transfigured in the *Diabelli*. Here the traditionally florid slow penultimate variation has become a series of three in the minor mode: Rococo decoration has completely disappeared, to be replaced in the last and most profoundly beautiful of the trio by a homage to J. S. Bach, with an imitation of the famous ornamented minor variation of the *Goldberg*. The powerful double fugue that follows is frankly Handelian; at the end, again as in the *Goldberg*, the dance returns— not Diabelli's simple waltz any longer, but the most delicate and complex of minuets, with a lavish play of sonorities that Beethoven rarely permitted himself. It is an ending conceived in the comic spirit (even the last chord is a surprise). In the *Diabelli*, as in the Quartet in F major op. 135 and, above all, the magnificent scherzando movement in D flat major from the Quartet in B flat major op. 130, Beethoven attained the witty combination of lyricism and irony that was part of Mozart's natural grace, and that Haydn was too good-humored to imitate.

In the structure of the *Diabelli*, there is a clear attempt to consider the variations in large groups, as if to find a unifying equivalent for the several movements of a sonata or symphony. The same grouping is even clearer in the choral finale of the Ninth Symphony, in which Beethoven has used the variation form to combine at once the symmetry of the sonata-allegro form and the larger conception of the four-movement symphony. Here, too, there is a return to an earlier experiment, the series of descending thirds of the F major Variations op. 34. In the choral finale, the successive modulations are no longer isolated events, but are comprehended within a larger scheme, the modulations justified in the same way as those of a sonata. More precisely, it is not the 'sonata' itself which provides the background against which the finale must be understood, but the classical concerto form. The choral variations begin, in fact, with the double exposition of a concerto (even the

439

opening solo recitative is astonishingly included in more elaborate form in the orchestral tutti); as in Mozart's concertos, the striking modulation is reserved for the solo exposition. Once the sonata is conceived as a set of proportions regulating tensions (or large-scale dissonances) and their resolution, it is easy to see that the purely orchestral fugue in the last movement of the Ninth Symphony plays the role of a development section (as well as standing in the place of the traditional second tutti of a concerto). The recapitulation (or resolution), with its return of the tonic, is equally set into relief.

Over this enormous sonata concerto form, a four-movement grouping which has equal weight is superimposed.[1] The opening expository movement leads to a B flat major scherzo in military style with Turkish music; a slow movement in G major introduces a new theme; and a finale begins with the triumphant combination of the two themes in double counterpoint. These groupings are not to be conceived as emphasized articulations, but as the result of pressures which give a more specifically classical shape to the variation form. About the shape itself there is no question: the proportions and the feeling for climax and expansion are solely those of the classical symphony, and even the use of the variation form itself fulfills the classical demand for a finale looser and more relaxed than a first movement. The ideals of the sonata style enabled Beethoven to endow a set of variations with the grandeur of a symphonic finale; until the *Eroica*, this form had been reserved for the lesser genres of the concerto and chamber music (lesser only on a scale of magnificence). The new principle can be felt already in the *Eroica* finale, but it is only in the Fantasy for Piano, Chorus, and Orchestra of 1808 that it became the principal shaping element.[2] With the Ninth Symphony, the variation set is completely transformed into the most massive of finales, one that is itself a four-movement work in miniature.

Beethoven's development of the fugue is best comprehended within the context of the transformation of the variation. The two fugal finales—the *Great Fugue* op. 133 (the last movement of the String Quartet op. 130) and the fugue of the *Hammerklavier*—are both conceived as a series of variations, each new treatment of the theme being given a new character. Like the last movement of the Ninth Symphony, they both have the harmonic tensions characteristic of sonata-allegro form, along with its sense of a return and extensive resolution. They both, too, impose upon this another structural idea of several movements: this is particularly evident in the *Great Fugue*, which

---

[1] This superposition of sonata-allegro and four-movement form is one of the rare experiments of the last years of Beethoven's life to have a genuine repercussion in the more original work of the first Romantic generation. The Liszt sonata is an attempt to repeat this conception. In spite of the frequent vulgarity of both his taste and his inspiration, Liszt was surely the composer of his generation who best understood Beethoven.

[2] The relation of the 'Choral Fantasy' to 'sonata-allegro' form was pointed out by Hans Keller in an article in *Score* (January, 1961).

has an introduction, Allegro, slow movement (in a new key), and Scherzo finale as almost completely separate divisions; but the D major section of the *Hammerklavier* Fugue also provides a perceptible sense of a slow movement before the stretto-finale.

No one model, however, can exhaust the variety of ways in which Beethoven was able to integrate the fugue into a classical structure. The simplest and most Haydnesque device is the use of a fugue for a development section, as in the last movement of the Piano Sonata op. 101, and the first movement of the *Hammerklavier*. The Sonata op. 110 uses the inversion of the fugue and a stretto of augmentation and diminution as both development section and preparation of the return of the original theme and tonality; the fugal texture is dropped once the tonic is reached. Perhaps the most remarkable integrations of the fugue within a larger plan are in the Quartet in C sharp minor op. 131, and the Piano Sonata in C minor op. 111.

Both Haydn's E flat major Sonata H. 52 and Beethoven's C sharp minor Quartet op. 131 have second movements in the Neapolitan major—that is, a half step above the first movement. Both are prepared, but on different levels of power and effectiveness. Haydn's E major slow movement is prepared by an emphasis on that tonality in the development section of the E flat major first movement, and by allusions to E major harmonies in the narrative thread of the recapitulation. In Beethoven's quartet, however, the D major movement is prepared at once by the opening theme of the initial fugue with its *sforzando* on A♮: this dominant of the next movement is dramatized throughout the fugue, and, played over and over with the theme transposed so that the *sforzando* falls on a D♮, it is the fulcrum which bears all of the expressive weight, and the pivot upon which everything else turns. The texture is given a directional force in the classical sense, totally alien to Baroque fugal style. The change to D major at the beginning of the second movement, therefore, seems at once as inevitable as it is astonishing; where Haydn's relationship is only prepared by the working-out of the previous movement, Beethoven's is implied by the main theme of the opening fugue, and is already potentially in the stuff out of which the form is created.

In the C minor Piano Sonata op. 111, the combination of fugue and sonata form takes a form almost the opposite of Mozart's brilliant solution in his G major Quartet finale, which Beethoven imitated in the last movement of the Quartet op. 59 no. 3. In the two quartet finales, the fugal texture of the opening measures gradually turns into the more normal *obbligato* writing of the late eighteenth century, in which accompaniments have only a shadowy independence given by their thematic significance. The Allegro con brio ed appassionata of the Sonata op. 111 starts with what is evidently a fugue theme, but withholds fugal texture until a good part of the statement has already taken place. When it comes at last, the actual sonority of fugal writing provides the increased animation demanded by sonata style.

The development is largely a double fugue in which the second theme is an augmentation of the first. The first four notes of the theme

are the basis for

in which, as so often, Beethoven is more interested in the shape of his theme than in the exact pitch relationship of the notes.

The first movement as a whole springs from the initial series of diminished seventh chords. The introduction has the following simple skeleton of three phrases:

Beethoven

The third diminished seventh is prolonged by a chromatic expansion over several measures before finding its resolution on an F minor chord (it is the length of this expansion and the consequent delay of the resolution that make the phrase spill over at once into the dominant of C minor). The main theme of the Allegro that follows is derived from these diminished sevenths and their resolutions:

although the melodic form is nowhere clarified in the introduction, which presents only the harmonic aspect (as the *Eroica* Variations begin with the bass alone). However, to make the derivation doubly clear, at the end of the movement Beethoven harmonizes the theme with the chords

where the diminished sevenths occur in the same order as in the introduction.

This order of the chords also fixes the harmonic structure of the development section almost in its entirety:

443

The three chords and their resolutions provide a basis for this development, and the order of the chords is once again always that of the introduction. The expressive significance of these chords needs no comment; they color most of the piece, appear with extreme violence at every important climax, and supply the dynamic impulse for most of the harmonic transformations.

Most of Beethoven's works in C minor from the *Sonate Pathétique* on rely heavily upon diminished sevenths at climactic movements. Yet none before the Sonata op. 111 fixes an order for these chords so firmly throughout a movement (the three chords and their inversions exhaust the range of possible diminished sevenths), derives the principal melodic material so directly from their sonority, and makes such a consistent attempt to integrate the whole movement by their means. It is this concentration upon the simplest and most fundamental relationships of tonality that characterizes Beethoven's late style most profoundly. His art, with all its dramatic force and its conception in terms of dramatic action, became more and more an essentially meditative one.

Beethoven

The aspect of many of these late works is not ingratiating; to many, the *Great Fugue* is disagreeably harsh. But when it is played, as it should be, as the finale of the B flat Quartet op. 130, there is nothing eccentric in this harshness, or in the broken sobs (marked 'strangled') of the *Cavatina* that precedes it. What makes some of these works appear wilful is that they are uncompromising. This was understood during Beethoven's lifetime by E. T. A. Hoffmann. Against those who granted Beethoven only genius without control, imagination without order, he wrote:

> But what if it were only *your* weak sight which misses the profound unity of inner relation [*innere tiefe Zusammenhang*] in each composition? If it were only *your* fault that the language of the master, understood by the consecrated, is incomprehensible, if the door to the holy of holies remains closed to you? In truth, the master, who is the peer of Haydn and Mozart in self-possession [*Besonnenheit*], carves his essential being [*sein Ich*] from the inner kingdom of tones, and reigns over it as its absolute ruler.

Since the Renaissance at least, the arts have been conceived as ways of exploring the universe, as complementary to the sciences. To a certain extent, they create their own fields of research; their universe is the language they have shaped, whose nature and limits they explore, and in exploring, transform. Beethoven is perhaps the first composer for whom this exploratory function of music took precedence over every other: pleasure, instruction, and, even, at times, expression. A work like the *Diabelli* Variations is above all a discovery of the nature of the simplest musical elements, an investigation of the language of classical tonality with all its implications for rhythm and texture as well as melody and harmony. There was no doubt an element of good fortune in his arriving on the scene to find a universe, a language already so rich in possibilities and resonances as the one formed by Haydn and Mozart. His singlemindedness, however, is unparalleled in the history of music, and it is this unrelenting high seriousness which can still create resentment.

Beethoven was the greatest master of musical time. In no other composer is the relation between intensity and duration so keenly observed; no one else understood so well, not even Handel or Stravinsky, the effect of simple reiteration, the power that can be drawn from repetition, the tension that can arise from delay. There are many works (the finale of the Eighth Symphony is only the most famous) in which an often-repeated detail becomes fully comprehensible only near the end of the piece, in which case we may quite literally speak of a logical tension that has been added to the familiar harmonic and rhythmic tensions of sonata form. Stravinsky once wrote that 'one misses in all so-called post-Webern music the tremendous leverage which Beethoven makes of time.' This mastery of time was dependent on a comprehension of the nature of musical action, or, rather, musical actions. A

445

musical event takes place on different levels; the fastest *perpetuum mobile* can appear immobile, and a long silence can be heard *prestissimo*. Beethoven never miscalculated the intensity of his musical actions, and the technique carried so far by Haydn and Mozart of endowing the proportions themselves with a weight both expressive and structural reaches the height of its development in Beethoven. The dissolution of classical articulation made its revival impossible.

The weight given within a work to duration alone (both of the whole and the parts) is by no means purely, or even principally, rhythmic in nature. Harmonic mass, the weight and scope of a line or of a phrase, thickness of texture—all these play roles equally influential. The fusion of these elements in Beethoven with a synthesis that not even Mozart knew[1] allowed him a command previously unknown over the largest forms. The slow movement of the op. 111 succeeds as almost no other work in suspending the passage of time at its climax. After almost a quarter of an hour of the purest C major, we reach what appears to be the cadential trill, and we must remember the temporal weight and mass of the preceding C major to understand the following:

---

[1] Tovey has remarked that Mozart is a more enchanting orchestrator than Beethoven because his greatest strokes stand out as such, whereas those in Beethoven's mature works seem inconceivable for any other instrumental pattern (nonsensical attempts to orchestrate the *Hammerklavier*, and the composer's financially motivated piano transcription of the Violin Concerto notwithstanding).

The only place in this movement where there is any harmonic motion is here, where the larger rhythmic motion is completely suspended: there is not the slightest directional force in these trills or in the modulation, and they are only a means of hovering before returning to C major and resolving the cadence. In the sense that a cadenza is a glorified cadence, this is a cadenza, and that is, in fact, its structural point. The mastery lies in Beethoven's understanding that a sequence does not move, that a diatonic circle of descending fifths within classical tonality does not exist on a plane of real action, so that the long series of tiny harmonic movements that prolong this immense inner expansion serve only as an harmonic pulse and in no sense as a gesture.

The trill is the culminating point in the rhythmic scheme of the movement. A long trill creates an insistent tension while remaining completely static; it helped Beethoven both to accept the static form of the variation set and to transcend it. The variation-set which proceeds by gradual acceleration—in which each successive variation is faster than the last—is common enough since the 16th century, but in no work before op. 111 are the gradations so carefully worked out. The sequence may be represented by the basic rhythm of each unit:

The fourth variation reaches almost undifferentiated pulsation, enforced by the continuous *pianissimo* and by the omission of the melody note from

447

the opening of every beat. The trill represents the complete dissolution of even this rhythmic articulation: the movement reaches the extremes of rapidity and of immobility. Its importance in the rhythmic structure of the movement as a whole accounts for the length of the trill and for its sonorous transformation into a triple trill. The trill returns on the last page, and the rhythm here is a synthesis of all that went before: the rhythmic accompaniment of Variation IV (the fastest measured motion) and the theme in its original form (the slowest) are both suspended under the unmeasured stillness of the trill. It is in this way that the most typical ornamental device is turned into an essential element of large-scale structure.

This power to suspend motion, seeming to stop the movement of time, which is measured only by action, is closely related to Mozart's exquisite feeling for a pause in harmonic movement before his recapitulations, but it became one of Beethoven's most personal traits. The development section of the first movement of the Quartet op. 130, with the continuous soft pulsation, the tiny ostinato theme, the long repeated lyrical phrase all combined into one, suspends motion in the same way as the quiet beginning of the development of the Ninth Symphony, with its syncopated and unaccented shifts of harmony that defer all sense of action: both build an intensity more terrifying and moving than any less inward motion could induce. With all their tension, these effects are essentially meditative in character, and they make one aware to what an extent the exploration of the tonal universe was an act of introspection.

Beethoven's Later Years and the Conventions of His Childhood

We think of Beethoven, particularly the Beethoven of the final years, as a deeply unconventional composer, and we generally assume that it was his deliberate flouting of the contemporary musical language and style that often made his work so difficult to understand and accept by his contemporaries. This must be right, of course, if we all feel it so, but it does not do complete justice to Beethoven's originality. In the first place, the demand for radically new invention in art that arose in the last decades of the eighteenth century made it almost a convention for composers to break with convention. It was already accepted that a new and original work must inevitably displease the public at first hearing. The poet Giacomo Leopardi, believing this to be more true of music than of the other arts, wrote in his *Zibaldone* on October 9, 1821:

> In fact, an absolute innovation in music cannot be anything else except discordant, because it would be unseemly to the general custom. Even in poetry and prose, that which is concerned purely with harmony and melody is almost not at all susceptible of innovation.

When Leopardi jotted down these sentences, the idea had been current for many years and his statement shows the incorrigible conservatism of Italian musical audiences. The Viennese were somewhat less wary of originality, at least at the beginning of the nineteenth century, and expected to be surprised and even shocked by new developments in art. Of course, they were upset when artists went too far—but going too far is obviously a built-in mechanism of the process.

Nevertheless, Beethoven's treatment of the conventions of the classical musical language was never simply an attempt to bypass them, to pretend that they were no longer valid. To the end of his life he continued to employ and even revive many musical procedures that he had known as a child in the 1770s and that younger contemporaries, like Weber, Schubert, and Mendelssohn, had abandoned as banal and old-fashioned.

In the final Adagio of op. 111, the harmonies preceding the trill quoted on page 446 are in fact exceedingly banal:

and the trill itself is also conventional, at least when it starts—it is the standard final trill used to close a movement or a long section. Beethoven prolongs this trill and then, paradoxically, transforms what should be a simple resolution on C major into the movement's only modulation to a distant key, a powerful effect after so much pure tonic C major. The passage is deeply moving precisely because the trill implies an immediate final resolution that is suspended for 24 measures by an aspiration toward a region far from both the expressive simplicity of the theme and the growing agitation of the variations. The trill restores the exquisite simplicity of the theme, but with a new complexity of harmonic structure. The convention is eventually fulfilled, the resolution achieved at last, but C major returns only when the main theme rises, almost imperceptibly, from within the texture of triplet thirty-second notes.

The final trill is one of the simplest of all classical conventions, and it receives its most spectacular transformation and fulfillment in this very late work. It is not, however, the first time that Beethoven played with this convention. A final trill at the end of a cadenza in a classical concerto or aria was standard. In the autograph manuscripts of his concertos, Mozart always notates the trill of the cadenza even when he does not write out the cadenza; the only exception occurs in the C minor Concerto K. 491. Did Mozart for once intend a cadenza without a trill here? Some have thought so, and Saint-Saëns even composed a cadenza that ends by going directly into the closing tutti.

Beethoven knew Mozart's C minor Concerto and it strongly influenced his own concerto in the same key, but we do not know if he heard Mozart play it and whether he had any idea what kind of cadenza Mozart intended. It is certainly possible that he had some knowledge of the composers cadenza, whatever it was. (Mozart's C minor Concerto was written and performed in 1786, and Beethoven came to Vienna briefly in 1787.) Nevertheless, in every important cadenza he wrote for his own concertos, the traditional trill is deprived of its expected ending.[1] In fact, in the immensely long cadenza to the First Concerto, the 'final' trill appears twice and is wittily frustrated each time, the second time spectacularly so:

---

[1] Two shorter and somewhat perfunctory cadenzas for the First Concerto have a more traditional ending; they are almost never chosen for performance.

The double trill is first accompanied by the opening motif of the movement and then turns into a triple trill—a sequence paralleled more than two decades later by the trill in op. 111.[2] The end of the cadenza is a pretext for one of Beethoven's least subtle but most effective humorous strokes. The soloist rounds off the brilliant passagework that follows the trill with a powerful dominant seventh chord, makes the conductor, orchestra, and public wait for the resolution—and then plays the chord again softly arpeggiated and makes everyone wait even longer. The resolution comes with a crash after the silence.

---

[2] Perhaps the earliest triple trill in Beethoven is in the coda-cadenza of the Sonata in C major, op. 2 no. 3. A double or triple trill with an important motif playing simultaneously is a typically Beethovenian effect. There is a similar detail in the double trill at the end of the finale of the *Waldstein* Sonata. Like the First Piano Concerto and the second movement of op. 111, all these works are in C major. Because Beethoven tended to give specific character to each key, the same devices recur in his works.

The cadenza to the Second Concerto, certainly written many years after the concerto was composed, evades even the suggestion of a final trill. The cadenza to the Third Concerto, by contrast, finishes with the trill unresolved and moving up to the leading-tone of the subdominant instead of down to the tonic. The final moments of this cadenza and perhaps even the rest of it were almost certainly planned when the concerto was composed, as they are conceived in terms of the following coda. There the soloist cooperates in the concluding ritornello, in direct imitation of the unique model established by Mozart in K. 491. Beethoven, however, enhances the Mozartean effect by prolonging the cadenza directly into the ritornello. He was to continue the experiment several years later and carry it even further. In the brief, written-out cadenza to the *Emperor* Concerto in the first-movement coda, the pianist begins the standard trill, but then moves it up to the dominant and extends it as the horns enter with their melody. (In this work, however, the function of the cadenza was largely displaced into the openings of the exposition and recapitulation.)

With the Fourth Piano Concerto in G major, Beethoven completely transformed the convention of the final trill into a structural device that determines the form of the movement and becomes, as well, the occasion for lyrical expression. In the first movement the final trills of the exposition, recapitulation, and cadenza are radically new. Not only do none of these trills ever reach the expected resolution, but they lead directly into one of the most expressive themes of the movement. In traditional, formal terms, a trill is a dissonant penultimate ornament to be resolved by the final harmony. In the G major Concerto, the dissonance remains unresolved and initiates the theme:

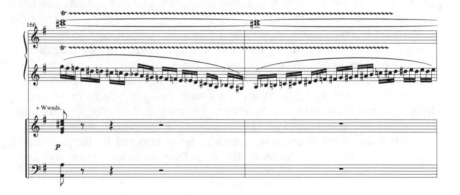

It is typical of Beethoven to take a conventional detail—here the emphasis on E, the main note of the trill—and to sustain it dramatically at an unprecedented length. The three quarter notes in the orchestra at measure 169 emphasize the E, and they are easily recognized as augmenting the rhythm of the main theme. The *cantabile* melody that follows continues the process of prolonging the trill and withholding resolution. Beethoven's refusal to allow the trill to follow its normal course and traditional function serves here to override the barrier between solo and ritornello. It breaks down the sectional character of the movement, allowing Beethoven to achieve a more complete integration of the concerto form than anyone had ever attempted before. Later the integration of solo cadenza and final section is achieved in the same way:

455

Beethoven

At this point the soloist takes over the orchestral extension of the original phrase with an extraordinary fluid decoration that continues the cadenza into the concluding orchestral section. One could say that the cadenza does not end before the final chord of the movement.

In these examples Beethoven directly engages the conventional aspect of the musical language and reveals it to us openly. He does not sidestep the most common procedures but—in a sense—reinforces them, prolongs their effect, and gives them greater power. Even when he appears to deform a stereotype most radically, it is always with a sense of its original purpose. In the finale of the Sonata in A major op. 101, the ornamental trill with an afterbeat in the fugal development seems to pervert the proper function of such an afterbeat:

The normal reason for existing of such an afterbeat is to resolve the trill either upward or downward, impelling the trill towards a cadence. It is an element so traditional that its presence is almost never worthy of remark: it

457

is simply taken for granted. Beethoven leaves it wittily hanging in the air with an initial effect of nonsense. This transforms the afterbeat from an ornament into a motif, but the original purpose is always present, very much in evidence. The irresistible comedy of the effect comes from the way the afterbeat is often cut short throughout the fugue, left unfinished, its function unfulfilled. And the pastoral good humor of the movement provides the context that makes the comic effect work.

The extent to which Beethoven manipulated conventions should not obscure how much he relied on them. Perhaps the most irritatingly banal convention of the late eighteenth-century concerto is the use of arpeggios by the soloist in the development, or central solo section (in the third quarter of the century the soloist was sometimes just given the harmonies and allowed to arpeggiate as he pleased). Mozart did not conform to this procedure in every instance (in the Piano Concerto in A major K. 488, for example, he substitutes more interesting passagework for the standard arpeggios). However, not only did Beethoven always retain these elaborate arpeggios in the development of every concerto, he exploited them in the *Emperor* at grandiose length. Even further, in those sonatas that are concertante in style, like op. 2 no. 3 in C major and the *Waldstein,* the regulation concerto-style arpeggios appear with great brilliance. These arpeggios in the development section differ strikingly by their improvisational character from those found in the exposition:

op. 2 no. 3

op. 53

In these two cases, and in the *Apassionata* as well, the arpeggios are a sign that the music is supposed to conjure up the public world of the concerto and transcend the traditionally limited genre of the piano sonata, intended for private or semi-private performance before a small group of listeners.[3]

In general, one may say that Beethoven's originality reveals itself most often not by frustrating the conventions that he learned as a child, but by magnifying them beyond the experience or expectations of any of his contemporaries. Every pianist who has played through the sonatas that Beethoven wrote when he was thirteen years old has remarked how similar some of the motifs are to those that Beethoven would use in his last works. (He had, for example, very early found the kind of musical material that later characterized most of his writing in C minor from the Piano Trio op. 1 no. 3 and the Sonata op. 10 no. 1 through the Fifth Symphony to the Sonata op. 111.) More profound, however, is his preservation of the traditional formal procedures of his youth until, at the end of his life, he was alone in continuing a late eighteenth-century style that he so transformed into the sensibility of a new age that he seemed to have reinvented it.

Two of the stereotypes that held sway in the 1770s and 1780s are a move to the relative minor or its dominant at the end of the development section and an emphasis on the subdominant soon after the beginning of the recapitulation. These formal procedures were already singled out by eighteenth-century theorists, in particular Heinrich Christoph Koch in 1791,[4] although they were commonplace at least two decades earlier. They may be briefly illustrated by Beethoven's Sonatina in G major op. 49 no. 2, written around

---

[3] Here again, Beethoven is following in Mozart's footsteps. The finale of Mozart's Sonata in B flat major K. 333 not only imitates concerto texture, the alternation of soloist and orchestra, but also has an elaborate cadenza. The cadenza, in fact, is introduced by a passage that sounds like an awkward piano reduction of an orchestral climax introducing some free brilliance:

[4] *Versuch einer Einleitung zur Composition,* Vol. III, Hildesheim, 1969, pp. 308 and 311.

1795. Here is the end of the exposition, the entire development section, and the beginning of the recapitulation:

Both these traditional harmonic schemes have latent expressive possibilities, barely exploited here by Beethoven, who employs them in this modest work largely for their formal convenience. The pause on V of vi, the dominant of the relative minor, enables the composer to return to the tonic just by going along the circle of fifths—in measures 63 to 67 he simply descends with B–E–A–D–G, and the four-bar pedal on B that precedes the descent adds a touch of dramatic tension that is not very interesting. It is clear that Beethoven did not take much trouble over this little piece for beginners and amateurs.[5]

Even less does he exploit the move to the subdominant in measure 73: he makes very little here of its expressive possibilities. The formal convenience of the harmony was important to late eighteenth-century sensibility (still earlier, fugues by Bach generally moved toward subdominant harmonies in the second half of the form). Schubert was to make frequent use of the

---

[5] The companion Sonatina in G minor, op. 49 no. 1, is more original. The G major Sonatina serves principally to place Beethoven's famous and popular minuet as its second movement.

subdominant in the recapitulation, and even, in the opinion of Donald Francis Tovey, to abuse it. The purpose of this turn to the subdominant is easily explained. One of the most basic relationships of triadic tonality is that the tonic is the dominant of the subdominant—in other words, a move from tonic to dominant in the first half of a piece can be reproduced by going from subdominant to tonic without any other change. A simple transposition of the second half of the exposition up a fourth will give us the rest of the recapitulation without the necessity of any further thought or invention.

More important, however, is the latent expressive force of the convention—the move towards the greater tension of the dominant in the exposition can be countered near the moment of recapitulation by the lesser tension of the subdominant, and this serves to reaffirm the return to the tonic and the feeling of resolution. The opposition of sharp (dominant) and flat (subdominant) directions on the circle of fifths is crucial in the late eighteenth century, although the feeling for it disappears almost completely with the generation of Chopin and Schumann. Beethoven, however, never lost his sense of this opposition. For example, the only piano sonatas in the major mode that do not allude to subdominant or subdominant-related harmonies soon after the recapitulation begins are the Sonata in D major op. 28 and two in E flat Major, op. 31 no. 3 and op. 81a. Because the main theme in both the latter two cases begins with the harmony of the subdominant, a move to the subdominant at the moment of recapitulation would bring about the subdominant of the subdominant unwelcome at this point, which traditionally demands a clear concentration on the tonic, so Beethoven defers full use of the subdominant in each case until the beginning of the coda:

op. 31 no. 3

Cadence and coda

op. 81a

As for op. 28, the main theme begins more radically with the dominant of the subdominant, and this gives the opening bars an extraordinary harmonic softness and absence of tension. A move to the subdominant in the recapitulation might lead the harmony too far from straightforward resolution, and in the very first bars of the development Beethoven initiates a complete statement of the principal theme in the subdominant (briefly giving us the V^7 chord on G, which is the dominant of the subdominant of the subdominant), a step backwards before he sets up the enormous climax at the end of the development (see also below, pages 477–80):

All these exceptional procedures satisfied the contemporary feeling for the harmonic balance of tonic, dominant, and subdominant, and they demonstrate how important this balance continued to be to Beethoven.[6] The expressive possibilities of the subdominant are basically metaphorical: both Mozart and Beethoven derived effects of great sweetness from the implied lessening of tension, and the traditional placing of this subdominant emphasis explains why moments of lyricism occur so often soon after the return to the tonic and to the main theme.

One example may illustrate the laconic effectiveness with which Beethoven employs the turn to the subdominant as a form of harmonic resolution, and how he deliberately, if briefly, goes beyond what is simply necessary to stay in the tonic and eliminate the exposition's excursion to the dominant. In the Sonata in B flat major, op. 22, the original establishment of the dominant is rapid:

---

[6] In addition to these piano sonatas, a few other works, like the Sonata for Cello and Piano in A major, postpone an emphasis on the subdominant until the coda. This generally occurs when the development section has given a preponderant role to the minor mode (which is a 'flat,' or subdominant, area).

It would have been easy to rewrite this in the recapitulation in order to stay in the tonic and continue everything as before but transposed down a fifth (or up a fourth if the texture seems better):

However, Beethoven wants the expressive allusion to the subdominant, and makes a slight change that renders the harmonic progression longer, delicately chromatic, and very much more mysterious:

Beethoven's play with the subdominant at this point of a sonata movement is often more elaborate than this, and so was Mozart's, but rarely more striking or more poetic. This simple formal junction of the form was an inspiration to Beethoven throughout his life.

The progression at the end of the development from the relative minor or its dominant back to the tonic, so commonplace in the late eighteenth century, may be illustrated by two examples from Mozart. The first is the Sonata in D major K. 575, written, like Beethoven's Sonatina, for beginners.

There is a letter in which Mozart claims that he was writing sonatas for children, but many have doubted that K. 576 was one of those works. The skepticism is understandable, as the first movement is very difficult, and even famous pianists sometimes play it badly. This, however, is due to Mozart's miscalculation. The only parts of the movement that create any technical problems are in simple two-part counterpoint. Like Bach, whose Two-part Inventions were also intended for the young, Mozart mistakenly thought that bare two-part polyphony would be easy to play. (This was not the first time he had overestimated the technique of his possible clients. He had been commissioned to write six quartets for piano and strings, and the order was cancelled after two of the quartets were completed, as the publisher complained they were too difficult for the amateurs who buy sheet music.) A composer who put three dance orchestras on the stage at one time (in *Don Giovanni*) performing in different rhythms with the second and third orchestras tuning up while the preceding one is still playing, and who wrote a comic opera containing a chorale prelude and an overture with a magnificent double fugue, was one of the most pretentious composers in history, and Mozart was clearly interested in showing off his contrapuntal skills: the exquisite sonata K. 576 displays all the possible two-voice combinations of stretto of the main theme.

As audacious as the contrapuntal art may be in this Sonata, the harmonic structure is the soul of convention, although realized, of course, with extraordinary grace. The development soon arrives at the expected harmony of F sharp (V of vi, the dominant of the relative minor). Then the standard progression takes us back to D major:

The bass proceeds simply through the fifths: F sharp, B, E, A, and pauses on the last, affirming it as the principal dominant.

Mozart needed no harmonic surprises to detract from his contrapuntal virtuosity in this movement. In another D major work, the rondo-finale of the *Coronation* Concerto, the simple, popular melodic material inspired a much more elaborate harmonic treatment of the conventional move from relative minor to tonic. Here the arrival at the dominant of the relative minor is unashamedly conventional, even banal, but it sets up the surprising modulation that Mozart now achieves:

The expected resolution to B minor is neatly evaded at the last moment, and in bar 187 B flat major arrives as a shock. It was this kind of chromatic modulation that Mozart's contemporaries found puzzling and that the composer Sacchini maintained was unintelligible to the general public. The music introduced is elegant and graceful, but it is clear that we are supposed to feel the new key as exotic—and Mozart reinforces the exotic chromaticism by turning to the minor mode (m. 196). B flat minor is indeed an alien harmony within a piece in D major, and Mozart hastens to restore equilibrium by returning to the B minor, where he should have been if tradition had held full sway, and finally to the subdominant G major, absolutely standard for a recapitulation, as we have seen. Nevertheless, the return to the conventional relative minor is one of Mozart's most remarkable effects. When B minor appears in passing (mm. 200–201) on a $^6_4$ chord, it has an even more exotic air than the alien chromaticism that preceded it. This is an aspect of the composer's art that Bernard Shaw observed in a letter to Ernest Newman (August 10, 1917).

> And don't *read* his scores: sing them and hear them. If you *look* at his blessed old dominant sevenths, they will never be anything but dominant sevenths to you. If you listen to them only, you will sometimes

find yourself going to the score to find what strange chord it is you have heard.[7]

Here it is not a dominant seventh but a simple $^6_4$ chord of B minor that sounds wonderfully strange. The passage is a lesson in Mozart's handling of conventional procedure. He never tries to avoid convention or disguise it, but realizes it with every appearance of ease—and then uses it as a pretext for the most unconventional development. It is this juxtaposition of the banal or commonplace in both melodic material and harmonic structure with the most unprecedented and disconcerting experiments that has sometimes made Mozart's work so difficult to assess, particularly as the commonplace elements are presented with such urbane grace that it is absurd to find them less important than the more original inspirations.

In order to appreciate this page from the *Coronation* Concerto, we must understand just how standard the move at the end of a development to the relative minor or its dominant was at the time (although Mozart often preferred to go through the tonic minor instead, perhaps because this facilitated a more dramatic chromaticism in the preceding development).[8] In particular, its repeated exploitation by Haydn would have made it a well-worn device, even a cliché, in Beethoven's eyes. The practice extends throughout Haydn's career.

In his six quartets op. 20 of 1771, the device appears in all four of the quartets in the major mode, in each case with decisive and even repeated full cadences on the relative minor. Ten years later, with the quartets of op. 33, Haydn decided upon a wittier use of the tradition. In the Quartet in E flat, the expected cadence on the relative minor arrives at the end of the development but is not allowed to finish, breaking off just before the last chord:

---

[7] *Collected Letters*, ed. Dan H. Laurence, Vol. III, London, 1965–1988, p. 500.

[8] One of the most impressive examples in which Mozart employs the transition from relative minor to tonic at the end of a development is illustrated by the G major slow movement of the Viola Quintet in D major K. 593 (pp. 285–286). The cadence on the relative minor is broken off at the last moment, and Mozart introduces the traditional sequence with the bass descending by fifths (C–F♯–B–E–A–D–G). It is typical of Mozart that he lavishes his most complex and exquisite contrapuntal art on the banal descent. The progression is used by absolutely everyone, but Mozart aims to demonstrate that no one can do it so well.

Beethoven

Resolution arrives after a brief pause as the main theme played in the relative minor supplies the missing end to the cadence, but this, too, breaks off
before it can resolve. After an even shorter pause, the tonic returns, entirely
unprepared, with the main theme. Haydn dramatizes the convention.

The process of dramatization continues with the other numbers of op. 33.
The quartet in B flat major, for example, reaches a powerful half-cadence
on V of vi, begins a recapitulation in the subdominant for two bars, and
then quickly shifts to the tonic. (Four years later, Haydn would repeat this
procedure even more surprisingly in the Quartet in E flat major op. 50 no.
3, where a C minor cadence is interrupted at the last moment, and the dominant seventh of A flat is substituted for the implied C minor harmony.) The
G major and C major quartets op. 33 make equally emphatic and eccentric
uses of the device.

With the Quartet in E major, op. 54 no. 3 of 1784, Haydn can dispense
not only with a full cadence on the relative minor but can even eliminate
any transition and jump directly from the dominant of the relative minor (V
of vi) back into the tonic and the return of the main theme:

This is the ultimate ellipse in the use of the convention.[9] It is evident that a full cadence on the relative minor before a return to the tonic had become decidedly commonplace, and the elliptical form was much more attractive. Nevertheless, at the end of his creative activity Haydn never abandoned the technique, and continued to use the full cadence as well as the ellipse. In the quartets of op. 76, which date from 1797, all those in the major mode retain the way of ending the development section with the relative minor. Where the first movements do not have the usual sonata structure, as in the fifth and sixth quartets of this set, the finales of both quartets incorporate the convention with great effect. The transition from relative minor to tonic in the finale of op. 76 no 6 in E flat major, quoted on page 340, has a savagely interrupted C minor cadence before its return to the tonic by a series of multiple syncopated accents.

It is understandable that Beethoven would try to get away from a procedure used so consistently by his teacher and employed frequently as well by Mozart, Dussek, and other composers. This makes his occasional use of it very idiosyncratic and his return to it in his last years all the more significant. At the beginning of his career, when he moved to Vienna, Beethoven was concerned as much with presenting proof of his originality as he was with demonstrating his mastery of the accepted patterns of the Viennese tradition. Showing that he could do both at the same time must have represented a special triumph. His appropriation of the well-worn convention we have been looking at is striking in the Sonata for Piano in F major, op. 10 no. 2, in which he uses it twice as no one else had done before.

We find it first in the wrong place, not at the end of the development but in the exposition, and very close to the beginning (mm. 13 to 22):

---

[9] The ellipse works best when the principal theme at the tonic begins with the third degree of the scale, the dominant of the relative minor. To go directly from this dominant acts like a mediant shift with the third degree as a pivot. For composers of the generation of Chopin, Verdi, and Schumann, this process was the most important method of changing key.

Here it is not a return of the tonic that is prepared by the relative minor but the move to the dominant, and it is the more radical elliptical progression that Beethoven uses, going directly from the E major dominant of A minor into the otherwise unprepared C major. For the public of 1798, this passage would have come as a shock, and it was no doubt attributed to the wild and uncontrolled humor that made up the essential part of Beethoven's early reputation. It still remains unique, as far as I know, as an approach to the dominant in a sonata exposition. In any case, the effect is too startling and eccentric to be used again by Beethoven.

Equally original in this sonata but very different in character is the appearance of the convention in its standard place, at the end of the development. It is set up in the ordinary way, although Beethoven at first pretends that he is returning to F major by way of the tonic minor (the method, derived from Mozart, that he generally preferred). He then shifts to the relative minor, D minor, breaks off the phrase at the end, and, after a pause, suddenly shifts to the major mode and begins the recapitulation in the wrong key, D major:

476

The false recapitulation lasts twelve bars. Then there are six bars of a return to F major (with the usual descent of the harmony by fifths—D, G, C). The proper recapitulation appears to start with the second phrase of the exposition, but the six bars of return to the tonic have in fact secretly replayed almost every essential element of the first phrase at the correct original pitch although without yet quite resolving into the tonic. The whole process is Haydnesque in character—particularly in its delicate use of a short and slightly comic motif; although I do not think that Haydn ever turned the relative minor into major at a similar juncture, it is a surprise in keeping with his usual wit, and the passage firmly establishes Beethoven as a master of his teacher's style.

Beethoven's next use of the convention in the piano sonatas is more specifically characteristic of his personal style and reveals the qualities that both gave him his immense prestige and caused (and can still cause!) bitter resentment of his characteristic manner. In the Sonata in D major (the *Pastoral*) op. 28, the convention is used properly at the end of the development with the harmony of F sharp major, which is the dominant of the relative B minor, and a brief but poetic retransition follows (descending harmonically as usual by fifths from F♯ through B and E to A):

Beethoven

Beethoven does not dress up the convention here: he displays it naked. Whatever force the dominant of the relative minor had in late eighteenth-century tonality, Beethoven wants us to hear it. For thirty-six bars, the pianist plays nothing but the harmony of F sharp major, first hammering away at it *fortissimo* with two *sforzandi* in every bar, then dropping to *piano,* and finally, after a swelling sonority, subsiding into an exhausted *pianissimo* extended by a fermata. In the following transition, the exquisite lyricism comes in part from an almost Schubertian play with major and minor: the relative minor is first changed to major and then back to the more traditional minor, and finally to the standard V^7 of I.

The extraordinary length of the insistence on the dominant of the relative minor may seem unprecedented, although in fact Beethoven was anticipated by Haydn at the end of the development of the *Emperor* Quartet in C major, op. 76 no. 3, which insists with unrelieved *forte* and unchanging *sforzandi* on the harmony of E major, with drone fifths (a basic signature of the pastoral style) that remain unaltered for eleven measures followed by four measures of E minor.[10] That is not quite as long as Beethoven's thirty-six bars of unremitting V of vi, but Haydn's tempo is slower than Beethoven's and the bars are longer. The lyrical transition in Beethoven that follows, however, is wholly his own, and the obsessive character of the preceding sus-

---

[10]This passage is reproduced and discussed in my *Sonata Forms,* rev. ed., New York, 1988 pp. 282–283.

tained harmony is considerably greater in the sonata. The atmosphere in Haydn is jovial and rustic as well as dramatic, but the rusticity almost disappears in Beethoven in spite of the general pastoral character of his sonata: the dominant of the relative minor is revealed at length, and turns out to be both powerful and mysterious. The basis of the method is simple duration and dynamics, and the F sharp major reveals its own strength.

Lewis Lockwood has pointed out to me that the *Spring* Sonata in F major for Violin and Piano, op. 24, published, like op. 28, in 1801, displays an example at once spectacular and austere of the modulation directly from the dominant of the relative minor to the tonic, at the end of the development:

Once the dominant of D minor has been reached, Beethoven continues a trill on A for eight bars, shifting it simply from one register to another, and then introduces the tonic F major and the opening theme, which begins on the A. This is the elliptical version of the stereotype given dramatic force by reducing it to its fundamental elements, the single note A, and sustaining it by a trill at great length.

It is interesting that the finale of the sonata recalls this device at exactly the same place—the end of the central section with the return to the main theme—but gives it a new twist. The central section is in D minor throughout, and once again Beethoven isolates the A with a trill:

481

The surprise here is not a return to F major, but a false recapitulation in D major which then modulates with great elegance back to the tonic. The passage combines Beethoven's notorious humor, here principally derived from Haydn, with an unbroken lyrical tone. In both movements what is extraordinary about the familiar transition from V of vi to I is the air of absolute simplicity.

In these examples from op. 24 and op. 28, as in so many other instances Beethoven appears to be trying not so much to achieve a form of expression as to allow the musical language to speak for itself. This transformation of a convention by stripping it down to its underlying essential function releases the strength that is latent within it. Beethoven treats harmonic conventions very much as he treats the themes of his variation sets: he aims less to decorate or vary them as to reduce them to their underlying skeleton.[11] He makes listeners hear what is most fundamental in the conventions of music. Only then can he use the musical language in a more strictly personal manner. E. T. A. Hoffmann defended Beethoven against the charge of being a wild savage genius (a child of Nature, like Shakespeare, in short), and emphasized his 'sobriety' and his prudence, because Beethoven, Hoffmann claimed, 'drew his very being from the kingdom of sounds.' Of course, the kingdom of sounds, for Hoffmann as for every other European of the time, was only late eighteenth-century triadic tonality (and there are still people who think the system is imposed by acoustics and, indeed, by Nature her-

---

[11] See the discussion of this process in the variation sets on pp. 435–436.

self). The controlled violence of Beethoven's style comes from his ability to cut away anything superfluous from the structure of the musical language and then demonstrate what power it has when it functions unimpeded by the constraints of decorum.

The brutality of some of Beethoven's writing has been emphasized often enough over almost two centuries, but it should be clear that the violence is not simply a matter of dynamics, or even the length at which he dwells on certain harmonies. It is true that Beethoven's music is much louder than Haydn's or Mozart's—as Jens Peter Larsen noted when arguing that their music could not be subsumed within the same stylistic pigeonhole as Beethoven's[12]—and his procedures sometimes go on at greater length (there are, of course, many other differences as well). Nevertheless, Beethoven rarely invests a dissonance with unremitting accents or prolongs it to any great length—the one exception, perhaps, is the hammering of insistent climaxes on a dominant minor ninth chord that precedes so many of his grandest resolutions to the tonic (this ninth acts usually as an enhancement of the more ordinary dominant seventh).[13] On the contrary, it is generally a consonant chord that is dwelt on and prolonged (as at the end of the development of the *Pastoral* Sonata) until it appears to give up its secret power to us. It has been said about certain sculptors (most often probably about Michelangelo) that they do not so much invent forms as reveal those hidden within the stone. In a similar way, Beethoven seems to discover the meanings and emotions buried within the musical language. The metaphor may be fanciful, but it describes the experience of hearing his works. Beethoven demanded an attention from his audience that was revolutionary for his time (his music may be held principally responsible for the industrial growth of academic musical analysis), a kind of listening that made many people uncomfortable from the start but that is clearly addictive.

A transition very similar to the one in op. 28 at the end of the development can be found in the finale of the Ninth Symphony at the end of the fugue, as William Kinderman has pointed out.[14] What I wish to emphasize here is how old-fashioned these procedures used by Beethoven had become (for example, neither Carl Maria von Weber nor John Field ever used this stereotype in their sonatas) and with what extraordinary simplicity he presented them, as if they had a value in themselves that needed merely to be exhibited to work their effect. His retention of these out-of-date forms and even his attempt to endow them with a new vitality in his last years indicates his growing isolation from the musical life in Vienna that accompanied his increasing and unshakable prestige. Many of his works were an inspiration

---

[12] In a talk given at the 1972 meeting of the American Musicological Society in Chicago.

[13] See the first movements of op. 7, op. 31 no. 1, and op. 57, and the finale of op. 53 among many other examples.

[14] *Beethoven,* Berkeley, 1995, p. 74.

ounger generation, although the attempt to use them as models ended
in disaster. What separated him from the composers of the 1820s
refusal to alter the fundamental aspects of the stylistic language he
...ed as a child, although he expanded the limits of this style in ways
that earned him the astonishment and incomprehension of his contemporaries. For a while his symphonies (like those of Haydn and Mozart, in whose
tradition he had now been fixed by his contemporaries) were played less
often. His deafness isolated him further, and threw him back upon himself
and upon his memories of the past. When he was fifty, he appeared like an
old man from a different age.

His dependence on out-of-date formulas and the formidable success with
which Beethoven gave them new life through a technique that was his own
and that could be imitated by no one is manifest throughout the *Hammerklavier* and strikingly so at the end of the development of the opening movement. Here he sets up the traditional move to the D major dominant of the
relative minor with massive effect (illustrated on pp. 412–413). At the arrival of the D major harmony (m. 191) the direction is *sempre fortissimo,*
and the bass, which has been descending steadily for pages, suddenly halts
on D and remains fixed for ten bars. Placed at the end of a development,
this is the old hackneyed formula undisguised. Beethoven then quickly re-
moves all harmonization from the D and directs the pianist to lift the pedal,
clear signals of an approaching modulation with the D as a pivot note. If he
had gone directly at this point to recapitulation, we would have a completely
convincing but exceedingly banal return:

Given the tradition, superannuated as it was, this is what everyone might
have expected, and it is the occasion for one of the most affecting of Beethoven's surprises: a *cantabile* and *espressivo* detour through the flat supertonic

B major that is harmonically the most original aspect of the entire movement. (Even this originality has a tradition behind it: as the examples from Mozart have shown, the arrival at V of vi could be the occasion for the most picturesque harmonic effects.) What this wonderful change of harmonic color replaces is the usual retransition by a sequence of fifths back to the tonic, but it leaves the rest of the convention intact. The end of the development juxtaposes an absolutely traditional form with an astonishing innovation.

As surprising as the modulation to the flat supertonic B major may sound, however, it too has a precedent—not in a stereotype, but in one of the most extraordinary uses of a stereotype in Haydn, the return to the tonic at the end of the development of the Sonata in E flat major, H. XVI 52. As usual, there is a half-cadence on V of vi, dramatically isolated this time by a fermata and followed by a sudden leap into the flat supertonic E major:

The emotional world is very different in Haydn, but at the identical point of the structure of op. 106 (the retransition from the end of the development to the return of the main theme) there is exactly the same harmonic relationship, a very rare one which is, as far as I know, without precedent in Haydn and does not reappear before Beethoven's use in the *Hammerklavier*. Even an analogue for Beethoven's lyricism in the retransition is found in Haydn's more relaxed texture by bar 73 after the scherzoso beginning, but the structure and contrast of tone in Beethoven is considerably tighter.

I do not suggest the passage in Haydn as a model for Beethoven, although it is highly unlikely that he did not know it, and I do not imply any essay at imitation. It was most probably a part of the unconscious stylistic baggage that he retained from his earliest years. What becomes clear from the comparison, however, is that after the experimental Romanticism of the cyclical works of the years from 1812 to 1816, the Sonatas opp. 101 and 102, nos. 1 and 2, along with *An die Ferne Geliebte,* Beethoven turned back, in his last phase, to the stylistic technique of his earliest years to initiate an extraordinary expansion of the style beginning with op. 106. The expansion was so formidable that its origins are clouded, but some of the power of the last works depends on Beethoven's incessant efforts to reincorporate the tradition that he knew best into what he himself believed to be a radically new conception of the musical work. Even the long fugato of the development section in the first movement of op. 106 is intimately related to Haydn's developments in symphony and quartet, although Haydn never transferred this to the piano sonata.

What Haydn cannot do with his E major flat supertonic is draw the consequences that Beethoven derives from the B major excursion,[15] as the return to the tonic is immediately succeeded by a move to G flat major (reached through the standard move to the subdominant E flat major and its minor mode), which leads to the electrifying climax on B minor. Here is one of the keys to understanding Beethoven's unique expansion of classical technique: there is no way that Haydn could have dealt with a climax of that nature or with the appearance in a recapitulation of a harmony as exotic as the flat supertonic minor. One must add, however, that even the stylistic principles of this Beethovenian expansion may be found in latent form in Haydn. Not only does Haydn exploit the unusual appearance of E major within the development of the first movement of the Sonata in E flat major by placing the slow movement in that key, but he even suggests the harmony of E major briefly within the recapitulation of the first movement in a passage of curiously mysterious character:

---

[15] In a fine and provocative talk (New York, April 1996) on one of the few surviving sketches for the first movement of op. 106, Nicholas Marston showed that Beethoven had originally intended to return to the tonic through an A major harmony (that is, extending the dominant of the relative minor, V of vi, by its own dominant). We cannot know whether the move to B major was determined by what Beethoven planned for the recapitulation, or whether the recapitulation was based on the new ending for the development.

None of these juxtapositions detracts from Beethoven's originality. On the contrary, we can see that his most radical ideas are not isolated inspirations but derive from the musical language he had inherited.

Beethoven had employed the old convention of closing the development in the relative minor almost in passing in the Sonatas opp. 78 and 81a, but not since the *Pastoral* Sonata had he made such an ear-catching display of it or exploited it for its dramatic potential as we find in the *Hammerklavier*. Nevertheless, three years later the Sonata in A flat major op. 110 revealed the most eloquent possibilities of this convention and also of the move to the subdominant after the beginning of the recapitulation. At first sight this may appear strange, as op. 110 is in many respects the most personal of all the sonatas; even opp. 26 and 27 nos. 1 and 2 have, it seems to me, more precedents in works of other composers. In fact, throughout op. 110 the most traditional elements of music are remolded in order to produce a work in which neither the formal structure nor the emotional expression has a parallel or analogue elsewhere, even in Beethoven's own work.

The conventionality of the development section in the first movement is disconcerting. At the same time, there is nothing else like it. The example begins with the last three measures of the exposition and its cadential theme:

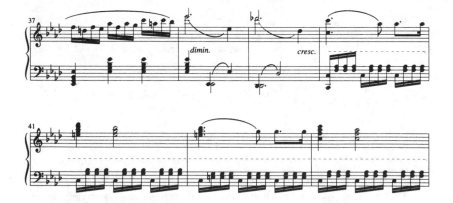

I do not know of another development section written after the 1770s in which the underlying structure is of such exaggerated simplicity, and even from that decade I can think of nothing as ostentatiously minimal as the melodic line. Just how little is taking place may best be perceived by simply isolating the melody from all the expressive counterpoint:

At the beginning, the melody of the two opening bars of the sonata at the original pitch is first reharmonized over a dominant pedal in the key of the relative minor and then repeated over and over, descending stepwise, until all the notes of the A flat major scale from C to C have been played. The formal character of this page can be seen clearly if we write out the bass, emphasizing the traditional groups of four measures:

This is our old friend the descent by fifths from V of vi to the tonic, with a beautifully controlled acceleration. The originality of the acceleration, however, should not be underestimated. Before this was written, most composers, including Beethoven himself, slowed down at the end of a sequence that returns to a tonic in order to set its final dominant in relief (see the example from Mozart's Sonata in D major K. 576 on pages 467–68 above). Beethoven here quickens the motion and sweeps directly into the recapitulation, which, at first, only continues the melodic process of the whole development.

In a real and very literal sense, this whole section is not a development at all but the traditional retransition to the tonic that eighteenth-century theorists specified should come after the development had closed properly in the relative minor. Behind this page lies Beethoven's knowledge and experience of the technique of Mozart, who deployed all his grace to make these transitions seem at the same time both inevitable and surprising. Although harmonically the page is only a retransition, motivically it operates as a development, but the motivic work is reduced to an unprecedented minimum in order to correspond to the harmonic character. The tone is lyric throughout, as the left hand alternates expressive tenor and bass lines antiphonally.

To start the process, the descent from E flat at the end of the exposition to the C, which functions as the dominant of F minor (mm. 38 to 40), is effected without harmonization. Beethoven had already made a similar move to the relative minor in the finale of the Sonata in E flat major op. 7:

However, the B natural here is much like the famous C♯ in bar 7 of the *Eroica* Symphony: a striking chromatic detail that has much more fateful consequences later in the piece. In the Sonata op. 7, it becomes the vehicle toward the end of the movement for the most magical harmonic alteration, to the dominant of E major:

Here, and in op. 110, we can see Beethoven stripping everything away from an element of structure so that it can make its point on its own. In op. 110, the unharmonized D flat and the C (see page 488), also left bare for a brief moment, may appear ambiguous at first, but they imply exactly what takes place. The D flat is dissonant in relation to the preceding five bars of dominant harmony and requires resolution to the C. The parallel unison motion over four octaves rules out the possibility of harmonizing the D flat with V^7 of I (the dominant seventh of A flat) and makes inconceivable a simple resolution into a first inversion of A flat, which would only be awkward. No chord is implied other than the $^6_4$ of F minor that actually appears. It is interesting that any harmonization of the D flat would be completely unconvincing: the transition is slightly mysterious and yet logical. The urge to force the single note, the single harmony, the single rhythmic gesture to release its implicit meaning manifested itself early in Beethoven's career, but it became more pressing in the final years.

Beethoven's treatment of the convention of moving to the subdominant after the beginning of the recapitulation is equally original and even more spectacular. The opening four bars of the exposition are first reconceived with a new rich texture that is a genuine development of another part of the exposition. Then the melody is transferred to the left hand for a simple transition to the subdominant, and bars 5 to 8 of the exposition appear transposed up a fourth.[16] The dynamics descend slowly to pianissimo as we reach the only modulation in the opening movement to a remote key. The most complex harmonic treatment takes place, therefore, not in the development but in the recapitulation, although the harmonic motion lacks any sense of the drive that would characterize a main central development. All harmonic action is suspended with this exquisite page. The transition to E major is a moment of intense lyrical expression, but the eventual return to the tonic is even more extraordinary:

---

[16] Bars 9 and 10 of the exposition already contain a trace of subdominant harmony, perhaps providing a stimulus for Beethoven's radical alteration of these and the following bars. However, I do not think that one can claim that the unusual turn to E major that amplifies the move to the subdominant in the recapitulation is implied by the thematic material.

Once again, as at the opening of the development, the listener must use his imagination to interpret the harmonic meaning of the last two notes of measure 77. This time there are two thirds (or tenths), not simple octave doublings, but there is a genuine ambiguity now, as the modulation back to A flat major does not take place precisely in phase between the two hands. The first note in the right hand, G♯, is the expected note in what is still heard as E major, while the E♯ in the left hand would have a possible explanation in E major (an added C♯, for example, would make it a much more ordinary chord), but any such elucidation is evaded. The second note in the right hand, G natural, however, seems to propose the oncoming dominant of A flat, but the E natural in the left hand continues to hold on to the tonality of E. Only with the E flat at the beginning of the next measure do we realize that the E♯ was an F natural, the E natural an appoggiatura to the E flat, and the G natural already a part of the returning tonic. (Any suggestion of E minor for the E natural and G natural has been made impossible by the previous E♯.) Harmonic explanation is left suspended until we hear the E flat. One could say that the passage holds a mystery, but that would not do justice to its exceptional modesty. After the fact, the importance of this juncture is marked by the *crescendo* and the *ritenente* of bar 78, and the secondary theme is now indicated *espressivo,* a direction missing whenever it was played before. The modulation to E major intensifies and reinterprets everything that comes after it.

As we have seen, Beethoven has reserved his most innovative conceptions for a transfiguration of the conventional elements of structure (the orthodox move to D flat major is changed to the minor mode with C sharp minor, and then slips almost without emphasis into E major). It would seem as if he was not so much inventing new effects as discovering what these old-fashioned devices had always held within them. The flatted submediant (E major) is, in fact, clearly treated here as a remote version of the minor mode of the subdominant (D flat or C sharp), as Mozart had also conceived it.[17] (It is in fact basic to the tonal system as Mozart and Beethoven and their contemporaries understood it that the subdominant or flat direction is intimately related to the minor mode—even the notation reveals this naively, as we transform C major into C minor by adding flats to the key signature). Using E major as an exotic version of the minor mode of D flat major gives this secondary development its strangely expressive character; and the appearance of the dominant harmony, E flat major, acts like a return to the major mode as well as a return to the tonic. Beethoven altered the system of tonality he had inherited very little, if at all, but he understood instinctively how it worked better than any of his contemporaries.

The most astonishing aspect of op. 110 is Beethoven's dramatic re-working, in the finale, of the most conventional elements of academic counterpoint: inversion, augmentation, and diminution. This reconception, however, needs to be understood in the light of his attempt to integrate all the movements of a sonata more thoroughly than he or anyone else had yet been

---

[17] See, for example, the famous C natural in the E major duet in the cemetery (second act of *Don Giovanni*), finally interpreted as part of a subdominant minor chord (illustrated on p. 311).

able to accomplish.[18] For this he engaged many of the basic elements of
form—theme, tempo, both large- and small-scale rhythm, long-range harmonic relations, and outer structure—and he created, not a dramatic program, but a purely musical analogue of one. An indication of his purpose is
the way each movement rises from the preceding one. He does not specify
attacca as he does in the Sonata in A major op. 101, or the Cello Sonatas
op. 102 nos. 1 and 2 (and we may add here the Sonata in E major op. 109,
in which the pedal designated at the end of the first movement is to be held
until the opening of the following *Prestissimo*). He does not need to. The
first bars of the scherzo and of the finale seem to take over from the preceding movements. The end of the first movement, although it beautifully
rounds off the piece, is just hesitant or inconclusive enough with its two
short, soft chords to make the scherzo sound as if it were a direct continuation. The main theme of the scherzo, in fact, starts with the last note of the
preceding cadence:

And the end of the scherzo itself presents the dominant of the first chord of
the next movement, which takes over the final F:

---

[18] James Webster has convincingly traced Haydn's early efforts to achieve a greater integration
of large-scale works. In the last quarter of the eighteenth century we find attempts to recapture
the thematic unity, admittedly superficial, of many Baroque suites. However, Beethoven went
further than his predecessors in attacking the independence of the single movements of symphony, sonata, and quartet.

Most pianists have remarked these thematic interrelationships and above all, the way the fugue theme can be found throughout the work. The parallel fourths of the theme are sufficiently idiosyncratic to call attention to themselves:

and they inescapably bring the main theme of the first movement to mind:

A secondary theme of the scherzo also presents rising parallel fourths:

and this theme is even recalled rhythmically in the finale by the diminution of the fugue:

The trio of the scherzo reworks the parallel fourths into a descending pattern:

which is heard as follows:

The figuration here is so curious that Beethoven understandably had great trouble shaping it: the manuscript of this trio contains pages of rewriting and he had to return to it after finishing the rest of the sonata.

Emphasizing only the recurrence of these fourths does little justice to Beethoven's conception of the thematic integration of the whole sonata, and makes it appear obsessively schematic. In fact, each movement alternates two types of motifs of very different character, allowing a play of expressive variety and contrast. In addition to the parallel fourths, there is a scale motif that outlines a sixth (a contour shared by so many of the work's motifs, including the theme of the fugue and the main theme of the first movement). This scale motif first appears in the opening Moderato, where it serves as a principal element of the second part of the exposition at the dominant leading to the most considerable climax:

The opening themes of the scherzo and of the *Arioso* (Adagio ma non troppo) in the finale invert this motif:

This thematic invariance leads to the perennial question raised by thematic analysis: are we supposed to hear the motif of the *Arioso dolente* as a return of the scherzo? I do not myself think that a perception of this identity has any great importance, and it would only disturb our sense of the different expressive character of the Adagio. The relation has a different theoretical interest: it shows that two themes formed of much the same pitches and with similar shapes can have radically opposed expressive values.[19] The different rhythms given to each version of the motif and their harmonic implications determine everything here: in the scherzo the strong beats in bars 1, 2, and 4 are consonant, and even the third bar, with its heavy repetition, gives a jolly swing to the rhythm; in the *Arioso*, the motif is arranged so that most of the notes on a strong beat are dissonant—the D flat, the B flat, and the A flat are all conceived as appoggiaturas, used throughout eighteenth- and nineteenth-century opera as an expression of grief: when the *Arioso* returns (losing force, grief-stricken), they are explicitly heard as sobs:

This texture closely resembles the central section of the Cavatina in the Quartet in B flat major, op. 130, where the first violin's part is marked *beklemmt* (choked), as if the lyric expression was impeded by tears.

What gives op. 110 its individual character is less the recurrence of themes (although this does, indeed, have its effect) than the recurrence of alternating and contrasting patterns—scale patterns as well as parallel fourths. To a great extent, this alternation is what Carl Dahlhaus has called 'subthematic'; along with the play of rhythm and spacing, it gives a unified character to the sound of op. 110, which has a sonority of its own unlike that of any of the other late sonatas. The alternation guarantees a richness of motivic forms, and prevents the parallel fourths from dominating as ex-

---

[19] Deryck Cooke in *The Language of Music* gave the theme of the Adagio to demonstrate that melodies descending the scale in minor from the fifth degree to the leading-tone are a natural expression of grief.

clusively as the descending thirds control the *Hammerklavier* or Neapolitan harmonies permeate the *Appassionata*.

The semi-programmatic aspect of op. 110 is signaled by the recitative that opens the finale as an operatic scena; the sobs of the *Arioso dolente* already appear here in the famous use of *Bebung* (an imitation of the 'trembling' vibrato of the clavichord, itself an imitation of the voice, to suggest grief). An arioso, for Beethoven, would still have signified a genre midway between aria and recitative, half lyric, half *parlando*. The operatic character of the finale, however, is cancelled by the fugue, Allegro ma non troppo, that follows the Adagio ma non troppo. Nevertheless, any disparity between arioso and fugue is overcome: the Adagio and Allegro may be in different tempi but they have almost the same pulse. Each tempo springs from the preceding, and there is little change as we move from one to the next. The Adagio is notated in 12/16, the Allegro in 6/8, and the sixteenth notes of the Adagio are equivalent to the eighth notes of the Allegro. On paper the Allegro is twice as fast as the Adagio, although the actual speed of the notes remains uniform or changes very little. Nevertheless, even if this equivalence were enforced metronomically (which is not what Beethoven's style demands), the Allegro would sound twice as fast as the Adagio since it has two strong beats per measure to the Adagio's four. Both sections, of course, need a certain freedom, and the Adagio in particular calls for considerable inflection, but any lurching change of speed at the junctures defeats Beethoven's conception.[20] This is amply demonstrated at the return of the Adagio after the first fugue:

---

[20] Schindler claimed that Beethoven wanted several tempo changes for the great Largo e mesto of the Sonata in D major op. 10 no. 3. It is dangerous to take anything that Schindler said at face value, but if we believe this often quoted statement, then we must also credit what followed: Beethoven added that only connoisseurs should be aware of the changes. In the finale of op. 110 it is the illusion of an identity of pulse that matters, not a metronomic identity.

The change from eighth notes to sixteenth notes here signifies a change of notation rather than of pulse. We can see this even more clearly from the autograph manuscript, where Beethoven at first put the change of notation later, and notated the G minor arpeggio of the Adagio still in eighth notes within the Allegro tempo, marking it *ritardando*. He later changed the tempo indication, wrote out the arpeggio in sixteenth notes, and removed the *ritardando* indication. This erasure of the *ritardando* implies either that there is a sudden change of pulse at this place, or that the Adagio ma non troppo and the Allegro ma non troppo are essentially the same. I have never heard a convincing performance that chose the first alternative, and the way that the second *Arioso* arises directly from the end of the fugue imposes a sense of rhythmic unity. The tempo of the *Arioso* is, freely and expressively interpreted, equivalent to the tempo of the fugue, although the accentuation of 12/16 naturally makes the large-scale rhythm sound twice as slow as the 6/8 of the fugue.

This type of tempo relationship was traditional at the time.[21] The finale of Beethoven's Third Piano Concerto changes at the coda from Allegro to Presto: in reality the beat remains the same, but the coda sounds much faster because there are many more notes to the bar. In the Sonata for Piano in C minor op. 111, the Maestoso introduction ends with a written-out trill in thirty-second notes that moves directly into the Allegro and is notated in sixteenth notes. Most pianists (including myself) play the Maestoso too slowly—it is not an Adagio—and have to accelerate the trill gradually (changing the tempo suddenly at the Allegro in the middle of the trill ought to be beneath consideration). The opening of Schubert's great Symphony in C Major (the introduction is marked *alla breve* in the manuscript although not in any published version) also implies that the Allegro that follows the Andante con moto is essentially in the same pulse; there are even performances nowadays in which this identity is clearly realized.

Tempo indications in Beethoven would create fewer problems if we understood that the metronome marks were not meant to be executed with dogmatic insensitivity. On the manuscript of a song, he wrote that the metronome mark was valid only for the first bars 'as feeling has its tempo, and this cannot entirely be expressed in this figure.'[22] In the *Prestissimo* of the

---

[21] Part of the problem with Beethoven's tempi and the metronome indications he chose for them lies in the fact that he continued to use Mozartean ideas of tempo to the end of his life, although writing music that was more difficult to play and to hear at these formerly standard tempos. The notorious ♩ = 138 of the *Hammerklavier* is a perfectly good Mozart Allegro. One should remember the circumstances in which 138 was put to the *Hammerklavier*. The indication was sent in a letter to Ries, who was correcting the proofs for the English edition in London. Beethoven asked him to change the tempo from Allegro assai to Allegro, and to add 138 as the metronome mark. This suggests that Beethoven was, in fact, revising the mark *down* to 138, and it certainly shows that the tempo was originally conceived as very fast and only slightly modified.

[22] *Thayer's Life of Beethoven*, ed. Elliot Forbes, Princeton, 1964, pp. 687–688.

Sonata in E major op. 109, Beethoven writes at one point *un poco espressivo;* eight measures later he specifies *a tempo.* Certainly for late Beethoven, and most probably for the earlier periods as well, *espressivo* indicates not exactly a different tempo but a relaxation of pace, with some freedom. In the opening movement of the Sonata in C minor op. 111, every indication of *espressivo* is accompanied by the indication *rit.* (which is *ritenuto,* a sudden *rubato,* and must not be confounded with the more gradual *ritardando,* always written out differently). In op. 110, the Adagio ma non troppo of the arioso is an expressive version of the tempo of the fugue, which becomes Allegro ma non troppo with the doubling of accented beats and the more flowing texture.

The importance of this relative identity of pulse in the finale of op. 110 becomes crucial with the extraordinary conceptual innovations of the final pages. The first half of the movement—recitative, Adagio, and Fugue—is wonderfully original in the working-out of its details, but it does not violate tradition in any way. The recitative modulates from F major, which ends the Scherzo, to the A flat minor of the Adagio; the Fugue is in A flat major. Both the coupling of Adagio and Fugue and the tonal scheme are hardly out of the ordinary. With the return of the *Arioso,* however, the structure is transformed. The Adagio ma non troppo suddenly reappears a half-step down, in the key of G minor, 'exhausted, lamenting,' as Beethoven indicates. The key relationship is unprecedented and works directly on the listener as symbolic. Taken down a half-step, everything sounds flat, depressing, less brilliant: the music literally induces the sense of despair that it expresses. The melody of the first Adagio ma non troppo is repeated complete in the second with no structural alterations but with elaborate changes of detail, as in a *double* from a Baroque suite. The changes, however, carry out a dramatic representation of exhaustion and lamentation. The phrase is continually broken as if a singer, choked with emotion, could breathe only with difficulty. The method is essentially the same (but without the humor or the irony) as that found in Mozart's quintet from the first act of *Così fan tutte,* 'Da scrivermi ogni giorno' (Write to me every day), where the lovers cannot sing more than a syllable without gasping through tears. After the serenity of the first fugue, the lament of the first Adagio is dramatically altered. The radical tonal relationship and the dramatic recasting of the melody create a huge structural dissonance that demands an elaborate and imposing resolution. After this, no simple return of the fugue or of the tonic A flat major will do.

The transition to the second fugue reinforces the harmonic tension, and the repeated, syncopated insistence on the single chord of G major contributes to a sense that the form is breaking down. We do not know what this obstinate, off-beat repetition portends. The heavy chords are all to be played *una corda.* The long *crescendo* with the *una corda* soft pedal held down resulted in a new sonority, a series of repressed thuds never tried before.

Beethoven's form of deafness allowed him intermittent moments of faint hearing. Did he know what this passage would sound like on his instrument?

An arpeggio rising from the lowest region of the bass gradually diminishes and clears away the concentration on a single harmony, and the second fugue arises out of the sonority:

Beethoven's mastery of fugue required a considerable act of will. He never had Mozart's unsurpassed facility for voice-leading, and his early contrapuntal exercises display astonishingly awkward mistakes. Perhaps it was this very difficulty that stimulated his drastic rethinking of fugal style. In the *Hammerklavier,* the way the pastiche of Johann Sebastian Bach's style (see p. 428) is cut off in the introduction to the finale is a statement without words of 'Nicht diese Töne!' Most teaching of composition in Beethoven's childhood consisted essentially of lessons in counterpoint. In the early 1800s, he mastered the technique of the late eighteenth-century concert fugue, in works like the *Eroica* Symphony and the Quartets op. 59 no. 3 and op. 95. In his last piano sonatas, he assumed the task of giving new vitality to the old contrapuntal forms. The gigantic shape of the *Hammerklavier* fugue was a manifesto. The first movement of op. 111 produced a synthesis of fugue and first-movement sonata form.

502

With the finale of op. 110, Beethoven reconceived the significance of the most traditional and academic elements of fugue writing: inversion, augmentation, and diminution. In the second *Arioso,* the dramatic scenario imagined by Beethoven had reached the lowest point of exhaustion and despair. The fugue theme, which originally outlined a sixth moving upward, is now replaced by its falling inversion. The implicit metaphor is not simply intellectual play: the new form of the theme is considerably weaker in tension and urgency. As a first fugue it would be sadly ineffective, but here it partially prolongs the sense of exhaustion conveyed in the preceding section. The movement returns to life only little by little (that is the composer's explicit direction: *poi a poi di nuovo vivente*). Following the *diminuendo* of the previous bars, Beethoven continues the soft pedal for 28 bars, and there are no dynamic indications whatever for the first 24:

503

Beethoven

After the first 16 bars the gradual return to life is accomplished by augmentation and diminution. When they arrive in bars 152–153 we hear again the original form of the theme that aspires rather than falls: it is played simultaneously twice as slow in the treble and three times as fast in the bass. At bar 160 a *crescendo* is indicated over 7 bars, and this implies a very gradual increase. Suddenly—a point that is the subject of some misapprehension—Beethoven writes all the rhythms twice as fast, but directs the pianist to play more slowly, Meno Allegro. (Kinderman has brilliantly called attention to the remarkable telescoping of the theme at this point, which is what makes it recall the Scherzo so closely.[23]) Like the change from the Allegro ma non troppo of the first fugue back to the Adagio ma non troppo of the *Arioso,* the Meno Allegro is not a change of tempo but of notation, and here it must be interpreted fairly strictly for the passage to make full sense and to sound natural. A few bars later the pianist is told to accelerate back into the original tempo again.

Beethoven reinvented tradition here. The techniques of inversion, augmentation, and diminution are among the most traditional in writing fugues: Beethoven gives them a totally new significance. Inverting the upward-moving theme became a symbol of exhaustion, the meaning enforced by texture and dynamics. Transforming the theme played at half tempo back to the original tempo renders the experience of a return of energy, and the diminution at triple tempo beginning softly represents the source of new life. For the first time in the history of music these commonplace elements of fugue take on a narrative content.

The second fugue, then, dramatizes the return of life and energy after the weakness and despair of the Adagio. To employ the aesthetic terminology

---

[23] 'A similarity [with the scherzo] is clearly audible, in part because Beethoven compresses the fugal subject in diminution, deleting the second of its three rising fourths.' William Kinderman, *Beethoven,* Berkeley, 1995, p. 229.

of Beethoven's age: the 'arbitrary' conventions are remade into 'natural' forms of expression. The abstract has become symbolic. As the augmentation accelerates the music little by little into the first tempo, the diminution has become an energetic accompanying figure. This caused a notation problem for Beethoven since he wanted to end in the original tempo, but he also wanted his augmented theme to accelerate into it. 'Little by little coming back to life' (*poi a poi di nuovo vivente,* or *nach und nach auflebend,* as the manuscript also has it) conveys Beethoven's intention of a very gradual return of energy. The direction to play louder and raise the soft pedal comes much later. In order to end with the original notation as well as the original tempo, Beethoven had to halve the tempo and double the notation, but the change is only on paper since, for the ear, the doubling and halving cancel each other out. Of course, at the point this happens the tempo cannot be precisely half of the original, as the direction 'little by little coming back to life' has been in force for thirty-two measures, and a very slight acceleration is the most logical means of realizing the effect. The idea of transforming a theme played at half tempo back into the original tempo was absolutely unprecedented and was not simple to notate. The essential innovation was to double the tempo only gradually, and every indication on these pages affirms that Beethoven wanted no sudden alteration: 'little by little coming back to life'; 'little by little raise the soft pedal'; 'little by little faster again.' All of these directions enforce the idea of an unbroken process.

The Meno Allegro does indeed represent a rhythmic change, but one that requires the relationship to be strictly observed so that it takes place as part of the continuous development. In fact, in order to make the continuity total, Beethoven initiates a different kind of rhythm some measures before the Meno Allegro and the new pattern moves into it. Starting in measure 161, although hinted at before, the diminution in the right hand fragments the motif and attacks every one of its phrases on the upbeat eighth-note. By the end of 161, indeed, it seems as if the bar-line has been displaced in the right hand by one eighth-note beat before the left. This makes the new form of the motif in bar 168 sound as if it began on a downbeat:

This interpretation of the shape of the motif is actually confirmed by the bar-line at 170. The out-of-phase relation among the different voices, and the return to equilibrium covers the irregularity of the gradual acceleration. It is a beautifully subtle example of cross accent, and it needs the sense of an uninterrupted flow to convey the sense of new life that is the principle of Beethoven's conception of this extraordinary page. When we remember that the Adagio ma non troppo moved seamlessly into the Allegro ma non troppo and back again, we can see that the drama of this third and final movement unfolds in one continuous impulse, culminating in the ecstatic joy of the final page.

The movement from despair to ecstasy needs to be put into perspective. Perhaps the indication at the very opening of the first movement should be recalled here. The first edition has *Avec amabilita;* the manuscript has *con amabilita* and explains this by the German *sanft.* Gentle, mild, lovely, good-natured—some combination of these should do for a gloss. Over the years we have become used to the heroic Beethoven, the tragic composer, the transcendent figure. We sometimes encounter the grossly humorous Beethoven, whose rough imagination reminded his contemporaries of the novels of Jean Paul Richter. We tend to forget the lyrical Beethoven—not the grand lyricism of the Adagio of the Ninth Symphony or the hymn-like slow movements of many of the piano sonatas, but the simple phrases of great sweetness that slip through his works without making any great claims. The transition from the Adagio of the Cello Sonata in C major op. 102 back to the opening Andante may serve as a reminder:

Marked *teneramente* (tenderly), these bars could be analyzed to show how they derive from the motifs at the beginning of the movement and how they

507

predict the return of the Andante. However, they exist essentially for their own sake, and they make no claims to transcendence.[24]

Most innovators try to forget the past or reject it, even when their dependence on earlier models is greater than they themselves or their disciples would like to believe. No composer has been more innovative than Beethoven, and he radically changed the nature and character of the music composed in the two centuries that followed his earliest works, but did less than Chopin, Schumann, Liszt, Verdi, Wagner, Schoenberg, Bartók, or Stravinsky—perhaps even less than Haydn—to alter the fundamental principles of the style he inherited. This may seem a paradox, but is in fact a straightforward account of his originality: he rejected no part of the eighteenth-century tradition. He continued to employ the contrast of character within a theme (see the first eight bars of the *Hammerklavier,* for example), a procedure that most of his contemporaries no longer found interesting. He insisted on the fundamental force of the dominant: even when he employed mediants within a sonata form, he always set them up and fully prepared them with a powerful dominant introduction, while his younger contemporaries preferred chromatic shifts. To the end of his life, he preserved the classical balance of dominant and subdominant, a dead letter to the generations that followed him and the reason it is rarely mentioned by nineteenth-century theorists, who had also forgotten it. He never abandoned the long final section in the tonic and the insistence on final resolution. His greatest innovations—and they cannot be overestimated—lay in the unprecedented expansion of the style. More than any other composer, he understood what was latent in the contemporary tonal language, and he knew how to exploit it to enlarge the possibilities of expression. That is why there has always been a problem in classifying him: those who lived when he lived placed him with Haydn and Mozart, even when they thought he was spoiling and perverting the grand tradition. More recent critics think of him as the beginning of a new era. As a metaphor for the nature of his innovative genius, we might choose the following passage from the opening page of his Sonata in D major op. 10 no. 3:

<hr />

[24] This Cello Sonata curiously parallels the structure of the Piano Sonata in A Major op. 101, written at the same time. Both start with a lyrical movement in 6/8 of similar tempos (Andante and Allegretto) and continue *attacca* with a vigorous march in dotted rhythm. Then in both works, a very slow movement with ornamental arabesque figures is followed by a fragmentary return of the first movement, leading with a trill directly into a brilliant Allegro in 2/4, very jolly and humorous in style. The scheme is an experiment in cyclical form that Beethoven evidently decided to repeat.

In this work of 1798, Beethoven produces a phrase demanding a low E that was not on his keyboard and follows it with another that requires a high F sharp that also did not yet exist on the instruments of his time. Even if these notes are not played, they are so clearly implied by the music that we think we hear them, or at least we imagine their existence. (Beethoven planned to rewrite his early works for piano to add the notes that were now possible, and he even did so with the Third Piano Concerto, originally conceived for a smaller keyboard range.) We may even experience a dramatic effect from the frustration that is inevitable when we play the music as written. Beethoven's innovations in harmony, phrase structure, large form, and even in emotional expression are analogous to his straining against the limits of the keyboard. He destroyed no part of his heritage. He continued to employ the conventions that he learned as a child even when he expanded them almost beyond recognition, because he knew what they meant and he understood how much energy they could release, how much expressive power they contained. His world was no longer the world of Haydn and Mozart, but we misconceive his achievement if we fail to recognize how much of their thinking is preserved within his and how much he attempted to retain their ease and grace. In this last matter his success was bound to be incomplete, but it was still formidable.

There is so much of Beethoven that appears incompatible with eighteenth-century style that it is hard to grasp how many of his grandest projects are essentially syntheses of late eighteenth-century ideals. For example, at that time there were several different traditional ways of ending a set of variations. A final fugue was one possibility. An adagio variation followed by a brilliant allegro was another. A variation in the minor mode succeeded by a return to the major was still another convention. One could also conclude with a free fantasy. Finally, one could bring back the original theme at the end. In the *Eroica* Variations for piano and in the *Diabelli* Variations as well, Beethoven decides to use all of these solutions. In the *Diabelli,* he even has three minor variations, including a very slow one that recalls the *Goldberg* Variations of Bach, and a grandiose and brilliant fugue in the style of Handel, with a virtuoso coda and a free development of the thematic elements so that we have a synthesis of the history of variation form in the previous century. He cannot bring back Diabelli's trivial waltz at the end after his monumental treatment of it, so he transforms it into a minuet, an evocation of the courtly grace of a world that has disappeared. It clearly acts as a surrogate for a return of the dance. The last five variations, in short, are an embodiment of a long stylistic development of the conventions of variation form in something like the same way that the introduction to the fugue of the *Hammerklavier* traces a history of counterpoint from simple imitation through the style of Bach to the new requirements of Beethoven's era.

I should like to emphasize the modesty of the concluding minuet ('Don't drag' ['non tirarsi dietro'] is Beethoven's indication), its exquisite urbanity, its elegance and its ultimate refusal of the sublime—its *amabilità,* in short. The coda, after some filigree passagework containing the most delicate sonorities, does not end *pianissimo* but concludes with a sudden startling *forte* on an offbeat, a reminder of the comic spirit that has informed the whole work. This minuet is one of those late works of Beethoven, like the String Quartet in F major op. 135 or the Eighth Symphony, that are sometimes labelled neoclassic. They call to mind the lightness and clarity of eighteenth-century Viennese style and do not exhibit any of the violence or the *terribilità* popularly associated with Beethoven. None of these works is pastiche like Mozart's great Handelian fugue in the Requiem or the chorale prelude in the *Magic Flute.* No eighteenth-century minuet ever sounded like the final variation of the *Diabelli* Variations, which, however, clearly functions as an evocation of the past. Hardly a phrase in op. 135 could conceivably have been written before 1800. If these works recall a past, it is one which still seems alive.

Vienna's musical life in the early eighteen hundreds was enriched more than that of any other European capital, not by public concerts but by small, semi-private performances that took place in the homes of the well-to-do middle class as well as in the mansions of the aristocracy. Beethoven's chamber works—his sonatas, quartets, and trios—disrupted the character of this musical life to some extent even while they exploited it. Although during his lifetime the piano sonatas were almost never played in public in Vienna but only in private or semi-private gatherings, many of them—the *Waldstein,* the *Appassionata,* the *Hammerklavier,* and others—implied a public domain. After his death, it was his instrumental compositions, rather than those of Haydn and Mozart, that became the staple of the serious public concert, to compete with the virtuoso works of the new generations.

The so-called neoclassic works reveal Beethoven's allegiance to the culture that produced his musical language, and not simply because some of these compositions may have been created essentially for semi-private performance. Their urbanity expresses an ideal of society in which his music was possible, even if many of his compositions amounted to an outrageous violation of that society's decorum and often provoked a musical scandal for that reason. The masterpiece of his sociable style is perhaps the third movement of the Quartet in B flat major op. 130, Andante con moto ma non troppo, a lyrical scherzo in D flat major of unparalleled charm and eloquence (*poco scherzoso* is the indication). It may appear to be a nostalgic reminiscence of Mozart and Haydn, but it is actually a modern and sophisticated achievement the equal of Beethoven's most heroic creations. Like the minuet-finale of the *Diabelli,* it ends humorously with a surprising *forte* on an offbeat. The moment of absolute grace in this movement is the traditional and all-too-familiar turn to the subdominant, postponed to the beginning of the coda. Here the lowering of tension and the lyricism inherent in the convention actually bring the movement to a halt and produce a brief and exceptional moment of stasis. The cadential trill is broken off with a pause, and the movement starts up again *non troppo presto* with a long scale in the first violin from which all overt virtuosity has been purged and which prolongs the stillness:

511

This moment of amiability, delight, and grace is an essential aspect of Beethoven's aesthetic, as much as his grotesque humor and his tragic vision. The autumnal regret inherent in this late and radical reinterpretation of an old convention is a reminiscence of a culture that had always lived mainly in the imagination. Just as the *Eroica* Symphony incarnated a political and public vision, this quartet movement is a musical image of an intimate and civilized society, one that certainly existed only as an imperfectly realized ideal. The ideal culture, however, was implicit in the musical language that Beethoven inherited and made his own.

EPILOGUE

On the whole, it looks as if the Sonata had run its course. This is as it should be, for we cannot repeat the same forms for centuries.

Robert Schumann (trans. Paul Rosenfeld)

———————

Ces grands novateurs sont les seuls vrais classiques et forment une suite presque continue. Les imitateurs des classiques, dans leurs plus beaux moments, ne nous procurent qu'un plaisir d'érudition et de goût qui n'a pas grande valeur.

Marcel Proust (*Classicisme et Romantisme*)

These great innovators are the only true classics and form an almost continuous succession. The imitators of the classics, in their finest moments, give us only a pleasure of erudition and taste which is of no great value.

Epilogue

Robert Schumann's homage to Beethoven, the Fantasy in C major, op. 17, is the monument that commemorates the death of the classical style. The beginning of the last song of Beethoven's cycle *An die ferne Geliebte* (a setting of the words 'Take these songs then, my love, that I sang')

is clearly quoted at the very end of the first movement of Schumann's work:

but also hinted at throughout the movement[1] in such phrases as

Nevertheless, in all significant respects of structure and detail the Schumann Fantasy is totally unclassical: even the appearance of Beethoven's melody is itself unclassical by its reference to a personal and completely private significance exterior to the work—the words of the Beethoven phrase are surely

---

[1] The motto of the Fantasy—four lines from Schlegel placed at the head—tells us that a hidden tone runs secretly through the whole. The homage to Beethoven is also suggested by the canceled titles to the movements: 'Ruins—Triumphal Arch—Starry Crown.'

present for Schumann as an autobiographical reference—and by its exposition of the definitive and basic form of the main thematic material only at the last moment.

Most important of all, this moment is the only stable one; the full reference to Beethoven on the last page of the movement is the first appearance in the work of the tonic chord of C major in root position. In other words, unlike every classical work, Schumann's Fantasy neither starts from a point of stability, nor reaches one until the last possible moment. (This was probably an instinctive procedure with Schumann; as a matter of strict truth there is a tonic chord in root position just a few measures before the final and complete reference to the secret motto, although it sounds there, indeed, not like a tonic but as a dominant of the subdominant, and makes only a minimal difference to the proportions and effect.) In spite of the thematic recapitulation in this movement, there is therefore no harmonic resolution until the very end. Most of the long symmetrical recapitulation is not even remotely in C major, but in E flat major, and the long, stable tonic section of the classical sonata is of no interest to Schumann.

The opening instability, as well, annuls the classical canon of a closed framework. The excitement of Schumann's first measures

is unparalleled in a classical work, and its emotional turbulence is conveyed by the accompaniment's shapeless version of the theme above it. In performance it is not easy to define even the rhythm of this accompaniment clearly, and there is no reason to suppose that Schumann expected a clear definition. The defining rhythmic framework of the classical style is rejected in favor of a more open sonority out of which the theme gradually assumes a shape. This shape is one which implies a direction, not to a classical dominant, but to the subdominant F major, and the movement does indeed go to F. The classical pattern of a rise in tension towards the center is consequently destroyed, and it would be difficult, after all, to imagine such a form starting from the violence of this opening. Most Romantic works of the 1830s imply a lowering of tension after the opening, and the succeeding fluctuations of tension evade the clear outline of the classical dramatic form.

In harmony and rhythm, as well as in formal outline, there is a return to the principles of the Baroque. The first movement of the Fantasy has a long middle section in the tonic minor and in a slower tempo, which gives it a shape closer to the Baroque ternary form, the da capo aria, than any opening movement of the classical period. The second movement of the Fantasy exhibits a similar form, and has also a relentless and obsessive use of a dotted rhythm that was almost unknown in the latter half of the eighteenth century, and which begins to reappear in music only with the post-classical style in the works of Schubert and Rossini. Like the homogeneous rhythmic texture of the Baroque, the rhythmic forms of the first generation of the Romantics are not syntactical (i.e., they do not depend on balance and ordering) but cumulative in their effect. Schumann set down only the literal truth when he wrote that his music (and that of Chopin, Mendelssohn, and Hiller) was closer to the music of Bach than to the music of Mozart. The impulsive energy of the Romantic work is no longer a polarized dissonance and an articulated rhythm, but the familiar Baroque sequence, and the structures are no longer synthetic but additive. The music of Schumann in particular (Chopin retains some of the classical clarity) comes in a series of waves, and the climax is generally reserved for the moment before exhaustion.

Romantic style is by no means a reactionary movement, in spite of the great influence of Bach. The 'revival' of the greatest of Baroque figures was not a cause but a symptom of the stylistic change; the homogeneous rhythmic structures of Schubert, for example, can have had nothing to do with Bach. Over a unified texture, the Romantic composer imposed a rigid periodicity derived from late classical music: this very slow beat of the fixed eight-measure phrase gives Romantic music a basic movement much less rapid than the classical style and yet retains the ideal of the symmetrical melody. One might say that the typical form of the Romantic style is Gounod's *Ave Maria*: that is, a Baroque movement of harmony and rhythm (in this case Bach's C major Prelude from the *Well-Tempered Keyboard*, Book I) with a post-classical melody superimposed.

With the change in style came a change in the tonal language itself. The chromaticism of Chopin, Liszt, and Spohr is only a surface manifestation of this change. Schumann's music is not exceptionally chromatic, and yet there

515

is an ambiguity of tonal relations in his work that has no precedent in the half-century from 1775 to 1825. The opening piece of the *Davidsbündlertänze* shifts so rapidly and so frequently from G major to E minor as to destroy any clear feeling for a tonal center. The *Kreisleriana*, like the great song-cycles, is written around a set of related keys, none of which is felt as more important than the others. This lack of a central reference arises, like Chopin's chromaticism, from a weakening of the tonic-dominant polarity. There are phrases by Beethoven, particularly in the *Diabelli* Variations and in the late quartets, which display a chromaticism as radical as anything outside Gesualdo, but they all imply a firm diatonic structure as a background. With Chopin it is the background that shifts chromatically as well. In such a fashion, even the classical harmonic pun—the violent fusion of two different harmonic contexts—is no longer possible, as the context no longer has sufficient clarity of definition.

The sources of the new style—if sources are understood not as causes but as inspirations freely chosen from the past—are easy enough to identify. They are, above all, Bach and Rossini, and a host of greater and smaller figures from the late classical period: Hummel, Field, Cherubini, Weber, Paganini, and others. Clementi, a figure from an earlier generation, remained a force in his development of loose, basically melodic structures; and by his importance for keyboard pedagogy, he transmitted a part of the heritage of Scarlatti. Haydn was almost completely ignored, Mozart admired but misunderstood, and the reverence for Beethoven can be accounted only a pernicious influence for at least a generation after his death, producing with few exceptions only the most lifeless and academic imitations of forms no longer either comprehensible or acceptable.

The disappearance of an old style is perhaps more mysterious than the birth of a new one. Is it abandoned because it is logically exhausted, written out? Have the needs and ideals of a new generation forced an old system into the shadow? Or is it merely a desire for novelty, and must we revive the threadbare historical mechanics of a change of fashion every twenty years? The figure of Schubert stands before us as a warning against generalization.

Except for a handful of works from his last years when he unexpectedly returns to a more thoroughly classical spirit, Schubert is in part the most significant originator of the new Romantic style and in part the greatest example of the post-classical composer. After the first tentative experiments, the principles on which most of his songs are written are almost entirely new; they are related to the *Lieder* of the past only by negation: they annihilate all that precedes. The classical idea of dramatic opposition and resolution is completely superseded: the dramatic movement is simple and indivisible. In those exceptional songs with a strong contrast, the opposition is not the source of the energy: on the contrary, in 'Die Post' from *Die Winterreise*, for example, the contrasting section brings only a deadening of the energy, a deadening which is not a resolution of tension but only a withdrawal before the final climax. The unvaried, anticlassical texture of the Schubert song reflects the singleness of its emotional vision.

Like the finest and most original works of the other Romantic composers, the songs of Schubert are largely cumulative rather than syntactical in effect. The extreme example is 'Der Leiermann' from *Die Winterreise*, in which there is a slight increase in intensity in the shape of some of the later phrases, but in which the heartbreaking effect depends largely on sheer repetition, and— which is only a reinforcement of the same principle—on the place of the song as the last of a long cycle. If this is an extreme instance, the weight of even an early song such as 'Gretchen am Spinnrade' is achieved by a similar iterative technique. Schubert's rhythm is unyielding by classical standards, but it is evident that these standards do not apply and are irrelevant.

On the other hand, in most of the chamber and symphonic pieces, Schubert works within the late and loosely organized post-classical style, in which the melodic flow is essentially more important than the dramatic structure. This is a degenerate style, judged solely as a style: the very looseness of organization prevented the dramatic concision, the close correspondence of part to whole and the consequent richness of allusion of the classical style. In this case, the classical standards can be considered relevant, but to apply them rigorously entails a failure to appreciate many works that, while never quite making virtues of their deficiencies, have virtues of their own that more efficiently organized music can rarely achieve.

Unfortunately, the classical standards cannot be set aside in the last analysis because Schubert is a classicizing composer, like Hummel, Weber, and the young Beethoven: that is, he constantly chooses specific classical works as models and thus admits their standards as he imitates them. Sometimes the thematic relationship with the model is so candid that one feels as if a deliberate allusion were intended. The minuet of Schubert's Symphony no. 5 in B flat major combines the third and fourth movements of the Mozart G minor Symphony:

so that one hears a blurred echo of the past in its outline. Even more disconcerting is the relation of the late Introduction and Rondo in B minor for violin and piano to the first movement of Beethoven's *Kreutzer* Sonata: here what is borrowed is trivialized, and every dramatic detail becomes petty and even decorative.

Schubert was not the first nor the last composer to write with specific models in mind, and Beethoven, for example, was older than Schubert ever was to become before his references to the past became allusive rather than direct. Brahms and Stravinsky, to name only two, continued the imitation of models

517

into their old age. But Schubert's imitations are too often more timid, less disturbing than the originals. For this reason, the structures of most of his large forms are mechanical in a way that is absolutely foreign to his models. They are used by Schubert as molds, almost without reference to the material that was to be poured into them. It is this post-classical practice, of course, which finally produced the idea of a 'sonata' as a fixed form like a sonnet.

The nature of Schubert's dependence on classical models can be seen most clearly in the last movement of the late A major Sonata which is based on the rondo finale of Beethoven's G major Sonata op. 31, no. 1. The two movements have themes that are alike in nothing but their firmly articulated rondo character:

Beethoven

Schubert

The borrowing is not of thematic shape but strictly of formal structure. The process starts the moment the theme has been played once: in both works it is immediately replayed with the melody in the left hand and a new triplet rhythm in the right:

Beethoven

518

Schubert

This new triplet motion continues for the second theme, and is transferred to the left hand for the return of the theme:

Beethoven

Schubert

and the development section begins, heavily contrapuntal, stormy in character, and largely in minor in both cases. For the second return of the theme, the accompaniment is reduced to pure pulsation and the harmony to a point of complete immobility:

Beethoven

Schubert

The most magical effect here in Schubert, the placing of this return not in the tonic but in the submediant, has no parallel in Beethoven's rondo. Schubert's coda, however, is once more subservient; nowhere is the presence of the model felt so strongly. Beethoven slows down his theme, breaks it into fragments, returns to the original tempo and slows down once more, separating the fragments by long pauses, and at the end follows the whole section by a brilliant and extended Presto. Schubert imitates him point for point, adding of his own invention mainly the extraordinary idea of a final phrase which is like a mirror version of the opening phrase of his own *first* movement.

What is most remarkable in this close imitation is its lack of constraint: Schubert moves with great ease within the form which Beethoven created. He has, however, considerably loosened what held it together, and stretched its ligaments unmercifully. Schubert's movement is very much longer than Beethoven's, although the opening themes of both are exactly the same length. This means that the correspondence of part to whole has been considerably altered by Schubert, and explains why his large movements often seem so long, since they are being produced with forms originally intended for shorter pieces. Some of the excitement naturally goes out of these forms when they are so extended, but this is even a condition of the unforced melodic flow of Schubert's music. It must be added that with the finale of this A major Sonata Schubert produced a work that is unquestionably greater than its model.

The relaxation of form typical of the post-classical style inspired Schubert's conception of the long-range sequence, particularly in development sections, a conception only partially based on Beethoven's practice. This device by which whole sections of a development are exactly repeated, only being transposed an interval up or down (almost always up to meet the rising tension), makes it possible to conceive developments in a form as symmetrical as an exposition and recapitulation.[1] It is one of the last stages in the

---

[1] This use of the sequence on the large scale reveals the extent to which the sequence in general had become the animating impulse.

complete systematization of the sonata, and no device was more abused by nineteenth-century symphonists, for whom it became almost a substitute for composition. The relaxed form, however, made it possible for Schubert to indulge in a play of sonority which not even Mozart in *Die Zauberflöte* could equal. The effects are so delicious as to be almost self-indulgent, and they are at their most remarkable in Schubert's extensive production of music for one piano four hands.

At the end of his life with the G major Quartet, the C major Symphony, and the C major String Quintet, Schubert returns to classical principles in a manner almost as striking if not as complete as Beethoven. The G major Quartet opens with a simple opposition of major and minor, and the whole first movement springs from the energy of the material:

This is not the normal major–minor coloring of Schubert, and the sense of pathos is almost completely absent. What is remarkable is the rebirth of the classical conviction that the simplest tonal relationships can alone provide the subject-matter of music. The investigation of these relationships is more diffuse than Beethoven's, but not essentially different. The C major Quintet, perhaps even more successful, is only apparently more complex. The C major Symphony, however, starts with a true Romantic introduction, a complete well-rounded tune, but the mastery of classical rhythm in the Allegro gives the movement a concision greater than that of any other symphonic work of Schubert (far more than the *Unfinished* Symphony, which works with a lavishness of material that the C major does not emulate). The shift of accent from

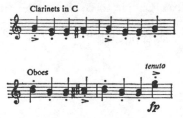

to

is a perfect recreation of Beethoven's rhythmic procedure. In all these works, the technique is more leisurely than Beethoven's, and even than Mozart's at his most relaxed, but the classical forms are no longer imposed from without, but rather implied by the material.

Epilogue

The synthesis of the means of expression we call the classical style was by no means exhausted when it was abandoned, but submission to its discipline was not an easy matter. A discontinuity of style between Beethoven and the generation that followed is an inescapable hypothesis for understanding the musical language of the nineteenth century. Schubert, however, cannot be easily placed into any one category—Romantic, post-classical, or classical—and he stands as an example of the resistance of the material of history to the most necessary generalizations, and as a reminder of the irreducibly personal facts that underlie the history of style.

A style, when it is no longer the natural mode of expression, gains a new life—a shadowy life-in-death—as a prolongation of the past. We imagine ourselves able to revive the past through its art, to perpetuate it by continuing to work within its conventions. For this illusion of reliving history, the style must be prevented from becoming truly alive once again. The conventions must remain conventional, the forms lose their original significance in order to take on their new responsibility of evoking the past. This process of ossification is a guarantee of respectability. The classical style could originally bring no such assurance: *Don Giovanni* and the *Eroica* were scandalous, the *London* Symphonies sublimely impertinent. But just as the Handelian fugue in Mozart served to match the high seriousness of a sacred ritual, the sonata-forms in the symphonies and chamber music of Mendelssohn and Schumann are essays in decorum and respect. In these works, sadly out of favor today, the evocation of the past is only incidental: the intent was to attain the prestige of the style imitated. The sense of the irrecoverable past, however, is omnipresent in the music of Brahms, resignedly eclectic, ambiguous without irony. The depth of his feeling of loss gave an intensity to Brahms's work that no other imitator of the classical tradition ever reached: he may be said to have made music out of his openly expressed regret that he was born too late. For the rest, the classical tradition could be used with originality only through irony— the irony of Mahler, for example, who employed sonata-forms with the same mock respect that he gave to his shopworn scraps of dance-tunes. The true inheritors of the classical style were not those who maintained its traditions, but those, from Chopin to Debussy, who preserved its freedom as they gradually altered and finally destroyed the musical language which had made the creation of the style possible.

Index of Names and Works

═══════

References to Haydn, Mozart, and Beethoven other than these relating to specific works are not indexed.

Abert, Hermann, 13, 177n.
Addison, Joseph, 166, 167
Alberti, Domenico, 28
Anderson, Emily, 13, 143n., 193n., 288n.
Aquinas, St. Thomas, 39
Ariosto, Lodovico, 317
Aristotle, 39

Bach, Carl Philipp Emanuel, 32, 44, 47, 48, 49, 79, 96, 107, 111, 112, 115, 116, 145, 239
Keyboard Sonata in B minor (1779), 112, 114–15, 115n.
Keyboard Sonata in F major (1779), 112–14
Symphony in D major, Wq. 183/1, 111–12
Bach, Johann Christian, 20, 37, 44, 47, 52, 79, 187
Piano Concerto in Eb major (1770), 189–90
Bach, Johann Sebastian, 20, 20n., 33, 36, 43, 46, 47, 50, 60, 63, 78, 80, 93, 101, 105, 107, 112, 115, 135, 146, 147, 167, 197, 227, 243, 264, 330, 345, 367–8, 375, 385, 387, 404, 462, 467, 502, 517, 518
Art of Fugue, BWV 1080, 26, 63, 368, 372, 385
Brandenburg Concertos, 45
   No. 4, in G major, 60–1
   No. 5, in D major, 196–7
   No. 6, in Bb major, 45
Cantata BWV 212 ('Peasant Cantata'), 330

Chaconne—see Partita for violin in D minor
Chorale Prelude, 'O Lamm Gottes,' BWV 618, 60–1, 93
French Overture, in B minor, 282
Fugue for Organ in A minor, BWV 543, 75
'Goldberg' Variations, 62, 63, 93, 95, 330, 331, 385, 395, 436, 439, 510
Inventions for keyboard, 385, 467
Italian Concerto, BWV 971, 77
Mass in B minor, BWV 232, 61n., 94, 367
Partita for keyboard No. 1 in Bb major, 89–90
Partita for violin No. 2 in D minor, 75
Passacaglia and Fugue for organ in C minor, BWV 582, 438
Passions, 168
   Passion According to St. Matthew, 70, 168
   Peasant Cantata—see Cantata BWV 212
Trio-Sonatas for keyboard, 281
Well-Tempered Keyboard, 63, 76, 368, 385, 426, 517
Bach, Wilhelm Friedemann, 44
Bartók, Béla, 137, 332, 434, 508
Bartolozzi, Theresa, 358, 360
Bauer, Harold, 104
Beaumarchais, Pierre-Augustin Caron de, 183, 302, 312, 313, 317, 323
BEETHOVEN
   Adelaide, Op. 46, 380
   An die ferne Geliebte, Op. 98, 379,

BEETHOVEN—*cont.*
   400, **402–3,** 403n., 404, 487,
      515–6
Bagatelles, Opp. 119 & 126, 405
Choral Fantasy—see Fantasy for Pi-
   ano, Chorus and Orchestra
Concertos for Piano and Orchestra
   No. 1 in C major, Op. 15, 258, 392,
      451–2, **451–2**
   No. 2 in B♭ major, Op. 19, 453
   No. 3 in C minor, Op. 37, **389–90,**
      450, 453, 500, 509
   No. 4 in G major, Op. 58, **64,** 69,
      198, 211, 213, 222, 256–7, 333,
      387–92, 399, 453–7, **453–5,**
      455–7
   No. 5 in E♭ major, Op. 73 ('Em-
      peror'), 198, 333, 391, 404, 453,
      458, 500
   In D major (sketch), 391
Concerto for Violin and Orchestra in
   D major, Op. 61, 89, 104,
      258n., 446n.
Fantasy for Piano, Chorus and Or-
   chestra, Op. 80, 440
Fidelio, 43, 103, 176, 180, 184n.,
   288, 379, 386, 399, 403 (*See*
   also Overtures)
Fugue for String Quintet, Op. 137—
   see Quintets
Great Fugue, Op. 133—see Quintets
'Kakadu' Variations, Op. 121a—see
   Trios
Masses, 47, 373–4
   Op. 86 in C major, 366, **373–5,**
      404
   Op. 123 in D major ('Missa Sol-
      emnis'), 53, 194, 275, 303, 366,
      374, **375,** 386, 404
The Mount of Olives, Op. 85, 366

Organ Prelude, 25
Overtures
   Leonore No. 3, Op. 72a, 9, 154
   Zur Namensfeier, Op. 115, 403
Quartets (String), 98, 145, 281
   Op. 18, 265
   Op. 18 no. 1 in F major, 79n.
   Op. 18 no. 5 in A major, 280n.,
      381

Op. 59 ('Rasumovsky' Quartets),
   399
Op. 59 no. 1 in F major, 280n.
Op. 59 no. 3 in C major, **441,** 502
Op. 74 in E♭ major ('Harp'), 404
Op. 95 in F minor, 94, 274, 404,
   502
Op. 127 in E♭ major, 383, 436
Op. 130 in B♭ major, 27, 275n.,
   280n., 383, 439, 440, 445, 448,
   498, 511, **511–2**
Op. 131 in C♯ minor, 403n., **441**
Op. 132 in A minor, 53, 319
Op. 133 in B♭ major ('Great
   Fugue'), 275n., **440–1,** 445 (*see*
   also Quartet Op. 130)
Op. 135 in F major, 280n., 439,
   510
Quintet for Piano and Winds, Op. 16,
   381
Quintet for Strings in C major, Op. 29,
   265–6, 382–3
Quintet (Fugue) for Strings in D ma-
   jor, Op. 137, 385
Septet in E♭ major, Op. 20, 381
Sonatas for Cello and Piano
   Op. 69 in A major, 404, 465n.
   Op. 102 no. 1 in C major, 403, 487,
      495, 507–8, **507**
   Op. 102 no. 2 in D major, 403, 405,
      487, 495
Sonatas for Piano, 46, 145, 352
   WoO. 47 (Three 'Kurfürsten' Sona-
      tas: 1782–3), 380, 460
   Op. 2 no. 3 in C major, 272, 380,
      382, 452n., 458–60, **458–9**
   Op. 7 in E♭ major, 483n., 490–1,
      490, 491
   Op. 10 no. 1 in C minor, 460
   Op. 10 no. 2 in F major, 52, 474–
      7, **475, 476–7**
   Op. 10 no. 3 in D major, 145,
      272, 382, 499n., 508–9, **508–**
      9
   Op. 13 in C minor ('Pathétique'),
      282, 444
   Op. 22 in B♭ major, **39–40, 422,**
      465–6, **465, 466**
   Op. 26 in A♭ major, 488
   Op. 27 no. 1 in E♭ major, 488

Op. 27 no. 2 in C♯ minor ('Moon-light'), 52, 91, 488
Op. 28 in D major ('Pastoral'), 463, 464, **464–5,** 477–9, **477–9,** 480, 482, 483, 488
Op. 31 no. 1 in G major, 81, 359, 382, 395, 396, 483n., **520–2**
Op. 31 no. 2 in D minor ('Tempest'), 38–9, 70, 81, 395
Op. 31 no. 3 in E♭ major, 81, 394, 396, 463, **463**
Op. 49 no. 1 in G minor, 462n.
Op. 49 no. 2 in G major, 460–2, **461–2,** 466
Op. 53 in C major ('Waldstein'), 49, 68, 70, 73, 79n., 134, 374, 383, 386, 392, **396–9,** 406, 452n., 458–60, **459,** 483n., 510
Op. 54 in F major, **61**
Op. 57 in F minor ('Appassionata'), 37, 62, 70, 76, **89,** 99n., 250, 381, **399–400,** 406, **438–9,** 460, 483n., 499, 510
Op. 78 in F♯ major, 350, 488
Op. 81a in E♭ major ('Les adieux'), 463, **464,** 488
Op. 90 in E minor, 394, 403
Op. 101 in A major, 68, 403, 403n., 441, 457–8, **457,** 487, 495, 508n.
Op. 106 in B♭ major ('Hammerklavier'), 34–5, 94, 108, 208, 280, 379, 383, 385, 396, 404–5, 407, **409–34,** 440–1, 446n., 484–8, **484,** 499, 500n., 502, 508, 510
Op. 109 in E major, 70, 145, 225, 436, 495, 501
Op. 110 in A♭ major, **67–8,** 300, 441, 488–500, **488–9, 489, 490, 492–3, 495, 496, 497, 498, 499,** 501–7, **502, 503–5, 506**
Op. 111 in C minor, 145, 225, 272, 383, 436, **441–4, 446–8,** 499–50, **450,** 452, 460, 500, 501, 502
Sonatas for Violin and Piano
Op. 24 in F major ('Spring'), 480–2, **480–1, 481–2**
Op. 47 in A major ('Kreutzer'), 277, 399, 519

Symphonies
No. 3 in E♭ major, Op. 60 ('Eroica'), 9, 35, 68, 77, 80, 225, 269, 275, 346, **350,** 386, **392–5,** 399, 437–8, 440, 490, 502, 512, 524
No. 5 in C minor, Op. 67, 36–7, 72, 147, 228, 275, 395, 404, 406, 407, 433, 460
No. 6 in F major, Op. 68 ('Pastoral'), **401–2,** 404
No. 7 in A major, Op. 92, 347, 349, 404
No. 8 in F major, Op. 93, 98, 275, 404, 445, 510
No. 9 in D minor, Op. 125 ('Choral'), 144, 225–6, 269, 272, 274, 275, 280, 332, 383, 386, 403n., 404, 405n., 427, 437, **439–40,** 448, 483, 507
Trios for Piano, Violin and Cello
Op. 1 no. 3 in C minor, 460
Op. 70 no. 2 in E♭ major, 282, 348, 403n., 404
Op. 97 in B♭ major ('Archduke'), 108, 404
Op. 121a in G major ('Kakadu' Variations), 198
5 Variations on 'Rule Britannia' (Publ. 1804), WoO. 79, **435–6**
32 Variations in C minor (1806), **400–1,** *WoO. 80,* 436
6 Variations in F major, Op. 34, **437,** 439
15 Variations in E♭ major, Op. 35 ('Eroica'), **437–8,** 439, 443, 509
33 Variations on a Waltz by Diabelli, Op. 120, 95, 372, 385, 404, 405, 436, **439,** 445, 509–10, 510, 511, 518
Wellington's Victory, Op. 91, 400, **401**
Bellini, Vincenzo, 101, 380
Norma, 306
Berg, Alban, 278
Berlioz, Hector, 176
Requiem, 176
Symphonie fantastique, 37, 402
Symphonie funèbre et triomphale, 401
Boccherini, Luigi, 47–8, 264, 265

Brahms, Johannes, 27, 33, 36, 83, 144, 169, 198, 213, 277–8, 379, 519–20, 524
    Cadenza to Mozart's Piano Concerto K453, 223
    Concerto for Piano No. 2 in B♭ major, Op. 83, 391
    Quintet for Clarinet and Strings in B minor, Op. 115, 119, 194
    Symphony No. 3 in F major, Op. 90, 275
    Symphony No. 4 in E minor, Op. 98, 407, 426
    Variations and Fugue on a Theme by Handel, Op. 24, 440
Brosses, Président de, 179
Bruckner, Anton, 394
Bukofzer, Manfred, 13
Bülow, Hans von, 399
Buxtehude, Dietrich, 36

Caravaggio, Michelangelo Merise da, 106
Cavalli, Pietro Francesco, 164
Chaucer, Geoffrey, 146
Cherubini, Luigi, 183, 386, 518
Chopin, Frédéric, 21, 22, 31, 33, 34, 36, 70, 72–3, 74, 101, 104, 169, 192, 203, 260, 277, 325, 368, 379, 380, 382, 385, 385n., 387, 390, 437, 463, 474n., 508, 517, 518, 524
    Ballade in G minor, Op. 23, 76
    Ballade in A♭ major, Op. 47, 382
    Ballade in F minor, Op. 52, 383
    Preludes, 25
Claude Lorraine, 162
Clementi, Muzio, 22, 23, 380, 518
Cooke, Deryck, 498n.
Couperin, François, 101
Crébillon, Prosper Jolyot de, 166
Czerny, Carl, 30, 101, 404

Dahlhaus, Carl, 498
Dancourt, Florent Carton, 312
Da Ponte, Lorenzo, 155n., 302, 313, 321, 322
David, Jacques Louis, 172
Debussy, Claude, 167, 524
    Pelléas et Mélisande, 351

Delacroix, Eugène, 29, 379n.
Della Porta, Giacomo, 313
Dent, Edward, 321
Deutsch, Otto Erich, 13, 177n.
Dittersdorf, Karl Ditters von, 22, 187
Dohnányi, Ernst von
    Variations on a Nursery Theme, 198
Donizetti, Gaetano, 367
Dussek, Jan Ladislav, 474
Dvořák, Antonin, 332

Einstein, Alfred, 13
Esterházy, Prince Anton, 83, 366
Esterházy, Princess Anton, 358
Esterházy, Princess Nicholas, 356

Favart, Charles Simon, 317
Feydeau, Georges, 312
Field, John, 384, 483, 518
Forbes, Elliot, 13, 500n.

Gay, John
    The Beggar's Opera, 341
Gershwin, George, 332
Gesualdo, Prince Carlo, 454
Giotto, 53
Gluck, Christoph Willibald, 19, 47, 145, 164, 166, 167, 169–80, 177n., 179–80, 289, 319
    Alceste, 172, 173
    Iphigénie en Tauride, 172, 175
    Orphée, 178n.
    Paride ed Elena, 174–6
Goethe, Johann Wolfgang von, 176–7
Goldmark, Karl, 402
Goldoni, Carlo, 162, 183, 313, 317, 318, 321
    Il Ventaglio, 312
Goldsmith, Oliver, 162
Gounod, Charles
    Ave Maria, 517
Gozzi, Carlo, 183, 314, 318, 321
    The Love for Three Oranges, 314, 318
    Memoirs of a Useless Man, 318
    Turandot, 318
Grieg, Edvard, 198

Handel, George Frideric, 20, 33, 37, 46, 47, 48, 53, 63, 71, 78, 105, 106–7, 135, 147, 164, 166, 167, 167–

9, 170, 197, 289, 333, 368, 374, 386, 387, 401, 445, 510, 524
Chaconne with 62 Variations, 63n.
Giulio Cesare, 167
Israel in Egypt, 60, 167, 368
Jephtha, 43, 169
Messiah, 20, 368
Suite No. 3 in D minor for harpsichord, 105
Susanna, 169
Hasse, 368
HAYDN
The Creation, 329, 348, 367, **370–3**
Concerto for Piano and Orchestra in D major, 185
Masses:
In C Major ('In Time of War'), 192n., **369–70**
In B♭ major ('Maria Theresa'), 369, 370
In B♭ major ('Windband'), 369
Quartets (String), 45, 74, 77–8, 143, 194n., 280, 296, 333, 351, 352, 392
Op. 9, 139
Op. 17, 137, 139, 146
Op. 20 ('Sun' Quartets), 116, 118, 119, 137, 139, 146, 151, 264, 265, 471
Op. 20 no. 1 in E♭ major, 68, **118**
Op. 20 no. 2 in C major, 117–8n.
Op. 20 no. 4 in D major, 57–8, **150**
Op. 33 ('Scherzi' or 'Russian' Quartets), 23, 47, 115, 116, 117, 118, 119, 137, 138, 139, 151, 208, 266, 471
Op. 33 no. 1 in B minor, 68–9, 91, **115–18,** 119, 120, 139, 140, 247, 399
Op. 33 no. 2 in E♭ major, 90–1, 139, 471–3, **472–3**
Op. 33 no. 3 in C major, **65–7,** 95–6, 108n., 267, 473
Op. 33 no. 4 in B♭ major, 97–8, 473
Op. 33 no. 5 in G major, 78, 473
Op. 42 in D minor, 138
Op. 50, 123, 138, 139
Op. 50 no. 1 in B♭ major, **120–5,** 128–9

Op. 50 no. 2 in C major, 138
Op, 50 no. 3 in E♭ major, 139, 473
Op, 50 no. 4 in F♯ minor, 136, 138–9
Op. 50 no. 5 in F major, **131–2**
Op. 50 no. 6 in D major, 73, 74, **125–9**
Op. 54, 139
Op. 54 no. 1 in G major, 139
Op. 54 no. 2 in C major, 139, 140, 275n.
Op. 54 no. 3 in E major, 140, **141–2, 473–4, 473–4**
Op. 55, 139
Op. 55 no. 1 in A major, 140
Op. 55 no. 2 in F minor, 140
Op. 55 no. 3 in B♭ major, **130–1**
Op. 64, 140
Op. 64 no. 1 in C major, **133–5,** 280
Op. 64 no. 2 in B minor, 140
Op. 64 no. 3 in B♭ major, 73, 74, 140
Op. 64 no. 4 in G major, **140–1,** 280
Op. 64 no. 5 in D major ('The Lark'), 61, **140–1,** 352
Op. 64 no. 6 in E♭ major, **132–3,** 286
Op. 71, 346, 349
Op. 71 no. 2 in D major, **335–6**
Op. 71 no. 3 in E♭ major, **345–6**
Op. 74, 346, 349
Op. 74 no. 2 in F major, 346
Op. 74 no. 3 in G minor, **346**
Op. 76, 474
Op. 76 no. 1 in G major, **336,** 346
Op. 76 no. 3 in C major ('Emperor'), 479–80
Op. 76 no. 5 in D major, 337, 345, 474
Op. 76 no. 6 in E♭ major, **339–40,** 474
Op. 77 no. 1 in G major, **74**
Op. 77 no. 2 in F major, 280
Op. 103 (Unfinished), 136
The Seasons, 185, 329, 370, **372–3,** 402
Sinfonia Concertante in B♭ major, H. 105, 157, 329

Index of Names and Works

HAYDN—cont.

Sonatas for Piano, 45, 46, 107, 144, 185, 292, 300
  H. 20 in C minor, 146, 358
  H. 31 in E major, 359
  H. 44 in G minor, 146n.
  H. 46 in A♭ major, 138, 146, **150–1**
  H. 48 in C major, 45
  H. 49 in E♭ major, 358
  H. 50 in C major, 358
  H. 51 in D major, 358
  H. 52 in E♭ major, 111, 115, 358, 441, 485–8, **485–6, 487–8**
Symphonies, 45, 46, 47, 77–8, **143–63, 185,** 193, 195, **329–50,** 351, 352
  No. 39 in G minor, 146
  No. 43 in E♭ major ('Mercury'), **149–50**
  No. 44 in E minor ('Trauer'), 146
  No. 45 in F♯ minor ('Farewell'), 146, 147
  No. 46 in B major, **147–9**
  No. 47 in G major, 94, **151–2**
  No. 49 in F minor ('La Passione'), 146
  No. 52 in C minor, 146
  No. 53 in D major ('Imperial'), 153
  No. 57 in D major, 346–7
  No. 60 in C major ('Il Distratto'), 153
  No. 62 in D major, 113–14, 151, **153**
  No. 73 in D major ('La Chasse'), 346–347
  No. 75 in D major, 151, **155–6,** 346–7
  No. 78 in C minor, **247**
  No. 81 in G major, **157–9**
  Nos. 82–87 ('Paris' Symphonies), 159, 192, 329, 333, 402
  No. 82 in C major ('The Bear'), 337
  No. 85 in B♭ major ('La Reine'), 73n., 287
  No. 86 in D major, 346–7
  No. 88 in G major, 157, 287, **338,** 408–9
  No. 89 in F major, **157**

  No. 90 in C major, 145, 159
  No. 91 in E♭ major, 145, 159
  No. 92 in G major ('Oxford'), 145, **159–62,** 296, 339
  Nos. 93–104 ('London' Symphonies), 193, 269, 300, 329, 333, 346, 350, 354, 369, 524
  No. 93 in D major, 338–9, **343–4**
  No. 94 in G major ('Surprise'), 337–8, 373, 438n.
  No. 95 in C minor, 346n.
  No. 97 in C major, **342–4,** 348
  No. 98 in B♭ major, 193, 195, 347, 373n.
  No. 99 in E♭ major, **334–5**
  No. 100 in G major ('Military'), 81, **334–5,** 347, 348
  No. 101 in D major ('Clock'), 97, 140, 339
  No. 102 in B♭ major, 45, 347, 361
  No. 103 in E♭ major ('Drumroll'), 90, 282, **331–2, 336–7,** 341, 348, 349
  No. 104 in D major, **330,** 337, 339, 347n.
Trios for Piano, Violin and Cello, 45, 46, 185, 264, 345, **351–65,** 392
  H. 1 in G minor, 355
  H. 7 in D major, **96–7**
  H. 12 in E minor, 356
  H. 13 in C minor, **355**
  H. 14 in A♭ major, **355–6**
  H. 15–17 (Piano, Flute and Cello), 354
  H. 18 in A major, **358**
  H. 19 in G minor, **83–8,** 358
  H. 20 in B♭ major, 137, 358
  H. 21 in C major, 356
  H. 22 in E♭ major, **356–7**
  H. 23 in D minor, 356
  H. 24 in D major, 360, 361
  H. 25 in G major, 360, 361
  H. 26 in F♯ minor, 45, 276, 360, **361–2**
  H. 27 in C major, 351–2, **358–9**
  H. 28 in E major, 358, **359–60**
  H. 29 in E♭ major, 358, **360**
  H. 30 in E♭ major, 354, **363–5**
  H. 31 in E♭ minor, **362–3**

Index of Names and Works

Haydn, Michael, 265, 354, 374
Herder, Johann Gottfried, 312
Herzmann, Erich, 13
Hiller, Ferdinand, 453
Hoffmann, Ernst Theodor Amadeus, 19, 36–7, 80, 162, 309–10, 315, 324, 325, 435, 445, 482
Houdon, Jean Antoine, 53
Hughes, Rosemary, 13, 331
Hummel, Johann Nepomuk, 22, 101, 103, 258, 260, 380, 381, 384, 390, 392, 394n., 437, 518, 519

Jannequin, Claude, 401, 434
Jansen, Theresa—*see* Bartolozzi
Jeunehomme, Mlle., 104
Joachin, Joseph, 27

Keller, Hans, 440n.
Kierkegaard, Søren, 324
Kinderman, William, 483, 505
Kleist, Heinrich von
 Der Zerbrochene Krug, 317
Koch, H. C., 87 n., 460
 Versuch einer Anleitung zur Composition, 460

La Fontaine, Jean de, 313, 317
Larsen, Jens Peter, 13, 483
Le Brun, Charles, 313
Ledoux, Claude Nicolas, 172
Lenz, Jacob Michael Reinhard, 317
Leonardo da Vinci, 228
Leopardi, Giacomo, 449
 Zibaldone, 449
Le Sage, Alain-René, 312
Lessing, Gotthold Ephraim, 312, 317
Liszt, Franz, 22, 77n., 101, 104, 198, 277, 440n., 508, 517
 Sonata in B minor, 440n.
Lockwood, Lewis, 13, 406, 480
Lowinsky, Edward, 13, 367
Lully, Jean-Baptiste, 168n.

Machaut, Guillaume de, 329
Mahler, Gustav, 278, 332–3, 344, 524
 Symphony No. 9, 275
Malherbe, François de, 111
Mallarmé, Stéphane, 434
Mälzel, Johann Nepomuk, 401

Manet, Edouard, 53
Maria Theresa, Empress, 323
Marivaux, Pierre Carlet de, 162, 183, 314
 Le Jeu de l'amour et du hasard, 314
Marston, Nicholas, 487n.
Marvell, Andrew, 162
Masaccio, 53, 146
Méhul, Etienne, 183, 386
Menander, 312
Mendelssohn, Felix, 379, 385, 403, 449, 517, 524
 Symphony No. 5 in D minor ('Reformation'), 401
 Variations sérieuses, Op. 54, 401
Metastasio, Pietro, 154, 166, 317
Michelangelo, 53, 483
Molière, 183, 312, 317, 321
 L'Avare, 313
 Le Médecin malgré lui, 312
 Le Misanthrope, 313
Monteux, Pierre, 351
Monteverdi, Claudio, 164, 173, 178
Mozart, Constanze, 373
Mozart, Leopold, 102, 191, 193, 288
MOZART
 Concerto for Clarinet and Orchestra in A major, K. 622, 192, **260–2**, 263
 Concerto for Flute and Harp in C major, K. 299, 214
 Concertos for Horn and Orchestra, 214
 Concertos for Piano and Orchestra, 36, 51, 101–2, 107, 144, **185–263**, 333, 352, 440
 K. 175, in D major, 219
 K. 246, in C major, 191, 193
 K. 271, in E♭ major, 23, **58–60**, 64, 82, 104, **198–214**, 215, 218, 219, 227, 241, 391
 K. 413, in F major, 208n., 218, 250
 K. 414, in A major, 208n., **218–19**, 243, 250, 260
 K. 415, in C major, 191, 191n., 208n., 218, 227, 251
 K. 449, in E♭ major, 208n., **219**, 220, 221, 227, 250, 251
 K. 450, in B♭ major, 208n., **220–1**, 241, 390

Index of Names and Works

MOZART, Concertos—*cont.*

K. 451, in D major, 102, 213, 220, **221,** 227, 241

K. 453, in G major, **221–6,** 275, 390, 391

K. 456, in B♭ major, 208n., 221, 241, 254

K. 459, in F major, 45, 139, **226–7,** 233, 241

K. 466, in D minor, 194n., **227–35,** 238, 240, 241, 245, 247, 248, 250, 253, 260, 278n., 390n.

K. 467, in C major, 213, 227, 228, 233, **235–40,** 241, 247, 248, 249, 260

K. 482, in E♭ major, 214, **240–1,** 250

K. 488, in A major, 211, **241–5,** 260, 458

K. 491, in C minor, 103, 104, 106, 213, 233, **245–50,** 276, 278n., 389–90, 450, 453

K. 503, in C major, 13, **251–8,** 391

K. 537, in D major ('Coronation'), **258–260,** 380, 468–71, **468–70**

K. 595, in B♭ major, 254, 260, **262–3,** 280

Concerto for Two Pianos and Orchestra in E♭ major, K. 365, 214

Concertos for Violin and Orchestra, 214, 219

Divertimento in E♭ major, K. 563—see Trios

Fantasy in C minor, K. 396, 92n.

Fantasy in C minor, K. 475, **91–3** (*see also* Sonata K. 457)

Mass in C minor, K. 427, 366, 368

Mass in D minor, K. 626 (Requiem), 366, 368, 510

'Messiah' instrumentation, K. 572, 20

Operas, 51, 69, 80, 92, 93, 99n., 184, 203, **288–325,** 352

La Clemenza di Tito, 164, 323

Così fan Tutte, 43, 80, 167, 179, 183, 184, 305, 306, 313, 314–17, 322, 323, 501

Don Giovanni, **94–5,** 95n., 104, 156, 167, 173, 179, 181, 183, 228, 233, 250, 257, 276, **296–303,** 305, 306, 306n., 309–12, **321–4,** 324–5, 360, 467, 494n.

Die Entführung aus den Serail, 43, 165, 167, 176–7, 182, 196, 289, 302, 306n., **307–8,** 309, 317

La Finta Giardiniera, 69, 181, **188–9,** 289, 302, **303–4,** 306

Idomeneo, 164, 167, 176, **177–81,** 182, 289, 304, **306–7**

Mitridate, 179

Le Nozze di Figaro, 43, 94, 103, 160, 165, 167, 173, **182–3,** 228, 240, **290–6,** 302, 304, 305, 306, **308–9,** 313, 323, 332

Zaïde, 288, 306, 306n.

Die Zauberflöte, 103, 156, 167, 173, 176, 178, 254, 260, 289, 305, 317, **318–21,** 323, 324–5, 330, 333, 368, 510, 523

Quartets for Piano and Strings, 46, 467

Quartets (String), 45, 250, 264

'Haydn' Quartets, 138, 266, 280, 281

K. 387, in G major, 275n., 441

K. 421, in D minor, 276, 278n.

K. 428, in E♭ major, **187–7,** 187n.

K. 458, in B♭ major ('Hunt'), **188, 407–8**

K. 464, in A major, 100, 280, 381

K. 465, in C major ('Dissonance'), **186,** 282, 347n., 348

K. 499, in D major ('Hoffmeister'), 266, 280

'Prussian' Quartets, 281

Quintets (String)

K. 174, in B♭ major, **264–5,** 286

K. 515, in C major, 258, **266–74,** 276, 277, 278, 280, 281

K. 516, in G minor, 88, 248, 258, 274, 276, **277–80,** 281, 324–5, 392, 402

K. 593, in D major, 65n., 269, **281–6,** 407, 471n.

K. 614, in E♭ major, 281, **286–7**

Requiem, K. 626—see Mass in D minor

Serenade for Thirteen Winds in B♭ major, K. 361, 152

Index of Names and Works

Sinfonia Concertante for Violin, Viola and Orchestra in E♭ major, K. 364, 211, **214–18**, 235, 264

Sonatas for Piano, 45, 243
K. 283, in G major, **78–9**
K. 284, in D major, 102, **102–3**, 105
K. 310, in A minor, 70, 223, 235, 276, 278n.
K. 311, in D major, 52
K. 330, in C major, 51–2
K. 331, in A major, 82, 102
K. 332, in F major, 81, 102, 103, 275
K. 333, in B♭ major, 45, 72, 270n., 460n., **460n.**
K. 457, in C minor, 105, 276, 278n. (*See also* Fantasy in C minor, K. 475)
K. 545, in C major, 52
K. 570, in B♭ major, 46
K. 576 in D major, 466–8, **467–8**, 490
Sonata for Piano, four hands, in F major, K. 496, 347n.
Sonatas for Violin and Piano
K. 304, in E minor, 276
K. 379, in G major, 225n., 269, 277
K. 526, in A major, **276**
Suite for Piano in C major, K. 399 (Fragment), 53
Symphonies
No. 34 in C major, K. 338, 72, 269n.
No. 36 in C major, K. 425 ('Linz'), 236, 347n.
No. 38 in D major, K. 504 ('Prague'), 233, 236, 258, 268, 269, 347
No. 39 in E♭ major, K. 543, 269, **334**, 347, **349**
No. 40 in G minor, K. 550, 13, 69, 228, 235–6, 254, **275–6**, 277, 278n., **324–5**, 334, 361, 395, 519
No. 41 in C major, K. 551 ('Jupiter'), **82–3**, 94, 235–6, 257, 269n., 272, 275n., **335**

Trio for Clarinet, Viola and Piano in E♭ major, K. 498, 240
Trios for Piano, Violin and Cello
K. 502, in B♭ major, 351
K. 542, in E major, 351
Trio (Divertimento) for Strings in E♭ major K. 563, 138, **280–1**

Newman, Ernest, 471
Nottebohm, Gustav, 13

Ockeghem, Johannes, 20
Offenbach, Jacques, 332

Paderewski, Ignac, 104
Paganini, Niccolò, 101, 518
Palestrina, Giovanni Pierluigi da, 319, 366, 374
Parny, Evariste, 166
Perrault, Charles, 331
Piccinni, Niccolò, 155, 302
Ployer, Babette, 219, 221
Pope, Alexander, 166
Poussin, Nicolas, 162, 171
Prévost, Abbé, 163
Prokoviev, Sergei, 337

Rabelais, François, 166
Racine, Jean, 167, 179
Raff, Joseph Joachim, 402
Rameau, Jean Philippe, 46, 50, 137, 164, 160, 167–8, 169, 289
Raphael, 171
Ratner, Leonard, 87n.
Redlich, Hans F., 191n.
Reger, Max, 36
Restif de la Bretonne, Nicolas-Edme, 163
Réti, Rudolph, 41
Richter, Jean Paul, 507
Riemann, Hugo, 36
Ries, Ferdinand, 426n., 500n.
Rimsky-Korsakov, Nicolai Andreyevich, 167, 344
Robbins Landon, H. C., 13, 143n.
Rossini, Giacomo, 101, 386, 517, 518
Le Comte d'Ory, 386
Rousseau, Jean-Baptiste, 166
Rousseau, Jean-Jacques, 172, 196
Le Devin du village, 341

Rudolph, Archduke Johann Joseph Rainer, 404

Sacchini, Antonio Maria Gaspare, 470
Sade, Donatien Alphonse François ('Marquis') de, 163, 323
　One More Step, 323
Saint-Saëns, Camille, 450
Salomon, Johann Peter, 193
Scarlatti, Alessandro, 164
Scarlatti, Domenico, 30, 43, 46, 50, 52, 57, 62–3, 79, 215, 518
Schenker, Heinrich, 13, 33, 34, 35–6, 40–1, 42
Schikaneder, Emanuel, 318, 319, 321, 323
Schindler, Anton, 145, 387, 499n.
Schlegel, Friedrich, 451n.
Schlösser, Louis, 405
Schoenberg, Arnold, 35, 329, 508
Schroeter, Johann Samuel, 243
Schroeter, Rebecca, 360
Schubert, Franz, 52, 137, 152, 215, 235, 239, 280, 332, 337, 379, 380–1, 384, 386–7, 394n., 402, 403, 434, 449, 462–3, 479, 517, 518–24
　Gretchen am Spinnrade, D. 118, 455
　Introduction and Rondo for Violin and Piano in B minor, D. 895, 519
　Der Leiermann—see 'Die Winterreise'
　Die Post—see 'Die Winterreise'
　Quartet (String) in G major, D. 887, **523**
　Quintet for Piano and Strings in A major, D. 667 ('Trout'), 384
　Quintet for Strings in C major, D. 956, **523**
　Sonata for Piano in A major, D. 959, **520–2**
　Symphony No. 5 in B♭ major, D. 485, **519**
　Symphony No. 8 in B minor, D. 759 ('Unfinished'), 523
　Symphony No. 9 in C major, D. 944, 500, **523**
　Die Winterreise, D. 911, 518–9
Schumann, Robert, 32, 70, 77n., 98, 198, 277, 324, 368, 379, 380, 381, 382, 383, 384, 385, 385n., 390, 402–3, 463, 474n., 508, 517–8, 524
　Carnaval, Op. 9, 37, 37n., 382
　Davidsbündlertänze, Op. 6, 382, 518
　Fantasy in C major, Op. 17, 382, 383, **515–7**
　Impromptus (Variations) on a Theme of Clara Wieck, Op. 5, 437
　Kreisleriana, Op. 16, 518
　Sonata, in F♯ minor, Op. 11, 350
Schuppanzigh, Ignaz, 379
Schweitzer, Albert, 330n.
Shakespeare, William, 482
　Comedy of Errors, 312
　Twelfth Night, 312
Shaw, George Bernard, 27, 471
Smart, Christopher, 166
Spohr, Ludwig, 387, 517
Stamitz, Johann, 22
Strauss, Richard, 144, 402
Stravinsky, Igor, 36, 170, 317, 337, 445, 508, 519–20
　The Rake's Progress, 317
Swieten, Baron Gottfried von, 373

Tchaikovsky, Peter Ilyich, 144, 194, 198, 325
　Concerto for Piano and Orchestra No. 1 in B♭ minor, Op. 23, 350
　Symphony No. 6 in B minor, Op. 74 ('Pathétique'), 274
Thayer, Alexander, 13, 379n., 386n., 387n., 405n., 407n.
Tost, Johann, 286
Tovey, Donald Francis, 13, 28, 38–9, 49n., 51, 69, 76, 100, 111, 115, 119, 140, 170, 180, 299, 351, 354, 390, 394, 400, 421, 446n., 463
Türk, Daniel Gottlob, 101
Turner, W. J., 315

Velasquez, 53
Verdi, Giuseppe, 166, 176, 333, 474n., 508
　Otello, 176
　Requiem, 409
Viotti, Giovanni Battista, 143

Index of Names and Works

Voltaire, Francois Marie Arouet de, 166, 167
  Candide, 163

Wagner, Richard, 21, 67, 88, 154, 165–6, 180, 277, 303, 317, 325, 379, 387, 508
  Parsifal, 67
Waldstein, Count Ferdinand, 19

Weber, Carl Maria von, 22, 258, 380–1, 384, 386, 394n., 449, 483, 518, 519
Webern, Anton, 445
Webster, James, 495
Wieland, Christoph Martin, 163, 168n., 177, 317
Winckelmann, Johann Joachim, 172n.
Wölfflin, Heinrich, 40